Islam in History

Islam in History

Ideas, People, and Events in the Middle East

New Edition, Revised and Expanded

Bernard Lewis

Open Court
Chicago and La Salle, Illinois

SECOND EDITION

First printing 1993
Second printing 1993

Printed and bound in the United States of America.

Library of Congress Cataloging-in-Publication Data

Lewis, Bernard
Islam in history : ideas, people, and events in the Middle East / Bernard Lewis.—2nd ed.
p. cm.
Includes bibliographical references and index.
ISBN 0-8126-9216-0.—ISBN 0-8126-9217-9 (pbk.)
1. Islam—History. 2. Middle East—Historiography. 3. Middle East—History—1517- I. Title
BP52.L46 1993
909′.0917′671—dc20 92-46218
CIP

CONTENTS

Preface to the Second Edition

The first edition of this book was published in 1973 and contained twenty-one articles on different aspects of Islamic and Middle Eastern history and historiography. In this new edition two of these articles have been deleted, one of them entitled "The Muslim Discovery of Europe," the other, "Semites and Anti-Semites." Each of these articles proved to be the nucleus of a book devoted to the same subject and published under the same title. I have however added thirteen new articles, all of them published since the first edition appeared and many of them dealing with recent and contemporary topics. This has also involved some rearrangement and reclassification of the articles. In preparing this new edition, I have also taken the opportunity to make a number of corrections and revisions, to take account both of the advance of scholarship and of the course of events. Some, especially the older ones, have been extensively revised; a few, entirely recast and rewritten. Almost all of them have been modified to some extent.

My thanks are due to the publishers and editors who gave permission to reprint material first published by them. In the first edition I offered my special thanks to Miss Bryan-Healing and Mrs. Alice Watson "for their hawk-eyed and dove-mannered editing of my text." For this edition I would like to add a word of thanks to Mr. David Steele and Mr. Edward Roberts, both of Open Court, for their many contributions to the improvement and production of this volume. Finally, I wish to express my appreciation to the reviewers of the first edition of this book, especially to those whose comments enabled me to make some changes for the better. I did not however feel obliged to defer to the judgments of those reviewers who in 1973 thought that I had underestimated "the gains made by secularism in the Muslim world" and that I had exaggerated the significance of religious movements in Iran.

Princeton 1992

PART I

THE WESTERN APPROACHES

The Study of Islam

1

During the nineteenth century the forms, language, and to some extent even the structures of public life in the Muslim countries were given a Western and therefore a secular appearance. In those countries which were under European domination, the process was slow, cautious, and incomplete; in those where Muslim rulers retained political independence, they were able to impose Westernizing reforms with greater ruthlessness and fewer fears or inhibitions. By nationalizing the *waqf* revenues and introducing modern—*i.e.* Western-style—law and education, they simultaneously deprived the ulema both of their financial independence and of a large part of their functions and influence, and reduced them in effect to a branch of the bureaucracy. The men of the faith now became servants and spokesmen of the state, who successively justified reform, reaction, liberalism, and socialism, from the same texts and by the same methods of exegesis.

The state itself, struggling for survival in a world dominated by the European powers, adopted European forms and procedures and drew increasingly, in the recruitment and promotion of its personnel, on those whose education and aptitudes enabled them to meet the needs of this situation—that is to say, on the minority who knew a Western language, had at least a tincture of Western education, and had therefore acquired some Western habits of behavior and perhaps of thought. From this time onwards, identity is defined and loyalty claimed on national rather than communal lines; criticism and aspiration are formulated in secular, not religious terms. New books replace the sacred and classical texts as the pabulum of the literate and governing elite; journalists, lawyers, and professors take over from the ulema; not theology, but politics provides the basis of argument and the form of expression.

The exponents of Islam have always been of two very different kinds, sometimes in conflict, usually interacting. On the one hand there were the ulema, the upholders of orthodoxy and authority, of dogma and of law; on the other the dervishes and their equivalents, preserving a tradition—or rather many local traditions—of popular religion and religiosity. Both groups have a habit of submission to political authority: the ulema of active support, the dervishes of passive if critical acquiescence—though the latter were often treated with mistrust by governments, because of the powerful pent-up emotions and energies which they could control or release.

The Westernizing reforms affected both groups adversely. The ulema, already to some extent associated with political power, now became completely subservient to it and lost touch with the people. The dervishes, together with the masses to whom they belonged, were separated by a widening gulf from the Westernized political and intellectual elites, who no longer shared the same universe of discourse or even wore the same clothes as the un-Westernized majority. Ulema and dervishes alike were out of touch with the modern world, against which the new elites were struggling and which at the same time they were striving to join.

In this new world, theology was seen as old-fashioned and irrelevant; dervish mysticism as a shameful and dangerous superstition. The only hope of salvation was economic, social, and above all political reform, conceived and, as it were, applied in accordance with a succession of imported European ideologies.

In the last hundred years Europe and, later, North America have seen the Islamic world through a distorting glass of European and, later, North American categories and terminologies. Muslims, for reasons of fashion, prestige, or perhaps even conviction, frequently describe the affairs of their countries in these Western terms. Western observers—journalists, politicians, scholars—gratefully accept these terms, for their own convenience and that of their readers. This has led to the curious but widespread belief that the authentic and significant forces in the Muslim world can be adequately denoted and classified by such parochial Western terms as nationalist and socialist, progressive and revolutionary—even, the ultimate absurdity, right-wing and left-wing. The results are about as informative as an account of a cricket match written by a baseball correspondent.

From time to time some incident, perhaps trivial in itself, allows a glimpse of the hard realities under the verbiage. On 25 April 1967 the Syrian army magazine *Jaysh al-Shaʿb* (The People's Army) published an article by one Second Lieutenant Ibrāhīm Khalāṣ, entitled "The Means of Creating a New Arab Man." The only way to build Arab society and civilization, the author argued, was to create

> a new Arab socialist man, who believes that God, religions, feudalism, capital, and all the values which prevailed in the pre-existing society were no more than mummies in the museums of history. . . . There is only one value: absolute faith in the new man of destiny . . . who relies only on himself and on his own contribution to humanity . . . because he knows that his inescapable end is death and nothing beyond death . . . no heaven and no hell. . . . We have no need of men who kneel and beg for grace and pity. . . .

This was the first time that such sentiments had appeared in print in any of the revolutionary Arab states.

The result was electrifying. The Syrian population seemed thoroughly cowed and had already passively acquiesced in a whole series of radical political and economic changes. The suppression of free speech, the control of movement, the confiscation of property all passed without incident—but an attack on God and religion in an officially sponsored publication revealed the limits of acquiescence, the final values for which a Muslim people was willing to stand up and resist.

In the face of mounting tension and hostility, the government beat a retreat. On 5 May the author of the article and the editors of the journal were arrested. The following day the semi-official newspaper *al-Thawra* (The Revolution) proclaimed its respect for religion, and shortly afterwards it was announced that the article was planted by the CIA and the resistance concerted with "the Americans, the English, the Jordanians, the Saudis, the Zionists, and Selīm Ḥāṭūm (a Druze opponent of the regime)." The troubles continued, and on 11 May the author and editors were sentenced by a military court to life imprisonment. Thereafter the problem was appositely overshadowed by a new crisis between Syria and Israel, which in due course led to the Six Day War.

There have been other occasions too—the passionate outburst of prayer and anathema after the Mosul massacres of March 1959,[1] the immediate response to the fire in the al-Aqṣā mosque in August 1969, the recurring clashes in India and Indonesia—which suggest that Islam is still the most powerful rallying-cry and that it is for Islam, more than for any other cause, that men are still willing to kill and be killed—provided of course that they are convinced that Islam, as they understand it, is really under attack, and not merely exploited, as so often, for political ends.

This is the crux. The response to the al-Aqṣā affair illustrates perfectly both the power and the limitations of Islam as a political factor. The anger of the Muslim masses at what they at first saw as a threat to the faith was strong and real—but the attempt to use that anger for political ends failed utterly. One reason for this failure was the patent insincerity of the attempt. The revolutionary Arab leaders made no secret of their desire to subordinate Islamic to Arab purposes; the conservative potentates were visibly more concerned about the oil in Alaska than about the fire in al-Aqṣā. Another reason no doubt was the gradual realization of the basic triviality of the incident—especially when contrasted with the unambiguous communal carnage in India at the same time.

Islam can no longer be harnessed, yet it remains a force—even when it ceases to command belief. As W. Cantwell Smith remarked of modernist Muslim intellectuals, they revere "Islam in history along with, or even instead of, God. . . ."[2]

It is curious that only two Muslim states, Turkey and Tunisia, have legally abolished polygamy. Neither would rank as "progressive" by the currently fashionable definition of the term—though both would qualify in an earlier, more conventionally liberal meaning of progress. The same cannot be said of the revolutionary states, which are intellectually and socially far more conservative and have in recent years become more, not less, self-consciously Islamic, both in their deference to their own religion and in their treatment of others. The lesson of April 1967 was well learnt. During the following three years, more mosques were built in Syria than in the previous thirty, while a Christian Arab writer described the feelings of the growing number of Christian emigrants in these terms:

> Christians [they say] have no future in a country which is becoming all the time more socialist and totalitarian. Their children are indoctrinated in the schools, where the syllabus is devoted more and more to Islam and their faith is in danger. Debarred increasingly from public office and from nationalised societies [*sic*], robbed of the property of their parents and unable to engage in profitable business in a society where almost everything is under state control, how can they survive?[3]

Even when Muslims cease to believe in Islam, they may retain Islamic habits and attitudes. Thus, among Muslim Marxists, there have been both ulema and dervishes, defending the creed and proclaiming the (revolutionary) holy war against the (imperialist) infidel. For a time, the ulema of Marxism inclined towards Moscow, the dervishes towards Peking or Havana. *"There is no God and Mao is His Prophet!"* Even when the faith dies, loyalty survives; even when loyalty fades, the old identity, and with it a complex of old attitudes and desires, remains, as the only reality under the superficial, artificial covering of new values and ideologies. For those who would understand the ways of Muslim peoples, some study of Islam, both formal and popular, is a necessity. It is important to observe Islam; and indeed Christendom, the closest neighbor and greatest rival of Islam, has been observing it for a long time.

It has not generally been the habit, in the past, for civilizations and religions to attempt a sympathetic study of their neighbors and rivals. Civilization meant our civilization, and the rest were barbarians; religion meant our religion, and the rest were infidels. Occasionally an author like Herodotus in ancient Greece or Rashīd al-Dīn in medieval Persia was moved by curiosity or other causes to attempt the study of remote peoples and alien cultures. They remained exceptions and found few if any imitators. The first civilization known to history which seriously undertook the study of others not in order to conquer or convert them but merely in order to know about them, is that of Western Europe. Its example has now spread to other parts of the world.

The observation of Islam from Christendom has been going on for many centuries. Though often marred by prejudice and interest, it has nevertheless produced an understanding which is far deeper, knowledge far more extensive and more accurate, than the corresponding and simultaneous observation of Christendom from Islam.

To medieval Europe, Islam was the great adversary, and its study was required for good practical reasons. One was polemic—to understand the rival faith in order to refute and destroy it. Another was to learn. There were men in Europe who, though good Christians, recognized that the Muslims in Spain and the East knew more than they did of science, medicine, and philosophy. They were anxious to learn from them, and some even learnt Arabic for this purpose.

Religious polemic against Islam was frequent in the Middle Ages, especially during the struggles in Spain and in the Levant, and many tracts were written, either to protect Christians from Muslim blandishments or to convert Muslims to Christianity. This literature died out when the one task was seen as unnecessary, the other as impossible. There was a brief revival during the period of the great Ottoman conquests, but broadly speaking, after the end of the Middle Ages, Islam was no longer regarded in Christian Europe as a serious intellectual rival. This is the more notable, in that this attitude continued even at the time when the great challenge of Ottoman military power constituted a major threat to Europe, and Ottoman social policies offered a dangerous attraction to European peasants.

Anti-Islamic polemic continued in a desultory sort of way in missionary and theological circles but is of no great importance except insofar as it affects and distorts the growth of scholarship in the West. To a remarkable extent theology has remained the starting point of those who undertake the academic study of oriental civilizations and religions. Though most—not all—are free from the prejudices and purposes of earlier days, these studies have not yet been entirely emancipated from their theological origins. The prejudices of the medieval schoolmen may still at times be detected lurking behind the serrated footnotes of the academic apparatus.

Broadly speaking, however, Western theologians, even missionaries, working on Islam no longer have it as their purpose—at least as their direct purpose—to convert Muslims to Christianity. Their approach to

Islam has rather been in the spirit of the Dutch poet and scholar Willem Bilderdijk (1756–1831), who argued that "Mohammedans must be brought to Christ through the Koran," by showing them that "Mohammed was a Christian at heart . . . a tool in the hands of a benevolent Providence, and pioneer of salvation to Pagans and Manicheans."[4] Similar views were expressed by the English missionary Charles Forster, who in his *Mahometanism Unveiled* (1829) saw Islam as a "half-way house"—a "middle term" between Christianity and paganism. "It is only by fairly acknowledging what they have," says Forster, "that we can hope to make them sensible of what they have not."[5] With the direct attack now generally abandoned as impracticable if not unnecessary, missionary interest takes other forms—sometimes in the guise of ecumenism, sometimes clothed in the desire to join forces against a common enemy, variously defined.

The earlier type of study of Islam for purposes of polemic and refutation reappeared in the twentieth century only in one place—in the Soviet Union. In the early days after the Revolution, Russian scholarship on the Islamic lands was dominated by the need to refute and undermine Islamic and nationalist movements in the Muslim territories of the former Russian Empire and to destroy Islam in order to prepare and facilitate the conversion of the Muslim peoples of the Union to communism. The anti-Islamic literature produced in Moscow in the 1920s and early 1930s in many ways closely resembles that emanating from the monasteries of medieval Western Europe. Their interpretation of Islam, based on *a priori* theoretical principles and directed to practical purposes, belongs to the literature of religious polemic rather than of scholarship. Much Marxist writing on Islam is similarly determined, though that which is produced outside the Soviet Union usually shows greater intellectual sophistication and less obvious polemic aims. In Muslim countries, no doubt for tactical reasons, Marxists often adopt, *mutatis mutandis,* a sort of Bilderdijk approach, presenting Muḥammad as a socialist at heart, a tool in the hands of the inexorable laws of history, and a potential pioneer of communism to Muslims. This approach has so far won little support, except from an occasional official ideologue of the regimes.

Apart from the work of a few scholarly broad-church Western Marxists, the literature of polemic, whether Marxist or Christian, shows little sign of intellectual curiosity or attempt at detachment—a quality which was indeed regarded by the one as a sin, by the other as an ideological error.

In the West, the polemicist was succeeded by a new figure, who came to be known by the odd term "orientalist." This word designates, with extreme vagueness, the object of the scholar's studies but gives no indication of his method or purpose. Usually, his disciplines were theology and philology, his motive scientific curiosity—though the opportunities to indulge his curiosity were often the result of political and economic needs.

The new phase began with the Renaissance, amid a uniquely favorable combination of circumstances. The classical revival and the voyages of exploration both contributed greatly to the growth of orientalist scholarship. The old authors, and especially Herodotus, provided the model for the study of remote and alien peoples; the new scholarship furnished the philological method that was required for such studies; the expansion of Europe provided at once the scope, the need, and the material.

While Europe was expanding at both ends, across the steppes and the oceans, Islam, now represented by the Ottoman Empire, was advancing through the Balkans towards Vienna. For a while, Turkey seemed to offer a major threat to the survival of Christian civilization—but at the same time her vast territories offered a great opportunity for European commercial enterprise. Both as enemy and as market, she was an important field of study.

Finally, the Reformation and Counter-Reformation injected a new religious concern into European affairs. Protestants and especially Unitarians showed for a while an interest in Islam—in this faith which, by its hostility to polytheism and images, seemed to offer some affinities with the Protestant challenge to Catholicism. Added to this was the tempting possibility of a Turkish alliance against the Catholic powers. Though all this came to nothing, it nevertheless left some effects on the growth of European scholarship.

European writing on Islam from the sixteenth century onwards is of two main kinds, with two very different approaches.

(1) The first of these is what one might call the scholarly, dominated by theology and philology, concerned primarily with the scriptures and with the classics of Islam. The Qur'ān and the ancient Arabian literature were studied in the same way and by the same techniques as the Bible and the classics of Greece and Rome had been studied in Europe. The greatest attention was devoted to Arabic, somewhat less to Persian. Characteristically, hardly any attention at all was given to Turkish which, though it was the major language of the Muslim world at that time, had the disadvantage of being a living language and therefore, like English, French, and German, unworthy of serious scholarly attention.

(2) A second group of writings was practical, concerned with the news from Turkey and, to a lesser extent, other Muslim countries. Many books were produced on the subject of the Turkish Empire, its resources, its population, its military strength, and of course, among other things, its religion, including the different forms of worship, of organization, and of belief which existed among the peoples of that Empire. This literature is based in the main on direct observation and is intended to satisfy the need for accurate practical information about this dangerous yet interesting neighbor of Christendom. It may be noted that this neighbor was still seen primarily in religious rather than national terms and that even such ethnic names as "Turk" and "Moor" were commonly used in a religious sense, as synonyms for Muslim. Eastern Christians were not normally called by either name, while a European who adopted Islam was said to have "turned Turk."

During the nineteenth century European scholarship on Islam received a tremendous new impetus. Several new developments contributed to this great growth. One of these was the application to Islamic studies of the critical historical method which was being developed by European and especially German scholars for the study of Greek, Roman, and European history. The use of these methods for the study of the early history of Islam, the life of the Prophet, the foundation of the Caliphate, the great Arab conquests and the like, carried these studies a major step forward and formed the basis for most subsequent writing, in the Islamic world as well as in Europe.

A second important development was the emancipation of the European Jews and the consequent entry of Jewish scholars into the

European universities. From the first, Jewish scholars made a major contribution to the development of Arabic and Islamic studies—a contribution which continues to the present day, as far as politically-minded administrators and benefactors permit. Like their Christian colleagues, most of them had a theological background, transferring from the rabbinical schools and seminaries where they had studied Hebrew and Talmud, to the study of Arabic and of Islam. They differed however in several important respects from their Christian colleagues. The Jewish scholar, unlike many of his Christian colleagues, had no missionary ambitions, no nostalgia for the Crusades, no concern with the Eastern question. He was free from the inherited fears, prejudices, and inhibitions that had often marred Christian scholarship.

On the contrary, in two important respects he was favorably inclined to the object of his studies. One of these was practical and real. Hebrew and Arabic are cognate languages; Judaism and Islam are sister religions, with many important resemblances between them. A Jew, particularly a learned Jew, had a head start over his Christian colleagues in the study of Islam and an immediacy of understanding which they could not easily attain.

There was in addition a further reason for Jewish sympathy with Islam. This was the period when old-fashioned religious anti-Judaism in Christendom was giving way to the new racially expressed anti-Semitism, and the Jew was being attacked no longer as an unbeliever (a charge unworthy of the enlightened nineteenth century) but as a racial inferior, an Asian alien in Europe. Rejected as an oriental intruder, he turned to other, more powerful orientals for support, rather as some American blacks look to Africa and even Asia at the present time, with about as much justification in either case. Though this affinity was largely imaginary and entirely unreciprocated, it was nevertheless an important factor in arousing Jewish sympathy for Islam and interest in Islamic studies. Jewish scholars were among the first who attempted to present Islam to European readers as the Muslims themselves see it and to stress, to recognize, and indeed sometimes to romanticize the merits and achievements of Muslim civilization in its great days.[6]

The major development of the nineteenth century which affected the growth of oriental studies was of course the rise of imperialism and the consolidation of European power over the greater part of the Muslim world. The main countries concerned were Britain, ruling India and, later, parts of the Middle East and of Africa; France, in North and, later, Western and Central Africa; Holland, which came to dominate the greater part of Muslim Southeast Asia; and Russia, which conquered the Muslim peoples of the Volga, the Crimea, the Caucasus, and the old Muslim Kingdoms of Central Asia. These were the four major imperial powers which divided the world of Islam between them. In addition, Germany and Austria developed a semi-colonial relationship with the Ottoman Empire; and later Italy, for a brief but important interval, ruled over parts of North and East Africa.

The charge is often brought, by orientals against orientalists, that they are the servants of imperialism and that their work is designed to serve the needs of the administrator, the trader, the diplomat, the agent, and the missionary. The charge is not entirely without foundation and finds added support in the occasional appearances of the orientalist in person in one or other of these roles. In the last European empire ruling over Islamic lands, that of Russia, scholarship was unmistakably—indeed avowedly—harnessed to the policies and purposes of the state.

Yet, as an assessment of the motives that impelled Western man, even till now almost alone among mankind, to undertake the study of alien civilizations, this charge is ludicrously inadequate. Empire and commerce may have provided the stimulus and also the opportunity to undertake such studies; they did not, in free societies, direct them. The missionary and the colonial expert have, on the whole, played only a minor part in the development of Islamic scholarship in the West, and their work, with very few exceptions, has won scant respect and enjoyed little influence among scholars. The major advances were the work of men whose driving force was the desire to know and to understand and whose methods were those of critical scholarship. Most of them were university teachers, independent of, and sometimes opposed to, the great imperial and commercial interests.

The first of the social sciences to give attention to Islam was history. Practical men wrote or sponsored histories of Ottoman Turkey, the last surviving Muslim great power; scholars examined the origins and early history of the Islamic faith and community. The former produced work which is now of interest only insofar as it is contemporary and first-hand; the latter laid the foundations of a great—and continuing—scholarly tradition.

It has been said that the history of the Arabs has been written in the West chiefly by historians who know no Arabic and by Arabists who know no history. If we add Persian, Turkish, and some other languages to the formula, it may be extended to cover the history of Islam as a whole. Even now it must be admitted, at whatever cost in professional self-esteem, that academic standards in Middle Eastern studies are recognizably lower than in other, more frequented disciplines. Nevertheless there has been progress; and during the past century-and-a-half a series of scholars who were both historians and orientalists have added substantially to our understanding of the history of Islam—and not only to our understanding but also to that of the Muslims themselves.

Even when writing of the past, historians are the captives of their own times—in their materials and their methods, their concepts and their concerns. Historians of classical Islam could not but be influenced by the contemporary Islam which they saw, and particularly therefore by that part of the Islamic world to which circumstances, personal or national, gave them access. British, French, Russian, or German Islamicists therefore tended to see Islam in an Indian, North African, Central Asian, or late Ottoman guise. The historian is also guided, in the questions he asks and the answers he finds, by the preoccupations of his own time and milieu. Edward Pococke, the first great English Arabist, working at Oxford during the Civil War, hinted at parallels, in the Caliphate of al-Ma'mūn, to the clash of forces and doctrines that he saw around him; nineteenth-century European scholars discerned currents of liberalism and nationalism in the religious and sectarian struggles of early Islam; twentieth-century scholars, looking in the mirror of history, found economic change and social conflict—and turned to the new techniques and concepts of the social scientists for help in understanding them.

The first European observers to make significant generalizations about Islamic society were—not surprisingly—travelers. Certainly the most influential of these was François Bernier (1620–1688), a French physician and natural historian who spent twelve years in India and shorter periods in Syria and Egypt. As well as describing Islamic society,

Bernier tried to analyze the causes of its relative poverty and backwardness in the arts, sciences, and agriculture. He found the explanation in the lack of private landed property and the seizure of the land by the ruler, which led, directly or indirectly, to a stagnant society and a despotic regime.[7] Bernier's ideas influenced many later writers, notably Montesquieu; they were also adopted by Karl Marx, and thus place him with Adam Smith and the English Utilitarians among the ancestors of the Marxist doctrine of the "Asiatic mode of production."

Another philosophical Frenchman, the famous Volney (1757–1820), spent three years in Egypt and Syria. Unlike so many travelers, he tells us nothing of his own journeys and adventures. Instead, he describes, systematically and in detail, the condition of the countries which he visited and examines the causes of what he describes. It is a somber picture that he paints—of poverty and fear, ignorance and backwardness, tyranny, brigandage and insecurity, and a general listlessness broken only by sudden fits of pointless violence. Volney rejects the theory, current in his day, that these evils are due to climate and its effect on character. The true cause, he argues, lies in social institutions—in government and religion, the despotic misrule of the one sustained by the quietist teaching of the other. Volney, writing again after the French Revolution, was optimistic, believing that what despotism had marred, liberty could mend. Social backwardness was a temporary setback on the march of progress, which change and reform would overcome.[8]

Half a century later Adolphus Slade (1804–1877), a British naval officer who was in Turkey during the great reforms of Sultan Mahmud II and his successors, took a different view. His books have not received the attention they deserve—partly no doubt because of their form as old-fashioned personal narratives, perhaps more because their findings clashed with the liberal orthodoxy of the time. Unlike most European observers, Slade was convinced neither of the iniquities of the old regime nor of the advantages of the new. A critical but sympathetic observer, he was aware of the defects of the old order, yet found much in it to admire; while seeing the need for some change he condemns the indiscriminate haste with which it was enforced and shows how liberal reform, by disrupting a traditional society, may lead to a loss of liberty. The old nobility, however ineffectual, had generosity, honor, and a certain grace;

the new nobility, thrown up by the reforms, was greedy, violent, and corrupt.[9] These judgments, with others of similar prescience, range Slade with Burke and Tocqueville as a conservative prophet of radical doom.

These—two French philosophers and an English sailor—are but three, among the best, of the many travelers who returned from the East to enlighten their compatriots about Islam. Their writings helped, even more than those of the historians, to form and shape the image of Islam and Islamic civilization, as reflected in Western thought and scholarship.

From the eighteenth century onwards most of the great political and social thinkers have something to say about the nearest neighbor of Christendom. In France, Montesquieu and Voltaire and later Tocqueville spoke of ideas and institutions; in Germany, Herder and Hegel discussed the deeper philosophical implications; in England, Burke considered the legal and political character of Muslim government as it affected the case of Warren Hastings, while Adam Smith, Richard Jones, and the elder and younger Mill commented on the economic and social structures of the Muslim Empires. At some distance after these came Spengler, Toynbee, and other exponents of metahistory, as it is now called, though catahistory might be a better designation for their endeavors.

In this connection one other group of writings may be mentioned in passing, though it has only minor relevance to the subject under discussion. In the literature of self-doubt and self-chastisement[10] which has become an essential part of the Western tradition, the Muslim—like other non-Westerners—is often used as a sort of lay figure, or rather a ventriloquist's dummy, with an assigned part to speak in a purely Western dialogue. All this has nothing to do with either Islam or scholarship and contributes about as much to our understanding of Islam as *Gulliver's Travels* or the *Lettres Persanes* to our knowledge of cartography or Persia—and far less to our edification.

Several of the founders of modern social science had something to say about Islam. For Auguste Comte, Islam, like Christianity, was medieval and superseded, and was doomed to make way for the new religion of scientific positivism; he followed the Ottoman reforms with sympathetic interest and had some impact on the Young Turks of the next generation, whose slogan "Union and Progress" was an adaptation of Comte's "Order and Progress." Max Weber died before he could add Islam to the other religions which he examined in detail, but his works contain numerous indications of his thinking on Islam, much influenced by the writings of Julius Wellhausen. Karl Marx, like other Victorians, saw the Ottoman Empire chiefly in terms of the Eastern Question, and the Arabs not at all. He did, however, devote some attention to India and Southeast Asia, and sketched the theory of the Asiatic mode of production, which was subsequently developed by others.

Not surprisingly, given the inadequate and inaccurate information available to them, the contribution of the sociological founding fathers to the understanding of Islam was of limited value—though some of them, notably Comte, Durkheim, and the otherwise unremarkable Gustave Le Bon and Edmond Demolins, had a considerable influence on Muslim writers. Of greater significance was the stimulus which they gave to the orientalists, to elaborate, or, more often, to refute their specific assertions, and—more important—to use their concepts and methods in new lines of inquiry. Since the beginning of this century a number of Islamicists have followed this path. Prince Caetani, a disciple of Comte, brought a positivistic analysis to bear on the career of the Prophet and the beginnings of Islam. Carl Heinrich Becker, a friend of Weber and Troeltsch, tried to prove that Islam was not by nature hostile to economic progress and that Islamic civilization, Hellenistic in origin, belonged with Christendom and not with the true Asia. Other social theorists—such as Pareto, Le Play, Breysig, Durkheim—have had their disciples among the orientalists, as have also more recent scholars, notably Robert Redfield of Chicago.

One case is of special interest—that of Karl Marx. Marxist analysis of Islam has been, broadly, of three types. One of these is the doctrine of the Asiatic mode of production. Briefly sketched by Marx and Engels, in modest recognition that their system of categories, derived from European history, might not be of universal validity, it was taken up by some later Marxist scholastics who, by combining passages or even single sentences, written at different times, some of them in letters, drafts, and newspaper articles, were able to construct a coherent system of revealed thought. Most discussion of the Asiatic mode of production has been concerned with China, some with India; the Islamic world has received little attention. Recently, however, the current revival of interest in this branch of Marxism has spread to Turkey, where a few young economists have tried to detect the Asiatic mode of production in the Ottoman Empire.[11]

The Asiatic mode of production, in which there is no private ownership of land and consequently no class war, only a simple opposition between the terrorized mass of the population and the all-encompassing state bureaucracy, is one of Marx's most accurate insights—not as history, but as prophecy. For some reason Stalin disliked the theory of the Asiatic mode of production and had virtually banned it by 1938.

After that, Soviet scholarship had to fit the history of Islam into the authorized sequence of the ancient (*i.e.* slave), feudal, and bourgeois modes of production. There was much argument on how precisely this was to be done. A good example of this literature, by the late Professor E. A. Belyaev, is available in English.[12]

Covering the period from the fifth to the tenth centuries, it presents what one might call a moderate Soviet Russian orthodox interpretation of the mission of Muḥammad and the rise of Islam, with a characteristic mixture of loyalties, concepts, and purposes. The Slavs make a brief and improbable appearance as those to whom "the working masses" of the Byzantine Empire looked "as their allies and deliverers." The endless sufferings, untiring energy, and "productive activity of the toiling masses" are duly contrasted with the perfidy, cruelty, and general villainy of their royal, feudal, and religious exploiters. Special stress is laid on the horrors of Arab conquest and rule in Central Asia, in much the same way as French historians of an earlier generation used to dwell on the devastation which the Arab raiders had wrought in North Africa—and no doubt for the same reasons.

Not the least interesting parts of Belyaev's book are the surveys of previous scholarly work at the beginning of each chapter. These deal with both Western and Soviet scholarship (modern Arab and other Muslim scholarship is contemptuously dismissed as worthless or at best secondary). Only two Arab authors, Bandali Juzi and Emil Tuma, both Marxists, receive special mention. By a curious coincidence both are

Orthodox Christians. Among Western historians of the Arabs, he considers Clément Huart and Philip Hitti the best and also speaks very highly of the Belgian Jesuit scholar Henri Lammens. Among Soviet scholars, the prime concern was how to fit Islamic history into the given, predetermined framework. Belyaev rejects the "merchant-capitalistic" theory of Islamic origins as "clearly at variance with the fundamental tenets of Marxism-Leninism," and also condemns the widely accepted "early feudal" interpretation, on the lesser charge that it does not accord with the evidence. The attempts by Morozov, Klimovitch, and Tolstov to prove that Muḥammad never existed are similarly rejected. In Belyaev's view, the motive force of Islam came from the slave-owning mercantile bourgeoisie of Mecca and Medina, which arose within a decaying primitive-communal society. The Qur'ān, which he considers to have been concocted after the death of Muḥammad, expresses the new ideology, justifying "inequality in property, slavery and development of exchanges." "A slave-holding Allah is described as a typical merchant, reflecting all the features of the trading community of Mecca." Only after the conquest, and under the Caliphate, did an early feudal order replace slave production. The main purpose of the early Caliphate was "to ensure by armed might the economic subservience of the laboring majority to the wealthy minority."

On the economic and social history of the early Caliphate, Belyaev makes a number of interesting and sometimes stimulating suggestions—not of course offered as such, but rather laid down with a certitude unknown to Western scholarship since the Reformation.

The purpose of this and many other writings of the same kind is basically polemical; to refute, rather than to explain, Islamic beliefs and to discredit any view of the Islamic past which might nurture Muslim pride and encourage opposition to Soviet rule in Muslim lands. Similar purposes, at an earlier date, inspired some British, French, and Dutch colonial historians—though these never enjoyed the right to silence those who disagreed with them. More recently there have been attempts at a less crudely propagandist Marxist study of Islam, by scholars like I. P. Petrushevsky in Russia and Maxime Rodinson in France, notably in the latter's *Islam et capitalisme* (1966). M. Rodinson declares his unorthodoxy and disclaims what he variously calls vulgar Marxism, demi-Marxism, pseudo-Marxism, pragmatist Marxism, philosophic Marxism, and institutional Marxism. He even complains of the imprecision of Marx's use of "feudal" and considers the term inappropriate to medieval Islamic society. Nevertheless, he remains a practicing Marxist, and devotes much effort to intra-Marxist disputation and to problems of the correct disposition of Islamic social and economic history in Marxist terms.

Many besides Marxists share the two underlying assumptions—first, that there is some universal pattern or sequence of economic and social development, and second, that a model or norm of this development can be constructed from Western experience, which combines the advantages of being the best studied and our own. Both assumptions are questionable.

For some time the contribution of social science to the study of Islam consisted of the *obiter dicta*—mostly ill-informed—of the great generalists and the responses or reactions of orientalists—mostly philologists and historians—who read their works. The next stage came when scholars trained in a social science discipline began to deal directly and at first hand with Islamic problems and undertake field work in Islamic countries. This happened in several stages.

Imperial administration naturally gave special importance to ethnography, the relevance of which will be clear to all readers of Rudyard Kipling's *Kim* and of *Sovietskaya Etnografiya*. In the British, Russian, French, and Dutch empires useful ethnographic surveys and monographs were produced, dealing with tribal and local customs, with local saint worship, with religious brotherhoods and much else. Most of this was purely descriptive—the only theoretical consideration, if indeed such it may be called, being the needs of the imperial administration.

In time this kind of descriptive ethnography gave way to anthropological studies, of which a considerable number have by now been published. Usually, these are studies in detail—a village in Turkey, a tribe in Arabia, a sect in North Africa, and the like. Until very recently they were carried out for the most part by techniques evolved for use in the study of primitive and non-literate societies.

Anthropologists working in Islamic countries have usually fought shy of generalizations about Islam. At one time they refused, almost as a matter of principle, to take cognizance of literary evidence or even of scholarship based on such evidence. Latterly, they have become aware of the rewards—and hazards—of literary and historical studies and have usually preferred to renounce the one and thus avoid the other.

Sociologists found greater difficulty than anthropologists in persuading themselves that the literary evidence of a literate society was irrelevant to their inquiries. For a long time they warily left the sociology of Islam to the orientalist, who, trusting in his philological sword and buckler to strike true and guard him from error, tackled sociology and history, theology and literature with equal readiness and often, alas, with equal competence.

A new phase began when social scientists, while remaining primarily concerned with their discipline, acquired sufficient linguistic and historical knowledge to become acceptable regional specialists—acceptable, that is, to those whose criteria were linguistic and historical. These are still very few and usually owe their rare combination of skills to personal circumstances—to the accidental opportunities of birth, war, and employment.

Professor Clifford Geertz's *Islam Observed* (1968)[13] is thus a work of courage as well as distinction. An anthropologist with field experience in both Morocco and Java, he had the interesting idea of studying and comparing the development and condition of Islam in these two countries, at opposite ends of the Islamic world. At first sight, this might seem a strange approach. What, one might ask, could a Muslim observer learn of Christianity by comparing the practice of the faith in, say, California and Ethiopia?

There are two answers to this question. The first is that an informed, perceptive, and rigorous Muslim observer might indeed learn a great deal about the nature of the Christian religion from such an inquiry, especially if he could speak and read both English and Amharic. The second, which is more immediately to the point, is that Islam has not yet undergone the differentiation which has overtaken Christianity in the last few centuries. Islam, not only chronologically, is in its fourteenth not its twentieth century; it has still to experience the processes of reform and secularization which have transformed and divided the once-united Christian world. In modern times, Islamic identity has been reinforced by a new shared experience—the penetration, domination, and (in most areas) the departure of European colonialists.

It is obvious that there is much that the social scientist can contribute to the study of Islam and that there are many things, in early as well as modern times, which he alone, with the special skills of his profession, is able to study and explain. Social scientists, or historians using social science concepts, have already made distinctive and important contributions to the study of Islam, and it may well be that these transplants will in time produce a flowering comparable with those of European oriental scholarship following the Renaissance, the Reformation, and the philogical golden age in the nineteenth century.

Before that can happen, however, there are certain difficulties that must be overcome. It may be noticed that among modern scholars using the sociological approach, the most successful are those who have also served a philological apprenticeship. For the others there remains the problem of how to understand a society for which the principal written sources of study are locked in a strange script, requiring the mastery of a difficult language to read them, and the intimate study of a civilization to interpret them. Most of the solutions propounded to the problem rest on one or both of two dubious assumptions: that it is possible for the social scientist to acquire within a short time a "working knowledge" of an oriental language which will be sufficient for his purpose and that the use of translators and informants is an adequate substitute for direct personal access to the evidence.

Some branches of Islamic civilization, such as art and architecture, can be studied without much reference to texts. But the greater part is beset with pitfalls for the unwary student who would venture into the field without adequate study of the language in which his sources are written and in which the people whose lives and endeavors he is examining think, write, and speak. Most modern techniques of field research in the social sciences relate to one of two situations: either the researcher is dealing with a sector of his own civilization, whose historical and cultural pattern is known to him as part of his own education and upbringing, or else he is dealing with a primitive society, where historical and literary evidence can be disregarded because it does not exist. What has not yet been adequately faced is the problem of field research in a literate, historical society other than that of the field-researcher himself. This, it seems to me, is the basic problem which must be solved before Western social science can make a really effective and autonomous contribution to the better understanding of Islam.

Some English Travelers in the East

2

Travelers who describe the countries and peoples of the Middle East have always attracted a wide readership. For the general reader they supply, so he believes, the superior knowledge and consequent superior wisdom of the man (or woman) who has Been There and Met Them and Knows. This belief even now miraculously survives the daily and weekly fatuities of special correspondents. For "experts" of various kinds, who wish to specialize on the Middle East without actually having to learn a Middle Eastern language, they offer the comforting appearance of inside information—a primary source for the historian, a field report for the social scientist, a first-hand informant for the political analyst.

There has been a long series of travelers from Europe to the East; pilgrims and crusaders in the Middle Ages, followed, with the growing sophistication of Christendom, by diplomats and spies, tourists and traders, renegades and missionaries, soldiers and politicians, artists, scholars and *littérateurs*, and some, in modern times, who manage to combine several or even all of these functions.

In our own day the traveler is enjoying a new popularity, in a new role. Some of the earlier functions of travel literature are now variously discharged by the monograph, the guide-book, the hand-out, and other works of reference; some by the cinema and television. The travel writer has however retained some of these functions; in addition he has found a new purpose, in part usurping the roles previously played by the novelist, the essayist, even the publicist and the historian. In turn discursive, reflective, and informative, he brings comfort to a wide circle of readers, including, as in the past, those who fear the cost and hardship of travel, reinforced by those who shun the rigors of scholarship.

Interest in the records of past and recent travel is reflected in the growing learned literature devoted to the subject—bibliographies, surveys, and monographs, dealing with the travelers by period and by language, by the countries from which they came and to which they went, and even by the libraries in which their books are to be found.[1] Travel, it is said, broadens the mind. Travel books certainly lengthen the bibliography, and travelers' tales have a not unimportant place in history, at least in that part of it which is concerned with the formation and projection of images. Such influence may extend from the past to the future, as politicians making decisions are swayed by memories and reports of journeys abroad, their own and others'.

But what are these memories and reports really worth, either as a source of information on the past or as a guide to conduct in the future? Some two hundred years ago the great orientalist Sir William Jones surveyed and deplored the state of European knowledge concerning the Ottoman Empire and remarked:

> It has generally happened, that the persons who have resided among the TURKS, and who, from their skill in the EASTERN dialects, have best been qualified to present us with an exact account of that nation, were either confined to a low sphere of life, or engaged in views of interest, and but little addicted to polite letters or philosophy; while they, who, from their exalted stations and refined taste for literature, have had both the opportunity and inclination of penetrating into the secrets of TURKISH policy, were totally ignorant of the language used at Constantinople, and consequently were destitute of the sole means by which they might learn, with any degree of certainty, the sentiments and prejudices of so singular a people. . . . As to the generality of interpreters, we cannot expect from men of their condition any depth of reasoning, or acuteness of observation; if mere words are all they profess, mere words must be all they can pretend to know.[2]

Sir William's judgment may seem harsh, but of the great majority of previous and subsequent travelers it is lamentably just. Even those whose professional duty it was to observe and report—the diplomats and journalists—are rarely better and sometimes worse than the more casual visitors. For the historian of, let us say, Turkey or Egypt, press reports and diplomatic despatches are an essential source of information on foreign activities and international relations—on the evolution of opinions, attitudes, and even, it may be, policies in the home country. But for the history of internal affairs, even at the personal and political level, they are only rarely and accidentally of value. The reports of such travelers on the countries in which they worked, the people among whom they lived, the forces and stresses of society, culture, and government, are usually trivial and frequently wrong, and the information they provide is insignificant compared with that which is available from indigenous sources—literary, documentary, even journalistic. Turning to more recent times, who can fail to remember—or be reminded of—the pathetic series of eminent dupes who had the honor of calling on Herr Hitler and returned to assure us of his essential moderation and peaceful intentions? It is customary nowadays to divide politicians into hawks and doves. An ornithology of travel might well classify these birds of passage into gulls and parrots.

The major disability of the travelers, of which their writings show the clearest evidence and the dimmest awareness, is ignorance. It is of many kinds—diffident and confident, simple and complex, ductile and rigid, elemental and compounded with prejudice, arrogance, and, latterly, guilt. The point was well made by Dr. Johnson: "Books of travel will be good in proportion to what a man has previously in his mind. . . . As the Spanish proverb says: 'He, who would bring home the wealth of the Indies, must carry the wealth of the Indies with him.' So it is in travelling; a man must carry knowledge with him, if he would bring home knowledge" (conversation of 17 April 1778). For visitors to lands of alien culture, the first essential is that to which Sir William Jones drew attention—knowledge of the language, "the sole means by which they might learn, with any degree of certainty, the sentiments and prejudices" of the people among whom they travel and about whom they write. Admittedly, knowledge of the language is no longer as important now as it was in Sir William's day, when it was unheard of for native Muslims to learn a Western language and associate with Westerners and when even written translations were few, scarce, and for the most part inaccurate. But even now, the student of, say, Turkish or Arab affairs who has no Turkish or Arabic is at a crippling disadvantage. He has no access to the history and culture of these peoples save at second hand—that is, through materials selected and processed by other men for other purposes. He is similarly cut off from the vernacular press and can use it, if at all, only through digests, summaries, and translations, which are sometimes tendentious, often defective, and always inadequate. In his personal contacts he is limited to those who have mastered a Western language and by this very fact are untypical and unrepresentative of their countrymen. In their conversations with the traveler, they will probably be untypical even of themselves, for no man talking with an inquiring foreigner in a foreign language, in the Middle East or anywhere else, will reveal himself in quite the same way as he would in the natural intimacy of his mother-tongue.

This means that the traveler is limited, in collecting information, to what is conveyed to him by members of a minority group. In earlier times, this meant members of a religious minority, usually Christians, occasionally Jews. Today this is no longer true, and there are many Muslims who have received a Western or Westernized education and can communicate freely with Westerners. It is now generally understood—though it was not at the time—that the Christian informants of Western travelers in the Ottoman Empire conveyed a sectional and therefore somewhat distorted view. It is not sufficiently realized that the informants of modern visitors to the Middle East, though nominally adherents of the majority religion and members of the majority nation, may also form a minority—cultural, social, political—which is in many ways more alienated and more untypical than were the Greek dragomans and Armenian merchants of the Ottoman Empire. The situation is not improved when the traveler and his informant are, respectively, the guest and spokesman of an autocratic regime.

The specialized guidance of their local informants was not the only kind of distortion to which the travelers were subject. Though unencumbered with any previous knowledge, the traveler might nevertheless carry other impedimenta, in the form of preconceptions, prejudices, purposes, and a variety of psychological and ideological baggage. For many, travel was a quest—a pilgrimage to the Holy Land or Hellas or The Thousand and One Nights; a search for the benighted heathen, the exotic oriental, or the noble savage; an inspection of the achievements of empire or the evils of imperialism; a visit to the heirs, custodians, or destroyers of ancient glories. Travelers' needs, if not previously known, were soon discovered; interest and courtesy combined to gratify their desires. There were few who did not return from their travels with their beliefs confirmed and their prejudices agreeably titillated.

There are of course exceptions, some of them outstanding. From time to time a traveler manages to achieve and communicate some new insight and thus to illuminate a patch of reality for his own and future generations. He may be a journalist or a diplomat, a soldier, sailor, or gentleman of leisure—even, it may yet be, a politician returning from a tryst in some presidential palace. The literature of Middle Eastern travel cannot as yet claim a Custine or a Madame de Staël. It does however include the writings of Niebuhr, Volney, Burckhardt, Lane, Burton, Doughty,[3] and some few others of comparable stature.

One of the most remarkable was Lady Mary Wortley Montagu, *née* Pierrepoint, who followed her husband to Istanbul, where he was ambassador, in February 1717, stayed there until July 1718, and recorded her impressions in a number of letters.[4] She had several advantages. As a woman she could enter freely into the harem and penetrate the exotic mysteries that had tantalized and preoccupied so many less fortunate males; as an ambassadress, she could enjoy the social opportunities without the political limitations of her husband's office. In addition, she had the advantage, perhaps even rarer, of being intelligent, cultivated, and perceptive.

Historically too Lady Mary went to Turkey at a fortunate moment. The overwhelming religious certitude, which for centuries had caused Christian Europeans to despise Islam as something irretrievably false, hostile, and inferior, had begun to falter; the new European mood of self-questioning, which in time and for some grew to self-doubt and self-hate, had hardly begun to work. Galland's translation of *The Thousand and One Nights,* the fountainhead of the new romantic cult of the East, had only just appeared. Lady Mary was between myths—the old one of the Muslim as barbarous infidel, the new ones of the oriental as the embodiment of mystery and romance and, later, as the paragon of virtue, wisdom, and wronged innocence. For her, Turkey was a country and the

Turks were people to be respected, studied, and as far as possible understood, through the medium of their own language and culture, and in reference to their own standards and values.

Lady Mary was keenly aware of the limitations of mere travel as a source of knowledge. "'Tis certain," she says in a letter dated 1 April 1717, "we have but very imperfect relations of the manners and Religion of these people, this part of the world being seldom visited but by merchants who mind little but their own Affairs, or Travellers who make too short a stay to be able to report any thing exactly of their own knowledge. The Turks are too proud to converse familiarly with merchants etc., who can only pick up some confused informations which are generally false, and they can give no better an account of the ways here than a French refugee lodging in a Garret in Greek street could write of the Court of England."[5] She returns to the subject, and in a letter dated 17 June 1717 admonishes a correspondent: "Your whole letter is full of mistakes from one end to t'other. I see you have taken your Ideas of Turkey from that worthy author Dumont, who has writ with equal ignorance and confidence. 'Tis a particular pleasure to me here to read the voyages to the Levant, which are generally so far removed from Truth and so full of Absurditys I am very well diverted with 'em. They never fail giving you an Account of the Women, which 'tis certain they never saw, and talking very wisely of the Genius of the Men, into whose Company they are never admitted, and very often describe Mosques, which they dare not peep into. . . ."[6] On 10 April 1718 she writes, in a letter addressed to Lady Bristol: "Since my Last I have stay'd quietly at Constantinople, a City that I ought in Conscience to give your Ladyship a right Notion of, Since I know You can have none but what is Partial and mistaken from the writings of Travellers. 'Tis certain there are many people that pass years here in Pera without having ever seen it, and yet they all pretend to describe it."[7]

Lady Mary spent just over a year in Turkey, during which time she had a baby. She also managed to learn some Turkish and was able to write to Alexander Pope about Turkish poetry. She met and conversed with a number of Turkish ladies, in their homes, and was even able to charm some Turkish gentlemen into discussing religion, literature, and public affairs with her. She is at her best in describing Turkish home life—food, clothing, interior decoration and amenities, the family and staff, social and domestic usage and entertainment, which she describes with accuracy, sympathy, and wit. Her observations are not however limited to such matters. Through her female informants she knew—and understood—a good deal about the life of the Palace and the great houses; on her journeys from the border to Edirne and Istanbul she saw something of Turkish provincial government and rural life and has sharp comments to make on both. She describes the role of the ulema in Ottoman government and society and the dance of the whirling dervishes; the merits and wiles of Turkish wives and the ferocity of the Janissaries; the interiors and congregations of both mosques and baths. Her last letter from Istanbul ends with an eloquent if somewhat wayward defense of what she conceives to be the Turkish way of life:

> Thus you see, Sir, these people are not so unpolish'd as we represent them. Tis true their magnificence is of a different taste from ours, and perhaps of a better. I am allmost of opinion they have a right notion of Life; while they consume it in Music, Gardens, Wine, and delicate eating, while we are tormenting our brains with some Scheme of Politics or studying some Science to which we can never attain, or if we do, cannot perswade people to set that value upon it we do our selves. . . . I allow you to laugh at me for the sensual declaration that I had rather be a rich Effendi with all his ignorance, than Sir Isaac Newton with all his knowledge.[8]

Lady Mary was no doubt being playful, but the cloud no larger than a woman's pen was already discernible in the sky.

Lady Mary enjoyed one distinction very rare among travelers—that of being translated into the language of the people among whom she traveled. It is a remarkable indication of the poverty of travel literature on the countries of the Middle East, that even in an age of massive translation and manic self-absorption in these countries, so few travel writers were thought to be worth the trouble of translation. One was Lady Mary Wortley Montagu;[9] another was Adolphus Slade, a British naval officer who first went to Turkey in 1829. He traveled extensively during the 1830s and published two books, the first in 1832, the second in 1837.[10] In 1849 he was lent to the Turkish Navy and remained there as adviser—Mushavir Pasha—for the next seventeen years. In 1867 he published an account of the Crimean War.[11]

Slade seems to have had some influence in Turkey, partly no doubt through his personal role as naval adviser, partly through his books. According to the economist Nassau W. Senior, who was in Turkey in 1857–58, Ahmed Vefik Pasha read and admired Slade's writings, which he praised for their "fidelity" and considered to be among the "best works on Turkey."[12] One of Slade's favorite themes, the role of the Janissaries as a "Chamber of Deputies" embodying the will and defending the rights of the nation, is taken up and developed by no less a writer than Namîk Kemal. This is probably not due to coincidence.[13]

In the West, Slade has been unjustly neglected; his books have never been reprinted and are rarely even cited by modern scholars. One reason for this may be the form in which they are cast. His major works are travel books—stories of personal experience and adventures which, though very well told, are of limited interest to the modern reader. Yet, interspersed with the narrative, there are passages of comment and analysis—political, social, cultural—which are profoundly interesting and reveal Slade as one of the few Western travelers in the Middle East whose works can be compared with the classics of Western travel.

Another possible reason for his neglect may be found in the nature of his insights. Slade's travels in Turkey were carried out during the period of the great reforms of Mahmud II and his successors, and much of what he has to say is concerned with these reforms. His approach however is strikingly different from that of most other European observers of his day. He does not share the common assumptions of the time, that the old order is irredeemably bad, that the only way of improvement is liberalizing reform, and that such reform is necessarily conducive to greater happiness, prosperity, and freedom. On the contrary, he finds much that is good and admirable in the old order and notes that the effects of the reforms have often been less happiness, less prosperity, and even—perhaps especially—less freedom. Though Slade was conservative, and at times perhaps reactionary in his views, he was not opposed to reform as such. What he criticizes is rapid, violent, and indiscriminate reform, which destroys the good as well as (or sometimes instead of) the bad parts of the old order and installs new and more efficient iniquities in their place. He is not unaware of the evils of traditional society and government, nor unwilling to mend them; but he is also deeply conscious of the virtues of the old order, which he describes with sympathy and knowledge, yet entirely without romanticism.

Part of his judgment was personal—respect and liking for Turks of the old school and mistrust of the manners and motives of their successors. Of Pertev Pasha, Slade remarks that he was "commonly styled the last of the Turks—of the Turks who were loyal without flattery, hospitable without ostentation, self-respectful without arrogance, and who with the vices possessed the virtues of a dominant race."[14] The new elite was quite different. "The men who had floated to the surface on the wreck of the orthodox Turkish party were in general needy, unillustrated by descent. They had to acquire wealth to gain influence and make partisans, in default of which they would be mere bubbles on a troubled sea. Each enriching himself had to wink at his colleague's infirmity, and partisans could only be retained on like conditions. The old nobility, profuse and open-handed, lived on their estates: their ovens were never cool; their pilaf cauldrons never empty. The State was the estate of the new nobility."[15] Slade may be biassed in his affection for the old aristocracy and gentry, but his final comment on the "new nobility" shows devastating accuracy and prescience.

Slade's defense of the old order must have shocked many of his readers, extending as it did to some of the legendary evils ascribed to "Turkish tyranny." He defends the Sultans, the Janissaries, and the ulema; he has much to say in praise, as well as in blame, of old-style Turkish practice and government and even of their treatment of the Greeks and other Christians, whose lot was in many respects better than under some Christian rulers. Slade protests repeatedly against the self-righteousness and superficiality shown by Western critics of Turkey and Islam. "Slavery sounds revolting to an English ear; change the name, where is the country in which it does not exist? The labourer is chained to his plough, the mechanic to his loom, the pauper to the workhouse."[16] Nor is the parallel limited to economic slavery. After describing the proceedings of a purchaser in the slave-market, Slade drily adds: "The waltz allows nearly as much liberty before hundreds of eyes."[17] He can even see some merit in public executions:

> Orientals are moved to reflection through the medium of their senses. The sight of one brigand hung on the theatre of his exploits has more effect than the report of a hundred brigands wasting away in chains in the bagnio. Whatever may be advanced against public executions, it will be admitted that punishment without example has the taint of vengeance—a reproach sure to be levelled in time against the cloistral imprisonment of the 19th century; the horrors of which cannot be imagined, nor conveyed even faintly to the imagination by the pen of a Sterne or a Dickens. Public execution is the only guarantee for the mass that criminals of a certain quality do suffer death, and in times of social excitement, that criminals of another stamp are becomingly dealt by.[18]

Once again Slade's judgments have not lost their relevance, even in modern times. Modernity takes different forms. In some countries public executions are abolished; in others they are televised.

Despite his aristocratic conservatism and his mistrust of the new men, Slade is not unsympathetic to the reforms. His judgment of the working of the Rescript of the Rose Chamber of 1839 is much more favorable than those of the impatient liberals: "This famous proclamation, conceived in a spirit of clemency and tolerance, inaugurated a new era for Turkey. The direct power of death by decapitation was taken from scores of vizirs; the indirect power of death by vexation, from hundreds of inferior station. Oriental ductility was severely tested. An ensanguined nation was ordered to be gentle, and the order was obeyed. Pashas used to rule with the sabre were required to rule by exhortation. Mudirs and agas, wont to admonish rayas with the stick, were enjoined to be civil to them. The exhaustion of the nation, after twenty years of unparalleled suffering, favoured the experiment; anything for quiet was the universal aspiration. The Ottomans, with the instincts of a dominant race, adapted themselves to altered circumstances; they leant upon their prestige, and it did not fail them."[19]

Slade's severest strictures are reserved for the autocratic reforming rulers, and above all for Sultan Mahmud II, whom he accuses of "the entire subversion of the liberties of his subjects."[20] Realizing that the use of this expression in relation to Turkey would startle his Western readers, Slade explains his meaning. Though the autocracy of the Sultan was nominally supreme, the people in effect possessed three great checks against tyranny. These were the *derebeys,* a hereditary nobility, whose domains "were oases in the desert";[21] the *ayān,* a provincial and urban magistracy; and the ulema, the "Mussulman hierarchy . . . a most powerful body, its existence, founded on religion, being cemented by the respect of the nation. It is the peerage of Turkey, sole intermedium now existing between tyranny and slavery. . . ."[22]

In his policy of centralization, Mahmud set to work to destroy or undermine all three. Slade does not object to his restraining the great pashas governing the provinces—"men who usually sprang from insignificance, owing their elevation to baseness, supporting it by tyranny—sycophants in the capital, tyrants in the provinces. . . ."[23] These men were an unmitigated evil, and had Mahmud contented himself with replacing them by "men of integrity, if such could be found, he would have given a solid proof of an enlarged understanding."[24]

It was however his appetite, not his understanding, that was enlarged. The *derebeys* "had two crimes in the eyes of Mahmoud II: they held their property from their ancestors, and they had riches. To alter the tenure of the former, the destination of the latter, was his object. The *derebeys*—unlike the seraglio dependents, brought up to distrust their own shadows—had no causes for suspicion, and therefore became easy dupes of the grossest treachery. The unbending spirits were removed to another world, the flexible were despoiled of their wealth."[25] In the same way he set to work to abrogate or enfeeble the intermediate powers of the *ayān* and the ulema and thus reinforce his own autocracy.

Slade views these changes with misgiving and is impatient with Western observers who hope for their success:

> It is strange that many Franks in Turkey hope that Sultan Mahmoud may succeed in overturning the ulema, as he has done the Janizzaries. They appear to think that no permanent reformation can take place while one of the ancient institutions exist. Who, when the machine is entirely disorganized, is to remodel

it,—when every element of discontent is loosened, is to allay them,—when the fabric of centuries is violently shaken, is to consolidate it?[26]

Who indeed.

Mahmud was unfortunate in his choice of example.

He took Mehemet Ali for his guide, and the rule of Mehemet Ali was to extort money from every source, by any means; to render himself sole proprietor of Egypt. An enlarged view of things, joined to unparalleled cruelty and duplicity, with a perfect knowledge of the evil ways of mankind in the East, gained during the various phazes of his life, (he has been a cavedgi, a tobacco merchant, a chavass, a klephte, a bim bashi, a pasha), enabled him to succeed. Excepting cruelty, Mahmoud had none of these advantages; truth never found the way to his ear, and he always saw with others' eyes—the natural consequences of his station. He thought that the other owed his success entirely to having overturned existing institutions, and he flattered himself, when he should have accomplished the same, to be able to rule Turkey and to till it.[27]

Slade's judgments of the results are worth quoting *in extenso:*

Travellers are apt to laud Mehemet Ali: but let them consider the condition of his subjects—let them recollect, what they must have seen, the multitudes labouring naked in the cotton and rice grounds, goaded on by overseers, the numbers perishing on the banks of the canal, or in the towns,—the only bar between life and death, of those who survive a few years, black bread and the water of the Nile, their only enjoyment—shared with animals, as transitorily and as soullessly—multiplying their wretched species,—they will not wish his doctrines to be extended to Turkey. If the attributes of civilization,—armies, fleets, canals, roads, palaces,—can only be obtained by similar means, humanity would decline them. . . .

Civilization, forced, is as inimical to a people's happiness as is a constitution abruptly presented. That deprives them of their liberties; this of their judgment: the shackles of the former are felt, before the corresponding silken bands are fitted to disguise the iron; the condescension of the latter is abused before its beauty is respected: the one sharpens the sword of state; the other puts clubs in the hands of the mob. For the former hypothesis look at Russia; for the latter observe France.

When a nation, comparatively barbarous, copies the finished experience of a highly civilized state, without going through the intermediate stages of advancement, the few are strengthened against the many, the powerful armed against the weak. The sovereign, who before found his power (despotic in name) circumscribed, because with all the will, he had not the real art of oppressing, by the aid of science finds himself a giant—his mace exchanged for a sword. In scanning over the riches of civilization, spread out before him for acceptance, he contemptuously rejects those calculated to benefit his people, and chooses the modern scientific governing machine, result of ages of experiments, with its patent screws for extracting blood and treasure,—conscription and taxation. He hires foreign engineers to work it, and waits the promised result—absolute power. His subjects, who before had a thousand modes of avoiding his tyranny, have not now a loop-hole to escape by: the operations of the uncorroding engine meet them at every turn, and, to increase their despair, its movement accelerates with use, and winds closer their chains. A people thus taken by surprise, and thrown off their guard, will be centuries before they acquire sufficient knowledge—every beam of which is carefully hid from them by the clouds of despotism—to compare their situation with that of their neighbours—(who, although ruled by the same means, have advantages to counterbalance its weight)—to assert human rights, and to dare to say "we are men". In the mean time, they are dispersed or collected, or worked, as cattle; suffered to perish of disease, or starve, as things of no import; compelled to march like puppets from zone to zone, for the caprice of one man—to slaughter and be slaughtered for his pleasure; and if any one, using his reason, pronounce such proceedings against the eternal fitness of things, he is denounced as revolutionary, an enemy of order, little short of mad, and unfit to live. Such are the fruits which civilization, so called, has produced in one country. Newspapers act as oil to the engine, are, under such auspices, the direst enemies of freedom and rational reform, simply because they dare only espouse one side of a question, the side which suits the powers that are. Even supposing, which is not probable, the editors to have any thing dearer at heart than their own profits, they dare not expose corruption in the heads of departments, and therefore, as a juste milieu is seldom the part of a newspaper, they applaud their measures, however tyrannical, the more particularly if they receive money for so doing. It is a long time in any state before the press acquires sufficient respectability, as well as independence, to expose abuses; until that time it only serves to abet them . . . the establishment of gazettes in Turkey, though exceedingly captivating in sound, quite refreshing to the ears of liberals, a harbinger of freedom, is in fact very anti-liberal, a corruption promoter, an aegis for the greatly wicked.

It is curious to observe the similarity of advantages which are enjoyed by nations in opposite spheres of knowledge, and separated by perfectly distinct manners and religion. Hitherto the Osmanley has enjoyed by custom some of the dearest privileges of freemen, for which Christian nations have so long

> struggled. He paid nothing to the government beyond a moderate landtax, although liable, it is true, to extortions, which might be classed with assessed taxes. He paid no tithes, the vacouf [*waqf*] sufficing for the maintenance of the ministers of Islamism. He travelled where he pleased without passports; no custom-house officer intruded his eyes and dirty fingers among his baggage; no police watched his motions, or listened for his words. His house was sacred. His sons were never taken from his side to be soldiers, unless war called them. His views of ambition were not restricted by the barriers of birth and wealth; from the lowest origin he might aspire without presumption to the rank of pasha; if he could read, to that of grand vizir; and this consciousness, instilled and supported, by numberless precedents, ennobled his mind, and enabled him to enter on the duties of high office without embarrassment. Is not this the advantage so prized by free nations? Did not the exclusion of the people from posts of honour tend to the French revolution? For this freedom, this capability of realizing the wildest wishes, what equivalent does the sultan offer? It may be said none.[28]

An interesting contrast with Slade's writings is provided by a far more famous book, Sir Charles Eliot's *Turkey in Europe*. Originally published under the pseudonym Odysseus in 1900, it was re-issued with additional material in 1908 and reprinted from the second edition in 1965.[29] The two authors have much in common. Both were active public servants—Slade a naval officer, Eliot a diplomat and, later, a university administrator. Both were superb writers—shrewd and accurate in their observation, clear, forceful, and often witty in their exposition. Both were helped by a knowledge of Turkish and a sympathy for the Turks; yet both were sustained by a confidence in their own civilization which, to the modern Western reader accustomed to fashionable self-abasement, may look rather like arrogance. They had standards, by which they were prepared to judge their own as well as other peoples and other peoples as well as their own. Eliot in particular often expresses judgments and clothes them in language, which to contemporary taste may seem offensive and even cruel. Much more than Slade, he views the East from a position of amused and comfortable superiority. His disapproval looks like disdain; even his sympathy smacks of condescension. This attitude, and the prejudices that go with it, will no doubt delight some readers and shock, offend, or irritate many others. But even these may appreciate his robust frankness, his freedom from the anxious and piacular humbug of much modern Western writing on the non-Western world.

Eliot's Turkey is different from Slade's. The reformers and, so it seemed, the reforms were dead and buried; Abdülhamid II, the arch-reactionary, was master. Liberal circles had given up all hope of the Turks and had espoused the cause of the subject peoples of the Turkish Empire; even conservatives were weakening in their traditional support for Turkish integrity, as the sultan on the one hand oppressed his subjects, on the other drew nearer to Germany. Eliot's sympathy for the Turks is much less pronounced than Slade's—but it is no less out of accord with the prevailing attitudes of his time. Still more discordant was his disenchanted view of the Christian subjects of the Turks—their characters and their aspirations.

There is another important difference between the two travelers. Eliot was an intellectual—a brilliant linguist who mastered more than a score of languages, a learned and imaginative scholar who later in life wrote standard works on Hinduism and Buddhism. While Slade's books are rambling, discursive, and personal, Eliot's *Turkey in Europe* is organized and analytical, combining direct knowledge with immense philological, historical, and even theological erudition. No other author has dealt as clearly and effectively with the different peoples, faiths, and institutions that made up the Ottoman Empire at the end of the nineteenth century.

He has his blind spots. A keen observer of the present and a learned student of the past, his scholarship is literary and linguistic rather than historical. Thus, he is capable of writing: "We must draw a distinction between the history of the Turks and the history of their Christian subjects. The former is a purely military record. Modern writers are unwilling to regard history as a mere catalogue of reigns and battles, and pay more attention to the various movements, political, religious, intellectual, social, and commercial which the life of each nation presents. This is very just in the case of nearly all nations; but the peculiarity of the Turks is at once apparent when we observe that their history is almost exclusively a catalogue of names and battles."[30] Despite Eliot's knowledge and intelligence, it does not seem to have occurred to him that the "peculiarity" he describes is one of historiography, not of history—a deficiency not of the Turks but of the books he had read about them. The same historical impercipience is shown in his insistence that despite all the reforms there had been no real change, that "without Janissaries, and without Phanariots, it [the Ottoman Empire] is still, in the first decade of the twentieth century very much what it was in the first decade of the nineteenth."[31] Slade, though without scholarly pretensions, would not have made such mistakes and indeed shows a keen awareness of social, economic, and cultural change. In the same spirit Eliot lays great stress on the eternal "nomadism" of the Turks, who after centuries of occupation, according to him, are still strangers in Europe—pastoral marauders who have used the country but contributed nothing to it and who have never really adapted themselves to urban or sedentary living. The point is made, with a characteristic blend of shrewdness and prejudice, in this description of the Yildiz Palace secretariat: "I have seen a number of secretaries and officials working in a room decked with red plush and the ordinary furniture of European palaces. Some were sitting curled up in armchairs, with their inkpots poised perilously on the arms, the idea of having a writing-table never having come into their heads. Some were squatting on the floor, eating with their fingers off broad dishes placed on a low table. One was taking a siesta in a corner. Nothing could have more vividly suggested the idea of a party of tent-dwellers who had suddenly occupied a European house, and did not quite know how to use it."[32] It seems a strange comment on an empire which had cherished and maintained such monuments of the past as Hagia Sophia and had added greatly to them.

Despite such lapses, Eliot has many insights to offer, especially in his thumb-nail sketches of persons and situations. Some of his dicta may still be of interest even to the contemporary student—of other places if not of Turkey. "When one reads European reports on the condition of the Turkish provinces, or reflects on the wonderful things one has seen with one's own eyes, one is inclined to think that the system cannot go on. It is annually proved that the machinery of government is collapsing; that there is no money and no food; that no one can pay any taxes, and that everybody must starve. Yet it all goes on next year eskisi gibi—'the same old way'. They that had been skinned are skinned again, and they that were starving are starving still, but not dead. . . . It may safely be affirmed that if any European Power were to undertake to finance Turkey, the whole place would be bankrupt in a week, and need years of recuperation. But political economy seems to be one of those things which must be accepted or rejected as a whole. Partial and blundering acceptance means collapse, but if, like the Sublime Porte, you reject it in toto, if you discard such conceptions as the National Debt, and pay no regard to the theory of wages, the theory of demand and supply, and all other theories what ever, it seems to make no difference."[33] There may still be a few places in the world where Eliot's economic wisdom is relevant. There are many more where students and practitioners of politics would do well to heed another of his warnings:

> Before I proceed any further I had better emphasize a distinction which has probably already dawned upon the reader—that between the real and the paper government of Turkey. If one takes as a basis the laws, statistics, and budgets as printed, it is easy to prove that the Ottoman Empire is in a state of unexampled prosperity. Life and property are secure; perfect liberty and toleration are enjoyed by all; taxation is light, balances large, trade flourishing. Those who had not an extensive personal acquaintance with Turkey may regard such accounts with suspicion and think them highly coloured, but they find it difficult to realize that all this official literature is absolute fiction, and for practical purposes unworthy of a moment's attention. Once in Russia, which is in many ways an Eastern country, I missed a steamer on the Neva owing to its having left a certain pier half-an-hour before the time advertised. I tried to appeal to the pier-keeper's sense of justice by pointing to the time-table displayed in his office, but he would not see the point of my argument, and merely replied, "You should never pay attention to what is printed." You never should, at any rate in Turkey. No reform is clamoured for which does not already figure in the statute-book; no complaint is made which cannot be disproved by statistics. This is partly due to the Oriental idea of literature. Just as no one would use the language of everyday life in the most trifling letter, so everyday facts are felt to be inappropriate to literary composition. You cannot write a letter without describing yourself as a slave and ascribing all virtues to your correspondent. Similarly you cannot write a history without describing the Sultan as ever-victorious, and you cannot write of his country without describing it as well defended and prosperous. The natural divorce between literature and facts is so complete that the Oriental attaches little more importance to striking statistics or to declarations of the Imperial clemency than he does to epistolary compliments. He feels that it would be rude and bad style to say anything else.[34]

The Decolonization of History

3

When the colonialists finally packed and departed from the countries they had ruled, their former subjects faced a new task. The present was saved, the future preserved from the colonialist grasp. There remained the task of liberating the past. The decolonization of history, as it was called, attracted considerable attention and energy in the new states of Asia and Africa. The line of argument was much the same in most of them and ran something like this. Ever since the advent of European rule, the writing of history had been controlled by colonialist historians and their native disciples. These historians had a purpose: to justify the establishment and facilitate the maintenance of colonial domination. This they did by blackening the pre-colonial era, which they depicted as an age of barbarism and backwardness, and whitewashing the colonial regime, which they presented as an instrument of enlightenment and progress. This kind of history, which was taught to both the rulers and the ruled, served the double purpose of demoralizing the latter and nerving the former for the sometimes disagreeable duties which they had to perform. A further aim was to divide the subject peoples by inventing fictitious national entities.

If, as was believed, this was a correct assessment of the historiography inherited from the colonial regimes, it was obviously unsuited to the schools and universities of the newly independent states. A new historiography was needed, which would rescue the forgotten—or rather the deliberately hidden—glories of the national past and set right the record of colonialism. In this way the citizens of the new states would attain the pride and self-confidence that come from the consciousness of one's national heritage and would abandon the unjustified and undignified deference which they had previously shown to their European mentors.

The first of the subject peoples to react in this way against imperialist historiography were those of the Russian Empire. The fall of Tsardom, the new revolutionary iconoclasm, and the temporary relaxation of imperial control brought a great wave of new historical thinking, in which Russian orientalists, in sympathy with the subject peoples, played no small part. National and religious leaders who had resisted Russian expansion were rediscovered and celebrated, and the remoter glories of the Turkish, Tatar, Iranian, and Islamic past studied and acclaimed. The Muslim peoples of Asiatic Russia were recovering their common identity—were learning that they were not an ethnic dust of broken tribes inevitably attracted to Great Russia but the scattered remnants of a great civilization.

This trend, strong in the 1920s, was slowed down in the 1930s and decisively reversed in the late 1940s—sometimes with some personal inconvenience to the scholars concerned. Two points were now firmly established; first that the Russian conquest of Asia, even under the Tsars, was "objectively" progressive and resistance to it therefore "objectively" reactionary; second, that the Uzbeks, Kirgiz, *et al.*, were separate and distinct peoples whose national identity had in the past been suppressed by Tatar, Iranian, and Islamic tyrannies and must not now be obscured by pan-Turkish, pan-Iranian, or pan-Islamic propaganda. Those who held otherwise were variously accused of chauvinism, racialism, clericalism, feudal idealism, and bourgeois objectivism. Particularly condemned was the racialist or clericalist idealization of the pre-Russian past.

Though the decolonization of history was halted and reversed in the Soviet Union, it was taken up with enthusiasm in other countries, notably in India, Egypt, and North Africa. Begun while the British and French colonialists were still in power, it has continued apace since their departure, and a considerable body of decolonized historiography, ranging from accurate scholarship to unbridled fantasy, has appeared. By a fortunate coincidence, Marxist scientific analysis, while condemning pan-Turkism and pan-Iranism, allows pan-Arabism; it also denies to the British in India or the French in North Africa the enlightened and progressive role played by Tsarist Russia in Central Asia and Trans-Caucasia.

M. Lacoste is a French Marxist, whose aim is to assist the people of North Africa in the liberation of their past.* The issue, he points out, is not an academic one, nor a mere intellectual exercise: it is directly relevant to the problems of under-development, which are the main concern of the Third World. Under-development is the result of colonial misrule—on this M. Lacoste has no doubts and uses no half-tones. It is therefore necessary to make a critical examination of the misdeeds of the colonialists and also of those factors in pre-colonial society which delayed or prevented economic, social, or political development and thus allowed the colonialists to enter. The great Arab historian Ibn Khaldūn is of particular value for this second purpose.

One of the gravest misdeeds of the French in North Africa, according to M. Lacoste, was the creation of a mythical version of North African history, which has no basis in historical reality. The word "myth" should not mislead us into thinking in terms of spontaneous generation and development:

> This myth is not the fruit of chance. It was consciously forged, and inculcated in the framework of colonialist ideology. This judgment, which may at first sight seem excessive and partisan, is only in conformity with the historic reality.

The content of the myth is the basic antagonism of nomads and sedentary peoples, of Arabs and Berbers. The method of the myth-makers is to portray the Arabs as destructive invaders, from whose yoke the Berbers were finally liberated by the coming of the French. The purposes of the myth were to divide Arab from Berber in order to rule both; to undermine any sense of nationality or patriotism which might arise among them; to prove the impossibility of any separate political existence for North Africa; to demonstrate the social, economic, and cultural backwardness bequeathed by the invaders; and, by these means, to justify

---

**Ibn Khaldoun: naissance de l'histoire, passé du tiers-monde* by Yves Lacoste (Paris, 1968).

and preserve the "civilizing mission of France." To sustain his argument, M. Lacoste quotes passages from such French writers on North Africa as E. F. Gautier *("un des plus brillants idéologues de la colonisation")* and Louis Bertrand *("chantre officiel du Gouvernement Général de l'Algérie")*.

The parallels between the French interpretation of North African history described by M. Lacoste and the Russian view of Central Asian history imposed during the past twenty years are obvious and striking: the French Berber policy and the Russian policy of local nationalities; the French disparagement of Arabism and the Russian rejection of both the Iranian and the Tatar heritages; the insistence of both on their own "civilizing" or "objectively progressive" role. There are of course two important differences: one is that M. Lacoste, in refuting the views of Gautier and Bertrand, is able to draw on a solid body of critical French scholarship; the other is that the French no longer rule North Africa.

M. Lacoste, though a believer in comparative studies, attempts no such comparison. Instead, he is concerned to rescue Ibn Khaldūn from the malice of colonialist historians, who have fraudulently *("frauduleusement")* distorted his writings for their own nefarious ends. Ibn Khaldūn's famous description of the enduring devastation brought to North Africa by the Bedouin migrations in the eleventh century has indeed been extensively used by Gautier and other French writers; together with other passages on the characteristics of the Arab nomads, it led an Egyptian philosopher (Ahmad Fu'ād al-Ahwānī, *Al-Qawmiyya al-ʿarabiyya*, Cairo 1960, page 98) to remark that the orientalists had only accepted Ibn Khaldūn because of his attacks on Arabism; it also led, for a while, to the banning of Ibn Khaldūn's works in the Republic of Iraq. M. Lacoste is at some pains to show that the events described by Ibn Khaldūn never happened and that in fact Ibn Khaldūn never described them.

Part of the book is devoted to finding alternative explanations of the factors exploited by colonialist historians, part to presenting and interpreting Ibn Khaldūn in a new light. There have been many studies of Ibn Khaldūn in which disciples of Durkheim, Breysig, *et al.*, have explained him as a precursor of Durkheim, Breysig, *et al.* He has even been presented (though not by a disciple) as a kind of Ur-Toynbee. M. Lacoste does not commit the error of making Ibn Khaldūn a Marxist: yet, by a sort of materialist election of grace, he admits him to Marxist salvation. Philosophically, M. Lacoste admits, he was no rationalist. On the contrary, he was religious, and at times subject to "mystical obscurantism." He was unable to define his essential ideas with precision, because the conceptual equipment of the time was too undeveloped and "objective realities" insufficiently differentiated. Yet, M. Lacoste believes, he came very near to historical materialism. To study Ibn Khaldūn with modern (*videlicet* Marxist) concepts thus involves no distortion or anachronism. It is the only way to discover and define his real meaning, which he himself could not define for lack of conceptual tools. Ibn Khaldūn's views are incomplete but not obsolete, according to M. Lacoste, and it is the task of the modern scholar to carry through the analysis which Ibn Khaldūn, apparently without realizing what he was doing, began in the fourteenth century.

M. Lacoste's approach to Islamic history is somewhat idiosyncratic. He believes that the fourteenth century was the most brilliant in the history of medieval Egypt; that Ibn Hawqal was an historian; that the Fāṭimid Empire represented the revolt of a group of mountain tribes. Some of his arguments bring much-needed corrections to established errors—as for example in describing the Hilali migration as a deportation and invitation rather than an invasion; others, in the absence of documentary as distinct from theoretical evidence, fail to carry conviction. The last part of the book is devoted to establishing the place of Ibn Khaldūn in the development of scientific historical thought and method and his relevance as an analyst of under-development to the present-day problems of the Third World.

For the reader who would like to know what Ibn Khaldūn himself actually said, the new volume edited by Mr. N. J. Dawood* provides an excellent introduction. Mr. Dawood has already shown his skill as a translator of the Qur'ān and of the *Thousand and One Nights*—two of the three Arabic books known by name in the West. He now turns his attention to the third, the *Prolegomena* of Ibn Khaldūn. Using as his base

---

* *The Muqaddima: An Introduction to History*, edited and abridged by N. J. Dawood. Translated by Franz Rosenthal (London, 1968).

the monumental three-volume translation by Professor Rosenthal of Yale, he has, by skillful abridgment and deft but unobtrusive editing, produced an attractive and manageable volume, which should make the essential ideas of Ibn Khaldūn accessible to a wide circle of readers.

On Writing the Modern History of the Middle East

4

The classical Western form of orientalism is an offshoot of the main tradition of European academic scholarship, which has grown up in the great universities of Europe since the Middle Ages. Orientalist studies—that is, studies of oriental civilizations by Western scholars—are a part of that tradition and have their roots deep in European history and culture. Their origins were in the sister disciplines of classics and theology, which for so long dominated the European universities. Through centuries of study of Latin, Greek, and Hebrew texts, and of Christian and Jewish belief and doctrine, the scholars of Europe perfected a philological and philosophical method and discipline which became, in their skillful hands, a precise and effective instrument of study and research. The achievement of the first great European orientalists was to take this instrument, fashioned for another purpose, and apply it to the study of Arabic and Islam. The labors of subsequent generations of orientalists have consisted largely of wielding this instrument and making such minor modifications to it as seemed necessary.

In the early nineteenth century the new European school of scientific history also found its disciples among the orientalists. The studies of Ranke and Niebuhr on European and Roman history inspired a number of orientalists to try and apply their methods to the study of Islam. The first pioneer was Gustav Weil (1808–1889), who in his biography of the Prophet and his history of the Caliphs made the first attempt to treat these topics in accordance with the methods and objectives of critical historical scholarship. Since then others have followed him, and Western orientalists have been able to make a profoundly significant contribution to the understanding of medieval Arab history—a contribution of incalculable importance to the historical self-awareness, at the present day, of the Arabs themselves.

It is, however, almost exclusively with the *medieval* history of the Arabs that the orientalists have concerned themselves. For one thing, it is in medieval history, based on chronicles and inscriptions, that the method of philological, textual scholarship is most effective—and it is in the use of this method that the orientalist is at his best and happiest. For another, it was the ancient and medieval periods that were intrinsically more interesting to these scholars. As long as Islam was an independent and distinctive civilization, it was a subject worthy of classical studies. In the periods of decline and change—particularly of change in the direction of a greater resemblance to themselves—it ceased to attract them. As Arabic literature became more European in its forms and themes, it became less interesting to European orientalists, who were drawn precisely by what was distinctive and unfamiliar in the classical Arab past. The modern Arabs were of no more interest to the old-style orientalist than were the modern inhabitants of Greece and Italy to the old-style Hellenist or Latinist.

In recent years some orientalists have begun to interest themselves in modern history and have produced work of value, particularly since the opening of the great Turkish archives has at last made possible the serious historical study of the Ottoman period. They are still, however, very few. On the history of the Middle East in modern times—that is, since the rise of European influence—the orientalists have little to say and have left the field to writers of another kind.

For some time now there has been a growing Western interest in the modern Middle East, and this has stimulated the production of a very large number of books, of varying purpose and value. Some are the work of European and American writers; others are written by authors of Middle Eastern nationality, of whom there are increasing numbers able to write in a Western language and for a Western reading public.

Many of these books, though purporting to be works of history, are in fact nothing of the kind but are exercises in quite different professions. One group may be best described as journalism. The honest and conscientious journalist follows an honorable profession, with a useful, indeed an essential function in the modern world. It may often happen that the journalist, with the special methods and insights of his craft, achieves a truer and deeper understanding of contemporary events than the historian and produces material of great value to present-day and future historians. Nevertheless he is not writing history. Reportage and news comment between hard covers are still journalism and belong fundamentally with the daily or weekly newspaper and periodical, rather than with the monograph of the critical historian.

The advocate too follows an honorable calling, at least when his character is clear and undisguised. Advocacy is not confined to courts of law. The writer who sets forth a version of events designed to convince an invisible judge and jury of the rightness of his client's cause is also an advocate, whether his client be a party, a nation, a class, a church, or a continent. From the clash of argument truth may emerge; but the advocate is not primarily concerned with arriving at the truth. That is the business of the judge and jury. The advocate's task is to state the best possible case for his client and leave his opponents to state their own. His writings, like those of the journalist, may be invaluable source-material for the historian. They are not history.

Propaganda has been defined as the art of persuading other people of what one does not believe oneself. The word has a respectable ancestry, having originally been used by the faithful of the propagation of their own religious faith. But in our own day, like so much else, it has gone through a process of devaluation, and only the most cynical will accept it as a definition of their own activities. Basically, the propagandist, as the word is used nowadays, is not concerned with the truth of what he preaches. He considers that it will benefit the cause or interests which he serves if certain people believe certain things; he therefore tries by all the means in his power to convince them of these things. Whether these things are true or false is irrelevant both to his purpose and to his chances of achieving it. It is hardly necessary to assert the distinction between propaganda and history; it is often however difficult to demonstrate it to the propagandist's victims.

To journalism, advocacy, and propaganda we may add a fourth category of non-historical writings on history, which for want of a better name we may call mythology. The ancient peoples expressed their religious beliefs and scientific principles—the two were much the same—in the form of myths; modern nations express their guiding and sustaining assumptions in the form of national historiographic myths, absorbed in childhood from home and school, and held through life without doubt or question. A depressingly large proportion of the so-called history in our school manuals is no more than mythology—deeply-held beliefs which gratify and solace those who hold them but which have little or no foundation in fact. In some countries the advance of historical research has been able to penetrate from the learned quarterlies into the school textbooks and to give people a more balanced and objective view of their national past and present. In other countries national history is still a twilight world of myth and fantasy, in which all virtue is with the patriots and all evil comes from foreigners (in certain situations this myth may be inverted, but the principle is the same). This is neither an adult nor a dignified posture; nor is it one from which one can conveniently step forward.

Of the vast literature published in recent years on the modern history of the Middle East, a large part, perhaps the greater part, belongs to one or other of these categories and cannot properly be classed as historical writing at all. Such works are written from the standpoint and in the interest of one or another party to Middle Eastern conflicts, and they offer only precarious guidance to the student of history.

If however we set aside the many books written to serve political or commercial purposes or to relieve personal tensions, there still remains a sizable body of work produced by professional scholars on the modern history of the Middle East. Some of it has been written by orientalists, but not much. In the main they have neglected this subject and have left it to the colonial (and anti-colonial) historian and to a variety of specialists in economics, politics, and international relations.

Between the modernist and the orientalist there has been remarkably little cooperation. While it would probably be an exaggeration to say that the twain never meet, one might not unfairly remark that they pass one another with cold and perfunctory greeting, sometimes even with averted eyes. Modern historians and political scientists anxious to work on the Third Republic or the Third Reich are not required to begin their studies with the *Chanson de Roland* or the *Nibelungenlied*, nor would such studies, however illuminating, be regarded as a sufficient disciplinary training. They are however expected to know French and German. While most would agree that the time has come to emancipate oriental history from philological domination, it is by now clear that we cannot afford to emancipate this study from all philological discipline.

The nineteenth century has fared badly at the hands of historians of the Middle East. The orientalists have, in the main, shown little interest in a period so near to our own, when the qualities which first attracted them to study Islamic society are attenuated and contaminated by contact with our own Western civilization and thus lose their attraction. The modernists have done useful work but have usually been ignorant of the languages of the Middle East and therefore limited to sources in European languages. They have thus been debarred from access to the material with which alone they could weave their narratives of external political and economic action into the texture of the internal history of the region—even, it might be said, from an adequate treatment of the political and economic events which are their primary concern. History moves at many levels, and it is only the surface movements of events which can be seen from the outside. It is generally conceded that the study of modern France requires some knowledge of the French language and of French writings. Why should the Arabs, Persians, Turks, or Israelis be different? It is true that their languages are more difficult, but that is not really an adequate answer.

There has long been a kind of diplomatic convention in the West that the Turks took no active part in the political struggle over Turkey and that there are no Turkish sources for its history—with parallel conventions for other countries of the Middle East. It is noteworthy, for example, that, leaving aside the archives, the great mass even of published Turkish documents and memoirs has passed almost unnoticed in the vast literature on the Eastern Question. The result has been a view of history in which the Middle East was no more than a stage, with the Ottoman Empire as backdrop, where European actors performed the main roles in the drama. Other writers *(quorum pars minima fui)* have erred in the opposite direction. Reacting against the exclusively Western approach of the historians of the Eastern Question, they have concentrated so heavily on oriental sources as to neglect not only the evidence of European documentation but also the effects of European action—without which, ultimately, the history of the Middle East in the nineteenth and twentieth centuries is not intelligible.

The emergence of a new generation of historians of Middle Eastern origin, trained in the methods and devoted to the standards of modern critical scholarship, might have been expected to carry these studies an important step forward. The results, for nineteenth-century history, have so far been rather disappointing. Most of these historians have been attracted by the times of ancient glory and current revival in the histories of their peoples and have turned away from a period which, in the main and in their eyes, was one of weakness and degradation.

There have, however, been some—recently increasing in number—who have taken the nineteenth century as their field. Much could be expected of these. Able to use both Eastern and Western sources, trained as historians and familiar with the language, culture, traditions, and attitudes of their own countries, they might have achieved that synthesis which in the West had eluded both the historian and the orientalist.

In the main it has eluded them too. There have, of course, been distinguished exceptions—obvious names will come to mind—but they are few, and most of them have concentrated on the early and late parts of the century.

A good deal of recent work has been devoted to the history of ideas—some of it using the arts of the taxidermist rather than of the historian. This is a comparatively new field of interest for historians of the modern Middle East. Some of these writings have been works of scholarship, throwing light into hitherto obscure corners of intellectual and indeed general history; others have been affected by a variety of polemic or apologetic purposes—to provide a past for some current ideological nostrum, to project an attractive image, or to assuage wounded pride. Indeed, of late the study of the politically sensitive nineteenth century has in a larger sense been menaced by new ideologies, which regard the past as another region to be "liberated" by assault and scholarship as another industry ripe for nationalization.

What is still lacking is good solid research on nineteenth-century history, conducted by the tried and tested methods of critical historical scholarship, using both Western and Middle Eastern sources and not governed by the desire to prove the virtue or villainy of persons, parties, classes, sects, or nations. There are such works, produced both in the Middle East and elsewhere, but their numbers are still lamentably few.

The student of modern history therefore has a difficult task. Without any really authoritative works to guide him, he must pick his way warily between imperialist, nationalist, and latterly ideological prejudice and propaganda and listen for the thin voice of truth almost drowned by the rolling of logs and the grinding of axes.

The question may be asked at this point whether there really is any possibility, in the Middle East or for that matter in any other area, of writing modern history in a scholarly, detached, and objective way. Where passion and interest are so strongly involved, where so much relevant information is withheld from the historian by official secrecy, is it possible for him to write history at all?

I believe that in spite of these very real difficulties, it is still possible to treat the modern history of the Middle East in a way that deserves the name of historical scholarship, provided that certain conditions are fulfilled. Of these I shall mention what seem to me the most important.

First, the historian must possess a scholarly knowledge of his subject. That is to say, in addition to the professional skills of the historian, he must be acquainted with the history, language, and culture of the people of whom he writes.

In other fields to state this is to state the obvious, but unfortunately in Middle Eastern studies the point still needs to be emphasized. Professional advancement, success, and reputation in this area are compatible with a degree of ignorance and incompetence which would not be tolerated in other more developed fields of study. This has led to low standards of entry, performance, and promotion in academic institutions and to the acceptance and acclamation as authorities, even as "standard works," of books of breathtaking superficiality and inaccuracy. Unfortunately such books really are "standard works" in the sense that they are cited, recommended, and even read by many people, in many places, for long periods.

The Middle Eastern historian, to achieve reasonable professional competence, must know the language of the people with whom he is concerned well enough to read their books and newspapers in the original and preferably also to converse with them in their own idiom. The use of translations and digests is legitimate for certain limited purposes but cannot replace this knowledge as a basis for serious historical study.

Second, the historian must strive to achieve as great a degree of objectivity as possible. This too is a truism which still needs emphasis in relation to the Middle East. This is an area in which there are violent disputes and one in particular which arouses strong emotions and stirs deep-seated prejudices and loyalties. It is also an area in which powerful material interests are involved. There are many who support one side or another in Middle Eastern conflicts because they have a material interest in doing so. This may be political, *e.g.* the pursuit of votes in domestic elections, or commercial, *e.g.* the pursuit of concessions or other commercial advantages in Middle Eastern countries. The elected politician responding to the wishes of his electors, the corporation employee advancing the interests of his stockholders, the public relations consultant diligently burnishing the image of his current or prospective client are all no doubt ennobling spectacles. None of them is a safe guide to the study of history—yet all of them try to penetrate the places where history is written and taught.

In the course of his inquiries the historian of the Middle East will have to review a great deal of evidence, some of which he will dismiss as irrelevant or untrue. The great danger is that he may use two standards of judgment, one for items favorable to his thesis, his loyalties, or his prejudices, the other for items that are not favorable. The scholarly historian must try, as far as he can, to select, evaluate, and interpret his sources according to objective and constant criteria and not according to the results at which he would prefer to arrive. No man can be entirely detached from the events of the time in which he lives; no scholar can become sufficiently interested in a subject to write about it without developing opinions and perhaps sentiments. The scholar, however, will not give way to his prejudices. He will recognize them, control them, allow for them, and by a process of intellectual self-discipline reduce their working to a minimum. There is an old Eastern proverb which runs: "Me and my tribe against the world; me and my clan against my tribe; me and my brothers against my clan; me, against my brothers!" The historian too is a man in a social context and will identify himself with different loyalty-groups in different circumstances. Thus, a Maronite Christian historian in Lebanon might, with equal sincerity, identify himself with the Arabs against the West, with the Levant against Egypt, with Lebanon against Syria, with the Christians against the Muslims, with the Maronites against the other Christians, with his clan against the rest. These loyalties may well influence his choice of subject of research; they should not influence his treatment of it. If, in the course of his researches, he finds that the group with which he identifies himself is always right, and those other groups with which it is in conflict are always wrong, then he would be well advised to question his conclusions and to reexamine the hypotheses on the basis of which he selected and interpreted his evidence; for it is not in the nature of human communities to be always right.

Finally, the historian must be fair and honest in the way he presents his story. That is not to say that he must confine himself to a bare recital of definitely established facts. At many stages in his work the historian must formulate hypotheses and make judgments. The important thing is that he should do so consciously and explicitly, reviewing the evidence for and against his conclusions, examining the various possible interpretations, and stating explicitly what his decision is, and how and why he reached it.

A single example from recent history may serve to illustrate these points—the rebuff offered to King Saud, during his visit to the United States in 1957, by Mayor Wagner of New York. Much has been written about this incident by journalists, advocates, propagandists, and mythologists—little if anything by historians. Let us imagine two propagandists, one a Zionist and the other an Arab nationalist; dealing with the same group of known facts, each will try to present them in a form creditable to his own side and discreditable to that of his opponent. Their presentations might run something like this.

The Arab nationalist could begin by attributing the Mayor's action to political vote-grabbing and point out how many Jews there are in New York. The Zionist would probably make no allusion to this aspect at all. If forced to admit that the presence of a large Jewish electorate had some bearing on the Mayor's action, he would argue that there is nothing wrong in a democratically elected officer acting in accordance with the wishes of his electors and might claim the Catholic electors as being equally opposed to a king who, he would point out, had outlawed the celebration of Mass by Americans resident in Arabia. He would of course lay great stress on the reasons given by the Mayor himself for his action—distaste for a ruler who practices slavery and religious discrimination in his country. The Arab nationalist would dismiss this as an excuse for pandering to the Jewish voters and might indicate nearer objects for the Mayor's moral indignation. He would avoid any discussion of slavery and religious discrimination in Saudi Arabia. In certain circumstances he might deny that they exist.

The Arab nationalist would accuse the Mayor of putting party before country and of sacrificing the national interests of the United States—for which he would profess great concern—for the sake of an advantage in New York City politics. The Zionist would play down this point and could argue that what are called the national interests of the United States are in fact the commercial interests of some oil companies. The argument could then continue with a discussion on the comparative merits of profits from Arabs and votes from Jews—which are more democratic, which are more sordid, which are more beneficial, and to whom? In conclusion, the Mayor, in acting as he did, could be either

(1) a sordid and irresponsible city politician, sacrificing the national interests of his country and insulting an honored guest in order to grab votes by pandering to a selfish sectional interest in the city—or

(2) a man of principle, who would not bow down before the sordid commercial interests of an oil company and refused to dishonor the great and free city of which he is the elected leader by welcoming a monarch whose hands are stained with slavery and persecution.

The same canvas, the same palette—and two quite different pictures. But what kind of picture will the historian paint? Probably, he will paint neither the one nor the other, but a composition containing elements of both. He is not precluded from forming and expressing a judgment on the motives of Mayor Wagner's action—indeed, it is his duty to do so. Where he differs from the controversialist is that in what he writes he will review all the evidence and not just the part that supports his opinion; all the possible interpretations and not just the one he adopts. Most important of all, he will, to the best of his ability, form his opinion by a dispassionate study of the facts and not in response to the call of blood or faith or the wishes of a paymaster. And when he has formed his opinion, he will state it clearly and give his reasons for it.

What he should not do is present an artificial selection of evidence, chosen to support his own view, and tacitly suppress the rest; he should not convey his assumptions and his judgments by implication, suggestion, or innuendo, nor by the use of emotionally charged language. For if he does these things he may be writing controversy—without the candor of the avowed controversialist; or journalism—without the professional competence of the journalist. He is not writing history.

On Nationalism and Revolution

5

In our permissive age we pride ourselves on a freedom of speech in which all the restrictions on discussion and criticism have disappeared. In fact, however, our freedom is not as great as we would like to believe. It is true that religion and sex are now deprived of the protection which they once enjoyed and have become so free that blasphemy and obscenity have lost their force, and those who seek outrage must find or invent new outlets. On the other hand the great political and social myths of our time still enjoy a surprising measure of protection. These are the beliefs which guide and inspire what may be called the liberal establishment. To deny them, even to question them, can involve risks to status, career, and even, in some academic circles, to personal safety. One of the most important myths of our time is the demiurgic struggle between imperialism and nationalism, ending in the triumph of the latter, a struggle which is never completed but always in need of ritual reenactment.

It is therefore with a sense of shock that one finds Professor Kedourie, in his long and brilliant introduction to his collection of texts on nationalism,* adopting an attitude of what might be called ideological agnosticism. Professor Kedourie does not believe in the primacy of economic causes; he is not convinced of the diabolic origin of imperialism; and he even harbors doubts about the virgin birth of Afro-Asian nationalist movements.

Professor Kedourie begins his discussion with an analysis of imperialism, the evil to which nationalism is said to have been a reaction. After briefly reviewing the earlier history and usage of the term he examines

---

**Nationalism in Asia and Africa*, edited by Elie Kedourie (London, 1971).

the economic definition of imperialism given by J. A. Hobson and later elaborated and made famous by Lenin. Since then their definition of imperialism—the subjugation and exploitation of colonial peoples for the benefit of investors and, behind them, of financiers in the metropolis—has been generally accepted, even by many whose political philosophies and purposes are very remote from those of Lenin or Hobson. Professor Kedourie questions the commonly accepted axiom and succeeds with surprisingly little difficulty in demonstrating its falsity. European activities in Africa and Asia were in origin primarily commercial; their subsequent development into imperial domination owed little to economic and financial interests. Professor Kedourie sees imperialism as basically a political force, determined by political, military, and sometimes cultural factors. Political domination and economic exploitation both existed, but the causal connection between them is the product of what Professor Kedourie calls "ideological and mystificatory" arguments.

Just as imperialism was not primarily an economic domination, so nationalism was not primarily an economic revolt, and currently popular explanations of the rising of the deprived and dispossessed against exploitation are equally "mystificatory." Imperial rule, Professor Kedourie argues, with all its defects, has in most cases brought much of value, both material and cultural, to the subject peoples, and if domination brought gain to the rulers, it also benefited the ruled. The immense influence and authority of the imperialist powers of Western Europe can be seen even in the manner in which their rule was opposed. In the eyes of Asian and African nationalists European civilization was inherently evil—yet every nation in Asia or Africa, in its own nationalist historiography, somehow claims the credit for having created that evil.

In Professor Kedourie's view not imperialism but nationalism itself is the great Western offense against the Afro-Asian world. This doctrine is an essentially Western importation, which runs counter to the experience and realities of most of these countries. The introduction of these ideas and the attempt to remold polities and societies in accordance with them have brought immense harm to the peoples of Asia and Africa. In the course of this revolt against European domination, the old order has perished, but no new one has emerged.

European expansion, with the inevitable pressure of stronger on weaker societies, brought grave disturbance. "This pulverisation of traditional societies, this bursting open of self-sufficient economies could not fail to bring about in those who were subject to this process a serious and distressing psychological strain." The old order was disrupted, the old relationships undermined, and the individual, stripped of his traditional supports and loyalties, was impelled to an essentially European aspiration for intellectual, moral, and economic independence. Failure to achieve this gives rise to feelings of "inadequacy and bewilderment" which sooner or later "erupt in violent and destructive action." Europe herself provides the ideas to express and direct this discontent; the imperial achievement of widespread literacy secures their rapid and extensive dissemination. Professor Kedourie asks why Europe has failed where Greece and Rome succeeded, in creating a new imperial civilization. He finds the explanation in the refusal of the European imperial masters—notably the British in India—to accept their assimilated imperial subjects as, in the last analysis, their equals. A Spanish or a Syrian provincial could rise to the highest office, even that of emperor, in Rome. The British in India refused to admit even Anglicized and loyal Indians to complete equality with themselves. In this refusal, in the mistrust which gave rise to it, and in the anguish and resentment which it engendered, Professor Kedourie sees the failure of imperialism and the beginnings of modern nationalism.

Professor Kedourie begins his series of excerpts from the writers of Asian and African nationalist movements with a passage from the great Greek scholar and patriot Adamantios Koraes. That a discussion of Afro-Asian nationalism should begin with Greece may seem at first strange, but it is right, for the Greeks were the first people outside Western Europe to accept the nationalist vision of identity and their place in history and to try to give it political expression. This is followed by extracts from writers in Turkey, the Arab countries, India, China, Africa, the Asian peoples of the Soviet Union, and the Blacks of the Western hemisphere.

One of the themes discussed by Professor Kedourie and exemplified in his extracts is what he calls secular millenarianism. This, under the fashionable name of revolution, forms the theme of Mr. Gerassi's very different collection.* For Professor Kedourie nationalism, with or without its millenarian aspects, is a false religion, which has brought untold suffering to mankind and of which Arabs and Jews, Indians and Pakistanis are equally the victims. For Mr. Gerassi, revolutionary doctrine of almost any kind is the true faith of the redeemer. While Professor Kedourie offers us a collection of specimens for analysis, Mr. Gerassi provides a canon of scriptures for our instruction. They are of varied provenance, including governmental statement of policy, the personal views of revolutionary leaders including that modern paradigm of the martyred god, Che Guevara, and a number of passages from the manifestos of organizations, some of major importance, others amounting in their own countries to no more than minor fringe groups. The Asian peoples of the Soviet Union are not represented. All the authors, except Lenin, have been edited and condensed. There are introductions to each section and a general introduction to the book as a whole. The flavor and quality of these may be judged from the following exerpts, the first from the general introduction, the second from the introduction to the section on Palestine:

> Freedom is not the right to say or do anything you want that does not infringe on [*sic*] the freedom of others. Freedom means having the material and psychological *power* to say or do that thing. Freedom is the real possibility of being relevant, of being meaningful, of being total.

> The governments of Jordan, Saudi Arabia, Kuwait and the Arab Gulf are feudal-fascist governments who are just as close to imperialism as is Israel. The Lebanese régime is run by a commercial and banking bourgeoisie in partnership with and dependent upon imperialism. The governments of Egypt, Syria and Iraq are petty-bourgeois—a class that, because it came to power without revolutionary struggle (via *coups d'état*) has no revolutionary consciousness (but lots of revolutionary sounding rhetoric). In all these countries the masses are agitated. They want or need a socialist revolution.

That "want or need" sums it up beautifully.

**Towards Revolution:* Vol. i, *China, India, Asia, the Middle East, Africa;* Vol. ii, *The Americas,* edited by John Gerassi (London, 1971).

Lenin once remarked that "the capitalists will sell us the rope with which to hang them." Capitalist publishers do not sell rope, but they are willing to supply, at a price, a manual on how to do the job. However, the danger is not great. Few genuine revolutionaries in Asia, Africa, or Latin America can afford a ten-guinea revolutionist's manual. And no one hanged with rope of this quality is likely to come to much harm.

Slade on Turkey

6

Sir Adolphus Slade[1] (1802–1877) was an officer of the Royal Navy, in which he reached the rank of Vice Admiral, and also served for a while in the Turkish Navy, in which he was promoted Admiral. He was the fifth son of Sir John Slade, a General in the British Army who had served under the Duke of Wellington in the Peninsular Wars. In 1815 he was one of twenty-six boys admitted to the Naval College in Portsmouth. His record was brilliant—he finished the course in two instead of the usual three years and won the gold medal. He began his service as midshipman on the South American station where he served until 1820. In 1824 he was present at the naval demonstration against Algiers and in October 1827 served at the Battle of Navarino, after which, on 27 November of the same year, he was promoted Lieutenant.

The outbreak of another Russo-Turkish war in 1828 aroused his interest. Gaining permission from the Admiralty to travel, he left England in January 1829 and, proceeding via France, Italy, and Greece, reached Istanbul in July. He attracted the attention of the Kapudan Pasha, Pabuççu-oğlu Ahmed Pasha, who invited him to sail with him in the Black Sea. This was the beginning of a long association with Turkey and more particularly with the Turkish Navy. In 1830 he sailed again in the Black Sea, this time as a guest on the British ship HMS *Blonde.* In 1831–32 he spent some eighteen months travelling, mostly in European Turkey and around the Bosporus. During this period he seems to have learned Turkish. In 1832 he published his first book, *Records of Travel in Turkey, Greece, etc. and of a Cruize in the Black Sea with the Capitan Pasha in the Years 1829, 1830, and 1831,* in two volumes.[2]

In 1834 he was appointed additional Lieutenant on HMS *Caledonia,* flagship of Admiral Sir Josias Rowley, and, between January 1834 and September 1837, served Rowley as liaison officer between the British Mediterranean squadron and Istanbul. In the course of his duties, he wrote reports on the naval and military strength of both the Russians and the Turks and also kept the Admiral informed on Turkish political matters. In 1837 he published his second book of travels about the Middle East, called *Turkey, Greece and Malta.*[3]

Between July 1838 and June 1839, again on leave, he travelled to Istanbul via Germany, Austria, and Russia, and in 1840 published his third book, entitled *Travels in Germany and Russia: including a steam voyage by the Danube and the Euxine from Vienna to Constantinople, in 1838–39.*[4] On 12 January 1849 he was advanced to post rank and later in the same year was sent to carry dispatches from the Foreign Secretary, Lord Palmerston, to the British Ambassador in Istanbul, Sir Stratford Canning, and the British Naval Commander, Admiral Sir William Parker. These dispatches apparently related to the crisis arising from the affair of the Hungarian refugees in Turkey. He again became involved in Turkish matters, and in March 1850 was appointed a special adviser to the Turkish Navy with the title Muşavir Pasha. He spent the next seventeen years in Turkish waters in the course of which he achieved the command of his own ship, the *Nusretiye,* became Admiral of the Port of Istanbul and of other ports and President of the Supreme Admiralty Court. He saw active service during the Crimean War on which he wrote a book entitled *Turkey and the Crimean War: a Narrative of Historical Events,* published in London in 1867.[5] His anxious concern for the Turkish forces under his command shows very clearly both in this book and in his dispatches. He left Turkey in 1867 and remained in London, in retirement, until his death on 3 November 1877.

Among the Western travellers who described Turkey in the nineteenth century, Slade has been strangely neglected. His first book, *Records of Travel,* was reprinted once, in 1854, but neither that nor any of his other books has, as far as I am aware, subsequently been reprinted. His writings do however seem to have attracted some attention in Turkey. A later English traveller, Nassau Senior, mentions a conversation with Ahmed Vefik Pasha, whom he found reading Slade's *Turkey* and who praised its fidelity.[6] There are other indications in Turkish authors of the time of some acquaintance with Slade's writings. Two of his books were even translated into Turkish, though these versions were not published until 1943 and 1945.[7]

Why was Slade so neglected? The most probable reason is that in general his attitudes were thoroughly out of accord with the commonly accepted opinions of nineteenth-century Europe. The first of these was that the non-Muslim subjects of the Ottoman state were downtrodden and depressed peoples, groaning under an atrocious tyranny. As will be clear from his writings, Slade was very far from sharing this opinion. A second element in the prevailing orthodoxy was the belief that the old order in Turkey was irretrievably bad, that the whole reform program, beginning with Selim III and continuing through the *Tanzimat* and after, was desirable and necessary, that it was good insofar as it was put into effect but failed because it was not put into effect. Its deficiencies, according to this view, were of application, not of content. Here again, Slade did not agree. For him, the old order was by no means wholly bad but on the contrary had many merits; the *Tanzimat*, including the earlier reforms which had led up to it, far from improving matters, had inflicted grievous harm on Turkey and that harm was compounded because, in his view, the reforms were indeed in many areas very effectively applied.

Time does not admit of any detail on this, and I would like to illustrate Slade's perceptions of Ottoman society in the first half of the nineteenth century by a few examples. The first is economic. Slade lays great stress in several places in his writings on the economic well-being of the Ottoman peasantry and of the Ottoman countryside, which he compares very favorably with conditions in many parts of Europe. Let me quote a passage from his first book, *The Records*. Speaking of the Balkan peasantry, particularly in Bulgaria, he says:

> No peasantry in the whole world are so well off. The lowest Bulgarian has abundance of everything: meat, poultry, eggs, milk, rice, cheese, wine, bread, good clothing, and a warm dwelling, and a horse to ride. It is true he has no newspaper to inflame his passions, nor a knife and fork to eat with, nor a bedstead to lie on, and therefore may be considered by some people an object of pity. A pasha, at any rate, is equally unhappy. Where, then, it may be asked, viewing the above true statement, is the tyranny under which the Christian subjects of the Porte are generally supposed to groan? Not among the Bulgarians

certainly. I wish that in every country a traveller could pass from one end to the other, and find a good supper and a warm fire in every cottage, as he can in European Turkey—the result of its being thinly inhabited.[8]

Slade attaches great importance to this last point and goes on to describe the economic and social benefits which it brings to the Christian peasantry:

For in the same ratio as population adds to a nation's greatness, it subtracts from its happiness. The soil, when over-occupied, fattens on man; when under-tenanted, man fattens on the soil: that is, in the former case unremitting labour is requisite to make it yield barely sufficient for the sustenance of numbers; in the latter case, nature requires very little aid to afford plenty for the few. The principal grievance of the Christian peasant in Turkey, is the harratch;[9] oftentimes he cannot pay it. What can the collector do? It is useless distraining his cattle, for on the plain are others wild. It is useless taking his furniture, for there is no vent for it. It is useless ejecting him, for no other occupier will be found for his tenement, every man having already more land than he requires, in a country without trade to consume the overplus of his produce. It is still more useless putting him in prison, for money is never gained *there*. He gives him the bastinado, or not, according as he believes that the man's poverty in specie is real or feigned. A few dozen blows decides the doubt, and he is undisturbed for another year. I venture to say that many a freeborn man, who boasts of liberal sentiments, of chartered rights, of equal laws, would gladly compound for his rent with a licking, and, instead of grumbling at his fate, bless heaven that he is not turned out on the high road with his family. At the same time I do not deny that the lower classes in Turkey often suffer grievous oppression under a rascally pasha or aga: but, take their position in the worst view, distorted by the film of slavery, they never see the most ruthless of tyrants—hunger. Their despots, though armed with whips and screws, and racks, cannot inflict any torture equal to the pang of a father who hears his children crying for bread, and crying in vain. They never feel this. Their rulers cannot check the fertility of nature;—cannot prevent the beasts of the field from multiplying; the trees of the forest from sprouting; nor the seeds thrown on the ground from springing into ears. They may have the mortification of seeing many of their children die when young, for want of medical aid; but they are certain that those who grow up will not be reduced to follow the career of vice—the sons on the highway, the daughters on the pavé—for subsistence. They are not tantalized by the constant sight of enjoyments beyond their reach; are not tempted by easy modes of conveyance, to leave their quiet villages for the fancy treasures of the capital; are not made discontented, by reading, with the state of life wherein destiny cast them; and, to sum up the advantages which the poor have in such (barbarous!) countries, it is worthy of remark, that the punishment of death rarely falls on them. For one poor man who loses his head in Turkey, 500 rich men lose theirs. How contrary to the practice of highly civilized states—elysiums for the wealthy, purgatories for the indigent—where the hungry and the naked—wretches whose greatest crime was want—are the principal offerings on the shrine of justice. Far be it from me to decry civilization and commerce. He would indeed be an unworthy Englishman who undervalued the levers which have raised his country to an unexampled pitch of greatness; but at the same time we cannot blind ourselves to the fact that they cause evil to a great proportion of mankind; by creating a thousand fictitious wants, which beget crimes, which build prisons and raise scaffolds; by unequally distributing wealth, to the great deterioration of social happiness; by drawing away the productions of countries, intended by nature for the support of the natives, to pamper strangers: *vide*, for example, the droves of cattle, sheep, and pigs; the cargoes of oatmeal, eggs, and flour, daily wheeled from the shores of Erin while her sons are starving. Without the active agency of commerce, they must remain where they are produced, and perforce be eaten there.[10]

According to Slade, it is not only the Christian peasantry that flourishes under Ottoman rule. He speaks too of the well-being of the new Greek middle class, and points out—probably the first to do so—that the reason for the Greek rising was not that the Greeks were falling back but that they were going forward; that for the previous forty years the Greek community under Ottoman rule had made immense progress, both economically and culturally.

This leads to a more general point about the nature of the resentment felt by the non-Muslim subjects of the Porte.[11] Slade insists repeatedly, with many illustrations and with considerable emphasis, that the hurt which they suffered, the oppression of which they complained, was largely psychological. What galled them was the status of inferiority assigned to them and the attitude of superiority maintained by the dominant group—a superiority which was the more difficult to endure, in that the generally liberal and tolerant policies of that dominant group made it possible for the subject peoples to thrive and to flourish and to achieve in many ways a higher standard of living and a higher level of education than those of their master. "The Turk committed an error and generated the grievance, when he allowed the Greek the wealth and pursuits of a free man, branding him at the same time as an inferior being. By permitting his Raya to become intellectually superior, he made submission painful."[12]

Slade found widespread discontent among the Greeks and other Rayas but rarely found any economic basis for it. On the contrary, the well-fed peasants and prosperous merchants whom he encountered were unable to conceive or believe the poverty and misery which existed in the advanced countries of Europe:

> . . . I have always heard similar complaints, but on enquiry about these hardships, I could never descend so low as *want of food, or of fuel, or of raiment;* and oftentimes I have excited disbelief by hinting at the state of pauperism in Europe. . . .
>
> In analysing the motive of this universal feeling among the rayas against the rule of the Ottomans, we find it to be not in the direct oppression which affects a man's physical state, but in the broad sentiment which makes an insult to be more resented than an injury—a taunt to be more felt than a blow. The Turk was porcelain, the Greek was clay. The Turkish clown might insult the educated Greek; the Turkish urchin pelt the Greek priest; the Turkish "dancing girl" mock the Greek lady. The rarer the outrage, the more bitterly was it felt; even though never committed, the liability to it would gall. . . . These were the real stings of Turkish oppression, the true causes of Greek revolt. . . . Such and such-like vexations, of dress and privilege, ideal when commented on, but sadly real when felt, weighed down the security of real property and the trade of the Empire in the other balance.[13]

Slade devotes considerable effort to criticizing and condemning the superficial and inaccurate comparisons which are so frequently drawn between Turkey and the West. On this he inveighs with equal vigor against Westerners, who are misled by names and judge Turkey by Western standards, and against Turks like Mahmud II who, in borrowing Western institutions or trying to adapt Western practices, "took the mask for the man, the rind for the fruit."[14] He discusses military reform, for example, and speaks with contempt of the adoption of European-type uniforms in the Turkish armed forces; these, he thinks, are in every way less suitable, less healthy, less comfortable, less adapted to the climate than the traditional dress worn by the Turkish military and have the further disadvantage of antagonizing the soldiers themselves, and thereby making them less willing to accept the necessary part of the military reform.[15]

While condemning some comparisons made by others, Slade is more than a little willing to make his own comparisons, and he does so very frequently, often to the disadvantage of his own country or, more generally, of the West. He finds a parallel for example in the situations of the Greeks in the Ottoman Empire and the Irish Catholics in what was then the United Kingdom of Great Britain and all Ireland. The Western world, he remarks, is asked to admire the fortitude of the Greeks in having retained their faith and their culture for so many centuries under Muslim rule.

> Much praise also is given to the Greeks for having adhered to their religion, notwithstanding the advantages which proselytism offered. Give them all credit; let us not analyse the feeling which induces man to cling to an oppressed cause, which has, in all ages, in all climes, caused the stake and the dungeon to be preferred to the mitre and the coronet; but let us be just, and while extolling the Greeks, let us not fancy them pre-eminently distinguished, but let us point to the Catholics of Ireland, who underwent a severer ordeal, *with a far less sacrifice of principle* to make, and with *brighter temptation.* The Greek, in apostasizing, still remained, even more immediately under the rod of the Porte. He stood alone. He was the butt of suspicion; he was cut off from his own people; he was rarely trusted by his new brethren; he descended in the scale of intellectual intercourse; he left the excitement of trade and society for the sofa and the pipe and "neh war neh yok" [*sic*];[16] he exchanged the love he might win, for the slave he could buy. Light was his gain, seldom more than the avenging of wounded pride, or the fancied cure of some morbid feeling, compared with the advantages held out to the Catholic: place, power, parliament, the smiles of his sovereign, the society of a superior endowed set, the incense of a great nation. Yet, how few yielded![17]

Slade reverts to the point that the Turk, "even more immediately under the rod of the Porte," is in many ways more exposed and worse off than the raya, and that, while the Greeks under Ottoman rule were extending their freedom, the Muslims were losing theirs.[18]

Slavery is another theme which gives Slade the opportunity to offer some sharp comments on the West and some words of extenuation for Muslim practice. He is contemptuous of the righteous indignation expressed by various Western commentators on Muslim slavery and observes that it ill befits the West, with its record of colonial and American slavery, industrial exploitation, and military conscription, to throw stones at a society which, because it recognizes an evil, is able to regulate it and soften its effects. Two passages, from different books, may serve to exemplify Slade's ideas on this topic.

> Anti-slavery and voluntary labour are pretty tunes to ring on, but experience sings a different song. Greece, in her days of glory, contained plenty of slaves; the Spartan warrior and the Athenian orator equally employed and made light of the poor wretches. Rome would have sunk much earlier but for the organised system of agricultural slavery in Italy. The woodsman's axe would still have remained unheard in some of the fairest portions of North America, and the cultivated plains of New South Wales would still be kangaroos' domain, but for the aid of the surplus numbers of English society. African sweat raised many of Spain's superb colonial cities: it sustains the prosperity of half of the United States. And the marvel of English industry arises from capital acting on population, which, if analysed, would produce a meaning not very gratifying to free ears.[19]
>
> It certainly seems very disinterested in us, who have already colonised largely by the aid of forced labour—who have convicts in great numbers—who have a people disposed to emigration, to put a veto on slavery. A veto on conscription would be more advantageous to mankind, and fully as humane. We shudder at the idea of a negro torn from Senegal to plant coffee in Martinique, but we see no particular hardship in leading a conscript away from Brittany to dig trenches in Algiers; exposed to die of fever in them, if he remain—or to be shot by a courtmartial if he run away.[20]

> Slavery sounds revolting to an English ear; change the name, where is the country in which it does not exist? The labourer is chained to his plough, the mechanic to his loom, the pauper to the work-house. Slavery ever has been, and must be a principle of society, under different names. Where the population is thin, the powerful force the weak to be their drudges, or import others; where the contrary is the case, necessity is the coercive power. Freedom, in connexion with the millions who depend on daily toil for daily bread, is a sophism. Since, therefore, slavery, barefaced or masked exists, as though a provision of nature, in all communities, barbarous or civilized, it should rather be the object of rulers to

> render it bearable by wise provisions, than to aim at the impossibility of abolishing it, thereby entailing greater evils on the sufferers.[21]

Even the *avret pazari*, the market for women, does not shock Slade as much as it shocks other Western travellers and indeed gives him occasion for some gentle irony:

> But a market where—horrid idea!—women are sold like beasts. God forbid that I would defend it!
>
> [However,] Decorum prevails. The would-be purchaser may fix his eyes on the lady's face, and his hand may receive evidence of her bust. The waltz allows nearly as much liberty before hundreds of eyes.[22]

One of the most interesting comparisons which Slade makes is an implicit one, suggested by some of the points he makes in condemnation of the whole reform movement from Selim III to Mahmud II and Reshid Pasha. A basic charge which he brings against the reforming Sultan is what he calls "the subversion of the ancient Turkish constitution" or "the subversion of the liberties of his (Turkish) subjects."

These expressions are strikingly reminiscent of the language used by the pro-Parliament jurists during the English Civil War of the seventeenth century and its aftermath. The doctrine of the ancient constitution of England and the immemorial rights of Englishmen are central to the arguments which were used to justify Parliament against the King in the Civil War and, in a different way, in the ensuing struggles of the later seventeenth and eighteenth centuries.

Consciously or unconsciously, Slade applied these characteristically English doctrines to the Turkish situation and, pursuing them in great detail, found that they fitted. In discussing the subversion of the liberties of subject, he is well aware that such expressions applied to Turkey would sound strange to his Western readers, and he therefore devotes a good deal of time and effort to explaining them.

Slade nowhere provides a fully worked out system. His writings on Turkey, apart from his narrative of the Crimean War, are essentially travel books, personal records of journeys, of encounters, of incidents interspersed from time to time with discursive passages in which he offers his reflections on various aspects of Turkish life. But from these, by juxtaposing and comparing different passages from the three main books written at intervals of years, one can trace the development of a quite consistent pattern of thought.

As Slade sees it, the traditional Turkish order is very far from being the capricious despotism imagined by some Western observers. Rather is it a limited absolutism, restrained by what he calls the ancient Turkish constitution, composed of three basic elements—the Holy Law of Islam, the edicts of previous Ottoman Sultans, and local custom where this is recognized and sanctified by usage. It includes the customs of other peoples and communities as well as the Turks.

Of all the evils of the *Tanzimat,* in Slade's opinion, the worst and most pervasive was centralization. This meant two things; on the one hand the reinforcement and extension of the central power, on the other the abrogation of intermediate powers—of those many groups and institutions in Ottoman society possessing and exercising authority and deriving it not from the central government but from tradition, inheritance, and popular acceptance. It was precisely in these two features—decentralization and the existence of autonomous powers—that he saw the main safeguards of "the ancient Turkish constitution" and the main guardians of the genuine and extensive liberties enjoyed by the peoples under Turkish rule.

Decentralization was of crucial importance and, indeed, was seen by Slade as the main reason for the survival of the Ottoman Empire. It affected not only regions but also functions and was the result, in his judgement, of a conscious and deliberate choice by the early Ottoman rulers:

> The Tartar conquerors of the Lower Empire saw nothing worth copying in Byzantine centralization. They judged the tree by its fruits and avoided it. Their ruling idea was to combine metropolitan predominance with modified provincial autonomy. Their ruling policy was to retain the superior administrative functions and military authority in their hands, leaving every community, every sect, every town, every village, to manage its own affairs. They organized their Empire in such a guise that it resembled a federation; or rather a congeries

of states bound to co-act with the sovereign, for imperial objects. They gave *eski adet* (old custom) the force to resist despotism. Vizirs, imperial delegates, ruled in the provinces; potentates within them, but responsible to the lord paramount for ruling according to law and usage. Invested themselves with the power of life and death, they were liable to be bowstrung on the strength of a simple mandate. Brought up in the imperial shadow, their sense of personal dignity and decorous manners impressed the provincials with respect. Wild Albanians, crafty Arabs, and supple Armenians admitted the moral superiority, the instinct of command, of the Ottoman. Each vizir was a Sultan in miniature. . . . [23]

The Ottoman dynasty respected national institutions and usages, and was *pro tanto* respected. Hence the spectacle of a vast heterogeneous empire kept together during centuries, by a government often vicious and contemptible, and without a regular army. . . . Decentralization also characterized the public expenditure. Every service had its distinct, inalienable revenue, derived from territorial sources. The state domain maintained the imperial dignity. The *vacoofs*[24] (endowments) supported the mosques, the *medressehs* (colleges), the *imarets* (almshouses), the *mektebs* (parish schools), the cemeteries, the fountains, and the pavement of cities; in fine all the pious and beneficent establishments. . . . The unassigned tithes, the salian,[25] and the kharatch[26] defrayed the expenses of the central government, the artillery, the fortresses, and the enrolled Janissaries. A district near the capital defrayed the expense of the gunpowder manufactory. The Navy—justly esteemed the right arm of an Empire with coasts bathed by the Mediterranean and the Indian Ocean, by the Red and the Black Seas, by the Persian and Venetian Gulfs, with numerous islands, some of them kingdoms in ancient days—was endowed with vast means, and its chief, the Capitan Pasha, held the third rank in the Empire. It was endowed with the revenues of Maina and of the sandjaks of Lepanto and the Negroponte, of the Thracian Chersonesus, of Biga, Codja-eili and Sighala, rich maritime provinces of Asia Minor, and of the Cyclades and Sporades in the Archipelago.[27] A Capitan Pasha then, ordered to build ships or construct docks, or reproached for keeping the seamen in arrears of pay, would have idly pleaded in excuse want of money—the excuse often justly pleaded since by successive capitan pashas. . . . Favoured spots in Scio and other islands supplied the ladies of the Imperial harem with aromatics and cosmetics. Works of general utility, such as dykes, mountain passes, *bendts* and bridges, were kept in order and mines were worked, by local personal service given in lieu of taxation with exemption from military requisition. The value of this privilege ensured cheerful fulfilment of the conditions; as long appeared in the comparatively flourishing condition of various communities.

This self-acting machinery, combining despotic power with municipal freedom, and providing ways and means independent of the calculations of a

> finance minister, was eminently fitted for an empire made up of various races, each tenacious of its own customs, with a traditional right of exemption from fiscal novelties. Purified of its manifold abuses, this system would, in conjunction with the humanizing spirit of the tanzimat and a regular organized police force, have given lustre to the throne, contentment to the people, and maintained the services of the empire on a becoming scale; that is, with the exaction, indispensable in an Oriental state, of personal responsibility.[28]

But instead of reforming it the statesmen of the *Tanzimat* abolished this system and enforced a new centralization. In this Slade sees a belated Byzantinization of the Ottoman Empire. At last, in his view, in the nineteenth century the Ottomans fell under the Byzantine influence which they had rejected when they arrived in the fifteenth century. But the new system did not work:

> Centralization has proved an inadequate substitute. Ministers virtually irresponsible may favour one department at the expense of the other, the capital at the expense of the provinces; may yield to the solicitations, pressed with varying urgency, of the favourite of the day; may defer to another, the necessary expenditure of the current year; while, dependent on the sovereign's favour, they rival each other in obsequious deference to his wishes. There have been, however, obstacles more than sufficient to prevail against the firmest will, coupled with energetic perseverance. Financial ability, statistical data, facile communications, and agents to carry out any scheme of a comprehensive character, have been wanting. Fraud, incompetence, and indolence have not had the check or the spur of publicity; they have, on the contrary, been encouraged by the cuckoo note of the official journals: all is for the best in the best of possible Empires.[29]

The reinforcement of the central power in Slade's view was accompanied and indeed facilitated by the simultaneous removal of those other powers which had previously served to limit its otherwise unrestricted despotism. The first of these consisted of what Slade calls the provincial nobility, gentry, and magistracy. These are his terms for the *ayān* and the *derebeys*. Slade greatly admired these and regarded their role in the Ottoman countryside as almost entirely beneficial, conducive to greater prosperity and security. In the successive limitation and destruction of the power of the *ayān* and the *derebeys* he sees one of the main reasons for the growing tyranny and dwindling power of the Empire.

Slade had little respect for the new ruling groups that emerged as a result of the reforms:

> Those with places, promotion, monopolies, or contracts to give, and in their default, those in a position to influence them, yielded to seduction in every form which ambition or avarice could suggest to render it acceptable; and so general became the weakness, giving point to the proverb, *Mal miri deniz dir itchmein domouz dur*,[30] as to lead, in a few years, to the formation of the Tanzimat Council: the rules emanating from which, with a remedial view, showed its gravity. Chamberlains and kislar agas traded with their influence; the kiayas and secretaries of chiefs of departments sang the praises of wide-awake aspirants for favours; cabinet ministers' ladies listened graciously to fair suppliants on marital or filial advancement. . . . Under the old regime only Imperial favourites and a few aspiring spirits willing to stake life against the Aladdin's lamp wealth dared openly indulge in malversation; and retribution, the poetical justice adored in the East, generally lighted on them sooner or later. Some purchased forbearance by expending part of their gains on public works, or on pious endowments.
>
> Allowance may in fairness be made for the necessities of the position. The men who had floated to the surface on the wreck of the orthodox Turkish party were in general needy, unillustrated by descent. They had to acquire wealth to gain influence and make partisans, in default of which they would be mere bubbles on a troubled sea. Each in enriching himself had to wink at his colleague's infirmity, and partisans could only be retained on like conditions. The old nobility, profuse and open-handed, lived on their estates: their ovens were never cool; their pilaf cauldrons never empty. The State was the estate of the new nobility.[31]

Slade had his own explanation of their failures:

> The ruling class of Turkey in that day were unequal to the position and did not clearly understand it. Wanting popular antecedents, they inspired little confidence: wanting earnest convictions, they failed to comprehend the enthusiasm of the nation. As much of the nation trusted in itself did they apparently distrust it. In olden days those only who had led armies in the field, or had ruled turbulent provinces, dared aspire to the dangerous honor of wielding the powers of the state in troublous times. They knew what the nation could do and with all their misreckonings they were never wanting in stubborn self-reliance. Their Epicurean successors, the bland smooth-tongued efendis of Constantinople,

> knew little of the nation from intercourse and the nation knew little of them save by report. They were, moreover, impressed more or less with the ideas of the men inlaid in every department, who had as youths been sent to Europe for education, to become the mirror for young Turkey. These youths had not been selected from the scions of the old race, with names to uphold and nursery traditions of their country's glory to dwell upon; they had been selected from among the slaves of pashas or the sons of obscure denizens of Constantinople. The young Circassians had no patriotic feelings and their companions aspired to no higher felicity than to live and die, as they had been born and bred, in the Sultan's shadow. After some years passed by most in desultory studies and idle pleasures, admiring the superstructure but giving no heed to the foundations of civilization, they returned home neither Franks nor Turks: without the knowledge of the former or the instincts of the latter. Their traditional contempt for the infidel had been succeeded by envy, mingled with discouragement. They had in general schooled themselves into neglect of their Prophet's self-denying ordinances and had weaned themselves from the practice of their national virtues. They had learned to view everything European with Turkish and everything Turkish with European eyes. . . .[32]

Slade clearly did not admire the first results of Western education on the new Turkish generation.

Another of the guardians of the ancient constitution in Slade's view was the ulema, the professional men of religion. Here again he has some sharp words to say in criticism of Western writers who attack them. Western writers, says Slade, particularly those of the liberal persuasion, are anti-clericalist. They see the ulema as priests, judge the Muslim religious hierarchy as a church, and then condemn the role of "the mosque" and of the ulema in terms not really relevant either to Islam or to Turkey at all but simply transposed from the circumstances of European history and the reactions of European anti-clericalism. The true situation, he says, was quite different, and he lays some stress on the constructive role of the ulema, notably through their control of the *waqfs*. "The vacouf (mosque lands) have been among the best cultivated in Turkey, by being free from arbitrary taxation. The mektebs (public schools) in all the great cities, where the rudiments of the Turkish language and the Koran are taught, and where poor scholars receive good gratis, are supported by the ulema. The medressehs, imarets, (hospitals), fountains, etc. are all maintained by ulema; add to these the magnificence of the mosques, their number, the royal sepultures, and it will be seen that Turkey owes much to the existence of this body, which has been enabled by its power and its union, to resist royal cupidity."[33] In fact however, the power of the ulema fell before the zeal of the reforming Sultan Mahmud II: "First he cut down the Janissaries, then he encroached on the mosque. For his intentions respecting the latter, he is lauded [in Europe]; lauded by men who raise the same watch-cry everywhere; who condemn certain institutions on account of a name, careless of how widely they may differ in various countries. Such come to Turkey and there finding a church establishment, rich, powerful and (what they may not have observed) respected; "Down with it" is the cry. Would they only take the trouble to inquire into the state of the mosque, their voice might be hushed."[34]

Slade goes on to elaborate on the differences between the Muslim religious establishment and the Christian churches and points out that the charges usually levelled by Western anti-clericalists against the clergy in their own countries do not apply. "What evils appear to counterbalance the above advantages? Tithe? ministers of religion chosen from particular classes? monastic seclusion? celibacy? Not one of the reasons ordinarily urged against a church-establishment is applicable to the mosque."[35]

If European observers see the Muslim ulema in the guise of a European Christian clergy, they look at the Ottoman Janissaries in terms of the Roman Praetorian Guard. Here again, Slade expresses opinions which must have been unpopular if not shocking to his Western readers. He refers frequently to the destruction of the Janissaries, an event which he regards as a disaster for Turkey. He is by no means a romantic defender of the Janissaries whom he describes in several places as unprincipled ruffians and as a menace to their compatriots. He does however see in the Corps of Janissaries, with all its faults, one of the essential safeguards of the ancient Turkish constitution. In several places he speaks of them as a "chamber of deputies" in the Turkish state. Their role as he sees it is a positive one, as defenders of the constitution and of old established custom both in the capital, where they restrained the caprice of the sultan, and in the provinces, where they limited the depradations of the pashas. In the Janissaries Slade saw one of the principal bulwarks against tyrannical rule. Their removal greatly increased the despotism of the central government, while weakening the defenses of the Empire against its enemies.[36]

Slade's professional judgement—he was, it will be recalled, an experienced naval officer—is interesting at this point. In his view the new military forces created by the reforms were in every way weaker and less efficient than the older ones which they replaced. The main reason for this was that "under the ancient system the nation and the army were identical. The forces on the frontier might be defeated; but the nation, with rights and liberties to defend, was behind." But with the advent of the new type troops, this ceased to be true, and a gap was opened between the government and the people. "Under the modern system, the army is the measure of national defence; and this expression, applicable elsewhere as well, has peculiar force in an empire with no ties of kindred and few bonds of sympathy with the outer world."[37]

Slade is not easy to classify. Certainly he was no liberal, whether in the sense of his day or of ours—indeed, the earnest liberal critic of Ottoman ways and customs is a frequent butt of his irony. But equally he cannot be dismissed as a mere reactionary, a defender of the past for its own sake, nor as a romantic doting on exotic peoples in remote places. Slade is well aware of the deficiencies and shortcomings of the old order and indeed discusses them at some length. He is neither an indiscriminate defender of the old nor an unthinking critic of the new, and his arguments, one way or the other, are invariably based on intimate knowledge, close observation, and careful reasoning.

Another characteristic feature of his writing is the deep feeling of compassion that so frequently emerges. As a good naval officer Slade was naturally concerned with the welfare of the men under his command. But his humanity is of wider range than that and can be seen in his remarks on many aspects of life in the Western world as well as in the Ottoman lands. He is perhaps best described as a philosophic conservative, with the conservative respect for established and functioning institutions and the corresponding mistrust of change for its own sake and with a deep-rooted concern for the individual human being, even in the improbable guise of a slave, a convict, a conscript, an Irish Catholic peasant, or a British factory worker.

Perhaps most remarkable is the extent to which he succeeded in penetrating, understanding, and even in some measure identifying himself with an alien society and civilization. His works deserve to be better known, and his writings of Turkey may not unworthily be ranked with those of Tocqueville on America and of Custine on Russia.

PART II

MUSLIM HISTORY AND HISTORIANS

Sources for the Economic History of the Middle East

7

The economic historian, even more than his colleagues in other fields of historical inquiry, has a liking for documentary evidence—a marked tendency to prefer archives to annals and other literature. The historian will of course be aware of the insights and even information that books can give him, and he will appreciate the relevance to his researches of the image of a society as reflected in the works of its authors and compilers. But whenever possible he will direct his main attention to the contemporary and immediate evidence or traces of historical events, in their original form, not as transmitted—and therefore transmuted—by a literary intermediary. The modern economic historian relies very largely on published and unpublished documentary and statistical materials. In the West, even the medievalist has at his disposal a mass of records, public and private, lay and ecclesiastical, central and local, on which to base his study of economic structures and economic change.

One of the classical difficulties of the historian of Islam is the lack of such evidence.[1] Without entering into the complex theoretical and philosophical problems of periodization, we may, for practical purposes, divide the history of the Middle East since the rise of Islam into three periods, defined by the availability and quality of documentary sources, and describe them by the neutral terms early, middle, and late. In the late period, which in most areas begins in the nineteenth century and continues to our own day, our knowledge is enriched—if that is the right word—by the multifarious bureaucratic activities of the state and of other agencies. Research into the recent economic history of the Middle

East can be based on material similar in form, if less so in content, to that appearing in other parts of the modern world and can be pursued by similar techniques. Which parts, and which techniques, are for the researcher to determine, and it is possible that in time students of some Middle Eastern countries will develop a particular technique of their own, analogous to those used by specialists in other regions where only published plans, reports, and statistics are available and where these pose distinctive problems of acceptance and evaluation.

The middle period, corresponding roughly to what European historians call early modern history, is also illustrated by archives, though of a different—an early modern—kind. The most important by far is the Ottoman archives, the existence and range of which in effect define this period. Apart from the major collections in Istanbul, there are others in Ankara and in a number of Turkish provincial cities. Archival collections, of varying types and sizes, have also survived in Egypt and Tunisia and in some of the former Ottoman lands in Europe and Asia. The Ottoman archives have already given rise to a considerable literature, much of it concerned with economic matters.[2]

In other parts of the region the position is much less satisfactory. There are Ottoman records for those provinces of Persia and Transcaucasia which for a time were incorporated in the Ottoman Empire;[3] for the rest of Persia, no archives have so far come to light. Outside the areas under Ottoman rule or suzerainty, there is only one region for which archives are known to exist. This consists of the Muslim Khanates of Central Asia, incorporated in the Russian Empire between 1865 and 1887. State archives and some private archives, dating for the most part from the period immediately preceding the Russian conquest, were preserved by the conquerors and contain data on land-tenure, taxation, and related matters.[4]

In addition to these, there are two other groups of archives, of considerable but unequal interest to the economic historian. The first, and smaller group, consists of records preserved among the non-Muslim communities within the Muslim world. These, by virtue of their coherence and institutional structure, often enjoyed a continuity lacking in the larger and more fragmented Muslim society and were thus able to accumulate and preserve records over long periods of time. The best known are the Armenian monastery of Ečmiadzin and the Greek Orthodox St. Catherine's monastery in Mount Sinai, the documents of which have recently been studied and, in part, edited. Christian and Jewish ecclesiastical and communal archives exist in various centers, but have so far been little explored.[5] Published documents deal, among other things, with such familiar topics as the assessment and collection of taxes, land-tenure, and disputes of various kinds, usually over money or property.

The second, and very much larger, group consists of the archives of foreign governments, trading companies, religious orders, and other bodies that have been involved in or concerned with the Middle East—first in the Italian states, then Austria, Russia, the countries of Western Europe, especially Britain and France, and latterly also the United States. These countries contain rich archive collections, almost all of which are freely open to researchers.

The Ottoman archives begin in the fifteenth century, and become really full in the sixteenth. For earlier periods of Middle Eastern history, and for areas outside the Ottoman Empire, there are, with certain limited exceptions, no archives at all.

This does not mean that there are no documents. Considerable numbers of documents have in fact survived and may be found in public and private collections. But these collections are not archives; they are fortuitous assemblages of individual documents, discovered by chance and distributed haphazard, with no order other than that imposed on them by curators, editors, and historians. Their value may be very great, but it can never be the same as that of a genuine record office in which documents are preserved in their original form, order, and sequence, as they emerged from the work and served the needs of the institution that created them. Much of the value of such records lies in their comprehensiveness, continuity, and cohesion. That such archives existed in medieval Islam is clear from the literary sources, but they have not survived. Archives are created and maintained for administrative use, not for the convenience of historians. The states of the medieval West survived and developed into the states of the modern West, and their archives, often still current, were preserved until a time when their historical importance was appreciated. This political continuity facilitated the survival of many other, local, institutions and the consequent conservation of their records. The church was another major element of stability and continuity, and the well-preserved and well-protected records of ecclesiastical offices and foundations are an invaluable source of information for the economic historian. The states of the medieval Middle East, with the exception of the Ottoman Empire, were destroyed, and their archives, ceasing to serve any practical purpose, were neglected, scattered, and lost. Islam had no church, and the character of Islamic society did not favor the emergence of corporative bodies below government level, of such a type and of such duration as to produce and conserve records.

There are some exceptions to the statement, frequently repeated and generally accepted, that there are no archives for medieval Islamic history. The most important of these exceptions have already been mentioned—the archives of foreign and of minority institutions. These are naturally less plentiful than for the Ottoman period but still contain much that is of interest. Italian and Spanish archives contain many documents relating to commerce, including a number in Arabic, which have received historically disproportionate attention from orientalists. Even the documents from St. Catherine's, reflecting the concerns of the monks and their dealings with the outside world, are not without economic interest. They include rulings from the Egyptian chancery on disputes between the monks and their Bedouin neighbors, who claimed a share of their lands and crops (wheat, barley, and fruit), and replies to appeals from the monks for the remission of taxes, tolls, and services.

Another exception is the pre-Ottoman material preserved in the Ottoman archives, most of it, unfortunately, in Ottoman copies or adaptations. Ottoman policy in a newly conquered province was usually very conservative and normally maintained, at least for a while, the existing fiscal and administrative practice. The Ottomans also recognized existing *waqf*, and the *waqf* registers compiled after the Ottoman conquest of Syria include many *waqfs* of the Mamlūk and even of the Ayyūbid period. The administration of *waqf*, together with other matters arising out of the application of the holy law, also gave rise to small groups of pre-Ottoman documents that have been preserved in the Ministry of *Waqf* and the court of personal affairs in Cairo.[6]

The European archives are often of considerable size and importance, but, in view of their external origin, are inevitably limited in the range of information which they can offer. Such Middle Eastern archives as survive, from the pre-Ottoman period, are vestigial and restricted and have on the whole been of more interest for diplomatics than for history.

In the absence of genuine archives, the surviving documents, despite their non-archival character, acquire considerable importance. There are several categories of such documents; most of them come from Egypt, where the dry climate on the one hand and a relatively high degree of political continuity on the other favored their preservation.

The first important group consists of some tens of thousands of miscellaneous documents and fragments, all but a few of them from Egypt, and written, for the most part, during the first four centuries of Islam. Some are in Greek, some in Arabic, some bilingual. A few are in other languages. They are known collectively as "the papyri," from the material on which they are written, and the special branch of scholarship concerned with their study is called papyrology.[7] This terminology, as Professor Claude Cahen has remarked, is unfortunate and conveys a somewhat misleading impression of the scope and purposes of these studies. "In reality, papyrology, when it is concerned with mere deciphering, is a branch of palaeography; when interpretation is involved, it is exclusively a branch of history."[8] In fact, there has been a tendency to make a distinction—which for the historian is of no importance—between documents written on papyrus and documents written on paper and to neglect the latter; there has also been undue separation between the study of Greek and of Arabic papyri, even where both date from the Islamic period and deal with similar topics.

Despite these limitations, and some others arising from the predominantly philological character of scholarship in this field, the study of the papyri has already significantly altered the accepted view of early Islamic history. Many of the papyri are administrative and financial documents. A comparison of these with similar documents from the late Byzantine period shows greater continuity and less change than was previously believed; a comparison of the evidence of the papyri with juristic expositions reveals the latter to be schematic and anachronistic and has led to a perhaps rather exaggerated reaction from the earlier habit of complete reliance on such sources.

In the work that has so far been done on the papyri, the main attention has been given to the workings of government—to such matters as provincial administration; the assessment and collection of taxes; land surveys and accountancy; the administration of justice; the recruitment, equipment, and supply of the armed forces. Much of this has an obvious relevance to economic history. Documents relating to the navy, for example, include information concerning the employment of skilled and unskilled labor in the shipyards, the supply of timber, nails, ropes, and other materials to them, and the provision of food for the sailors and workers. In addition, there are numerous other papyri, of both official and private origin, dealing with the transfer of commodities by purchase, requisition, or taxation, the employment of labor for wages or by *corvée,* and similar topics. After the pioneering work of Karabacek, Becker, and Bell, published work on the papyri has, in the main, taken the form of editions, translations, and evaluations of individual documents or groups of documents, with some work on administration, taxation, and law. The systematic use of the papyri by economic historians is still at a very rudimentary stage; given the unsystematic character of the evidence, and the arduous philological apprenticeship required for its study, this situation may well persist.

During the tenth century papyrus gradually went out of use and was replaced, even in Egypt, by paper. Documents on paper, apparently of the same types as the papyri, have survived in considerable numbers. Not being papyri, these have been almost entirely disregarded by orientalist scholarship, and little is known about their range and content.

One important group of papers, also of Egyptian provenance, has received serious attention. These are the documents from the so-called *Geniza,* the repositories in which the Jews of Cairo placed written papers which were no longer required, to protect the name of God, which might occur in them, from desecration.[9] Leaving aside literary manuscripts and "mere scraps," the number of whole documents and self-contained fragments in the *Geniza* has been estimated by Professor S. D. Goitein at about 10,000. These date mainly from the Fāṭimid and Ayyūbid periods, with a small number from Mamlūk times. There is in addition *Geniza* material of the Ottoman period, which has not so far been used.

Like the papyri, the *Geniza* documents are subject to certain limitations. They are not archival; they all come from Egypt—and they are further limited, by their Jewish provenance, to such matters as concerned the members of one religious minority. The first of these limitations, the non-archival character of the documents, is of major importance and severely restricts the use that can be made of data on such matters as prices and wages, in the *Geniza* as in the papyri. The other limitations, though serious, are less so than would at first appear. The papyri, largely of governmental origin and concerned with such very local matters as taxation and provincial administration, tell us little about conditions outside Egypt; apart from the very few papyri found in Southwest Asia,[10] the best they can offer is comparative material, which may occasionally be of use in elucidating data obtained from other sources. The *Geniza* includes documents of governmental origin, but the greater and most valuable part, for the economic historian, is of private origin—business and family correspondence, accounts, receipts, contracts and other commercial documents, and legal deeds and reports of various kinds. The commercial and social relations reflected in these documents are by no means limited to Egypt but extend westwards to the Mediterranean lands, eastward to India.[11] They provide fuller information on the life and activities of the commercial classes in medieval Egypt than is available from any other source.

No third group of documents, comparable in scale and importance with the papyri and the *Geniza,* has so far been brought to light. Many documents exist, however, of which only a small proportion have been studied. As in the earlier periods, Egypt is the richest source. Besides the papyri, large numbers of Egyptian documents written on paper, and dating from the tenth century onwards, are kept in public collections; some 28,000 are reported in Vienna alone.[12] These documents, said to be of the same general type as the papyri, have hardly been touched by modern scholarship. A small group of documents from Damascus, discovered by D. and J. Sourdel, include some deeds of sale dated 310/922–23, the title-deeds of an estate, dated 604/1207–8, and a letter announcing the restoration of property previously confiscated by the sovereign.[13]

After Egypt, Iran and the neighboring lands in Transcaucasia and Central Asia provide the most important nonarchival collections of documents. Original Persian documents from the pre-Mongol period are very few indeed. The earliest is a private letter from a Jewish merchant, written in Persian in Hebrew characters, possibly in the eighth century. It was found near Khotan. Others include a Judaeo-Persian law report of 1020 from Ahwāz, a deed for the sale of land, dated 501/1107, from the region of Khotan (?), and a group of six documents from Bāmyān of which one is dated 607/1211.[14] There are rather more documents from the period of the Il-Khāns and their successors, but it is not until the time of the Safavids that we find them in any great numbers. Those that have already been found, in public and private collections in Iran and elsewhere, include many that deal with fiscal, commercial, and other matters of economic interest.[15]

Besides all these, two other groups of documents have survived in the Middle East, because they were written on metal and on stone. Coins and inscriptions are available in great numbers and have been extensively studied by numismatists and epigraphers.[16] The documentary information inscribed on coins is inevitably meager and repetitive, but even such modest data as the year and mint of issue can usefully contribute to the inferences drawn from the weight and metallic composition of coins, and from the place, quantity, and company in which they are found. Probably the best known example is the series of hoards, containing many thousands of Muslim silver *dirhams,* that have been found in the countries around the Baltic, and especially on the Swedish island of Gotland, then an important commercial center. These coins come mainly from Iraqi, Persian, and Central Asian mints, and carry dates ranging from the turn of the seventh/eighth century to the early eleventh century. Until about the middle of the tenth century, the coins found in these hoards consist almost exclusively of Muslim *dirhams.* From the second half of the tenth century, the hoards include a growing proportion of other coins, Byzantine, West European, even Anglo-Saxon. Towards the middle of the eleventh century Muslim coins disappear entirely from these silver hoards. These hoards, together with similar finds in Poland and Russia, especially in the regions of Kazan and Kiev, on the one hand, and in Western Europe on the other, have given rise to a vast literature on the trade between the Muslim lands and the North.[17] The problem, as Professor Tadeusz Lewicki has remarked, is still anything but clarified.[18]

Islamic inscriptions are extant in great numbers, with a very wide range of countries and periods of origin. Their range of content is, however, disappointingly narrow. One of the greatest of Arabic epigraphers, Max van Berchem, remarked that almost all of them "are centered on one of the two predominant ideas in the Muslim world: divine power and absolute political authority. On the one hand, the Koran, invocations, and pious phrases, confessions of faith, mystical allusions, and prayers for the dead; on the other hand, the names of the sovereign, his titles, exploits, and his perpetual praise."[19] Though some of us may wish to dissent from the particulars of van Berchem's formulation, we must surely agree with his conclusion, that the inscriptions of Islam have far less documentary value than those of Greek and Roman antiquity. "In this world," said Benjamin Franklin in a famous phrase, "nothing can be said to be certain, except death and taxes." The Muslim inscriptions may be said to reflect a parallel preoccupation with the two ultimate certainties, but differently expressed—as God and the government. It is at the point of contact or conflict between these two concerns that the inscriptions are most informative. Two groups of inscriptions are of particular interest to the economic historian. The first consists of the texts or summaries of *waqf* deeds, inscribed on pious foundations, to protect the service of God from the depredations of the state; the second deals with taxes, tolls, and levies of various kinds—usually in the form of the pious abolition of illegal taxes by a pious new ruler.[20] Though never, as far as can be seen from the record, reimposed, these illegal taxes are reabolished with monotonous frequency. Between the papyri and the Ottoman archives, inscriptions provide the best documentary evidence concerning taxation. Also of interest are the inscriptions on metrological objects (weights, coin-weights, measure-stamps, vessel-stamps, tokens), and trade-marks or certificates on manufactured articles, especially textiles and metalwork.[21]

For the second and third of the three periods we have considered, the economic historian of the Middle East, apart from some problems of physical and linguistic access to documents, is not significantly worse off than his European colleague—indeed, he may find that the Ottoman archives offer material of a wealth and diversity not found elsewhere. For the first, or medieval, period, however, the documentary evidence available to him is very much poorer. In compensation, he has at his disposal a body of literary material of incomparable richness, "larger perhaps than any other civilization has produced until modern times."[22]

It would be pointless to attempt a survey of the literary sources for the economic history of the Middle East, which potentially include the whole vast literature of the area. It may, however, be useful to look at certain classes of writings and to consider the type of information that they offer.

The first group of texts to be considered are those that deal directly and explicitly with economic questions, both theoretical and practical. The earliest prescriptive statements are in the Qur'ān itself, notably in the final pages of *Sūrat al-Baqara.* "God has permitted buying and selling, and forbidden usury. . . . O you who believe! Be pious towards God, and forgo what is owing to you from usury, if you are believers. If you do not do this, then expect war from God and the Prophet, but if you renounce [usury], your capital will remain with you, and you will neither inflict nor suffer injury."[23] Other passages confirm the lawfulness of honest trading and touch on such matters as fair weights and measures, debts, contracts, and the like.[24]

Qur'ānic approval of buying and selling is amplified in a large number of sayings, attributed to the Prophet and to the leading figures of early Islam, in praise of the honest merchant and of commerce as a way of life. Some sayings go further and defend the more expensive commodities which the honest merchants sold—such as silks and brocades, jewels, male and female slaves, and other luxuries. "When God gives wealth to a man," the Prophet is improbably quoted as saying, "He wants it to be seen on him." Even more striking is a story told in an early Shīʿite work. The Imām Jaʿfar al-Ṣādiq, it is said, was reproached by one of his disciples for wearing fine apparel (a variant says: clothes from Marw), while his ancestors had worn rude, simple garments. The Imām is quoted as replying that his ancestors had lived in a time of scarcity, while he lived in a time of plenty, and that it was proper to wear the clothing of one's own time.[25] These and similar attempts to justify luxurious living mark a reaction against the strain of asceticism in Islam and no doubt reflect the interests of the luxury trades.

As in many other fields, the earliest known Muslim work on economic ethics consists very largely of a collection of sayings attributed to the Prophet and the early heroes of Islam entitled *Kitāb al-Kasb,* "On earning"; it was written by a Syrian of Iraqi *mawlā* ancestry called Muḥammad al-Shaybānī, who died in 804.[26] Shaybānī's purpose is to show that earning a livelihood is not merely permitted but is incumbent on Muslims. Man's primary duty is to serve God, but to do this properly he must be adequately fed, housed, and clothed. This can only be achieved by working and earning. Nor need his earnings be limited to providing for the bare necessities of life, since the acquisition and use of luxuries is also permitted.

Another point which Shaybānī is anxious to make is that money earned by commerce or crafts is more pleasing in God's eyes than money received from the government for civil or military service. The same point is argued by al-Jāḥiẓ (d. 869) in an essay entitled "In praise of merchants and in condemnation of officials"[27] and is echoed by many later writers. Jāḥiẓ stresses the security, dignity, and independence of merchants in contrast with the uncertainty, humiliation, and sycophancy of those who serve the ruler and defends the piety and the learning of merchants against their detractors.

The discussion in ethical and religious terms of gainful employment, usually equated with commerce and crafts, was continued by a number of subsequent writers, occasionally in separate works, more frequently within the framework of more extensive treatises.[28] A tenth-century encyclopaedic work of Ismāʿīlī inspiration includes a detailed survey of arts and crafts, classified in several different ways—by the materials they use, by the tools and movements they require, and by "rank." Under the last heading crafts are divided into three main groups: The first, or primary, group provides basic necessities and is subdivided into three subgroups—weaving, agriculture, and building, providing the three basic needs for clothing, food, and shelter. The second, or "ancillary," group consists of accessory and finishing trades, ancillary to the first. The third main group is concerned with luxuries such as silks, brocades, and perfumes. A final cross-classification is by the "merit" of the crafts, which may derive from their indispensability, as agriculture; their precious materials, as jewellery; their skilled workmanship, as the making of astronomical instruments; their public utility, as the work of bath-attendants and scavengers; or, finally, the nobility of the craft itself, as painting and music.[29]

It would be easy to assemble other traditions, and writings of ascetic tendency, that say just the opposite and condemn commerce and those engaged in it. It is, however, noteworthy that centuries before Christian writers were prepared to defend and define the ethics of commerce against ascetic criticism, Muslim writers were willing to do so and that even a major theologian like al-Ghazālī (d. 1111) could include, in his religious writings, a portrait of the ideal merchant and a defense of commerce as a way of preparing oneself for the world to come.[30]

Besides religious writings on commerce, there are others, of a more practical nature. The best known is the *Kitāb al-Ishāra ilā maḥāsin al-tijāra* (Indication of the merits of commerce) written in the eleventh or twelfth century by Abū'l Faḍl Ja'far b. 'Alī al-Dimashqī. Greek philosophic influences are already apparent in the tenth-century encyclopaedia cited above. They appear again in al-Dimashqī's treatise, in a more specifically economic form—from Plato's *Politics,* Aristotle's doctrine of the golden mean, and, in particular, the *Oikonomos* of the neo-Pythagorean "Bryson."

For al-Dimashqī, gain is a good thing for its own sake. Though he includes some theoretical and moralistic discussion, his main purpose is to provide practical guidance for merchants. He discusses, among other topics, the types, qualities, and prices of merchandise; the roles of the three classes of merchants, the wholesaler *(khazzān),* the exporter *(mujahhiz),* and the traveling merchant *(rakkāḍ);* the dangers of fraud and waste; and various problems such as the appointment of agents, the obtaining of information about market prices, the fixing of prices, the delivery of goods, and financial and commercial administration.[31]

Even more practical are works dealing with specific problems. "A Clear Look at Trade" *(al-Tabaṣṣur bi'l-tijāra),* probably written in ninth-century Iraq, discusses the qualities, values, and ways of evaluating gold, silver, pearls and precious stones, scents and aromatics, textiles, skins and other commodities, and lists the goods imported from the provinces of the Islamic Empire and from foreign countries.[32] An eleventh-century author wrote "On the purchase of slaves"—a sort of slave-trader's vade-mecum, with a classification of slaves by race and country of origin and much fascinating information on the slave-trade in all its stages. This work is also, incidentally, a useful source for the history of Africa.[33] A common theme of the practical handbooks is the need for precautions against swindlers and fakers, whose methods are often described in fascinating detail. A thirteenth-century Syrian author devotes a whole book to the subject of trickery and fraud. Beginning with false prophets, spurious priests, thaumaturges, alchemists, astrologers, mountebanks, and the like, the author goes on to discuss the distinctive malpractices of dishonest grocers, cooks, horse-copers, money-changers, physicians, and other trades and professions.[34]

Farmers seem to have been less articulate—or less represented in book-writing circles—than merchants. There is, however, a literature on agriculture, which deserves more attention than it has received. The earliest known work is the so-called "Nabataean Agriculture" *(al-Filāḥa al-nabaṭiyya)* written or translated into Arabic by Ibn Waḥshiyya in 291/904, and purporting to convey the agronomic knowledge of the pre-Arab inhabitants of Iraq. It was followed by a parallel compendium of Greek agronomy, *al-Filāḥa al-rūmiyya,* translated into Arabic from a Greek original. These and other, later, works deal with the different types and qualities of land; with agricultural implements and methods of work; with fertilizers, irrigation, animal and vegetable pests; and with the various problems of planting, tending, and reaping crops, including cereals, vegetables, bulbs, fruits, and flowers for perfume.[35]

Mining and metallurgy also received some attention. The South Arabian antiquary Ibn al-Ḥā'ik al-Ḥamdānī (d. 945) devoted a book to gold and silver, including a list of places from which they are obtained, with some information about the mines, and an account of the methods used in mining, smelting, and assaying.[36] A thirteenth-century Egyptian mint official, Ibn Baʿra, deals more specifically with the use of gold and silver for coinage. Besides much technical detail, he also offers useful information on monetary matters.[37]

A very rich source of information on economic matters is the vast bureaucratic and administrative literature of medieval Islam. Written by civil servants for civil servants, these works vary from manuals dealing with the working of one office or official to immense encyclopaedias of bureaucratic usage and procedure. A major concern of these writers is of course finance—revenue, financial administration, expenditure. The information they offer is by no means limited to the financial activities of the state. Discussions of tolls and customs-dues tell us something about trade and industry; works on the land-tax throw some light on agrarian conditions. To quote one rather striking example, an eleventh-century handbook of mathematics written for the use of tax-assessors in Iraq deals with problems of money, wages, and prices, with trade and manufactures (work in gold, gold thread, fine stuffs), and with both the technical and administrative aspects of irrigation.[38]

Taxation and the regulation of commerce also take up much space in another major branch of Muslim literature—that of the law. At one time the jurists were treated with excessive respect, and their statements taken as a sufficient description of the functioning of Muslim institutions. A reaction followed, in the course of which scholars remarked that lawyers in general are concerned with what ought to be rather than with what is and that Muslim lawyers in particular are inclined to construct ideal systems which may have little to do with the real facts of life. Recent scholars have adopted a more balanced attitude, neither accepting the statements in the law books at face value nor rejecting them out of hand. Muslim law has not been static; it has undergone a long and complex development. A careful scrutiny of juristic texts can produce valuable information on the changing conditions, pressures, and influences to which the jurists were subject.[39] Another body of legal material, of considerable value, is the Jewish Responsa—the answers given by rabbis to questions put to them. Many of these deal with matters of economic interest—disputes arising out of trade, manufacture, employment, partnerships, tenancies, inheritances, and the like. The Rabbinic Responsa are very rich for the Ottoman period and by no means negligible for earlier times.[40]

Most other branches of the scientific and scholarly literature of the area are potentially relevant—military writings, chemistry and physics, religion—especially heresiography and hagiography, geography, even philology. Among the most important are works of narrative history and biography. The value of the chronicles is self-evident. Of special value are the numerous local histories, which frequently record in detail such things as floods, earthquakes, famine, and plague, as well as scarcities and gluts, harvests, market prices, and other data of economic interest. Useful information, independent of the Muslim historiographic tradition, may also be found in the chronicles and other literature of the Christian populations under Muslim rule.[41]

Biography offers particular promise and interest. In the biographical appendices to the annals, in the largely biographical local histories, and in the biographical dictionaries arranged by centuries or devoted to certain professions and other groups, Muslim literature offers us a great treasure-house of information for social, cultural, and economic history. The possible contribution of these biographies to narrative history is obvious; less obvious, but far more important, is the cumulative value of these tens of thousands of life-histories, many of them of men of no great individual significance, in building up a picture of the society in which these men were born and educated, lived and died. In recent years, Western historians have made increasing use of the method of prosopography—that is, the approach to the study of historical phenomena through the examination and comparison of as many as possible relevant individual facts concerning as many as possible individual participants. This method, like any other, has its dangers and its limitations. It also has tremendous potentialities, especially for a society like that of Islam, where the mass of available biographical information goes far beyond the customary restricted oligarchies of power and privilege.[42]

Finally, there remains the vast mass of poetry and *belles lettres*, from which the historian can gather and piece together the countless fragments of information that he needs. The poet, in traditional Islamic society, often has an important public function. The political function of the poet—and the consequent political relevance of poetry—is well known. The economic uses of poetry are less explored. Two final examples, both from the Arabic Book of Songs *(Kitāb al-Aghānī)*, must suffice. An Umayyad governor of Iraq, in the eighth century, forcibly expropriated a piece of land, needed for the extension of the irrigation system. The famous poet Farazdaq, on behalf of the landowner, composed a poem attacking the governor and accusing him of oppression. The second story also comes from Umayyad times. A merchant went from Kūfa to Medina with a consignment of veils and sold all but the black ones, which the ladies apparently did not like. He complained to a poet, who obliged him by composing some verses, in which he spoke of his love for "the beauty in the black veil." The poem was set to music and sung all over Medina, every lady of refinement *(ẓarīfa)* bought a black veil, and the Iraqi merchant sold his entire stock. Thus, in a dark hour, with a black veil, the singing commercial was born.[43]

In Search of Islam's Past

8

For Muslims, history is important. The mission of Muḥammad and the promulgation of the Qur'ān are events in history, and knowledge of them was preserved and disseminated through historical memory and record. In this respect Islam takes the same view as its two predecessors, Judaism and Christianity, and indeed the earliest Islamic narratives bear a generic resemblance to those of the Jews and Christians, in scripture and elsewhere. The Muslims too had their kings and their prophets, their saints and their martyrs, and preserve the memory of their lives and their deaths in history and biography, in tradition and commemoration.

But there is more. Judaism began among a small group of migratory tribes, grew among the inhabitants of a small kingdom, overshadowed and often dominated by mighty neighbors, and achieved its greatest flowering among a people who were conquered, subjugated, and ultimately dispersed. Christianity first appeared as the faith of a small minority in a subject province of the Roman Empire and remained through its early formative centuries a religion of the downtrodden and the oppressed. Islam, in contrast, triumphed during the lifetime of its founder, who created a state which, under his immediate successors, the caliphs, became a vast empire. The Christianized Roman Empire strove, albeit with limited success, to preserve the language, the laws, and the institutions of pagan Rome, and even the barbarian conquerors who

---

A review of *Islamic History: A Framework for Inquiry, Revised Edition* by R. Stephen Humphreys, Princeton University Press, from *The New York Review of Books*, 5 December 1991.

became its real masters paid at least lip service to the state and church which they had conquered. The situation in the Islamic caliphate was totally different. The Muslim Arabs, unlike the Western barbarians, brought their own scripture, in their own language, and created their own imperial system and structure. Though much remained of the Roman and Christian past in the former Roman Christian provinces of the Levant and North Africa, it evoked no respect and conferred no legitimacy. Its survival was, so to speak, surreptitious, and ultimately vestigial. In the new Islamic polity and society, only Islam conferred legitimacy; only Islamic precedent, that is, the Islamic past, could validate government and law.

Even during the lifetime of the Prophet, and much more frequently after his death, pressing problems arose for which the Qur'ān provided no explicit answers. At an early date the principle was adopted that the Prophet was divinely guided in all his actions and utterances and that after his death the divine guidance was given to the Muslim community as a whole. "My community," the Prophet is cited as saying, "will not agree on an error." The practice of the Prophet and the decisions made by the early caliphs thus constitute a body of precedents, ranking second only to the Qur'ān itself among the authoritative sources of the *Sharīʿa*, the holy law of Islam. It is designated by a variety of terms, the commonest being *sunna*, meaning, approximately, the corpus of custom and example left by revered predecessors.

But between the Qur'ān and the *sunna* there was an important difference. The Qur'ān was scripture, in the Muslim view literally divine, having been dictated to the Prophet by an angel. A written and authorized text was established at an early date, and, apart from a few minor and insignificant variants, there is no argument about the accuracy or authenticity of the canon. The *sunna*, on the other hand, though divinely inspired, was human, and therefore subject to error and even fraud. It consists of a multiplicity of traditions, orally transmitted for generations before they were committed to writing. Human memory is always fallible, and the bitter religious, social, and political struggles of the early Islamic period encouraged the distortion or even the fabrication of traditions, designed to support an argument, a faction, or a cause.

From an early date Muslim scholars recognized the danger of false testimony and hence of false doctrine, and developed an elaborate science for criticizing tradition. "Tradition science," as it was called, differed in many respects from modern historical source criticism, and modern scholarship has often disagreed with the evaluations of tradition scientists about the authenticity and accuracy of ancient narratives. But their careful scrutiny of the chains of transmission and their meticulous collection and preservation of variants in the transmitted narratives give to medieval Arabic historiography a professionalism and a sophistication without precedent in antiquity and without parallel in the contemporary medieval West. By comparison, the historiography of Latin Christendom seems poor and meager, and even the more advanced and complex historiography of Greek Christendom still falls short of the historical literature of Islam in volume, variety, and analytical depth. For Sunni Muslims—the Shīʿa take a different view—God's community was the embodiment of God's design for mankind, and its history, providentially guided, revealed the working out of God's purpose. An accurate knowledge of history was therefore supremely important, since it could provide authoritative guidance in both the profoundest problems of religion and the most practical matters of law.

History was important—that is to say, Muslim history. The history of non-Muslim states and communities, which did not accept God's final revelation and did not obey God's law, offered no such guidance and possessed no such value. Muslim historians therefore paid scant attention to non-Muslim history, whether of their neighbors in Christian Europe and elsewhere, or of their own Christian, Zoroastrian, and pagan ancestors. Some knowledge of the immediately pre-Islamic past was retained and included in the corpus of historic knowledge. Of the great civilizations of the ancient Middle East, all that Muslim historiography knew was what was related in the Qur'ān, with some additional explanatory matter, mostly derived from Jewish and Christian informants. The rest of the ancient past was forgotten and, often literally, buried beneath the ground. Perhaps even more remarkable was the almost total disregard of Europe which characterizes Islamic writings in Arabic, Persian, and Turkish from the beginning of historiography until the nineteenth century, when the advancing power of Europe demanded, and finally received, attention.

For a long time, European Christian historians showed a similar lack of interest in non-Christian history. They were of course very much concerned with the advance of Islam, which had wrested the eastern and southern shores of the Mediterranean from Christendom and which for a thousand years threatened Europe itself from both ends, the Arabs in the West, the Turks and Tatars in the East. But the study of Islam in medieval Europe, such as it was, was religious. It was pursued principally in monasteries and had as its primary aim to protect Christians from conversion to Islam—a very real danger at the time—and, ultimately, to launch a Christian counter-mission for the conversion of the Muslims to Christianity.

By the end of the Middle Ages, it was becoming increasingly clear that the first task was no longer necessary, the second impossible. But if the Islamic religion was no longer seen as a serious rival, Islamic power, now embodied in the rising empire of the Turks, remained a major threat. European writers, their concerns aroused by the Turkish conquests, their curiosity whetted by the adventures in ideas of the Renaissance, their methods sharpened by the new learning, devoted increasing attention to Turkish history and produced a considerable body of writing on the subject. By the beginning of the seventeenth century, an English clergyman, Richard Knolles, was able to publish an immense volume on the history of the Turks, based on a wide range of continental European writings, some of them translations from Turkish originals.[1]

But all this was what we would nowadays call modern and contemporary history, with some minimal necessary background. This literature paid little attention to classical Islam, and it had no place in the universities or in the research and teaching carried out under their auspices. The universities of the time were not interested in modern languages like Turkish, any more than they were interested in French or German: they were not interested in the history of Turkey, any more than in the history of Germany or France. The only history worthy of the attention of academic scholars was ancient history, based on classical and scriptural sources, and it was to this aspect of Islam that, in due course, scholars in the European universities began to devote their attention.

The first chair of Arabic in France was established by King Francis I at the Collège de France in 1529; the first chairs of Arabic in England at

Cambridge and Oxford in 1633 and 1636. Others appeared at about the same time in the German states and, notably, at the University of Leiden in Holland, which from the seventeenth century onward became a major center of Arabic and Islamic studies. Those engaged in these and similar studies came to be known as Orientalists, a term coined on the analogy of the Hellenists and Latinists whose intellectual discipline and rigorous philological method they adapted to the study, and later to the edition, translation, and annotation, of Oriental texts. These texts were principally in Hebrew, Syriac, and Arabic, and the third led naturally and inevitably to the study of scriptural and then classical Islamic history—that is, the life of the Prophet and the history of the medieval caliphate.

Like the Jewish scholars who helped the first Christian Hebraists, so also Christian Arab scholars from the Middle East contributed significantly to the early development of Arabic scholarship in Europe. These early modern scholars performed a task of the greatest importance in discovering, editing, analyzing, and interpreting the original sources for early Islamic history. In doing so they laid the foundations of virtually all modern scholarship in this field, in the Arab lands as well as in the West. At first they published most of their work in Latin, still at that time the common language of European scholarship. But soon, especially but not exclusively in Protestant countries, they began to use their own languages. By the nineteenth, still more the twentieth century, the serious student of classical Islamic history required a wide range of linguistic equipment, giving him access not only to the indispensable original sources but also to scholarly monographs in all the major and several of the minor languages of Europe.

Arabic and Islamic studies presented—to some degree still present—special difficulties, as compared with Latin and Greek, or even with medieval European studies. The quantity of surviving texts was enormous, but in the early days of Orientalism they were almost all still in manuscript, scattered through countless libraries, many of them difficult or impossible of access. Very few were printed, and the small production of published texts was for long due largely to the efforts of Western scholars. Printed editions of classical texts did not appear in Middle Eastern countries until the mid-nineteenth century; critical editions not until the twentieth. Because of their small numbers and the magnitude of their tasks, the Arabists of Europe fell far behind the Hellenists and Latinists.

The relative backwardness of Orientalist scholarship gave rise to, and was in turn aggravated by, the lack of certain basic research tools which before long were taken for granted in other fields of study. The medieval Arab scholars had left a magnificent legacy of studies on the grammar and vocabulary of their language, but the task of transforming this into modern philology and lexicography took many generations. The medieval Islamic states and societies left vast hordes of coins and innumerable inscriptions, but the science of Islamic numismatics and epigraphy, though begun in the sixteenth century, did not achieve major results until the twentieth, when it also benefitted from contributions by scholars in the Muslim lands.

Despite all these difficulties, substantial progress was made. Already by the late seventeenth century, when a French scholar called Barthélemi d'Herbelot published a multivolume alphabetical dictionary of Oriental civilizations,[2] he was able to draw on a substantial body of printed scholarly work. A century later, when Edward Gibbon was writing the Arab and Turkish chapters of his *Decline and Fall of the Roman Empire,* sufficient material was available to him, both translated sources and recent studies, for him to perform this task with his customary flair and distinction.

But there were still many gaps in the equipment of the Arabist. He did not have—we still do not have—a historical dictionary of classical Arabic, or even a satisfactory dictionary of classical Arabic usage. The preparation of a comprehensive Arabic dictionary is now underway, for the first time, under the auspices of the Arabic Language Academy in Cairo, with the cooperation of many scholars in Arab and other lands. When this work is completed, it will be an immense boon to scholarship concerned with all branches of Arabic and Islamic studies.

Another deficiency, particularly felt by students, was the lack of the kind of bibliographical and methodological handbooks available in most other fields of historical and philological studies. Muslim scholars—Arabs, Persians, Turks, and others—had been writing bibliographical works since the high Middle Ages, but this literature, like that of the classical lexicographers, had not been reshaped in accordance with modern bibliographical standards and practices.

A first Orientalist bibliography was published in Leipzig in 1846.[3] It contained a classified list of published texts in Arabic, Persian, and Turkish, most of them, as was inevitable at that date, printed in Europe. An Italian work,[4] published in 1916, provided invaluable guidance to several generations of scholars and students; it formed the basis of a more recent work in English.[5] These provide detailed information about reference works, sources, libraries and archives, and centers of study; they offer, however, no methodological guidance and no critical examination of either the problems discussed or the solutions propounded. Gustav Pfannmüller's handbook of literature on Islam, published in 1923, does offer such discussions, but only of Western literature and not of the Arabic sources, with which he was apparently not acquainted.[6] It is still useful as a guide to the early European travel and scholarly literature.

The first who attempted to do for students of Islamic history what scholars like Ernst Bernheim and Louis Halphen did for historians of the West, the one in his handbook of historical method, the other in his initiation to the study of the Middle Ages,[7] was a French Orientalist called Jean Sauvaget, whose introduction to medieval Islamic history was published in Paris in 1943.[8] Conditions in wartime Paris were not favorable for the preparation of full and up-to-date bibliographies, and the bibliographical part of Sauvaget's book is now badly out of date. It remains, however, invaluable for its methodological chapters, in which he enumerated the various categories of source material and the ways of approaching them, and for his incisive and often pungent comments on previous work in the field, sometimes of a severity nowadays usually reserved for political and ideological opponents and not, as previously, for flawed scholarship. A revised edition was prepared by Claude Cahen and published in 1961, in which Cahen added a great deal of bibliographical information but removed most of Sauvaget's sharper critical notes. An English translation of this edition was published by the University of California Press in 1965.[9] A new and entirely recast French text was published by M. Cahen in 1982.[10] There are a number of other bibliographical works,[11] but basically the sequence of works by Sauvaget,

Sauvaget-Cahen, and Cahen alone have continued to provide the most basic and comprehensive guidance available. There has hitherto been no other work of comparable scope, depth, and value.

To these however we must now add a new book by Professor R. Stephen Humphreys, already known for his studies on Syria and Egypt in the later Middle Ages. The first edition of this important work was first published apparently for limited circulation by the Bibliotheca Islamica of Minneapolis in 1988. It has now been reissued, in a revised and updated version, by the Princeton University Press. Professor Humphreys offers something less, and very much more, than the works described above. Only the first two chapters—one a critical, classified bibliography of works of reference, the other an analytical survey of the sources—provide the kind of bibliographical and technical guidance given by Cahen and Sauvaget, whose work they usefully supplement but do not replace.

The remaining ten chapters deal with a series of problems that have particularly preoccupied students of Islamic history in recent years. They include such topics as the reassessment of early historical tradition on the beginnings of the Islamic state; the mid-eighth-century revolution that overthrew the Umayyads and installed the ʿAbbāsids as caliphs, thus transferring the center of the Arab-Islamic empire from Syria to Iraq and transforming both its social base and political structure; the role and status of the ulema, the professional men of religion in medieval Islamic society who were at once jurists and theologians, though not, in the Christian sense, a priesthood; and urban topography and society, with special reference to late medieval Damascus.

Several chapters deal with problems arising from classical Islamic historiography in both Arabic and Persian and with the complex double problem of the importance of Islamic law in Islamic history and the use of Islamic legal texts by the historian. The first Orientalist students of Islam, impressed on the one hand by the central role of law in Islamic society and religion, on the other by the mighty structure of Islamic jurisprudence, tended to treat the normative statements of the jurists as descriptions of real events and usages. In this, they were both preceded and followed by historians within the indigenous tradition. A later generation of scholars, becoming aware of the often wide disparities between the principles of Islam as prescribed in the law books and the practice of Muslims as revealed in documents, went to the opposite extreme and dismissed the whole juristic literature as a system of ideals unrelated to reality—"as if it embodied only the vain dreams of aged *'ulama'* cloistered in their mosques, and did not hope to mold the affairs of everyday life." As Professor Humphreys remarks, "until very recently historians of Islam have been extremely reluctant to regard law and jurisprudence as a significant source for social and economic life. For anyone familiar with the importance of law in the study of Roman or English history, such behavior must seem simply obtuse."

Professor Humphreys traces the stages in the evolution of scholarly thought and method on this matter and offers guidance on the place of law in Islamic history, the difference between Muslim and Western perceptions of the nature of law, the range of Muslim legal texts and the studies based on them, and the manner in which these texts can and should be used for both legal and general history.

The two final chapters deal with two non-elite groups—in a brief but interesting argument, Professor Humphreys gives his reasons for avoiding the term "minorities," preferring to speak of groups "systematically excluded by law or custom from the enjoyment of all the benefits which that society has to confer." Islamic law recognizes three categories of legal inferiors: slaves, women, and unbelievers. Human nature, in defiance of Islamic law and morality, created other categories of inferiors, both racial and social. Professor Humphreys has chosen two groups of inferiors, one de jure and one de facto—the non-Muslims and the peasantry, whom he describes as "the voiceless classes of Islamic society." He examines the important work of A.K.S. Lambton and I.P. Petrushevsky on agrarian relationships in Iran and some studies on the fiscal and land-tenure systems of the Arab Mediterranean countries and, more briefly, of the Ottoman Empire, which for the most part falls outside the chronological range of the book. The chapter ends with a short review of more recent work on the condition of peasants in the Middle East and a discussion of how such studies can help a better understanding of the past.

For the non-Muslims, there is extensive documentation, both from the Islamic side and from the non-Muslim communities themselves, and a very considerable body of scholarship. The discussion of the role and status of the *dhimmis,* the tolerated non-Muslim, in Muslim society and under the Muslim state has probably produced more nonsense than any other topic in Muslim history, ranging from bitter complaints of Hitler-style oppression at one extreme, to myths of an interfaith utopia at the other. Professor Humphreys restores some balance to this question and also reviews the important matter of conversion to Islam both by individuals and by groups—when it occurred, in what circumstances, and with what response from coreligionists in both the abandoned and the adopted religions.

Much less is known, and much less has been written, about the rural population and, more generally, about what went on in the countryside. Contrary to popular mythology in the West, medieval Islamic civilization was overwhelmingly urban; its historiography, its literature, and its laws discuss urban problems and reflect urban conditions. Not until Ottoman times do we have archives, from which it is possible to study in detail the day-to-day life of the peasantry; not until very recent times do we find much literature depicting the life of the peasants—even less, peasant literature. Professor Humphreys's chapter on the countryside is therefore of necessity limited to such matters as the physical setting, technology, land use, and land tenure, and in a brief final section, "Agriculture and the Social Order."

Each of the chapters follows more or less the same pattern. First, a problem is identified and stated in broad terms and then is studied in one or two examples in a carefully defined time and place. Professor Humphreys then goes on to examine the sources—their variety, their evidence, and their deficiencies—and to look critically at both earlier and recent scholarship. Young scholars will be especially grateful for his frequent suggestions on work still to be done.

A book of this kind, in the nature of things, cannot be comprehensive, either in the range of topics that it covers or in the scholarly literature reviewed for each of the topics included. Every specialist reader will no doubt note and regret some omissions under both headings. The treatment of legally established inferiors is limited to non-Muslims and does not extend to the other at least equally important groups, slaves and women. The treatment of the lower social classes is limited to the countryside and says little about the urban working class or about the social fringes described in C.E. Bosworth's fascinating volumes on the vagabonds and beggars and other "groups outside the pale of normal society" in medieval Islam.[12] Bureaucracy, warfare, and sects might also have deserved separate treatment in a study of a society in which bureaucrats, soldiers, and religious dissidents played so important a part. There are also a few bibliographical omissions, even in the topics that are covered in the book. Thus, for example, in the treatment of the tenth-century Buyids, a dynasty of Shīite Iranians, whose rise to power marks a turning point in medieval Islamic history, mention is made of only one of Joel L. Kraemer's two volumes on the cultural and intellectual world of that time—a major contribution to the intellectual history of medieval Islam.[13]

Two omissions may be noted in the chapter dealing with the recent critical study of the beginnings of Islam and the first Islamic polity. It might have been useful to mention the very radical criticism of the biography of the Prophet, the Qur'ān, and the early Caliphate propounded by a group of Soviet scholars in the late 1920s and early 1930s.[14] Most of them were inspired primarily by polemical and ideological motives, sometimes reminiscent of those of the religious controversies of the Middle Ages. Much of their work was published under the auspices of a body known as "The League of the Militant Godless" and formed part of a three-pronged attack on the three religions surviving in the USSR. These writers did however anticipate some of the points, or at least some of the questions, raised by more recent scholars in the West, including such highly sensitive matters as the historicity of Muḥammad and the actual manner and period of the composition of the Qur'ān.

Soviet scholarship is not the only omission in this chapter; the Muslims are missing, too. The critical study of Jewish and Christian scripture and sacred history has almost entirely been the work of Jewish and Christian scholars. The critical study of early Islam has overwhelmingly been undertaken by non-Muslims. For that reason special interest attaches to the small number of recent Muslim scholars, writing in Arabic, who have contributed to this discussion and have raised questions of a kind now commonly accepted among contemporary theologians and Biblical scholars in the West, but not yet heard in Muslim debate. Perhaps wisely in these dangerous times, Professor Humphreys has refrained from naming them; for the same reasons I shall not name them here.

All these are comments, not reproaches. Professor Humphreys's book, as it stands, will henceforth be indispensable to teachers of Middle Eastern history, invaluable to serious students in the field, and extremely useful to scholars whose fields of study abut on medieval Middle Eastern Islam, either in time: Ancient Middle East, Modern Middle East—or in space: Byzantium, Mediterranean Europe, Africa, India.

But there is another, and larger, sense in which Professor Humphreys has rendered a service. At this time, when both the study and the neglect of other civilizations are condemned—by different critics, sometimes even by the same critics—Professor Humphreys's review of a great tradition of scholarship provides an answer to both. With the deep knowledge and understanding of the "insider," but at the same time with that unsparing critical analysis that is the hallmark of the Western scholarly tradition at its best, Professor Humphreys shows, through his chosen examples, how Western scholars approach and study the history of another civilization, the principles and methods that inspire them, the mistakes they can make, and the results they can achieve, notably through the discovery and elucidation of the documents and monuments that remain. And, at the same time—and in this too, he is an authentic representative of the best, but by no means the whole of Western scholarship—he has a deep and sympathetic understanding of both the concerns and the achievements of the civilization that is studied.

The Use by Muslim Historians of Non-Muslim Sources

9

Herodotus, the father of history, wrote of the "great and wonderful actions" of both Greeks and Barbarians and pursued his study into the past of alien lands and remote times. Though excluded by the hierophantic mysteries from access to oriental writings, he tried to make good the deficiency by travel and personal inquiry in Eastern lands. Some fifteen centuries later another European, William, Archbishop of Tyre in the states of Outremer, wrote a history of the Islamic Empires. He too sought his information from oriental sources and, better placed than Herodotus, was even able to read them in the original.[1]

These first European students of oriental history were, however, exceptional. Herodotus, though acclaimed as the father of history, was not accorded the respect of classical historians, most of whom preferred to follow the precept and practice of Thucydides and limit their concern to the deeds of their contemporaries and compatriots. The medieval European chroniclers were for the most part content to follow their example, and it is no accident that while William of Tyre's history of the Crusaders in the East—the *Historia rerum in partibus transmarinis gestarum*—was widely read and even translated into French, his *Gesta orientalium principum* has not, as far as is known, survived in a single manuscript. It was not until the Renaissance had awakened a new European curiosity and the Discoveries had whetted it with the sight of remote and alien peoples that European historians began to show interest in other lands and societies and to seek out and pass on information and opinions about them.[2] This universal historical curiosity is still a distinguishing, almost an exclusive, characteristic of Europe and her daughters. Oriental societies study their own history; perforce they also study the history of the West which has influenced or dominated them. They still show little interest in one another.[3]

The medieval Muslim, like the citizens of most other societies that have appeared among men, was profoundly convinced of the finality, completeness, and essential self-sufficiency of his civilization. Islam was the one true faith, beyond which there were only unbelievers—the Muslim equivalent of the Greek term barbarians. The Islamic state was the one divinely ordained order, beyond which there were only tyranny and anarchy. Universal history was the history of the Islamic community, outside which were lands and peoples whose only interest was as the settings and objects of Muslim action.

These lesser breeds were not unknown to Muslim historiography. Sometimes there were intrepid travelers who ventured among them. With many there were the normal exchanges of commerce, war, and diplomacy. From some there were acknowledged borrowings of useful knowledge and crafts. But none of these led to any interest in the history of the infidel peoples. To fight the Greeks it was necessary to have political and military intelligence; to learn from the Greeks it was useful to have philosophic and scientific training. For neither was there any need to inquire into the history of the Greek past. For centuries the Muslim Caliphate stood face to face with the Byzantine Empire—the House of War *par excellence* of medieval Islam. The Muslim chroniclers have much to say of the war on the frontiers; the Muslim geographers have ample information, probably drawn ultimately from secret service files, on the topography, administration, and strength of the enemy Empire, and even on the scandals of its court and capital. But at no time did they attempt to consult Greek historical sources or to deal in a connected form with the history of the Greek Empire.

Still more striking is the case of the Crusades. For two centuries the Muslims of the Middle East were in intimate if hostile contact with groups of Franks established among them—yet they do not seem to have developed the least interest in them. As Professor Gabrieli has pointed out,[4] the Muslims, unlike the Christians, did not regard the

Crusades as something separate and distinctive, nor did they single out the Crusaders from the long series of infidel enemies whom from time to time they fought. The chroniclers report in detail the smallest skirmishes between Muslims and Frankish troops—but they have little to say about the internal affairs of the Frankish states in the Levant and even less about their countries of origin. The omission is the more remarkable in that the geographers and cosmographers have some information, mostly derived from western Muslim sources, about the Franks and their countries. Yet with one or two minor exceptions, the historians of Islam made no attempt to relate their narrative of the Syrian wars to this information, to trace the invaders back to their countries of origin, or to inquire into the mighty yet invisible movement that had launched them.[5]

The Crusades opened the way to closer diplomatic and commercial relations between the Muslim and Christian states of the Mediterranean. These are reflected in the manuals of civil service usage of the Mamlūk period. In the encyclopaedic bureaucratic vade-mecum of Qalqashandī, and similar works, we find lists of the European sovereigns with whom the Sultans of Egypt had corresponded, with the correct names, titles, and forms of address for each, and some allusions to earlier exchanges of letters or embassies. We find nothing about the history of those countries.

All this does not mean that Muslim historians never concerned themselves with non-Muslim history. For the Muslim, the Islamic revelation is not a beginning but a completion, the final link in a chain of revelation—and the Islamic community is thus no new creation but a revival and improvement of something that had existed long before. The history of Islam therefore did not begin with Muḥammad; it included the history of the earlier prophets and their missions, and something also of the peoples to whom they were sent. The earlier history is chiefly biblical and Arabian, within a framework defined by the historical allusions in the Qur'ān. The development of this history and the use made of biblical sources and of Jewish and Christian informants have been discussed by Professor Rosenthal.[6] The Prophet also speaks of Caesar and Chosroes, and here too some historical elaboration was permissible—was even required for the explanation of the sacred tradition. For this too information was to hand—Persian converts to Islam, with memories of and access to Persian historical writings, Eastern Christians with knowledge of the histories of the pagan and Christian Roman Empires. Through them some accounts of Persian and Roman history found their way into the Arabic language and, together with the Judaeo-Christian biblical material, became part of the common stock of Muslim universal history.

This stock, acquired in the early days when the Islamic community was still malleable and receptive, received few later accretions. It appears chiefly in the general introductory matter, leading up to the establishment of the Islamic oecumene; it is interesting to note that it is not normally supplemented by any discussion of the conditions in any specific country prior to the Islamic conquest. The Islamic community as a whole has some earlier history; the individual Islamic countries begin theirs with the advent of Islam.[7]

The external interests of Islamic historiography were thus limited to the prehistory of the Islamic community itself and were moreover confined to the earlier period. With few and rare exceptions, they did not extend to the history of alien peoples or cultures or even to the pre-Islamic history of the peoples and countries brought into Islam. In other words, Muslim historians were concerned only with their own civilization and its immediate ancestors—and in this they resembled the historians of most other human communities, including, until comparatively recent times, our own.

There were some exceptions. The universal curiosity of Masʿūdī led him even to Frankish history and enabled him to give a list of the Frankish kings from Clovis to Louis IV, based, he tells us, on a book prepared by a Frankish bishop for the Andalusian prince al-Ḥakam in 328/939.[8] The transcendent genius of al-Bīrūnī carried him across the impenetrable religious barrier of an alien script, to study Sanskrit and learn something of India—though his interests were philosophical and scientific rather than historical. These were however few and unrepresentative; even as great a historian as Ibn Khaldūn, in his universal history, does not go north of Spain or east of Persia.[9] Within that area he tried very hard to deal with non-Muslim as well as Muslim history and made use of such non-Islamic sources as were available to him—as

Orosius on Rome and Josippon on the Jews.[10] But he did not go beyond the limits of his own civilization and its known and recognizable predecessors—like the authors of most of the so-called universal histories written in Europe until very recently.

The first genuine universal history in Islam—probably in the world—is that of Rashīd al-Dīn. The Mongol conquests, by uniting for the first time under one dynasty the civilizations of Southwest Asia and the Far East, created new opportunities for social and cultural contacts between societies previously separated by political and religious barriers. At the same time they opened the door to new contacts with Europe, as a number of Europeans availed themselves of the opportunity offered by the presence of non-Muslim rulers in the Middle East to explore the overland routes to China. The *Jāmiʿ al-tavārikh*—a universal history prepared by Rashīd al-Dīn for the Mongol Ghāzān Khān—is a product of these new contacts. To carry out his task, he assembled a team of collaborators, including two Chinese scholars, a Buddhist hermit from Kashmir, a Mongol specialist on tribal tradition, and a Frankish traveler, probably a monk who had come as envoy from the Papal Curia. Through him Rashīd al-Dīn made the acquaintance of a European chronicle which has recently been identified as that of the thirteenth-century chronicler Martin of Troppau, also known as Martin Polonus. From this source, brought up to date by his informant, Rashīd al-Dīn was able to include a brief chronicle of the Holy Roman Emperors as far as Albert I and the Popes as far as Benedict XI. Both are correctly described as living at that time.[11]

Rashīd al-Dīn's venture into occidental and oriental scholarship, made possible by the brief interlude of Mongol power, found few imitators. His account of European history, the first since Masʿūdī's king-list, was the last until the sixteenth century, when the Ottoman need for political intelligence about Europe began to grow into an interest—albeit still a faint and disdainful one—in European history.

In the Saxon Landbibliothek in Dresden, there is a Turkish manuscript containing a history of France from the legendary Faramund to the year 1560. It was made by order of Ferīdūn Bey—compiler of the famous *Munshe'āt-i Selāṭīn* and Reis Efendi from 1570 to 1573—and was the work of two men, the *terjumān* Ḥasan b. Ḥamza and the *kātib* ʿAlī b. Sinān. The book was completed in 980/1572.[12]

This work may well have been the first translation of a European historical work into Turkish. It was followed by an account of the discovery of the New World, adapted from European sources, which reflected the growing Turkish concern at the vast expansion of Western maritime power.[13]

During the seventeenth century several other Turkish historians show signs of an interest in European history and an acquaintance with European sources. Ibrāhīm Mülhemī (d. 1650) is said to have written a *Tārīkh-i Mulūk-i Rūm ve-Ifranj*, of which unfortunately no copy appears to have survived.[14] His more famous contemporary Ḥājjī Khalīfa (d. 1657) was also interested in Europe. Ḥājjī Khalīfa's researches into European geography are well known and followed a line of inquiry opened, for practical reasons, by Ottoman map-makers and navigators in the previous century. Ḥājjī Khalīfa incorporated European material in his world geography, the *Jihānnümā*, and, with the assistance of a French priest, converted to Islam and known as Sheykh Meḥmed Ikhlāsī, prepared a Turkish version of the Atlas Minor of Mercator and Hondius. Probably with the help of this same Frenchman, Ḥājjī Khalīfa also prepared a Turkish translation of a history of the Franks—*Tārīkh-i Firengī*. Mordtmann, who believed this work to be lost, guessed that it was a translation of the Byzantine history of Chalcocondyles.[15] At least one copy, however, has survived in private possession in Turkey, and parts of it were actually published, in serial form, in the newspaper *Taṣvīr-i Efkār*, in 1279/1862–63. In his introduction Ḥājjī Khalīfa names his source—the Latin Chronicle of Johann Carion (1499–1537), which he used in the Paris edition of 1548.[16] In addition to these translations, Ḥājjī Khalīfa also wrote a short "original" work on Europe, which has only recently come to light. It provides an outline of the Christian religion, some definitions of European forms of government, and a brief review of some of the states and rulers of Europe. Ḥājjī Khalīfa's purpose, he explains, was to rouse the Muslims from their "sleep of negligence" and give them accurate information about the numerous and powerful peoples of Europe, in place of the "lies and fables" told by the Muslim historians. His treatise serves, in the words of Professor

Ménage, "by its very triviality, as an index of the ignorance of Europe which prevailed in his day among Ottoman men of learning."[17]

Of quite a different character was the use made of European sources by another Ottoman historian of the early seventeenth century, Ibrāhīm-i Pechevī (1572–1650). Pechevī was not concerned with universal history; still less was he interested in writing or translating the history of the infidel kings. His concern, like that of most Ottoman historians, was with the history of the Empire of which he was a subject, and more especially of the wars fought by the Ottoman armies in Europe. His history covers the events of the years 1520–1639. For the later period he relied to a large extent on his own knowledge or on the reports of old soldiers; for the earlier period he seems to have made use of the writings of his predecessors in Ottoman historiography. But in addition to those Pechevī had the revolutionary idea of consulting the historians of the enemy. He was interested above all in military history and seems to have been fascinated by the stories of the great battles fought by the Ottoman Sultans and other rulers, dwelling with loving attention on every detail. But sometimes the Muslim chronicles were sadly lacking in details—and so Pechevī had recourse to the accounts written by the enemy. "In our country," he says, "there are men without number able to read and write Hungarian."[18] It was therefore a simple matter to have Hungarian chronicles read to him and to translate some of them into Turkish.[19] A number of passages, Pechevī says, he thought fit to incorporate in his own chronicle. These include an account of the battle of Mohacs and other narratives of the wars in Hungary. Though Pechevī does not name his Hungarian sources, two of them have been identified by Kraelitz as Kaspar Heltai and N. V. Istvanfy, whose histories were published in 1575 and 1623 respectively.[20]

Pechevī was not, as has sometimes been stated, the first Ottoman historian to use Western sources. He does however seem to have been the first to compare foreign accounts with native accounts of the same events and to weave them into a single narrative. In this he can have had but few predecessors anywhere. He certainly had few successors.

Meanwhile, however, the more general interest in Western history continued. A lesser-known historian of the late seventeenth century was Ḥüseyn Hezārfen (d. 1691), most of whose works are unfortunately still unpublished. Like Ḥājjī Khalīfa, whom he cites with admiration, he was a man of wide-ranging curiosity and seems to have been especially interested in the geography and history of remote countries, as well as in the earlier history of his own. To an extent rare if not unique among Muslims of his day, he made the acquaintance of European scholars and men of letters, not a few of whom visited Istanbul. He is known to have been acquainted with Count Ferdinand Marsigli and Antoine Galland. It seems likely that he also knew Prince Demetrius Cantemir and Pétis de la Croix. It was perhaps in part through the good offices of these and other European friends that Ḥüseyn Hezārfen was able to gain access to the contents of European books and incorporate them in his own works.

The most important of these, for our purpose, is his *Tenqīḥ al-Tevārīkh,* completed in 1673. This is divided into nine parts, of which the sixth, seventh, eighth, and ninth deal with history outside the Islamic oecumene and its accepted predecessors. Part 6 deals with Greek and Roman history, including some account of the Greek philosophers; part 7 with the history of Constantinople since its foundation, including the Byzantine period; part 8 with Asia—China, the Philippines, the East Indies, India, and Ceylon; part 9 with the discovery of America. Oddly enough, Ḥüseyn Hezārfen does not seem to have included Europe in his survey, but his accounts of both Asia and America are based almost entirely on European sources, mostly via the *Jihānnümā* of Ḥājjī Khalīfa. His accounts of Greek, Roman, and Byzantine history are also based on European works. These served to augment the meager stock of Islamic knowledge of classical antiquity.[21]

With the work of Aḥmed b. Luṭfullah, known as Münejjimbashı (d. 1702), we return to universal history in the grand manner. His great *Jāmiʿ al-Duval*—the title is an obvious echo of Rashīd al-Dīn's *Jāmiʿ al-Tavārīkh*—is a universal history of mankind from Adam to the year 1083/1672, based, so the author tells us, on some seventy sources. The Arabic original of the work is still unpublished, but a Turkish translation, prepared under the direction of the poet Nedīm, has been printed.[22] The bulk of the work, as one would expect, is concerned with Islamic history. A large part of the first volume is, however, devoted to the history of the pre-Islamic and non-Islamic states. The former, as usual, included the Persians and Arabians on the one hand, and the Israelites and Egyptians on the other, discussed on more or less traditional lines. Münejjimbashı's ancient history, however, goes beyond the common Islamic stock. His accounts of the Romans and of the Jews clearly derive from Roman and Jewish sources, already in part available to him in the adaptation of Ibn Khaldūn. Münejjimbashı has however much fuller information than Ibn Khaldūn and is able to deal with such peoples as the Assyrians and Babylonians, the Seleucids and the Ptolemies, previously barely known to Islamic historiography. For these a European source must have been used. This becomes certain when we come to Münejjimbashı's chapter on Europe, which includes sections on the divisions of the "Frankish" peoples and on the kings of France, of Germany, of Spain, and of England. The source of these would appear to have been the Turkish translation of the chronicle of Johann Carion, though, since Münejjimbashı continues his narrative down to the reigns of Louis XIII of France, the Emperor Leopold in Germany, and Charles I of England, he must have had later supplementary material at his disposal. He reports the English civil war and the execution of King Charles. "After him the people of England (Anglia) did not appoint another king over them; we have no further information about their affairs" (i, 652).

Münejjimbashı's outside interests were not limited to Europe. For his account of the kings of Armenia, he tells us he made use of translations of Armenian chronicles (i. 652). For the ancient history of the Jews, he had recourse to Hebrew sources, made available to him by Jewish informants (i. 684). From his accounts of his dealings with these informants, and of his painstaking attempts to verify and compare material in languages unknown to him, we may get some idea of the far-ranging curiosity and meticulous scholarship of Münejjimbashı. Even China and Hindu India are included in the history, though here Münejjimbashı's information is meager and poor.

During the eighteenth century the nature of Ottoman interest in Europe underwent a radical change. The peace treaty of Carlowitz, signed 26 January 1699, marked the end of an epoch and the beginning of another. For a long time the growing internal crisis of Islamic civilization had been masked by the imposing military façade of the Ottoman Empire, protecting the Muslim heartlands both from foreign attack and from self-realization at home.

Now this façade was, for the first time, dangerously shaken. There had been unsuccessful campaigns and inconclusive wars before now. But the disastrous retreat that followed the second Ottoman failure at Vienna, in 1683, was the first clear and unmistakable defeat. At Carlowitz the Ottoman Sultan, for the first time since the foundation of the Empire, was compelled to accept terms dictated by a victorious infidel enemy.

A Turkish document, written shortly before the treaty of Passarowitz (1718), records an imaginary conversation between a Christian and an Ottoman officer, in which they discuss the military and political situation. The purpose of the writer seems to have been to prepare Ottoman ruling circles to accept defeat, by depicting as darkly as possible the unfavorable situation of the Empire. The conversation also makes a comparison between the Austrian and Ottoman armies, to the great disadvantage of the latter, and would appear to embody a plea for military reform.[23]

The impact of military defeat, and the resulting desire to seek out and make use of the talisman that had brought victory to the enemy, opened a new phase in the relations between Islam and the Western world—one which, with some important modifications, has continued until today. The new interest was at first limited to the weapons and military science of Europe, but it was inevitable that it should be extended at least to as much of European culture as seemed necessary for their effective application. In 1721, when the famous Yirmi Sekiz Chelebi Meḥmed Efendi was sent as ambassador to Paris, his instructions were "to make a thorough study of the means of civilization and education, and report on those capable of application" in Turkey.[24] One of these "means of civilization" was printing, the establishment of which among the Turks owed much to the initiative and enthusiasm of the ambassador's son, Saʿīd Chelebi. Closely associated with him in this work was Ibrāhīm Müteferripa, a Hungarian convert to Islam.

The first book appeared in February 1729. By the time the press was closed in 1742, seventeen books had been printed, most of them dealing with history, geography, and language. They included an account by Meḥmed Efendi of his embassy to France, a treatise by Ibrāhīm Müteferrika on the science of tactics as applied in European armies, and a translation of a European account of the wars in Persia. Editions of earlier works included the sixteenth-century history of the discovery of the new world—*Tārīkh al-Hind al-Gharbī*—and part of the geographical treatise of Ḥājjī Khalīfa.

The new interest in Europe was primarily concerned with military matters. But once the barrier separating the two civilizations had been breached, it was no longer possible to keep a strict control over the traffic passing through. A concern with military science on the one hand, and a need for political and military intelligence on the other, led to an interest in recent European history which, desultory and sporadic at first, became more urgent as the realization spread that the very survival of the Empire might depend on an accurate understanding of European developments.

Besides the books printed at the Müteferrika press, a small number of manuscripts in Istanbul collections testify to this new interest in European history. A manuscript of 1135/1722, entitled *Nemche Tārīkhi,* gives an outline history of Austria from A.D. 800 to 1662 and was translated from the German by the interpreter ʿOsmān b. Aḥmed. Of rather a different kind are two anonymous manuscripts, written in about 1725, giving up-to-date and first-hand information about contemporary Europe. On internal evidence both appear to be the work of Ibrāhīm Müteferrika himself.[25] Another report "on some historical circumstances of the states of Europe," dated 1146/1733–34, was made by the famous Aḥmed Pasha Bonneval, a French nobleman who joined the Ottoman service and was converted to Islam. It discusses events in Austria, Hungary, Spain, and France and was translated into Turkish from the author's presumably French original. An outline survey of the major dynasties—the *Fihris-i Düvel* of ʿAbd al-Raḥmān Münīf Efendi (d. 1742)—includes the pagan and Christian Roman emperors, the Byzantine emperors, the kings of France in Paris, and the kings of Austria in Vienna. Towards the end of the century a survey of European affairs—*Ijmāl-i aḥvāl-i Avrupa*—discusses Prussia under Frederick William II and France in the revolutionary period, and in 1799 an Istanbul Christian called Cosmo Comidas prepared, in Turkish, a handlist of reigning European sovereigns, with their dates of birth and accession, their capitals, titles, heirs, and other useful information.[26]

These works, or others of the same kind, became known to Ottoman historians, and some of the information they contained found its way into the mainstream of Ottoman historiography. The first of the Imperial Historiographers who himself learnt a Western language and made use of Western sources was ʿAṭāʿullāh Meḥmed, known as Shānīzāde (1769–1826). By education one of the ulema, he was a man of encyclopaedic knowledge and became Imperial Historiographer in 1819. He seems to have learnt several European languages and made a study of European medicine and other sciences. His major work was a Turkish translation, probably made from an Italian version, of an Austrian medical textbook. He also made a translation in 1220/1805 of the Instructions of Frederick the Great to his commanders—*Viṣāyānāme-i seferiyye*. It was therefore natural that, when called upon to write the history of the Empire for the years 1808–20, he should make some use of European sources.

The vast, swift campaigns of the Revolutionary and Napoleonic wars drove the lessons of the new warfare deep into the lands of Islam, while the new, secular ideas of the Revolution, untainted in Muslim eyes with any recognizably Christian origin, could for the first time penetrate the barrier that had hitherto excluded every movement of ideas from Europe and thus provide the Muslim peoples, in their new liberalism and nationalism, with the ideological foundations of Westernization.

In the first half of the nineteenth century there were two main centers of Westernizing reform in the Middle East—Turkey and Egypt. In both of them the preparation and publication of translations of Western books played an important part. In Egypt under Muḥammad ʿAlī Pasha there was an organized, state-sponsored program of translation, for the like of which we must go back to medieval times. Between 1822 and 1842, 243 books were printed at the Būlāq press, the greater part of them translations. Of these, rather more than half were in Turkish, most of the remainder in Arabic. Under Muḥammad ʿAlī's rule Turkish was still the language of the ruling elite in Egypt, and we are therefore not surprised to find that works on military and naval subjects are almost all in Turkish. The same is to a large extent true of pure and applied mathematics, which were chiefly needed for military purposes. Works on medicine, veterinary science, agriculture, and grammar, on the other hand, are mostly in Arabic. History would seem to have been regarded as a matter for the Turkish-speaking rulers, since the few historical books issued from the press in the early period are all in Turkish. The first was a translation of Castera's *Histoire de l'impératrice Catherine II de Russie,* translated by the Greek Yakovaki Argyropoulo and published in 1244/1829. It was reprinted in Istanbul in 1287/1870. Another early translation was an extract from the *Mémorial de Sainte Hélène,* published in 1247/1832 under the title *Tārīkh-i Napolyon Bonapart.* It is also known as *Napolyon sergüzeshti.* Then came versions of Botta's *Storia d'Italia* and of the memoirs of the Duc de Rovigo, both published in 1249/1834. These four books complete the historical translations from Western languages in the early period, though there were also one or two translations from Arabic into Turkish. Thereafter there was an interval of several years until the next historical translation appeared—a version of Voltaire's *Histoire de Charles XII,* published in 1257/1841. This time it was in Arabic, as were also a number of subsequent translations of historical works by Voltaire, Robertson, and others.[27]

In Turkey the movement began more slowly. The translations made in Egypt seem to have been known and studied, but it was not until the middle of the century that translations of European historical writings begin to appear in Istanbul. In 1866 a Turkish translation appeared, by Aḥmed Ḥilmī, of an English *Universal History*—probably the first world history in modern Turkish literature. Thereafter the translation movement developed quickly, especially in Turkey and Egypt, and rapidly altered the world picture as it appeared to Muslim students and readers.[28]

The Cult of Spain and the Turkish Romantics

10

Towards the end of the nineteenth century the Muslim Orient began to rediscover the lost and long-forgotten glories of Muslim Andalusia. The time was one of defeat and retreat for the Muslim peoples. The expansion of Europe—by sea from the west, by land from the east—was still bringing great and ancient Muslim cities under Christian rule. The French in North Africa, the British in India, the Russians in Central Asia, all seemed to be converging on the heartlands of Islam, and, at the same time, political and military defeats were matched by the retreat of traditional Islamic concepts and values before the advance of new notions emanating from Europe. Only the Ottoman Sultanate remained as an independent Muslim Great Power—by now the accepted leader and spokesman of Sunnī Islam; and even then the survival of the Ottoman Empire was gravely threatened by foreign invasion, domestic dissension, and the spread of new and disruptive ideas.

It was in these circumstances that the cult of Andalus emerged and, responding to a deep emotional need, spread widely among Muslim intellectuals. In a time of humiliating weakness and backwardness, they could find comfort in the spectacle of a great, rich, powerful, and civilized Muslim state in Europe—the leader and guide, as they saw it, of European civilization. In a time of decay, they could find a melancholy satisfaction in the contemplation of the sunset splendors of the Alhambra, in the long, sad epic of defeat and withdrawal. Before long, the rise and fall of Muslim Andalusia became favorite themes and settings of poets and novelists; the glories of Cordova served as a Golden Age for the romantic and apologetic school of Islamic historiography that was growing up in the Middle East and especially in India.

M. Henri Pérès, in his invaluable book on Muslim travelers in Spain, has dated the Muslim rediscovery of Andalusia from the year 1886.[1] It sprang, he says, from two sources—the attendance of Muslims at the international congresses of orientalists, where they made the acquaintance of European orientalist scholarship, including its work on Spain, and the action of the Ottoman Sultan Abdülhamid II, in sending prospectors to Spain in search of Arabic manuscripts.

Of the two, the latter had the more immediate effects. In 1886–87 the Sultan, at the suggestion of his minister of education Munīf Pasha, appointed and sent Ibn al-Talāmid al-Turkuzī al-Shinqīṭī, an Arabic scholar of Moorish origin, to Spain to search for remnants of the bygone glories of Andalus.[2] He was the first of a long series of Muslim pilgrims, westward bound on a similar search.

The Sultan may well, as M. Pérès suggests, have been inspired by the Lebanese scholar Fāris al-Shidyāq, who was engaged in the search for and publication of Arabic texts at the time.[3] It is however more than likely that the Education Minister, Munīf Pasha, was himself actively concerned in the matter. Munīf Pasha (1828–1910),[4] a well-known Turkish publicist and public servant of the time, played an important role in the introduction and dissemination of modern knowledge and ideas in Turkey. Trained and for a time employed in the Translation Chamber of the Sublime Porte—Turkey's open window to the West—he published as early as 1859 a group of translations from Fontenelle, Fénélon, and Voltaire and in 1860 founded the Ottoman Scientific Society (Jemiyet-i ʿIlmiye-i ʿOs̱maniye), modelled on the Royal Society of England. Its journal, the *Mejmūʿa-i Funūn,* includes a wide range of articles on history, geography, and philosophy as well as the natural sciences and played a role in nineteenth-century Turkey in some ways analogous to that of the *Grande Encyclopédie* in eighteenth-century France. Munīf Pasha was a man of many interests and projects—even including a reform of the Arabic alphabet for typographical purposes. As Minister of Education from 1884 to 1888, he was at least formally responsible for al-Shinqīṭī's mission, which he himself appears to have suggested. Al-Shinqīṭī was invited to go from Arabia to Istanbul by one Haji Ibrahim, a Turkish professor of Arabic at the Dār al-Taʿlīm in Istanbul, who had studied under him in the Hijāz when his father, Sherīf Pasha, was governor there. In Istanbul al-Shinqīṭī associated on familiar terms with many prominent Turkish officials and scholars, notably with Munīf Pasha, in whose house he lived as a member of the family.[5]

There is a further reason for believing that the project originated in Istanbul. In our time, when Turkey has abandoned all pan-Islamic activities and the Turkish language is little known in the eastern world, it is important to remember that in the nineteenth century Turkey was still generally recognized, by Muslims, as the leading Muslim power. It was in Turkey that the new problems of religion and nation, country and state, were first formulated and discussed. Turkish publications were read by the Turkish-educated Arab intellectuals of Aleppo, Damascus, and Baghdad; some too were published in now-forgotten Arabic translations, and the ideas they contained filtered through to widening circles of Muslims in both Asia and Africa. Many of the characteristic themes and arguments of Arab literature towards the end of the nineteenth century are anticipated in Turkish some decades earlier, and the cult of Andalus is no exception.

The origin of this cult can be traced, with precision, to a book. It is the *Essai sur l'histoire des arabes et des Mores d'Espagne* of Louis Viardot, published in Paris in two volumes in 1833. A Turkish translation was prepared by Ziya Pasha and published in Istanbul, under the title *Endelüs Tarihi,* in A.H. 1280 (=1863–64). It was reprinted, in four volumes, in 1304–5/1886–87—that is, immediately before al-Shinqīṭī's mission.

The translator, Ziya (1825–1880), was one of the leading figures in nineteenth-century Turkish literature and notably among the group of liberal patriots known as the Young Ottomans.[6] The son of a clerk in the customs house at Galata, he was educated at the grammar school which Sultan Mahmud II had opened by the Süleymaniye mosque and entered the civil service at the age of 17. In 1855, thanks to the influence of the great reforming minister Mustafa Reshīd Pasha, he joined the staff of the Imperial Household, as third secretary to the Sultan. There he attracted the attention of Edhem Pasha, then Marshal of the Palace *(Mabeyn Ferīki),* who urged him, allegedly as a cure for depression,[7] to learn French. Ziya set to work with a will and before very long was ready to undertake the translation of Viardot's book. Edhem Pasha encouraged him and perhaps assisted him in this task.

The translation was not a distinguished effort. The original was of limited scholarly value; the translation the work of a beginner just mastering the language. Tanpınar has pointed to the translator's ignorance of history, Gibb to the heavy bureaucratic style which he adopted. Yet with all these defects the book had a great impact. Widely read at the time, it served to inspire a series of Turkish poems, plays, and stories which made the glories of Andalus familiar to a new generation of Turkish readers.

By far the most important of the writers concerned was the great poet and dramatist Abdülhak Hamid (1852–1937).[8] At the age of 11 he accompanied his father on a mission to Paris, where he went to school for a year. In 1876 he returned to Paris, as second secretary to the Turkish Embassy. It was at that time, in Paris, that he wrote his famous drama *Ṭāriq*, a passionate defence of the glory, greatness, and nobility of Islam. Its hero is Ṭāriq b. Ziyād, "the conqueror of Spain." In this drama of love, hate, and jealousy, of war, death, and glory, Hamid manages to assert his conviction of the profound ethical values of Islam, to express his ideas on patriotism and progress,[9] and to make some indirect comments on the political and social problems of the Ottoman Empire. It was, no doubt, because of these that the book was banned and seized after its publication in 1879. It was however reprinted and circulated secretly and republished after the Young Turk Revolution.[10]

In the same year, 1876, Hamid dealt dramatically with a theme from the end of the Muslim history of Spain. *Nazife* is a one-act dialogue, in verse, between the Spanish King Ferdinand and Nazife, an Arab girl. The King, who loves Nazife, withdraws the permission he had previously given her to go to Morocco. The girl kills herself to save her honor. Some years later he wrote a sequel to this play, called *'Abdallah al-Saghīr*. Also in verse, it tells of the love of 'Abdallah, the last Muslim ruler in Spain, for a Spanish girl called Carolina.

In 1879 Hamid wrote another drama on a Spanish theme—*Tezer,* also called *Melik Abdurrahman-i S̱alis̱*. This play, also in verse, is situated in Cordova under the Umayyads and tells the tragic story of a Spanish girl called Tezer (probably intended as Terez, Thérèse, Teresa). Loved by 'Abd al-Raḥmān III, she allows herself to be used, in a plot against him, by her former lover Richard, the leader of an anti-Arab Spanish faction.

Tezer, however, actually falls in love with ʿAbd al-Raḥmān and in the ensuing dénouement loses her life.

In 1881, while living at Rize, on the Black Sea, Hamid returned to the theme of Ṭāriq and produced a second full-length drama, in prose. *Ibn-i Mūsā,* or *Zāt al-jamāl,* continues the complex story of the conquerors of Spain and follows them back to Syria and Arabia, to show the working-out of their destiny at the Umayyad court. Once again the themes are love, hate, and jealousy, and the tragic clash of honor and passion.[11]

The influence of the French classical theatre on Abdülhak Hamid is obvious, notably of *Le Cid* and *Bérénice.* But if Corneille and Racine provided the manner, the humble Viardot provided the matter and served as the starting point of a new and significant literary and intellectual trend.

Abdülhak Hamid was by no means the only Turkish author to turn to Viardot and the history of Andalus for inspiration. Muallim Nājī (1850–1893),[12] for example, wrote an historical poem called *Ḥamiyet,* describing the heroic Muslim defenders of Granada during the final struggle in 1492, and others could be added. He was, however, the most important and influential. Though in our time he has lost much of his influence, he was in his own day widely read and admired, not only in Turkey. His play *Tezer,* for example, is said to have been translated into Arabic and Persian, as well as into Serbian and Muslim Bosniak.[13] His three-year stay as Turkish consul-general in Bombay (1883–85) may also have brought his work and ideas to the attention of Indian Muslims. Following on Ziya's translation of Viardot, his work did much to popularize the romantic revival of interest in medieval Spanish Islam and to encourage the cult of Andalus that is so noteworthy a feature of recent and modern Islamic writing.

PART III

MUSLIMS AND JEWS

The Pro-Islamic Jews

11

When Lord Beaconsfield, Prime Minister of England, returned from the Congress of Berlin, he received the somewhat mixed welcome which democratic societies usually offer to their leaders. His achievement, as he saw it, had been to save Turkey from dismemberment by the victorious Russians, and thus to preserve both the peace of Europe and the interests of Britain. For his supporters, he had indeed fulfilled his claim to "peace with honor"; for his opponents, he had brought shame and strife to his country, by pursuing policies which were harmful and wrong.

The dispute was an old and bitter one in English politics. On the one hand were those who believed, in Lord Palmerston's words, that "the integrity and independence of the Ottoman Empire are necessary to the maintenance of the tranquillity, the liberty, and the balance of power in the rest of Europe"—and, in addition, that the protection of Turkey against Russia was a vital British interest. On the other, there were those who rejected the Turks as infidels, barbarians, and aliens in Europe and saw no reason to obstruct the Russians in the work of removing them. The quarrel between the Turcophiles and the Turcophobes aroused strong passions and at times split not only the nation but also parties and even families.

Nineteenth-century polemic was notoriously violent in tone, and the controversies on the Eastern Question in particular provide some really outstanding examples of political scurrility. Attacks on Disraeli sometimes contain hostile references to his Jewish origin. These are not on the whole frequent and would not be remarkable in an age noted for uninhibited personal abuse. They can be easily paralleled by similar hostile references to other ethnic and religious groups in the country. It is, however, significant that the anti-Semitic theme occurs most frequently, most persistently, and most extensively in the discussion of Disraeli's Eastern policy and takes the form of a specific accusation—that he was applying a Jewish, not an English policy, and was subordinating British interests to Jewish (or Hebrew, or Semitic) sentiments and purposes.

Disraeli's accusers give two reasons for regarding his pro-Turkish policies as Jewish. The first is that Russia persecuted the Jews and that Disraeli as a Jew was, therefore, determined to thwart Russia and help her enemies—a line of argument familiar in other times and places. The second, and in contemporary eyes far more important, reason was that Disraeli, as a Jew, was bound to rally automatically to the Turkish side. The Jew, even the baptized Jew, remained an Oriental; in the struggle over the Eastern Question, his loyalties were with Asia against Europe, with Islam against Christendom.

To the modern reader, such theories may seem fanciful to the point of absurdity. They were not so to Disraeli's critics and commanded belief in surprisingly wide circles. The friendship of the Jew for the Muslim was taken for granted as a fact; the policy of Disraeli seemed to follow naturally from it.

A few examples may suffice to give the flavor of these writings. A Liberal member of Parliament, T. P. O'Connor, discussing the Russo-Turkish war of 1877, wrote:

> One of the most remarkable phenomena in the course of the war between Russia and Turkey was the extraordinary unanimity with which the Jews of every part of the world took the side of the Sultan against the Czar. People living within the same frontiers, speaking the same language, professing the same creed, with exactly the same interests, have held the most opposite views upon this Russo-Turkish question. In this country—to take the most striking example—the people, agreed for the most part on the main question of religion, of the same race, with the same great interests to conserve, differed with a bitterness almost unexampled in their domestic or in their foreign controversies. But here are the Jews, dispersed over every part of the globe, speaking different tongues, divided in nearly every sympathy,—separated, in fact, by everything that can separate man, except the one point of race,—all united in their feelings on this great contest! . . . For many ages—more in the past than in the present, of course—there has been among large sections of the Jews the strongest sympathy with the

> Mohammedan peoples. A common enemy is a great bond of friendship, and as the Christian was equally the enemy of the Mohammedan and the Jew, they were thereby brought into a certain alliance with one another. This alliance has been most close on many occasions. In the time of the Crusaders, the Jews were the friends who aided the Mohammedans in keeping back the tide of Christian invasion which was floating against the East, and in Spain the Jews were the constant friends and allies of the Moorish against the Christian inhabitants of the country. The alliance must have been very close in the past indeed to have left such deep traces behind. . . . His [*i.e.* Disraeli's] general view then upon this question of Turkey is that as a Jew he is a kinsman of the Turk, and that, as a Jew, he feels bound to make common cause with the Turk against the Christian. . . . From first to last his policy was persistently, uniformly, without interruption, a policy of friendship to the Turk and the oppressor, and hate to the Christian and the oppressed.[1]

Such views were not confined to professional politicians and pamphleteers. They are also found in the writings of historians like J. A. Froude, Goldwin Smith, and E. A. Freeman. The last was particularly virulent:

> But there is another power against which England and Europe ought to be yet more carefully on their guard. It is no use mincing matters. The time has come to speak out plainly. No well disposed person would reproach another either with his nationality or his religion, unless that nationality or that religion leads to some direct mischief. No one wishes to place the Jew, whether Jew by birth or by religion, under any disability as compared with the European Christian. But it will not do to have the policy of England, the welfare of Europe, sacrificed to Hebrew sentiment. The danger is no imaginary one. Every one must have marked that the one subject on which Lord Beaconsfield, through his whole career, has been in earnest has been whatever has touched his own people. A mocker about everything else, he has been thoroughly serious about this. His zeal for his own people is really the best feature in Lord Beaconsfield's career. But we cannot sacrifice our people, the people of Aryan and Christian Europe, to the most genuine belief in an Asian mystery. We cannot have England or Europe governed by a Hebrew policy. While Lord Derby simply wishes to do nothing one way or another, Lord Beaconsfield is the active friend of the Turk. The alliance runs through all Europe. Throughout the East, the Turk and the Jew are leagued against the Christian. . . . We cannot have the policy of Europe dealt with in the like sort. There is all the difference in the world between the

> degraded Jews of the East and the cultivated and honourable Jews of the West. But blood is stronger than water, and Hebrew rule is sure to lead to a Hebrew policy. Throughout Europe, the most fiercely Turkish part of the press is largely in Jewish hands. It may be assumed everywhere, with the smallest class of exceptions, that the Jew is the friend of the Turk and the enemy of the Christian.[2]

The attempts of Freeman and Goldwin Smith to launch German-style intellectual anti-Semitism in England, like the later attempts by Chesterton and Belloc to import the French clerical variety, had very little success. But the belief in the "Semitism" of Disraeli's Eastern policy went far beyond such circles. "I have a strong suspicion," Gladstone told the Duke of Argyll, "that Dizzy's crypto-Judaism has had to do with his policy. The Jews of the East *bitterly* hate the Christians, who have not always used them well."[3] As late as 1924, in a paper which Sir James Headlam-Morley wrote as historical advisor to the Foreign Office, he remarked that Disraeli "in his sympathies . . . was consistently a Jew and a Zionist [*sic*]. . . . Not without reason did his enemies publicly attribute his Near Eastern policy to his 'Semitic instincts' . . . the conviction can scarcely be avoided that the charge contained part of the truth, and that if 'Semitic sympathies' be added we get yet nearer to Disraeli's inner personal motives."[4]

The charge against Disraeli's patriotism is obviously absurd. His policy of defending Turkey against Russia had been anticipated by such impeccably Christian and English gentlemen as Palmerston, Castlereagh, Canning, and Pitt, and had long been an important, though not uncontested, principle of British diplomacy. But that is not the whole story. Disraeli's most recent biographer has reminded us that "historians do not always sufficiently weigh the influence of the conditions, prejudices and sympathies of early youth upon the choice of sides made by statesmen later, when they are confronted with the great political questions of the hour."[5] Like Churchill, Lloyd George, and so many others, Disraeli may well have been affected, in his mature attitudes and decisions, by the formative influences of his youth. Disraeli's pride in his Jewish ancestry is well known. His novels and letters amply attest his profound sympathy for the Turks, the Arabs, and Islam, and his belief in the basic kinship between Jews and Muslims. Like so many Englishmen, he was fascinated by the desert and the Arabs; better than others, he was able to identify himself with both. Assertions of such identity recur frequently in his writings, in which the terms "Arabia" and "Arab" have an almost mystical significance. The Jews are "Mosaic Arabs" or even "Jewish Arabs," kinsmen and predecessors of the Muslim Arabs; "the Arabs are only Jews upon horseback." Judaism, Christianity, and Islam are all Arabian religions: "On the top of Mount Sinai are two ruins—a Christian church and a Mohammedan mosque. In this, the sublimest scene of Arabian glory, Israel and Ishmael alike raised their altars to the great God of Abraham. Why are they in ruins?"[6]

Disraeli's sentimental Semitism, however well documented, does not explain his pro-Turkish feelings; still less does it throw any light on the general attitude of European Jews to the Turks and Islam. As his biographer Buckle remarked, had Disraeli been guided by racial feeling, "the race which that feeling would have led him to support would have been . . . the Arab, and not the Turk."[7] In any case, Disraeli's racialism—his obsession with race in general and the Jewish race in particular—owes more to his Christian education than to his Jewish ancestry and has no parallel in the writings of authentic Jews of the time. It was in Christian Europe that the great racial myths, with the accompanying rejection of "inferior stocks," had begun to influence ideas and events; Disraeli's hymns, or rather fugues, on the theme of Jewish power and Jewish glory are no more than inverted anti-Jewish stereotypes, with as little foundation in reality as their originals.

Yet, beneath the distortions and slanders of Disraeli's political enemies, there was an important element of truth. Disraeli *was* an admirer of Islam, of the Persians and Turks as well as the Arabs, and in his youth had even thought of joining the Turkish army as a volunteer. Moreover, his pro-Turkish sentiments were connected with his vestigial Jewishness and are typical of a good deal of Jewish opinion at the time. O'Connor, despite his malicious exaggerations, was not far wrong in speaking of the Jews in nineteenth-century Europe as a pro-Turkish, and more generally pro-Muslim, element.

One field in which the Jewish interest in Islam made a significant impact was that of scholarship. In the development of Islamic studies in European and, later, American universities, Jews, and in particular Jews of Orthodox background and education, play an altogether disproportionate role. In one of his early novels, Disraeli puts in his hero's mouth a lively plea for Oriental literatures: "Why not study the Oriental? Surely in the pages of the Persians and the Arabs we might discover new sources of emotion, new modes of expression, new trains of ideas, new principles of invention, and new bursts of fancy . . ." and praises "the Persians, whose very being is poetry, the Arabs, whose subtle mind could penetrate into the very secret shrine of nature."[8] Jewish scholars did much to bring these achievements of the Islamic genius to Western notice and inculcate in the Western mind a less prejudiced and more sympathetic understanding of Islam.

One such scholar was Gustav Weil (1808–1889), a rabbinical student who became Professor of Arabic at Heidelberg. He mastered Persian and Turkish as well as Arabic and spent some time in Algiers, Cairo, and Istanbul. In 1843 he published his first major work—on the life and teachings of the Prophet Muḥammad. There had been many biographies of Muḥammad in Europe; Weil's was the first that was free from prejudice and polemic, based on a profound yet critical knowledge of the Arabic sources, and informed by a sympathetic understanding of Muslim belief and piety. For the first time, he gave the European reader an opportunity to see Muḥammad as the Muslims saw him, and thus to achieve a fuller appreciation of his place in human history. Weil's other publications on the beginnings of Islam include an historical and critical introduction to the Qur'ān, a translation of the major Arabic biography of the Prophet, and a five-volume history of the Caliphs. In terms of scholarship, these books have to a large extent been overtaken by subsequent research; in their day, however, and for long afterwards, they were standard works, and they remain as landmarks in the Western discovery of the East.

Many Jewish scholars came directly from Hebrew to Arabic studies and made important contributions to both—particularly in the areas where the two overlap. Salomon Munk (1805–1867) and Moritz Steinschneider (1816–1917) were both specialists on Judaeo-Arabic literature, but their work was of great value to Arabic and Islamic studies generally. Munk's work on medieval Islamic philosophy, Steinschneider's studies and bibliographies on the translation movement —from Greece to the Arabs and from the Arabs to Europe—throw a flood of light on the cultural history of Islam and on the Muslim contribution to European civilization. Christians of Jewish origin also play a part. Karl Paul Caspari (1814–1892), a Lutheran theologian of Jewish parentage, wrote what was for long the standard European treatise on Arabic grammar. David Abrahamovitch Chwolson (1819–1911), a baptized Lithuanian Jew, became a professor at the newly founded faculty of Oriental languages at St. Petersburg. Though primarily a Hebraist, he was also a competent Arabist and through his writings and his influence as a teacher ranks among the founders of the Russian school of Arabic studies. To these may be added David Samuel Margoliouth (1858–1940), an Anglican clergyman who held the Laudian Chair of Arabic at Oxford University and was one of the major Arabic and Islamic scholars of his day.

With the advance of emancipation during the later nineteenth and early twentieth centuries, Jewish scholars play an increasing part in the European universities, notably in Oriental studies. A Turkish Jew, Joseph Halevy (1827–1917), and two Austrians, David Heinrich Müller (1846–1912) and Edward Glaser (1855–1908), were among the pioneers of South Arabian studies; a German rabbinical scholar, Hermann Reckendorf (1863–1923), whose father incidentally had translated the Qur'ān into Hebrew, wrote the standard work on Arabic syntax. Julius Hirschberg (1843–1925), Julius Lippert (1866–1911), and Max Meyerhof (1874–1945) devoted themselves to the recovery and study of Muslim science and medicine. Other important figures are the Iranist Wilhelm Bacher (1850–1913), Siegmund Fraenkel (1855–1909), Max Sobernheim (1872–1932), Josef Horovitz (1874–1931), Eugen Mittwoch (1876–1942), and the art historian Leo Aryeh Mayer (1895–1959), one of the pioneers of the new and flourishing school of Islamic studies in Jerusalem.

It was chiefly in Germany and Austria that Jewish scholars, half way between the traditionalism of the East and the emancipation of the West, were able to achieve the most effective combination of old-style learning and modern scholarship. But the Jewish role in Oriental studies can be seen very clearly in other countries, too: David Santillana (1855–1931) and Giorgio Levi Della Vida (1886–1967) in Italy; Joseph Derenbourg (1811–1895), his son Hartwig Derenbourg (1844–1908), the Iranist James Darmesteter (1849–1894), the historian of Spanish Islam Evariste Lévi-Provençal (1894–1956) in France; the Persian scholar Reuben Levy (1891–1966) in England; Richard Gottheil (1862–1936) and William Popper (1874–1963), pioneers of Arabic studies in the United States. Probably the greatest of all was Ignaz Goldziher (1850–1921), a pious Hungarian Jew whose magnificent series of studies on Muslim theology, law, and culture rank him, by common consent, as one of the founders and masters of modern Islamic studies.

The role of these scholars in the development of every aspect of Islamic studies has been immense—not only in the advancement of scholarship but also in the enrichment of the Western view of Oriental religion, literature, and history, by the substitution of knowledge and understanding for prejudice and ignorance. In recent years the revival of learning in the East has given these scholars a new importance, as their works, in the original and in translation, are read by the Muslims themselves and help to shape both their knowledge of past achievements and their awareness of present problems. It is said that when the Turkish historian Ahmed Refik, returning from a tour of Europe at the beginning of this century, was asked by his friends what was the most remarkable thing he had seen on his travels, he replied: "The University of Budapest, where I found a Jewish professor expounding the Qur'ān to a class of Christian pupils." The Jewish professor was of course Ignaz Goldziher. Since then, some of his writings have been translated into Arabic and are used for teaching Muslim Arab pupils their own heritage. Not a few other Jewish scholars have been translated and adapted in the same way.[9]

Impact and influence are not always the rewards of accurate and original scholarship, and the reputation of these men rarely reached beyond the academic circles in which they lived and moved. There were others, however, whose impact was more strongly felt, and more extensive. Three in particular found readers and disciples in unexpected places.

The first of these was Arthur Lumley Davids (1811–1832), an English Jew who died of cholera shortly before his twenty-first birthday.

An infant prodigy, he mastered Hebrew, Arabic, Persian, and Turkish at an early age and undertook a vast program of research. His most important work, published three weeks before his death, was his *Grammar of the Turkish Language*, the first in English since 1709. More significant than the grammar itself was the 78-page "Preliminary Discourse," in which, on the basis of an astonishingly wide range of learning, Davids surveys the origins and history of the Turkish peoples, the classification and characteristics of the Turkish languages, and the principal monuments of Turkish literature.

This "Discourse" was the first attempt of its kind to bring to the Western reader a balanced account of the Turks, their achievement and their place in history, and thus to correct the vulgar errors and prejudices that were current concerning them. It is inspired by a spirit of profound sympathy and admiration.

Davids's *Grammar* was published in English in 1832 and in a French translation, prepared by his mother, in 1836. Though no doubt a remarkable effort for so young an author, the book is of limited scholarly value and was on the whole neglected by the world of Oriental scholarship. It was, however, greatly admired by the well-known Turcophile writer David Urquhart, who in his *Spirit of the East* (1839) quotes extensively from the "Preliminary Discourse."

Rather more important than Davids's influence on the Turcophiles was his influence on the Turks themselves, to whom his "Discourse" brought a new awareness of identity and a new pride of achievement. Already in 1851 Fuad and Jevdet Pashas, the co-authors of the first modern Turkish grammar in Turkish, drew on Davids's work. Their book, which was enormously influential in Turkey, has been regarded as the starting-point of the renovation of the Turkish language. In 1869 another Turkish author, Ali Suavi, wrote an article extolling the past glories of the Turkish race, for which his sole source was Davids's "Preliminary Discourse." This article was one of the earliest statements of an entirely new trend among the Ottoman Turks—that of nationalism. In adapting this new and essentially alien idea to their own needs, Turkish—and later also other Muslim—nationalists relied very heavily on Western literature. In this respect the most influential works were not necessarily the most scholarly.[10]

Another author, of rather doubtful scholarship and far greater influence, was David Léon Cahun (1841–1900), an Alsatian Jew who went on a tour of the Middle East in his youth and thereafter remained a passionate enthusiast. Cahun wrote and lectured extensively on the countries and peoples of the area, especially on the Egyptians and the Turks, and from 1890 gave courses at the Sorbonne on the history and geography of Asia. His writings include a number of romantic historical novels, several with Turkish and Muslim heroes; a wide range of geographical and ethnographical books and papers; and a number of books and articles on Islamic and Asian history. The best known of these was his *Introduction générale à l'histoire de l'Asie* (1896), a sustained hymn of praise to the greatness of the Turkish peoples and their immense creative role in the history of Asia and indeed the world. A history of the Arabs remained unfinished at his death.

This *Introduction Générale* was published in a Turkish adaptation in 1899 and exercised a powerful attraction on successive generations of Turkish readers, not only in Turkey but also in the Russian empire. Modern Turkish historians regard this book as one of the seminal influences in the development of pan-Turkism and of Turkish nationalism. Cahun's influence was not limited to his books. A committed liberal, he cultivated the Turkish and Egyptian émigrés in Paris and served their cause both in person and through his writings.[11]

Among European Jews who became involved in Muslim countries and affairs, one was outstanding, both for his genuine scholarship and for his political influence. Arminius Vambéry (1832–1918) was the son of a Hungarian Talmudist and was brought up in Orthodox Judaism and grinding poverty. His subsequent career was in every sense unorthodox. After an irregular and largely self-administered education, he went as a young man to Istanbul, where he lived from hand to mouth by giving lessons. In time he mastered Turkish so well that he became one of the leading authorities in Europe on Turkish studies and one of the founders of the new science of Turkology. Between 1862 and 1864, disguised as a wandering dervish, he traveled in Persia and Central Asia; in 1865 he became professor of Oriental languages at the University of Budapest, where one of his pupils was Ignaz Goldziher. His numerous books and articles were read not only in Europe but in Turkey where his friends included men in the highest positions. Both through his writings and his personality, he had a considerable influence on cultural and, to some extent, on political developments in Turkey.[12]

The Turks admired and responded to Davids, Cahun, and Vambéry because they recognized, in all three, a genuine and deeply-felt sympathy for themselves. There is no evidence that their Turkish readers and disciples were particularly aware of the Jewish origin of the three men or attached any importance to it; still less is there any sign of belief, among nineteenth-century Turks or Muslims, in a Muslim-Jewish bond of brotherhood such as was imagined by O'Connor, Freeman, and others. Yet the prevalence of Jews—and especially of conscious Jews—among Orientalists and Turcophiles is more than coincidental. Weil, Reckendorf, Vambéry, Goldziher, and many others started with a Biblical and Talmudical training. Even such Westerners as Davids and Cahun had a more than nominal connection with Jewishness. Davids, his mother tells us, wrote on many subjects, "notably" on Jewish emancipation; Cahun wrote a book on the customs of the Jews of Alsace, with a preface by the Chief Rabbi of Paris.[13] Even converts like Disraeli and Chwolson show an active concern, not only in their writings but also in their actions—the one by his stand for Jewish emancipation, the other by his testimony against the blood-libel.

Why then did these Jews and ex-Jews rally to the Islamic and Turkish side, to such an extent that in Europe, though not in Turkey, their pro-Turkish attitude was treated as an acknowledged fact? Certainly not because of any agreement or alliance, for the devotion of some Jews to Muslim studies and causes aroused no corresponding interest or sentiment on the other side.[14] Some romantics, however, like the young Disraeli, seem to have dreamed of such an alliance and seen its fulfillment in the golden age of Muslim Spain, "that fair and unrivalled civilization" in "which the children of Ishmael rewarded the children of Israel with equal rights and privileges with themselves. During these halcyon centuries, it is difficult to distinguish the followers of Moses from the votary of Mahomet. Both alike built palaces, gardens, and fountains; filled equally the highest offices of the state, competed in an extensive and enlightened commerce, and rivalled each other in renowned universities."[15]

This kind of romanticism affected a number of Jewish writers of the time and has a curiously mixed origin. Basically, it was part of the romantic cult of Spain, which reached its peak in Victor Hugo's *Hernani* (1830) and was extended to the Muslim Middle Ages by Washington Irving's highly successful *Chronicle of the Conquest of Granada* (1829) and *The Alhambra* (1832). Jewish romantics found an additional point of interest in the tragic fate of their own ancestors in Spain—a fate which was becoming better known through the labors of historians. One of these was Disraeli's cousin Elias Haim Lindo, whose *History of the Jews in Spain and Portugal* appeared in 1846.[16] The broad outlines of the story, in the simplified and dramatized form in which great historic events so often reach the popular imagination, were well defined. The Jews had flourished in Muslim Spain, had been driven from Christian Spain, and had found a refuge in Muslim Turkey.

The reality was of course more complex, less idyllic, less one-sided. There had been times of persecution under the Muslims and times of prosperity under Christian rule in Spain—and many Christian states, as well as Turkey, had given shelter to the Spanish Jewish refugees. Even at its best, medieval Islam was rather different from the picture provided by Disraeli and other romantic writers. The golden age of equal rights was a myth, and belief in it was a result, more than a cause, of Jewish sympathy for Islam. The myth was invented by Jews in nineteenth-century Europe as a reproach to Christians—and taken up by Muslims in our own time as a reproach to Jews.

Like most powerful myths, this story contains an element of historic truth. If tolerance means the absence of persecution, then classical Islamic society was indeed tolerant to both its Jewish and its Christian subjects—more tolerant perhaps in Spain than in the East, and in either incomparably more tolerant than was medieval Christendom. But if tolerance means the absence of discrimination, then Islam never was or claimed to be tolerant but on the contrary insisted on the privileged superiority of the true believer in this world as well as in the next. The great conflict of the Crusades, and later the European counter-attack against the Turks, brought a harshening of Muslim attitudes, directed primarily against the Christians but to a lesser extent also against the Jews. Both minorities suffered from the decline in Muslim power, prosperity, and standards. In more recent times the position of the Jews had become relatively worse, since unlike the native Christians they were unable to invoke the protection of the Christian powers. European travelers to the East in the age of liberalism and emancipation are almost unanimous in deploring the degraded and precarious position of Jews in Muslim countries and the dangers and humiliations to which they were subject.

Jewish scholars, acquainted with the history of Islam and with the current situation in Islamic lands, can have had no illusions on this score. Vambéry is unambiguous: "I do not know any more miserable, helpless, and pitiful individual on God's earth than the *Jahudi* in those countries. . . . The poor Jew is despised, belabored and tortured alike by Moslem, Christian and Brahmin, he is the poorest of the poor, and outstripped by Armenians, Greeks and Brahmins. . . ."[17]

In view of this, it is the more striking that Jewish scholars and writers should in general have felt and expressed so much sympathy for Islam. In part this was based on a well-grounded feeling of gratitude. In medieval Spain there had indeed been a great age of Jewish creativity, which owed much to Muslim tolerance; in modern Turkey many Jews, fleeing from Christian persecution, had found a new home under Muslim rule.

To the European Jews of the early nineteenth century, facing the opportunities and frustrations of emancipation, there were some further points to note. In medieval Spain, at least so it appeared, there had been a degree of social and cultural communication between Jew and Gentile such as was impossible in medieval Christendom and was only just becoming possible, against many obstacles, in Europe in their own day. In the world of Islam, governments might discriminate against non-Muslims, including Jews; but they rarely persecuted them. There might be contempt, degradation, even occasional repression, but there was nothing in Islam to compare with the specific hatred, both theoretical and popular, that was directed against the Jews in Christendom.[18] In the age of secularism, theological anti-Judaism was far from dead; the newer, racial anti-Semitism was already making itself felt.

Although the term anti-Semitism was not invented until 1862, the racial ideology that gave rise to it was already well established in the early nineteenth century. Instead of—or as well as—an unbeliever and

"Christ-killer," the Jew was now labelled as a member of an alien and inferior race, variously described as Semitic, Asiatic, and Oriental. The old-style religious Jew, secure in his faith, was untroubled by religious hatred, except of course in so far as it endangered his life and liberty; the new-style emancipated Jew was deeply disturbed by racial rejection, which wounded his spirit even when it spared his body. Told that he was a Semite or an Asian, he looked to other Semites and other Asians for comfort—just as the Czechs and Serbs looked to their Slavic big brother in Russia. The obvious choice was Islam—which in the nineteenth century meant the Ottoman Empire, the last surviving Muslim great power. In Europe, the collocation of Jews and Moors, Jews and Saracens, Jews and Turks was bitterly familiar from a thousand pogroms and Crusades, bans and banishments, inquisitions and persecutions—familiar, that is, to the Jews, who were the nearer and easier victims of the anger directed against both. The worst massacres of Jews in medieval Christendom were perpetrated by Crusaders on their way to fight the Saracens; the expulsion of the Jews from Spain was the climax of the reconquest from the Moors; the deadliest enemies of the Turks were the Russians, the most inveterate Jew-haters of modern Europe. A fellow-feeling, even if unreciprocated, was understandable.

Gratitude, sentiment, fellow-feeling—all play their part in the growth of pro-Muslim sentiment among Jews. But underlying them all there was something more powerful—an affinity of religious culture which made it possible for Jews, even emancipated, liberal West European Jews, to achieve an immediate and intuitive understanding of Islam. It is fashionable nowadays to speak of the Judaeo-Christian tradition. One could as justly speak of a Judaeo-Islamic tradition, for the Muslim religion, like Christianity, is closely related to its Jewish forerunner. Judaism has more in common with each of its two successors than either has with the other and thus in many ways occupies an intermediate position between the two. The Judaeo-Christian affinities are well-known and are at last being recognized. The Judaeo-Islamic affinities include such things as inflexible monotheism, austerity of worship, the rejection of images and incarnations and, most important of all, submission to an all-embracing divine law, enshrined in scripture, tradition, and commentary, which regulates and sanctifies the most intimate details of daily life.[19] Not only were the sacred texts similar in spirit, but they were written in cognate languages. The same word, *din*, means 'religion' in Arabic, 'law' in Hebrew; the connection between the two meanings is obvious to any Jew or Muslim. A Hebraist could learn Arabic, a Talmudist understand the *Sharī'a,* with greater ease and with greater sympathy than his Protestant or Catholic colleagues. This feeling of affinity was expressed by the most illustrious of Jewish Islamicists, Ignaz Goldziher, in a letter written shortly before his death, to an Arab pupil: "It is for your people and for mine that I have lived. When you return to your country, tell this to your brothers."[20]

Palestine: On the History and Geography of a Name

12

The word *Palestine* comes from 'Philistine' and originally denoted the coastal region north and south of Gaza which was occupied and settled by the Philistine invaders from across the sea. The name was familiar to their ancient neighbors, occurring in Egyptian as *Purusati,* in Assyrian as *Palastu,* and in the Hebrew Bible as *Pĕleshet* (Exodus 14:14; Isaiah 14:29, 31; Joel 3:4). In the English Authorized Version, Peleshet is rendered *Palestina* or, in Joel only, Palestine. In the Revised Version, followed by the New English Bible, Palestina and Palestine disappear from the Old Testament and are replaced by *Philistia,* an obvious gain in accuracy.[1] In the New Testament the name Palestine does not occur at all.

The coast and its hinterland were known by a number of names in antiquity, and several of these are attested in Egyptian, Assyrian, and other writings. The earliest in common use was *Canaan*, an ethnic term. The Jews called the country *Eretz Israel,* 'the land of Israel,' and used the names *Israel* and *Judah* to designate the two kingdoms into which the country was split after the death of King Solomon. The latter name, in the forms *Ioudaia* and *Judaea,* passed into Greek and Latin usage.

The form Palestine, used by Greek and Latin authors, is first attested in the history of Herodotus and occurs in a number of later classical texts.[2] It occasionally appears as a noun but more commonly as an adjective in apposition to Syria. In normal usage *Palaistinê Syria* or *Syria Palestina* seems to have meant the coastal plain formerly inhabited by the Philistines. It was sometimes extended to include territories further east but was not usually applied to Judaea, which in Roman times was still officially and commonly known by that name.[3]

Official Roman usage of the name Palestine to designate the area of the former Jewish kingdom seems to date from after the Jewish risings and their suppression. The Emperor Hadrian made a determined attempt to stamp out the embers not only of the revolt but of Jewish nationhood and statehood. The ruined city of Jerusalem was rebuilt in A.D. 135 as a Roman colony with a new name, *Aelia Capitolina,* in honour of the Emperor, whose full name was Titus Aelius Hadrianus, and of the gods of the Roman Capitol. A temple of Jupiter, with an equestrian statue of Hadrian, adorned the Temple area; a temple of Venus was built on Calvary. Access to the city was forbidden to Jews, including those converted to Christianity, on pain of death. The Christians in the Holy City had to find a new bishop of gentile birth. It would seem that the name Judaea was abolished at the same time as Jerusalem and the country renamed Palestina or Syria-Palestina with the same intention to obliterate its historic Jewish identity.

The earliest attempts at a territorial definition of the country later known as Palestine are in the Bible and represent three successive phases in the evolution of the concept of the Promised Land. The first is God's covenant with Abraham, enumerating the areas promised to the patriarch and his descendants, "from the river of Egypt unto the great river, the river Euphrates."[4] This, of course, includes the descendants and lands of Ishmael as well as of Israel. The second is the land promised to Moses and occupied by the Israelites after the exodus from Egypt.[5] The third set of boundaries are those mentioned in connection with the return of the exiles from the Babylonian captivity.[6] The promise to Moses defines the land of Israel as extending from a line passing through Levo Hamath in the north to Nahal Misraim in the south. Levo Hamath (the Authorized and Revised Versions read "the entrance of Hamath") is probably the modern Labwa, on the Orontes River in North Lebanon. Some scholars have identified this border with the northern frontier of the Egyptian province of Canaan, as delimited after the war with the Hittites, while others have seen it as a projection backward of the later, short-lived expansion of Israel under the early monarchy. The Authorized Version translates Nahal Misraim as "the river of Egypt"; the New English Bible has "the torrent of Egypt." The medieval Jewish commentator Saadiya is probably right in saying that what is meant is the Wadi of al-ʿArīsh, to which neither epithet, river or torrent, seems very appropriate.

In practice, the ancient Jewish state had varying frontiers at different times, under different rulers and dynasties. Even when Jewish independence was finally extinguished and no Jewish political entity with frontiers existed, the rabbis found it necessary to formulate a legal definition of the limits of the land of Israel. This was not just an intellectual exercise; it was required for both fiscal and ritual purposes, since rabbinical law makes distinctions in both respects between Jews living in the land of Israel and those living outside. This definition was based on the areas resettled by Jews after the return from Babylon. The place names mentioned in the relevant rabbinical texts as marking the limits of the land of Israel have not all been identified, but it is clear that this delimitation excludes some areas in the far north and south of the present-day state of Israel and includes a substantial part of Transjordania.[7]

The Roman province of Palestine was usually attached to Syria, of which it was considered a part. During the later Roman and Byzantine periods a number of changes were made, in the course of which Roman Palestine was extended by the annexation to it of neighboring territories and then subdivided. Under Diocletian, the province of Arabia, founded by the Emperor Trajan in the year 105, was attached to Palestine, but in 358 this area, consisting of the Negev and southern Transjordan, was constituted a separate province and named *Palestina Salutaris*. In about A.D. 400 Palestine proper was split into two provinces known respectively as *Palestina Prima* and *Palestina Secunda,* while Palestina Salutaris was renamed *Palestina Tertia*. Palestina Prima with its capital in Caesarea was the central part of the country. It included the coastal plain as far south as Rafa and the historic lands of Judaea and Samaria together with Edom, and it extended eastwards into Transjordan into the region known in classical times as Peraea. It was bounded in the north by Palestina Secunda and in the south by Palestina Tertia. Palestina Secunda had its capital at Scythopolis, the Hebrew *Bethshean* or Arabic *Baysān,* and included the valley of Esdraelon, Galilee, northern Transjordan, and the Golan area. Palestina Tertia, with its capital at Petra, included the Negev, southern Transjordan, and part of Sinai.[8]

After the Arab conquest in the seventh century, the new masters of the country seem substantially to have retained the existing administrative subdivisions; Palestina Prima and Palestina Secunda remained but with new names and new capitals. The first became *Filasṭīn,* an obvious Arabic adaptation of the Roman name, and was administered first from Lydda and later from Ramla. Palestina Secunda was called *Urdunn,* that is, Jordan, after the river, and had its capital at Tiberias. Jerusalem, which in the earliest Arabic texts is referred to by its Roman name of Aelia, was not a provincial or even a district seat of government. The boundaries between the two provinces seem to have varied somewhat from time to time but in the main followed the Roman lines. In the Arab as in the Roman periods, the division between Palestine and Jordan was not, as in modern times, vertical between west and east, but horizontal between north and south, with both districts extending, one above the other, from the Mediterranean across the Jordan River to the eastern desert.[9]

The former Roman Palestina Tertia or Salutaris seems to have ceased to exist as a separate entity. Most of it belonged to the area which the Arab historians call *Tīh Banī Isrā'īl,* the land of the wanderings of the Children of Israel, usually known simply as Tīh. This included the Negev and the greater part of the Sinai desert and was sometimes attached to the district of Filasṭīn. This attachment meant very little in practice. Medieval governments generally made no attempt to extend their direct rule over the desert, which they regarded in much the same way as modern states regard the sea, or did until recently. The deserts between southern Palestine and the Nile valley were thus in fact subject to neither. Only when both parts were under a single rule, as sometimes happened, was any attempt made to police the desert between them, and even that was usually intermittent and ineffective.

In early medieval Arabic usage, Filasṭīn and Urdunn were subdistricts forming part of the greater geographical entity known as Syria or, to use the Arabic term, the land of *Shām.* This was one of the major geographical entities named in common Arabic usage, the others being Egypt, Jazira (Mesopotamia), Iraq, Arabia, and the Yemen. These, though never constituting countries or nations in the modern political sense, were nevertheless generally recognized as social, cultural, and to some extent even economic and political entities with a continuing identity. The land of Shām comprised all the territories bounded by the Taurus in the north and Egypt in the south, the desert in the east and the

Mediterranean in the west. The two districts of Filasṭīn and Urdunn constituted the southernmost third of the land of Shām.

Under Roman, Byzantine, and Islamic rule, Palestine was politically submerged. It reappeared only under the Crusaders. The Latin Kingdom of Jerusalem began as a very small unit which grew steadily and at its largest extended from a point north of Beirut to the Sinai desert, and along both sides of the River Jordan. There are interesting parallels with the modern situation in the continuing conflict over the southern border and in the role of what one might call the Ascalon Strip, a stretch of territory with Ascalon as its center, retained by the rulers of Egypt after the Crusaders had conquered the rest of Palestine. Crowded with refugees and troops, this area served as a base for raids and attacks on the Crusader principalities until it was conquered by the Crusaders themselves and used in turn as a base for an attack on Egypt. During the period of the Crusades the name Palestine or Filasṭīn fell into disuse. The Muslims no longer administered it, and the Crusaders preferred to call the country which they had conquered the Holy Land and the state which they had established the Kingdom of Jerusalem.

After the Muslim reconquest, the names Filasṭīn and Urdunn disappear from administrative usage. Under the successors of Saladin and still more under the Mamlūks who ruled from the mid-thirteenth to the early sixteenth centuries, the country was redistributed in new territorial units, usually known by the names of towns which were district administrative centers. For most of the late medieval period the two banks of the Jordan were divided into six districts with their capitals in Gaza, Lydda, Qaqun, Jerusalem, Hebron, and Nablus, all six districts forming part of the province of Shām, with its capital in Damascus. At certain times Gaza, Lydda, and Qaqun appear as separate provinces. In the late Mamlūk period, most of Palestine seems to have been divided into the *Niyābas* (lieutenancies) of Gaza and Safad, comprising the southern and northern parts of the country. The Niyāba of Safad included much of what is now south Lebanon, with the districts of Tyre and Tibnin. All these came under the rule of the viceroy of Damascus.

After the Ottoman conquest in 1516–17 there was again a redistribution, and the country was divided into the Ottoman *Sanjaks* (administrative districts) of Gaza, Jerusalem, Nablus, and Safad in Cisjordania and

'Ajlun in Transjordan. An additional district, that of Lajjun on the west bank, was later added. All these again were subject to the authority of the *beylerbey* (governor-general) of Damascus. These districts were from time to time subdivided and rearranged during the four centuries of Ottoman rule. In the final phase of this rule before the British conquest, the center and north of the country were part of the vilayet of Beirut, the whole of Transjordan was incorporated in the vilayet of Damascus (renamed vilayet of Syria under Abdülhamid), and the remainder of Palestine constituted as the independent district of Jerusalem (*i.e.*, independent in the sense that it was directly dependent on the capital and not subject to any of the pashas of the neighboring provinces).

The name Urdunn, or Jordan, seems to have gone out of use entirely, except for the river, from the Middle Ages until its reappearance in the twentieth century. The name Filasṭīn, or Palestine, had a somewhat different history. It had never been used by Jews, for whom the normal name of the country, from the time of the Exodus to the present day, was Eretz Israel.[10] It was no longer used by Muslims, for whom it had never meant more than an administrative sub-district, and it had been forgotten even in that limited sense.

It was, however, widely adopted in the Christian world. In the Middle Ages, Christian writers had usually spoken of "the Holy Land," or even of Judaea. The Renaissance and the revival of interest in classical antiquity gave a new currency to the Roman name Palestine, which came to be the common designation of the country in most European languages. European influence brought it to the Arabic-speaking Christians, the first of the country's inhabitants to be affected by Western practices and usages. The second Arabic newspaper to appear in Palestine, published in 1911, was called *Filasṭīn* and was edited by an Arab Christian of the Orthodox Church.

An expression as vague as the Palestine of Christian usage could of course have no very precise geographical definition. The 1910 edition of the *Encyclopaedia Britannica*, published when all these lands were still part of the Ottoman Empire, defines it as follows:

> Palestine, a geographical name of rather loose application. Etymological strictness would require it to denote exclusively the narrow strip of coastline once

> occupied by the Philistines, from whose name it is derived. It is, however, conventionally used as a name for the territory which, in the Old Testament, is claimed as the inheritance of the pre-exilic Hebrews; thus it may be said generally to denote the southern third of the province of Syria. Except in the west, where the country is bordered by the Mediterranean Sea, the limit of this territory cannot be laid down on the map as a definite line. The modern sub-divisions under the jurisdiction of the Ottoman Empire are in no sense co-terminous with those of antiquity, and hence do not afford a boundary by which Palestine can be separated exactly from the rest of Syria in the north, or from the Sinaitic and Arabian deserts in the south and east; nor are the records of ancient boundaries sufficiently full and definite to make possible the complete demarcation of the countries. Even the convention above referred to is inexact; it includes the Philistine territory, claimed but never settled by the Hebrews, and excludes the outlying parts of the large area claimed in Numbers xxiv as the Hebrew possession. . . . Taking as a guide the natural features most nearly corresponding to these outlying points, we may describe Palestine as the strip of land extending along the eastern shore of the Mediterranean Sea from the mouth of the Litany or Kasimiya River (33° 20′N) southward to the mouth of the Wadi Ghuzza; the latter joins the sea in 31°28′N, a short distance south of Gaza, and runs thence in a southeasterly direction so as to include on its northern side the site of Beersheba. Eastward there is no such definite border. The River Jordan, it is true, marks a line of delimitation between Western and Eastern Palestine; but it is practically impossible to say where the latter ends and the Arabian desert begins.

It will be noted that this territorial definition differs in several important respects from that laid down for the British mandate only a few years later. For the writer, it clearly includes the east bank of the Jordan as part of Palestine—common usage at the time. In addition, it includes what is now southern Lebanon but excludes the Negev Desert and its extension southwards.

With the British conquest in 1917–18 and the subsequent establishment of a mandated territory in the conquered areas, Palestine became the official name of a definite territory for the first time since the early Middle Ages. As a modern state with modern neighbors, Palestine now had to have properly demarcated and recognized boundaries, which were fixed by the new masters of the Middle East.

The delimitation of the frontiers of mandatary Palestine is of some interest. In the south, the boundary had for centuries been purely administrative. Under the Ottomans, and before them under the Mamlūk sultans, Egypt and Palestine had been under a common sovereignty. In general, the effective southern limit of the Palestinian districts was at Rafa; the effective northern limit of Egyptian jurisdiction was in the neighborhood of Faramā, the ancient Pelusium, in the eastern corner of the Nile delta. Between the two was a desert no-man's-land, inhabited only by a few roving Bedouin, variously attached to one or the other or, most commonly, neither.

The modern process of delimitation began with Muḥammad ʿAlī, the Ottoman Pasha of Egypt and founder of the modern Egyptian state. By the London Convention of 1840, the Sultan agreed to assign to Muḥammad ʿAlī the hereditary pashalik of Egypt with the addition of a personal pashalik of Acre and the right to administer southern Syria, the southern border of which was defined as follows: "From the western shore of the Dead Sea . . . it shall extend straight to the Red Sea, which it shall strike at the northern point of the Gulf of Aqaba, and from thence it shall follow the western shore of the Gulf of Aqaba, and the eastern shore of the Gulf of Suez, as far as Suez."

This is very clear. But such impolitic clarity was inevitably of short duration. After further fighting, Egyptian troops withdrew from the Syria-Palestine area and a new frontier was laid down in the Sultan's firman to Muḥammad ʿAlī of 1 June 1841. This omits Syria-Palestine and assigns to the Pasha the government of Egypt only, "within its ancient boundaries, such as they are to be found in the map which is sent to you by my Grand Vizier now in office. . . ."

There were, it seems only two copies of the accompanying map, and when a border dispute arose between Turkey and Britain, as the occupying power in Egypt, neither was available. The British stated that the Egyptian map had been lost in a fire in Cairo; the Turks claimed possession of a copy but did not produce it.

The issue was raised in 1892, some ten years after the British occupation of Egypt. The Sultan issued a firman of investiture for the new *khedive* ʿAbbās Hilmī in which he pointedly referred to Egypt only, and thus, by implication, withdrew Sinai and the other areas as personal to Muḥammad ʿAlī and not part of Egypt, and reclaimed Aqaba. One reason for this change was the Ottoman concern with the Hijāz and the project for a Hijāz railway, then already under discussion; another was the line of communication to the Yemen where the Ottoman authorities were having some difficulty in maintaining their authority.

The British ruler of Egypt, Evelyn Baring, later Lord Cromer, at once sent a protest to Constantinople, and the Grand Vizier replied by agreeing to leave Sinai to Egypt provided that the Red Sea forts were left to the Ottomans. Baring published a statement interpreting the Grand Vizier's telegram as recognition of a frontier from just east of al-ʿArīsh to the head of the Gulf of Aqaba. The Ottoman authorities were silent, neither agreeing nor objecting at that moment.

While the Ottomans were concerned about their route through Arabia, the British were increasingly anxious for the safety of the Suez Canal. From 1903 onwards, the British operating from Egypt began to advance their outposts into Sinai, and in 1906 a small force of Egyptian gendarmes commanded by a British officer went to Aqaba. This led to a crisis between the Ottoman Empire and Great Britain. The Turks began by rejecting the very idea of a frontier between Palestine and Egypt, since in their view both were Turkish provinces and all that could exist between them was an administrative boundary. They also rejected Baring's earlier statement, which, they argued, was purely unilateral. The Turks wished to limit the Egyptian part of Sinai to two triangles, bounded by lines from Rafa (north of al-ʿArīsh) to Suez and from Suez to Aqaba; the first of these, they said, was the administrative boundary fixed in 1841. This would have left the central part of the peninsula, bounded by the lines Rafa-Suez-Aqaba, under Turkish control. The British, however, objected strongly to any Turkish presence in Sinai, and Muhtar Pasha, on behalf of the Turks, then proposed a compromise partition, a straight line down Sinai from al-ʿArīsh to Ras Muhammad, just south of Sharm al-Sheikh. A Turkish sketch map in the Yildiz Palace papers, now in the archives of the Prime Minister's office in Istanbul, shows two lines, one marked as the border on the map given to Muḥammad ʿAli in 1841, the other as the compromise line proposed by Muhtar Pasha.[11] The former line, running from north of al-ʿArīsh to Suez, reappears in a map published in 1926 by the Egyptian Foreign Ministry and obtained from Turkey. This publication was apparently later withdrawn from circulation.[12] In the event, the Turks yielded to a British ultimatum, issued with

French and Russian support, whereby the frontier was fixed at the point where it remained until 1948.

At the northern end, the frontier of Egypt was shifted some twenty miles east from al-ʿArīsh to Rafa; in the south a Turkish officer, Rüshdi Bey, managed to hold on to the head of the Gulf of Aqaba, denying it to British-Egyptian rule and thus preserving it for Palestine, Jordan, and Israel in a then inconceivable future.[13] During the dispute, the Egyptian nationalists favored the Turks against the British and thus ultimately against themselves. At the time, it seemed to them more important not to

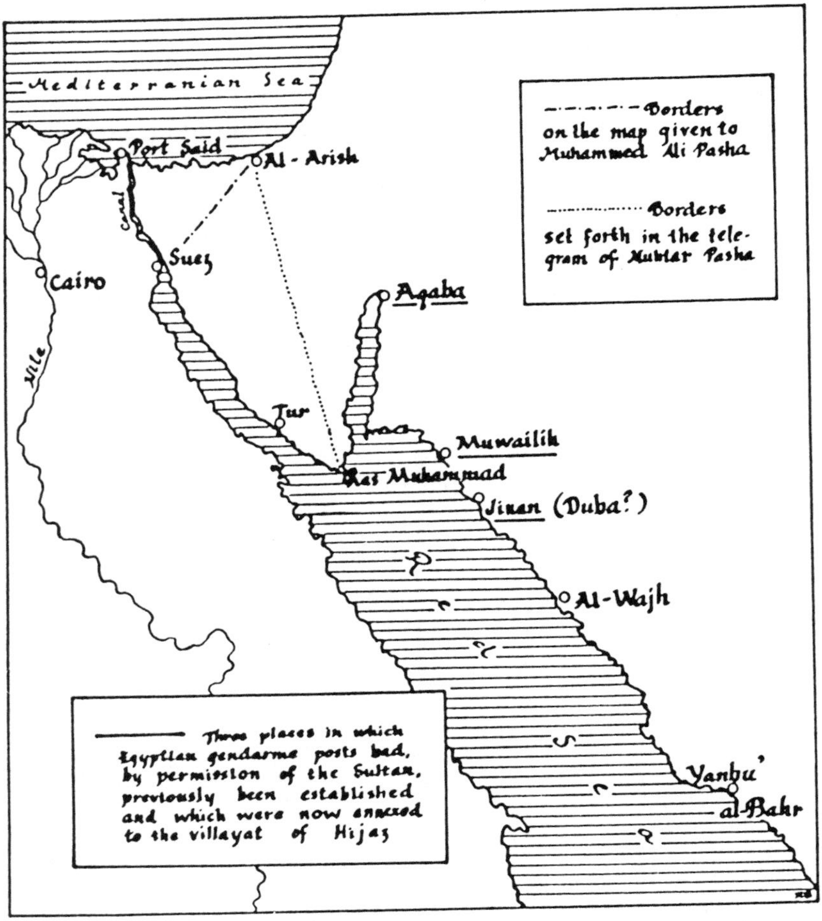

extend British influence at Muslim expense. In the north and east there were no frontiers until Palestine as a political concept re-emerged in the aftermath of the First World War. It became a reality in the post-war settlements.

With much wrangling, delimitation of the frontiers proceeded through three stages. In the first of these, the area was called Occupied Enemy Territory Administration South. This lasted from 1918 to 1920 when, after the San Remo agreement, a civil administration was established which continued until 1923. This, in turn, was replaced by the British Mandate approved by the League of Nations.

A preliminary Franco-British Convention was signed in December 1920, containing a preliminary definition of "the French Mandate of Syria and the Lebanon on the one hand and the British mandates of Mesopotamia and Palestine on the other. . . ." Palestine at that time included both banks of the Jordan. Under the terms of this convention a commission was set up which worked for some time on the terrain and submitted its report in February 1922. The agreement was finally signed between Britain and France in March 1923. Between the 1920 and 1923 agreements, a few small changes were made—small, but in the light of subsequent events important. Their purpose usually was to avoid splitting village lands or estates, and allocation of a district to one side or the other was frequently determined by the place of residence of the local large landowner. Thus the western Golan Heights, including the Quneitra triangle, were transferred to Syria from Palestine, to which they had been assigned in the 1920 agreement, in order to avoid splitting the property of the Amīr Maḥmūd al-Fawr al-Faḍl, a landowner and Bedouin sheik; similarly, the lands south of Lake Tiberias were transferred from Syria to Palestine because their owner, ʿAbbās Efendi, resided in Haifa. In the meantime, the border between Western Palestine and the newly created principality of Transjordan was fixed by British officials.

On 29 November 1947 the General Assembly of the United Nations adopted a resolution approving the partition of mandatary Palestine into three components: a Jewish state, an Arab state, and an international zone. As the Mandate came to an end, the Jews began to form their state; the Palestinian Arab leaders and the Arab governments rejected the partition resolution and went to war to prevent its implementation. The ensuing military operations led to a new, de facto partition in which the new Jewish state, called Israel, occupied a part of mandatary Palestine, larger than the area assigned in the partition resolution, and the rest was divided between three Arab states. Gaza and the Gaza Strip were held and administered by Egypt, the little town of Al-Ḥamma on the Sea of Galilee by Syria, and the West Bank, with East Jerusalem and points south, by Jordan. The Egyptians did not annex the Gaza Strip but administered it as occupied Palestine. Al-Ḥamma was treated as part of Syria. In the spring of 1950 the Jordanians formally annexed the areas under their rule and conferred full citizenship on the inhabitants, who were declared to be Jordanians. Indeed, the Jordanian nationality law offered Jordanian citizenship on request to all citizens of the former mandatary Palestine.

The lines dividing Israel from her neighbors were ceasefire lines, subsequently regularized as 'Armistice Demarcation Lines' in four conventions signed by the parties between February and July 1949. The wording of the conventions—ironically, on Arab insistence—makes it clear that these lines are not frontiers. Thus, the earliest of the four, the Israel-Egypt convention, signed 24 February 1949, states: "The Armistice Demarcation Line is not to be construed in any sense as a political or territorial boundary and is delineated without prejudice to rights, claims and positions of either Party to the Armistice as regards ultimate settlement of the Palestine question" (Article V, Sub-Section 2). Similar reservations appear in two of the other conventions. The Jordanian convention, signed 3 April 1949, reads: "The provisions of this article shall not be interpreted as prejudicing, in any sense, an ultimate political settlement between the Parties to this Agreement. The Armistice Demarcation Lines defined in Articles V and VI of this Agreement are agreed upon by the Parties without prejudice to future territorial settlements or boundary lines or to claims of either Party relating thereto" (VI, SS. 8, 9). The Syrian convention of 20 July 1949, is more emphatic: "It is emphasized that the following arrangements for the Armistice Demarcation Line between the Israeli and Syrian armed forces and for the Demilitarized Zone are not to be interpreted as having any relation whatsoever to ultimate territorial arrangements affecting the two Parties to this Agreement" (V, SS. 1). Only the Lebanese convention, signed 23 March 1949, departs from the pattern: "The Armistice Demarcation Line shall follow the international boundary between the Lebanon and Palestine" (V, SS. 1).

The Palestine entity, formally established and defined by Britain, was formally abolished in 1948 with the termination of the Mandate. The subsequent history of the idea of Palestine is another story.

An Ode against the Jews

13

Little is known of the life of Abū Isḥāq.[1] His name is given as Abū Isḥāq Ibrāhīm b. Masʿūd b. Saʿīd al-Tujībī al-Ilbīrī. Tujībī indicates that he was descended from the famous Arab family of Tujīb, which played a role of some importance in the history of Muslim Spain; Ilbīrī suggests that he came from Elvira. He appears to have been born towards the end of the tenth century and probably moved to Granada, along with the rest of the inhabitants of Elvira, when that city was sacked by the Ṣanhāja Berbers during the insurrection of 1010. In 1012 Zāwī b. Zīrī, the founder of the Berber Zirid dynasty, made Granada his capital.

A jurist by training, Abū Isḥāq served as secretary to the *qāḍī* of Granada and also acted as a teacher. His career coincided with the reign of Bādīs b. Ḥabbūs (reigned 1038–1073), the Zirid monarch who was the patron of Samuel ibn Nagrella, known in Jewish literature as Ha-Nagīd, and of his son Joseph. At some point Abū Isḥāq seems to have fallen foul of authority; by order of Bādīs he was banished from Granada and went to live in a convent called Rābiṭat al-ʿUqāb, in the Sierra de Elvira. According to Ibn al-Khaṭīb, he was banished because of the slanders of the Jewish minister Joseph ibn Nagrella, but a poem which Abū Isḥāq composed at al-ʿUqāb suggests that other influences may have been at work:

I settled there and it dispelled my troubles,
and soothed me, and I did not feel estranged there.
Though there are many wolves around it, yet
I find the wolf less dangerous than the jurist (faqīh)

Nor do I regret the absence of any brother, for
I have seen that a man's ruin comes on him from his brother.
What has made me despair of our times is that
honor does not go to the honorable.[2]

From these verses it would seem that Abū Isḥāq blamed his misfortunes on co-religionists and colleagues—on brother Muslim jurists, rather than on Jews. Later, however, he turned his anger against these and composed his famous *qaṣīda*, or ode, attacking Joseph ibn Nagrella in particular and the Jews of Granada in general. He lived long enough to witness, and presumably approve, the death of Ibn Nagrella and of many other Jews in Granada on 30 December 1066, and he himself died shortly after, in 1067.

The poem was first made known to modern scholarship by the Dutch orientalist Reinhart Dozy, who found a biography of Abū Isḥāq, including this and some other poems, in a Berlin manuscript of the *Iḥāṭa fī ta'rīkh Gharnāṭa*, by the fourteenth-century Granadan author Ibn al-Khaṭīb, and published the Arabic text of this passage, with a French translation.[3] This was used by Heinrich Graetz[4] and subsequent Jewish historians. The poem, with some lines omitted, appears again in another work by Ibn al-Khaṭīb, the *A'māl al-a'lām fī man būyi'a qabl al-iḥtilām min mulūk al-Islām.*[5] A unique manuscript of Abū Isḥāq's *Dīwān*, preserved in the Escorial library, was published by E. García Gómez, with an introduction.[6] The anti-Jewish poem was reprinted and partially translated into English by A. R. Nykl[7] and again partially translated and analysed by M. Perlmann.[8]

The following is a new translation of the poem.

Go, tell all the Ṣanhāja[9]
the full moons of our time, the lions in their lair
The words of one who bears them love, and is concerned
and counts it a religious duty to give advice.[10]
Your chief has made a mistake
which delights malicious gloaters
He has chosen an infidel as his secretary
when he could, had he wished, have chosen a believer.

Through him, the Jews have become great and proud
and arrogant—they, who were among the most abject
And have gained their desires and attained the utmost
and this happened suddenly, before they even realised it.[11]
And how many a worthy Muslim humbly obeys[12]
the vilest ape[13] *among these miscreants.*
And this did not happen through their own efforts
but through one of our own people who rose as their accomplice.[14]
Oh why did he not deal with them, following
the example set by worthy and pious leaders?
Put them back where they belong
and reduce them to the lowest of the low,
Roaming among us, with their little bags,[15]
with contempt, degradation and scorn as their lot,
Scrabbling in the dunghills for colored rags[16]
to shroud their dead for burial.
They did not make light of our great ones
or presume against the righteous,
Those low-born people would not be seated in society
or paraded[17] *along with the intimates [of the ruler].*
Bādīs! You are a clever man
and your judgment is sure and accurate.
How can their misdeeds be hidden from you
when they are trumpeted all over the land?
How can you love this bastard brood
when they have made you hateful to all the world?
How can you complete your ascent to greatness
when they destroy as you build?
How have you been lulled to trust a villain
and made him your companion—though he is evil company?
God has vouchsafed in His revelations
a warning against the society of the wicked.[18]
Do not choose a servant from among them
but leave them to the curse of the accurst!
For the earth cries out against their wickedness
and is about to heave and swallow us all.
Turn your eyes to other countries
and you will find the Jews there are outcast dogs.
Why should you alone be different and bring them near
when in all the land they are kept afar?

—You, who are a well-beloved king,
scion of glorious kings,
And are the first among men
as your forbears were first in their time.
I came to live in Granada
and I saw them frolicking there.
They divided up the city and the provinces
with one of their accursed men everywhere.
They collect all the revenues
they munch and they crunch[19]
They dress in the finest clothes
while you wear the meanest.
They are the trustees of your secrets
—yet how can traitors be trusted?
Others eat a dirham's worth, afar,
while they are near, and dine well.
They challenge you to your God
and they are not stopped or reproved.
They envelope you with their prayers[20]
and you neither see nor hear.
They slaughter beasts in our markets[21]
and you eat their trefa.[22]
Their chief ape has marbled his house
and led the finest spring water to it.
Our affairs are now in his hands
and we stand at his door.
He laughs at us and at our religion
and we return to our God.[23]
If I said that his wealth is as great
as yours,[24] *I would speak truth.*
Hasten to slaughter him as an offering,
sacrifice him, for he is a fat ram
And do not spare his people
for they have amassed every precious thing.
Break loose their grip and take their money
for you have a better right to what they collect.
Do not consider it a breach of faith to kill them
—the breach of faith would be to let them carry on.
They have violated our covenant with them
so how can you be held guilty against the violaters?
How can they have any pact[25]
when we are obscure and they are prominent?

Now we are the humble, beside them,
as if we had done wrong, and they right!
Do not tolerate their misdeeds against us
for you are surety for what they do.
God watches His own people
and the people of God will prevail.

Abū Isḥāq's verse tirade is of interest in two respects—as an example of the public and social function of poetry and as evidence on the position of a Jewish community in a medieval Muslim society.

According to a ninth-century Arabic author, poetry has four functions—to command, to forbid, to give information and to elicit it. These functions are discharged in eulogy, satire, elegy, apology, love-making, comparison, and "reports of happenings."[26]

The modern observer might describe many of these functions of the medieval poet as journalism, publicity, propaganda, public relations—even as broadcasting. Medieval Islamic society was, by comparison with contemporary Christian Europe, highly literate and sophisticated; the Arabs, at all times, have shown a unique skill in the art of words, a ready appreciation, and a swift response.[27] In such a society, information and image could be of great significance, and the success, even the survival of a ruler or minister might depend on their manipulation. Lacking the mass media which serve the present-day holder or seeker of power, the medieval had recourse to his poet who, in return for a consideration, produced a version of events, a statement of opinions, or an image of a person which was vivid, memorable, and conducive to his patron's requirements. Eulogy served to present the patron to the public in the most favorable light, satire to tarnish the images of his rivals and opponents. Politics, opinion, and news were not the only concerns of this kind of poetic journalism. The poet could also provide a social column, by celebrating or commemorating in verse the births, marriages, and deaths of the great; he could promote special interests of various kinds; he could even, in a prefigurement of the singing commercial, advertise goods for sale—and, anticipating another type of modern journalism, he could extort money by the threat of scurrilous abuse.[28]

The poet may seek to advance his own personal interests or those of a patron whom he serves or hopes to serve or those of a group or faction to which he feels himself to belong.[29] This group may be tribal or ethnic, religious or sectarian, political or personal—sometimes, though rarely, even local. Normally, the poet's aim is propagandist—that is to say, he seeks to influence men's opinions and attitudes, to persuade or dissuade, to win or divert their support. Sometimes, his aim is more direct and immediate—incitement to action rather than mere suasion. Probably the most famous instance recorded in Arabic historiography is the massacre of the Umayyad princes after the accession to power of the ʿAbbāsids. In several different versions, an inflammatory poem declaimed by a hostile poet is said to have been the cause of the massacre, or at least the signal for the killers to begin their work.[30]

Such stories are no doubt exaggerated and dramatized—but they do reflect an important aspect of the function of poetry and the poet in public life. The anti-Jewish *qaṣīda* of Abū Isḥāq is clearly intended to produce results and not merely to relieve the author's feelings. The form and style are noteworthy. The meter is short and sharp, the language simple and direct, the statements forceful and concrete—aimed at the Ṣanhāja Berber soldiery, who could not be expected to appreciate or even understand the intricate prosody, abstruse vocabulary, elaborate imagery, and recondite allusions that were customary in formal Arabic poetry.[31] This time Abū Isḥāq wanted to be understood by a wide public—and it seems that he got what he wanted.

Abū Isḥāq, says Ibn al-Khaṭīb, brought about the destruction of Joseph ibn Nagrella, by means of "a poem, which was memorized, in which he incited the Ṣanhāja against him . . . so that they killed him, and also attacked his people."[32] "This *qaṣīda*," he concludes, "was the cause of their extirpation."[33]

The rather vague statements of Ibn al-Khaṭīb have been taken to mean that the poem was the immediate cause of the outbreak in which Joseph ibn Nagrella and thousands of his co-religionists perished.[34] This seems unlikely. The Jewish accounts of the massacre make no mention of Abū Isḥāq or his poem;[35] neither do the earlier Arabic sources, which give a more detailed account of the outbreak, explaining the circumstances in which it occurred, without reference to the poet agitator.[36] The story that the poem was the direct and immediate cause may be dismissed as dramatic exaggeration of a familiar kind; it may however safely be assumed that this piece of verse propaganda, with its fierce and plain appeal to hate, envy, and violence, will have helped powerfully to prepare the way.

Abū Isḥāq speaks for himself, not a patron. His immediate objective was a powerful Jewish statesman against whom he appears to have had a personal grudge, and Dozy and García Gómez are probably right in attributing his rage to frustrated personal ambition.[37] But his invective and his accusation are aimed at the Jews in general, not merely at Ibn Nagrella as an individual; and it is upon the Jews as such that he invokes the vengeance and punishment of the outraged Muslims.

Outrage is the dominant theme of the poem. In striking contrast to the anti-Judaism and anti-Semitism of Christendom, Abū Isḥāq does not deny the right of the Jews to life, livelihood, and the practice of their religion. On the contrary, he is well aware that these rights are legally guaranteed by the *dhimma,* the contract between the Muslim state and the tolerated non-Muslim communities to which it extends its protection and which are thence known as *dhimmīs.* Abū Isḥāq was, it will be recalled, a jurist. He does not seek to deny or to minimize the contract; indeed, even in his fury, he is at some pains to reassure his hearers (and no doubt himself) that in killing and robbing the Jews they will not be acting illegally, *i.e.,* violating the provisions of a contract sanctified by the Holy Law of Islam. The contract, he argues, has already been violated by the Jews and has therefore ceased to be operative. The Muslims and their ruler are therefore absolved from their obligations under the contract and are free to attack, kill, and expropriate the Jews, without illegality—*i.e.,* without sin.

Abū Isḥāq indicates how, in his judgment, the Jews have broken the contract. In the simplest terms, they have failed to keep their proper place—to remain in the station which is assigned to them. The law relating to the *dhimma* makes it clear that the protected communities must recognize the primacy of Islam and the Muslims of this world as well as the next and must accept certain fiscal disabilities and social limitations, in token of their submission. These conditions are specified in the law-books but were in general not very strictly enforced by Muslim governments. In contrast to the treatment of parallel problems in

Christian countries, in Islam practice was usually more tolerant than precept, and Christians and Jews enjoyed greater rights and opportunities than would have been accorded to them with the strict enforcement of the law.[38]

There was nevertheless a very definite feeling that the non-Muslim communities had their place and should not be allowed to exceed it. Abū Isḥāq makes clear, if with some exaggeration, what that place was to be. Diatribes like his, and massacres like that of Granada in 1066, are of very rare occurrence in Islamic history. When they do occur, the circumstances are almost invariably the same. Members of a minority community, sometimes Jews, more often Christians, have waxed rich and powerful; they are accused of flaunting their wealth and abusing their power and thus forfeit their rights and bring retribution on themselves.[39] The word most commonly used of the Jews is *dhull,* which means "humility, abasement,"[40] and Abū Isḥāq clearly expected his Jews to remain poor, humble, and degraded. In practice, considerable latitude was allowed to Jews, as to other minority groups, but too striking and visible a departure from the approved condition of *dhull* was apt to arouse popular anger.

The position of Jews and Christians under traditional Muslim rule certainly fell a long way short of the inter-faith utopia imagined by modern romantics and apologists, but it was one which enabled them to survive and at times to flourish. To the modern ear, "second-class citizen" has a harsh and evil sound—yet second-class citizenship which is rooted in tradition, respected by law and custom and effectively maintained, is better than first-class citizenship on paper only. Constitutional rights, in countries where such concepts have little meaning, are a poor substitute for entrenched privileges. To the citizen of a liberal democracy, the status of *dhimmī* would no doubt be intolerable—but to many minorities in the world today, that status, with its communal autonomy and its limited yet recognized rights, might well seem enviable.

The Sultan, the King, and the Jewish Doctor

14

One of the most popular motifs in the saga of Maimonides as a Jewish culture hero is the story of how he was invited to go and treat the King of England, Richard Lionheart, who had gone to Palestine with the Third Crusade—and refused the invitation. This story, which appears in almost every biography of Maimonides and in most popular histories of the Jews, assumes several forms. The simplest version merely states that on some occasion King Richard sought the services of Maimonides as a physician. Others develop this into an offer of employment as body-physician, sometimes with the further suggestion that Maimonides accompany the King back to London. The reason given for his refusal is, usually, his satisfaction with his court post in Cairo, sometimes also disquiet about conditions in London.[1]

The birth, growth, and luxuriance of this story provide a curious and instructive example of the methods and validity of popular historiography. It derives from a single source—the *Ta'rīkh al-Ḥukamā'*, or *History of Physicians,* of the Egyptian Muslim writer Jamāl al-Dīn Abu'l-Ḥasan ʿAlī ibn Yūsuf al-Qifṭī (1172–1248). He was born in Qifṭ, in upper Egypt, to a family of scholars and officials. When he was fifteen years old his father was appointed first assistant to the chief minister al-Qāḍī al-Fāḍil, the patron and benefactor of Maimonides. Later his family moved to Palestine and after many travels al-Qifṭī eventually settled in Aleppo, where he remained until his death. Among his closest friends there was the Jewish physician Joseph ibn Yaḥyā ibn Shimʿōn, a pupil of Maimonides, who may possibly be identical with the famous Joseph ibn ʿAqnīn. Al-Qifṭī thus had the opportunity of collecting information for the biography of Maimonides which he included in his book. This work, a biographical dictionary of physicians, was written between 1230 and 1235. The full text is unfortunately lost, but an abridgment made by Muḥammad ibn ʿAlī al-Zawzanī about a year after al-Qifṭī's death has survived. An edition of the Arabic text did not appear until 1903,[2] and the work has not yet, so far as I am aware, been translated into any European language. The passage relating to Maimonides, however, became known to European scholarship very much earlier, when the Maronite scholar Casiri (Al-Ghazīrī) published the Arabic text, together with a Latin translation, in his catalog of the Arabic manuscripts in the Escorial library, printed in Madrid in 1760.[3] This Latin version was used by Heinrich Graetz and other nineteenth-century writers on Maimonides.

The relevant passage in al-Qifṭī's text may be rendered as follows:

> . . . He left Spain and travelled to Egypt with his family, and settled in the town of Fusṭāṭ, among the Jews there. He revealed his religion publicly and lived in the quarter called al-Maṣīṣa. He earned a living by dealing in precious stones and the like, and people studied philosophy under him. This was in the last days of the Egyptian ʿAlid dynasty. They wanted to employ him among the other physicians and to send him out to the king of the Franks in Ascalon, who asked them for a physician. They chose him, but he refused this service and refrained from participating in this affair. And when the Ghuzz ruled in Egypt and the dynasty of ʿAlī collapsed, the Qāḍī al-Fāḍil ʿAbn al-Raḥīm b. ʿAlī al-Baysānī took him under his wing and showed him favor and assigned a salary to him.[4]

Since Casiri's Latin version has, directly or indirectly, formed the basis of most subsequent writing on the subject, it may be useful to quote that part of it that deals with the Frankish king:

> Interea Philosophicas disciplinas publice praecepit; adeoque in Medicorum album adscriptus, & Francorum Regis *Ascaloniae* ipsum maxime optantis Medicus electus est: quod tamen munus & honorem omnino recusavit.

It will be noted that Casiri's translation is rather different in form and emphasis from the original. Moreover, both his text and translation omit the important phrase: وذلك في أواخر أيام الدولة المصرية العلوية — "This was in the last days of the Egyptian ʿAlid dynasty."[5]

From this reference back to the primary source, several important points emerge:

1. The name of the Frankish king is not given.
2. There is nothing to show whether permanent employment or merely a visit was involved.
3. There is no suggestion whatever of accompanying the Frankish king back to his own country in Europe.
4. No reason is given for Maimonides' refusal.
5. No date is given for the episode, but there is a strong implication that it took place early in Maimonides' career in Egypt—before the fall of the Fāṭimids in 1171 and before he had established himself as a successful physician in Cairo.

Who then was the Frankish king? Casiri, assuming that the incident took place during the first Frankish occupation of Ascalon (1153–1187), contents himself with noting that there are four possibilities—the four kings who reigned in the Latin kingdom of Jerusalem in that period. Graetz seems to have been the first to assert that it was Richard Lionheart and was sufficiently confident of this identification to incorporate it, without qualification, in the text of his narrative, where we read:

> Maimuni's Ruf war so gross, dass ihn der englische König Richard Löwenherz, die Seele des dritten Kreuzzuges, zu seinem Leibarzte ernennen wollte. Maimuni schlug aber diesen Antrag aus.[6]

In a footnote to this sentence Graetz cites the Latin version of al-Qifṭī, and remarks:

> Dieser מלך אלפרנג בעסקלאן kann nur Richard Löwenherz bedeuten, welcher Askalon wieder aufbauen liess und zum Stützpunkte für die kriegerischen Unternehmungen gegen Jerusalem machte.

It will be seen that Graetz is not responsible for the invitation to London, which would seem to be a gloss by Yellin and Abrahams to Graetz's hypothesis, nor did he put forward any of the reasons later adduced for Maimonides' refusal. He did make, however, with a confidence which I hope to show was quite unjustified, the identification of the unnamed Frankish king with Richard Lionheart and also introduced two other elements to the story for which the original source provides no foundation.

We may at once set aside Graetz's assumption that it was Maimonides' reputation that led King Richard to wish to appoint him as his physician. From our text it seems clear that the Frankish king merely asked for *a* physician and that it was "they"—the authorities in Cairo—who chose Maimonides. It has already been pointed out that the text speaks merely of sending a physician and says nothing whatever of an appointment as body-physician. This, too, therefore must be set aside as pure imagination.

Nor, despite Graetz's confidence and the repetition of so many subsequent writers, is there any certainty—or even likelihood—that the Frankish king in question was really Richard Lionheart.

If we accept the authenticity of al-Qifṭī's narrative—on which the whole story rests—then the episode must have taken place between two dates: 1165, when Maimonides arrived in Egypt, and 1192, when under the peace-terms signed in that year Richard withdrew from Ascalon and the fortress was demolished. From the wording of al-Qifṭī's narrative there is, moreover, a strong probability that the limits must be drawn more narrowly. "This was in the last days of the Egyptian Fatimid dynasty. *They* wanted to employ him among the other physicians and to send him out to the king of the Franks in Ascalon, who asked *them* for a physician. *They* chose him, but he refused. . . ." The identity of the "they" who did these things is not quite clear from the text, but it would seem that these events took place before the coming of the Ghuzz. Max Meyerhof assumed that it was the Fāṭimid court, and therefore inferred that Maimonides was already a court-physician under the last Fāṭimid Caliph, al-ʿĀḍid.[7] Claude Cahen has taken it to be the guild of physicians in Cairo, to whom, he assumed, such a request would have been referred.[8] In either case the text would seem to make it fairly clear that it was under the Fāṭimids that "they" wanted to employ Maimonides, that it was under the Fāṭimids that a request was received from the Frankish king for a physician, and that "they" chose Maimonides to go to him. If we accept this, then the *terminus ad quem* for the incident is the year 1171, when the Fāṭimid dynasty was finally overthrown by Saladin—twenty years before King Richard Lionheart set foot in the Holy Land. Meyerhof, in a passing allusion, did in fact place the incident in the Fāṭimid period and suggested that the Frankish king was probably Amalric.

This is, however, not in itself conclusive. The text that we possess of al-Qifṭī's work is not the original but a later abridgment. Though al-Qifṭī was in general an accurate and conscientious scholar, his biography of Maimonides does contain some errors, and it is therefore just conceivable that the story of the request from the Frankish king in Ascalon, though authentic in itself, has fallen out of its proper place in the chronological sequence. We may therefore, for the time being, retain Richard Lionheart, together with other later kings, as possible candidates, though their candidature will seem weak in comparison with that of the Frankish king who came to Ascalon before the fall of the Fāṭimid Caliphate in 1171.

At this point it may be useful to digress briefly in order to review the history of the town of Ascalon in this period. It first came into prominence in the year 1099, when, after the capture of Jerusalem by the Crusaders, the retreating Egyptian army entered and held Ascalon. For the next half-century it was an Egyptian fortress and was used by them as a bridgehead and a base for raids into the Frankish-held territory in Palestine. With its population swollen by Muslim refugees from the areas conquered by the Crusaders and with its garrison maintained and regularly reinforced from Egypt, it became a major military center and a key objective in the struggle between the Crusaders and the Muslim rulers of Egypt. The Crusaders, gravely perturbed by Egyptian raids from Ascalon, built a ring of fortresses round it to neutralize the threat which it offered to Jerusalem. Finally, in 1153, after a siege of seven months, the Crusaders captured the town by a combined sea and land attack.

Having previously been a base of Egyptian action against the Franks, it now became a springboard for Frankish political and military adventures in Egypt. The Fāṭimid Caliphate was tottering to its end, and the rival viziers who disputed for power in Cairo, in their desperate struggle for allies, had no hesitation in calling on Frankish as well as Muslim help from Syria. In the sixties of the twelfth century the Crusaders were even able to exact an annual tribute from Cairo, and on two occasions, in 1164 and 1167, the King of Jerusalem, Amalric, led an army of Crusaders into Egypt, ostensibly to come to the rescue of the vizier or the Caliph. A third Frankish expedition set out in December 1168, but this time the rival Egyptian factions joined forces and compelled the Franks to withdraw. Thereafter, with the consolidation of Saladin's power, the Crusaders fell back on the defensive, and in 1187, after their defeat by Saladin at the decisive battle of Ḥaṭṭīn, they were compelled to surrender Ascalon, together with most of their other strongholds in Palestine, to the victorious leader of the Muslim counter-Crusade.

The second, and very brief, Frankish occupation was a result of the Third Crusade. After his defeat at Arsūf in 1191, Saladin found himself unable to hold Ascalon against Richard Lionheart. He therefore destroyed the town and evacuated its population. Richard arrived at the desolate site in January 1192, and at once began work on rebuilding the fortress. He demolished it and withdrew, in accordance with the peace terms signed in the autumn of the same year. A third occupation by the Franks in the thirteenth century does not concern us, as it took place after Maimonides' death.[9]

Within the wider period determined by the arrival of Maimonides in Egypt and the withdrawal of Richard Lionheart from Ascalon, four kings reigned over the Latin kingdom of Jerusalem: Amalric (1163–1174), Baldwin IV (1174–1185), Baldwin V (1185–1186), and Guy de Lusignan (1186–1192). To these we may add two other names: Count Raymond III of Tripoli, who acted as Regent of the kingdom from 1174 to 1177 and again in 1185–1186 and might easily have been described as king *(malik)* by a Muslim author; and, finally, King Richard Lionheart of England.

Of all six candidates Richard Lionheart is the least likely. He is the latest of them and came to Ascalon at a time when Maimonides was already an established and celebrated figure in Cairo—yet both the wording of al-Qifṭī's text and the inherent probabilities of the situation imply that the incident took place when Maimonides was an unknown newcomer. Richard, newly arrived from the West, would be less likely than the acclimatized Syrian Franks to seek the services of an Eastern physician. His stay in Ascalon was brief, lasting only a few months—and most of that time he was engaged in active hostilities against the Muslims.

Finally, Richard was well-known to Arabic historiography under the name of al-Inkitār ("the king of England") and is therefore less likely than a king of Jerusalem to be described simply as "the king of the Franks."

In August 1192 King Richard fell sick, probably of typhus fever. This illness is mentioned both by Richard's biographer Richard of Devizes and by Saladin's secretary and biographer Bahā' al-Dīn. Both of them agree that the Muslim leaders took a sympathetic interest in Richard's welfare; Richard of Devizes tells a story, probably apocryphal, of how Saladin's brother al-ʿĀdil came to visit him and commiserate with him; Bahā' al-Dīn says that Richard kept on sending messengers to Saladin to ask for fruit and snow, for which he craved in his fever. "The Sultan," says Bahā' al-Dīn, "granted him this, hoping to obtain intelligence through the relays of messengers."[10]

It was no doubt of this occasion, though he does not specifically mention it, that Graetz was thinking when he assumed a request from Richard to Cairo for the services of a physician. The fact remains, however, that although Richard's sickness is discussed by both Frankish and Muslim sources, none of them, to my knowledge, gives any hint of any such request—an omission which is the more remarkable in view of the liking of the chroniclers for the theme of the mutual, chivalrous respect of Richard and Saladin and the friendly contacts between them.

Of the other kings, all had some connection with Ascalon. Amalric was often there and used it as the base for his expeditions to Egypt. Baldwin was present at the defense of Ascalon against Saladin in 1177. Guy de Lusignan held the fief of Ascalon before becoming king.

Of all the candidates, Amalric is by far the most probable. Already on the throne when Maimonides arrived in Egypt, he continued to reign for three years after the deposition of the last Fāṭimid Caliph and is thus the only one who would qualify for consideration if, as seems most likely, we must place the incident between 1165 and 1171.

There are other arguments to support this identification. Amalric, unlike any of the others, was active in Egyptian affairs and took part in an Egyptian civil war, in alliance with one of the Egyptian factions. The period of his political and military association with the vizier Shāwar provide the likeliest set of circumstances when such an invitation from the Muslim authorities in Cairo to attend a Frankish king in Ascalon might have been issued.

That the Franks established in Syria and Palestine respected the superior medical knowledge of the East and at times consulted Eastern physicians is in general known from other sources. In the particular case of Amalric, we have actual references to two such consultations. One of them is the story told by William of Tyre, of how when Amalric was dying he called for physicians "of the Greek, Syrian, and other nations noted for skill in diseases."[11] It is conceivable that this was the occasion when Maimonides' services were sought, though it should be noted that this death-bed consultation took place three years after the end of the Fāṭimid Caliphate.

On the whole it seems more likely that the incident was connected with Amalric's Egyptian adventure. For this we find indirect confirmation in a story related by the author of another biographical work on physicians, the Syrian Ibn Abī Uṣaybi'a (1203–1270). Speaking of the Christian physician Abū Sulaymān Da'ūd, born in Jerusalem but resident in Egypt, he says:

> The physician Rashīd al-Dīn Abū Ḥalīqa, the son of al-Fāris, the son of this Abū Sulaymān, told me when King Amalric came to Egypt he was astonished at my grandfather's medical skill, and asked the Caliph for him. Then he took him and his five children to Jerusalem. . . .[12]

The pious Rashīd al-Dīn's attribution of Amalric's choice to his wonderment at Abū Sulaymān's skill is strikingly reminiscent of Graetz's story of Maimonides' fame reaching Richard Lionheart. Perhaps the two may be explained as examples of the same kind of ancestral piety. What seems most likely is that Amalric simply asked for a doctor—and got Abū Sulaymān Da'ūd. May we guess that on this occasion Maimonides was asked, and refused, and that Abū Sulaymān was then asked—and accepted? The Jew might well have hesitated before placing his life in the hands of the Crusaders. The expatriate Christian need have had no fear of returning to his native city under Christian rule.

Amalric went twice to Egypt, in 1164 and 1167. Ibn Abī Uṣaybi'a does not say on which of the two occasions Abū Sulaymān was invited. If the occasion was the same as that described by al-Qifṭī, then it must have been the second visit. In 1164 Maimonides had not yet arrived in Egypt. In 1167 he had been there for two years.

One final question may now be considered—that of Maimonides' service with Saladin. Several of the modern writers who have told this story assert that, after becoming the physician of al-Qāḍı al-Fāḍil, Maimonides also won the favor of Saladin, who appointed him as his court- and body-physician. Some even adduce this appointment as the reason for his refusal of Richard's invitation.

If, as has been suggested, the Frankish king in question was Amalric, then it will be obvious that neither Saladin nor al-Qāḍī al-Fāḍil can have played any part in the story, since neither of them achieved a position of power or eminence until several years later. It may be that Maimonides was already at that time a court-physician to the last Fāṭimid Caliph, as has been suggested by Meyerhof; but this is purely a hypothesis based on an interpretation of a line in al-Qifṭī's text.

There is no doubt that at a later stage Maimonides served as physician to al-Qāḍī al-Fāḍil, who was his friend and patron and who enjoyed great power as the chief minister of Saladin. It also seems fairly certain that in his last years Maimonides attended patients in the royal household, as he says himself in his letter to Samuel ibn Tibbon, dated 30 September 1199:

> The Sultan lives in Cairo and I live in Fusṭāṭ, a distance of two Sabbath-days journey. Every morning I must call on the Sultan, and if he, or one of his children, or one of his wives is sick, I spend the whole day there. Even when there is nothing special I never get home before the afternoon. . . .[13]

But Saladin himself had left Egypt in 1174 and again, finally, in 1182. Was Maimonides ever in his personal service?

The story of Maimonides' service with Saladin, unlike that of his invitation by Richard Lionheart, does at least rest on an early text. It occurs in one of the earliest biographical notices on Maimonides—that of Ibn Abī Uṣaybiʿa, a contemporary and colleague of Maimonides' son Abraham. Ibn Abī Uṣaybiʿa, in the course of a very laudatory account of Maimonides, says: "The Sultan al-Malik al-Nāṣir (that is, Saladin) held him in high regard, and was attended medically by him. So, too, was his son al-Malik al-Afḍal."[14]

That Maimonides was a court-physician under the successor of Saladin is confirmed by other sources, not least by Maimonides himself. Neither he, however, nor any other early source alludes to service with Saladin, and it is difficult to believe that so distinguished a patient would have escaped mention either by Maimonides—who was not averse to speaking of his professional successes—or by his admirers.

Ibn Abī Uṣaybiʿa's book was first published in 1884. His remarks on Maimonides were, however, briefly cited, in a French translation by Silvestre de Sacy in 1810,[15] and again used in 1840 by Wüstenfeld, who incorporated the Saladin story in his own account of Maimonides.[16] From these sources the story was repeated by many later authors.

It is, however, almost certainly untrue. The first to doubt it was Graetz, who points out that it is in effect contradicted by Maimonides' letter to Ibn ʿAqnīn.[17] In this letter, written some years after Saladin had left Egypt, Maimonides speaks with satisfaction of his successful practice among the great: "I must tell you that in the practice of medicine I have achieved much fame among the great, such as the chief judge, the amīrs, the house of al-Fāḍil, and other great ones of the city. . . ."[18]

The implication of the passage would seem to be that this success is fairly recent—and, moreover, it contains no allusion to a court appointment. The letter is dated *Marheshvan* 1503 Sel. (October 1191). As Munk, the editor of the letter, pointed out,[19] the date must be erroneous, and most subsequent authorities have agreed on an earlier date. The earliest would be 1187, when Ibn ʿAqnīn, to whom the letter is addressed, left Cairo. The most probable dates are 1187 or 1190. It would thus seem clear that Maimonides' appointment as an Ayyūbid court-physician must be placed some time between the letter to Ibn ʿAqnīn—when it had not yet happened—and the letter to Ibn Tibbon of 1199. It seems likely that the appointment took place towards the end of this period, since Saladin's son al-Afḍal, who is named as Maimonides' patron and to whom he dedicated a book, did not seize power in Egypt until 1198. In any case, the appointment must have taken place after Saladin's final departure from Egypt in 1182 and probably after his death in 1193.

Maimonides, the story-books tell us, the court-physician of Saladin in Cairo, was invited by Richard Lionheart but refused, preferring his appointment in Cairo. That Maimonides ever served Saladin rests on a single, unsupported statement, almost certainly untrue; that he was ever invited by Richard rests on a guess, almost certainly mistaken. The subsequent popularity of both are an interesting confirmation of the words of the great American poet Robert Frost:

A theory, if you hold it hard enough
And long enough, gets rated as a creed.

PART IV

TURKS AND TATARS

The Mongols, the Turks, and the Muslim Polity

15

Some thirty years ago a well-known Swiss writer on Middle Eastern affairs published an article on patriotism and nationalism among the Arabs. Discussing the attitude of nationalists to the past and their tendency to substitute fanciful constructions for serious history, he quotes "a high Syrian government official" as saying, "in deadly earnest": "If the Mongols had not burnt the libraries of Baghdad in the 13th century, we Arabs would have had so much science, that we would long since have invented the atomic bomb. The plundering of Baghdad put us back by centuries."[1]

This is of course an extreme, even a grotesque formulation, but the thesis which it embodies is not confined to, and was not invented by, romantic nationalist historians. Deriving ultimately from the testimony of contemporary sufferers, it was developed by European orientalists, who saw in the Mongol invasions the final catastrophe which overwhelmed and ended the great Muslim civilization of the Middle Ages. As the barbarians had destroyed the Roman Empire, it was thought, so the Mongols destroyed the Caliphate—except that the destruction was more terrible and more permanent, and the new masters, unlike the Germanic barbarians in Europe, could neither learn from others nor themselves create anything new. This judgment of the Mongols, sometimes extended to include the Turkish invaders who had preceded them out of the steppe, was generally accepted among European scholars and was gratefully, if sometimes surreptitiously, borrowed by romantic and apologetic historians in Middle Eastern countries as an explanation both of the ending of their golden age and of their recent backwardness. It was expressed with characteristic force by the famous English orientalist

Edward Granville Browne, who saw in the Mongol invasion "a catastrophe which . . . changed the face of the world, set in motion forces which are still effective, and inflicted more suffering on the human race than any other event in the world's history of which records are preserved to us."[2]

To Browne, writing in Cambridge in the early years of this century, it may well have seemed that the Mongol conquest was a calamity of unparalleled magnitude and that a civilization so stricken could never fully recover. But for the less innocent historians of a less tranquil age, the horrors of the past assumed a milder aspect. The great Russian orientalist V. V. Barthold, writing in Moscow in 1917, was able to achieve a more tolerant view of Mongol destructiveness and a more robust assessment of the recuperative powers of their victims.

> It would be a mistake, however, to consider that cultural life could only continue in these localities which had escaped the inroads of the Mongol troops. It is true that a cultured land had been conquered by a wild people still believing in the efficacy of human sacrifice. When a town was taken, except for the artisans who were needed by the conquerors, the inhabitants were sometimes subjected to total massacre. People, who had survived these horrible experiences, naturally thought that the country will [*sic*] not arise again for another thousand years. Influenced by the opinion of writers contemporary to that epoch, European scholars have believed that the Mongols dealt a heavier and more devastating blow to the cultural life of Asia and Eastern Europe than, for example, was dealt to the cultural life of Southern Europe by the Great Migration of Peoples. In reality, the results of the Mongol invasion were less annihilating than is supposed. . . . Besides a not numerous military contingent the Mongol Khans brought with them their cultured councillors [*sic*] who helped them to establish their rule and to apply to the new country that harmonious and well-constructed governmental and military organization which had been elaborated at the time of Chenghiz Khan himself.[3]

Since then, a more intimate experience of catastrophe on the one hand, and a deeper knowledge of Islamic history on the other, have confirmed some—though not all—of Barthold's insights. In our own time we have seen, in the heart of Europe, rulers and armies compared with whom the Mongol Khans and the Tatar hordes appear almost as angels of mercy—and we have seen the swift recovery of the lands they ravaged. Not all scholars would now fully accept Barthold's views on the benevolent and progressive character of Mongol rule. They were well received in Mongol, Tatar, and Turkish circles; others however have suggested some revisions, and among Russian scholars in particular there was at one time a sharp reaction against them and against what was called the "racialist-nationalist idealization of the Turco-Tatar nomads" by pan-Turkist writers. Professor I. P. Petrushevsky formally declared that Barthold's evaluation of the consequences of the Mongol invasions for the economic development of Iran and neighboring countries "cannot be accepted by Soviet historiography."[4] This statement is obviously prescriptive, not descriptive, and, like other such decisions recorded on behalf of Soviet historiography, may not be determined exclusively by the findings of historians and the evidence of the sources. A clue may be found in hostile allusions, without citation of authors or titles, to "pan-Turkists," *i.e.*, those who ascribe a common identity and purpose to the Turkic peoples inside and outside the USSR. Barthold is declared innocent of complicity in such villainy. His errors are attributed to his lack of Marxist discipline, not to sinister pan-Turkist motives. But even Professor Petrushevsky affirms that the processes of development, interrupted by the catastrophe of the thirteenth century, were resumed and completed in the fourteenth and concedes that Barthold had some reason to react against the one-sided presentation of the Mongols as destructive savages. Most scholars would now agree that the harmful effects of the Mongol conquests were not as great, as lasting, or even as extensive as was once thought.

The reconsideration of the impact of the Mongols on the Islamic world has been concerned with three periods—before, during, and after their irruption—and with three questions: what did they destroy, what did they achieve, and what did they leave behind them? The traditional answer to the first of these questions is that they destroyed the Caliphate, and with it the great Arabic-Islamic civilization that had flourished under its aegis. "Islam," says a contemporary Syrian historian, "has never suffered a greater and more decisive disaster than this,"[5] and other historians, of that and later ages, have shared this opinion. The destruction of the Caliphate, still, even in its decay, the legal center of Islam and the symbol of its unity, and the establishment of a heathen domination in the Islamic heartlands were indeed a bitter blow to Muslims, and it is not surprising that their anguish has echoed through the centuries. But the real significance of this act of destruction has been much exaggerated. The golden age of classical Islamic civilization had long since ended, and the Mongols conquered a society that was far advanced in decay. The Caliphs had lost most of their effective power, and by abolishing the Baghdad Caliphate the Mongols did little more than lay the ghost of something that was already dead. Even some modern nationalist historians, their perceptions sharpened by more recent reverses, have begun to appreciate this. "Some of us still believe," says Professor Constantine Zurayk, "that the attacks of the Turks and the Mongols are what destroyed the Abbasid Caliphate and Arab power in general. But . . . the fact is that the Arabs had been defeated internally before the Mongols defeated them. . . ."[6]

In another respect, too, the effects of the Mongol conquests have been exaggerated—in the extent and consequences of the material damage done by them. Certainly, the damage was great. The immediate blows of the Mongols, though no doubt trivial by modern standards, were terrible and overwhelming. Even the Persian historian Juvaynī, a servant and admirer of the Khans who sees in them the instruments of God's purpose, tells how they destroyed whole cities and massacred or deported their inhabitants. Their ravages were not confined to the cities; in many areas the extirpation of the military aristocracy, the death or flight of the peasantry, left vast lands untenanted, uncultivated, and unclaimed, often permanently abandoned to nomadic herdsmen. Recent studies have shown that the damage done by the Mongols to the economy of Persia was not limited to the actual destruction during the campaigns of conquest. The ill effects of depopulation and the neglect of irrigation works were aggravated by harsh and extortionate policies, which degraded and impoverished the peasants and set back the development of agriculture and of the rising feudal society of the immediately preceding period.[7]

Yet these effects, however terrible, were limited both in extent and duration. Egypt, which by this time had become and has ever since remained the chief center of Arab Islam, was never conquered by the Mongols and was thus only indirectly affected by their coming. Syria suffered only raids and, after the defeat of the Mongols by the Mamlūk army of Egypt at ʿAyn Jālūt in Palestine in 1260, was incorporated in the Egyptian Sultanate and protected by Mamlūk power from Mongol attack. Arab Africa was never invaded; Turkish Anatolia was long dominated by the Mongol state in Persia but suffered little direct interference and survived to cradle the last and greatest of the Islamic Empires—that of the Ottomans. Persia, indeed, was hard hit—but even here by no means the whole country was affected. In South Persia, the local dynasties submitted voluntarily to the Mongols, and their cities, not looted by the invaders, continued to flourish. Even in those parts of Persia which were actually overrun and devastated, there was some recovery, and before long some Persian cities were again centers of industry, trade, and culture.

Only in one country did the Mongol conquest leave permanent injuries—in Iraq, once the metropolitan province of the Caliphate. Here, as elsewhere, the immediate effect of the invasion was the breakdown of civil government; in Iraq this also meant the decline of the elaborate irrigation works on which the prosperity, even the life of the country depended. But whereas in Persia there was a partial recovery once the new regime was firmly in control, in Iraq there was hardly any.[8] The Mongol Il-Khans of Southwest Asia, like the Seljuks before them, made Persia, not Iraq, the center of their power; Tabriz, their residence, grew into a great and wealthy city. Even before the Mongol conquests, Iraq had lost much of her importance; the coming of the Mongols, the destruction of the Caliphate, and the emergence of new centers finally ended it. The Mongols conquered Persia and Iraq but failed to conquer Syria and Egypt; these, under the Mamlūk Sultans, formed the base of the most important Muslim military power of the day and the most dangerous adversary of the Il-Khans. Iraq now became an outlying frontier-province, abandoned to the destructive inroads of the Bedouin, who moved into the breaches made by the Mongols and, unlike them, did not pass on, but stayed. The valley of the Tigris and Euphrates was cut off from the Mediterranean lands by the Mongol-Mamlūk conflict; it was overshadowed by the rise of the new Persian center to which it was subordinated and outflanked by the flourishing Turkish states in Anatolia, now under Mongol suzerainty. Iraq could no longer serve as a channel for east–west trade, which now passed through two other, competing routes—the Mongol northern route, through Anatolia and Persia, and the Mamlūk southern route, through Egypt and the Red Sea. Bereft of the Caliphate and ruled by a Mongol governor, Baghdad could no longer be the center and the rallying point of Islam. This role passed to Cairo and later to Constantinople, leaving the fallen city of the Caliphs to centuries of stagnation and neglect.

The dethronement of Iraq and the partial devastation of Persia are the significant exceptions in the general picture of gradual recovery and renewed activity in the Muslim Middle East. Clearly, such a revival could not have been accomplished under the heel of destructive and unteachable savages, such as the Mongols of the conventional image. The opposite extreme is expressed, in a lyrical passage, by the Polish Altaist Wladyslaw Kotwicz.

> *Dans leur empire,* [he says] *les Mongols firent régner l'ordre et le droit, organisèrent une administration uniforme, entreprirent l'œuvre de reconstruction des pays en ruines, de relèvement de l'industrie et du commerce, développèrent des rapports culturels avec les territoires les plus reculés de l'ancien monde.*
>
> *Leur autorité énergique fit effectivement régner, sur la plus grande surface de cet ancien monde, une vraie* Pax mongolica.[9]

Even allowing for the natural affection of a Mongolist for the Mongols and for the revisions imposed by more recent research, there is a certain element of truth in this picture. Once the conquests, with their attendant horrors, were completed, the Mongols were quick to appreciate the advantages of peace and order, and the *pax mongolica* became a reality in their vast dominions.

Some beneficial effects of Mongol rule in Persia are discernible almost immediately. Once firmly established, the Khans brought a measure of security and stability. In contrast to barbarian Europe, there was no permanent reversion from a money economy to barter, from an urban to a rural way of life. The merchants raised their heads again, and the Il-Khans, for their own good reasons, gave them every encouragement. Their interest was more than that of the greedy savage who has learnt to tend instead of killing his dairy cattle—though even to learn that, in so short a time, would have been no small achievement. The Il-Khans gave active help to what they regarded as useful sciences, such as medicine, astronomy, and mathematics; after their conversion to Islam at the end of the thirteenth century, they extended their patronage to Islamic learning, and by the fourteenth century Muslim Khans were raising magnificent edifices for Islamic worship and scholarship.

In one respect the Mongol conquests actually brought some advantage to the lands of Islam—through the broadening of Muslim horizons. The Mongol world was not limited to the familiar Muslim lands of the Middle East and Central Asia. It included southern Russia and, most important of all, the Far East, with which Muslim Western Asia was now united for the first time in a single imperial system. In this way Persia was opened to Chinese influence, notably in art and technology. The Mongols also exposed the Muslims to other contacts, as Europeans seized the opportunity offered by their presence to explore the land and sea routes through Persia to China and India. The benefits of these journeys, it may be noted in passing, are more apparent in Europe than in the Middle East.

A good example of the wide outlook and interests of the Mongol era in Persia is the *Jāmiʿ al-tavārīkh,* the Assembly of Histories, by the Persian historian Rashīd al-Dīn (1247–1318). Rashīd al-Dīn was a Jewish convert to Islam, a physician, scholar, and minister, who was entrusted by the Il-Khans with the task of preparing a universal history. He assembled a team of collaborators and informants, including two Chinese scholars, a Buddhist hermit from Kashmir, a Mongol specialist on tribal tradition, and a Frankish monk, as well as a number of Persian scholars, and with their help composed a vast history of the world, from Ireland to China. In thus attempting a universal history, going beyond the confines of their own civilization and its accepted precursors, Rashīd al-Dīn and his colleagues anticipated European historical scholarship by half a millennium.

The Mongols, then, though they ravaged some of the lands of Islam and abolished the Baghdad Caliphate, did not destroy Islamic civilization, which was far advanced in the decline before they came and which, in new forms, rose again after their coming. But their advent marked the turning-point in a process of change which, in the course of time, transformed the whole pattern of society and government in the Middle East. The Mongols were relatively few in number; their direct rule in the Middle East was limited to the northern tier and to a brief period. They bequeathed neither a language nor a religion to the lands they conquered, and whether their dominion was "historically progressive" or "historically reactionary," as Soviet scholars of successive generations argued, its effects in either direction were exhausted within a century. Yet the historical instincts of those who, from contemporaries onwards, saw in the Mongol conquests the end of one era and the beginning of another, were fundamentally sound; their error was the common one of telescoping a long and complex evolution into a single dramatic event. The great change in medieval Islam cannot be understood only in terms of the brief episode of Mongol conquest and domination; it must be seen against a broader background, involving a longer period than the reign of the Khans and the movement of more numerous peoples than the Mongol tribesmen of Jenghiz and his heirs.

Professor Zurayk, it will be recalled, links the Turks with the Mongols as the invaders of the collapsing Arab Caliphate. The association is not new. "It is a remarkable thing," says a thirteenth-century Damascene chronicler, discussing the defeat of the Mongols by the Mamlūks at ʿAyn Jālūt, "that the Tatars were defeated and destroyed by men of their own kind, who were Turks."[10] Rashīd al-Dīn also links the two together. The Assembly of Histories begins, as one would expect, with "the present masters of the world." Volume I is in two parts, the first dealing with the steppe peoples in general, the second with Jenghiz Khan and his successors. The first, concerned with the divisions, genealogies, and legends of the tribes of the steppe, includes Turks as well as Mongols and in time became a source-book for Turkish heroic and historiographic myths. Even a Turkish tribal origin-myth, as Professor Hatto has remarked, is "fused with a wishful travesty of the saga of the more dazzling Mongols . . . at the poetic level of myth and folk-tale."[11]

The Turks and the Mongols were ethnically, culturally, and linguistically distinct; yet they had much in common. Both came into the Middle East from the steppe-lands of Central and Northeast Asia, where they shared a common way of life and were subject to similar influences. These affinities brought the Mongols closer to the Turks than to any of the other peoples they had conquered. Jenghiz Khan himself made use of Uygur Turkish advisers and ordered the adoption of the Uygur script for the Mongol language. The Mongols, few in number, leaned heavily on Turkish support in both war and government. In time, the Mongols in the Islamic lands were merged into the mass of their Muslim subjects and even lost their language, adopting various forms of Turkish in its place. The very name "Tatar," once that of a section of the Mongols, has for a long time been applied to the Turkish-speaking Muslim inhabitants of the territories that were once ruled by the Mongol Khans of the Golden Horde.

The great migrations of the steppe peoples into the Middle East began in the tenth century, when the Turkish tribes of Central Asia crossed the Jaxartes and began their march of conquest westwards. They ended in the period after the death of Timur or Tamerlane, the last of the great Turkish world-conquerors, in 1405. Even then, the trickle of Central Asian tribes continued for a while, until it was stopped by the double barrier of Safavid and Ottoman power on the plateaux of Iran and Anatolia.

In the establishment of Turkish power and the spread of Turkish customs over the lands of Islam, two periods are particularly significant. One was that of the Seljuk Great Sultans, who ruled for about a century from the conquest of Baghdad in 1055 to the death of Sultan Sanjar in 1157. The other was that of the Mongol conquests of the thirteenth century and the period of Mongol supremacy and influence that followed them.

The Seljuks had entered Islam as condottieri and had served various Muslim rulers, including the Ghaznavids, before they carved out an independent state of their own. They were devout and earnest Muslims, and, as their Russian historian has remarked, "it is quite natural that the first Saljuqids . . . were better Muslims than [the Ghaznavids] Maḥmūd and Mas'ūd, just as Saint Vladimir was a better Christian than the Byzantine Emperors."[12] They were also free Turks, with their roots in Central Asia and with memories both of the older Turkish kingdoms and of the tribal traditions of the Oghuz. We can point to many Turkish elements among the titles, ranks, and emblems of the Seljuk Sultanate; we can also see the first phases of a profound transformation of Islamic state and society, part of which must surely be attributed to the incursion of the steppe peoples.

The transformation is completed with the second and greater of the steppe Empires—that of the Mongols. Their rule, though of brief duration, was of great significance, for it was at this time that the main characteristics of the post-Mongol phase of Islamic government were formed. The first Mongol rulers of Persia were pagans—the first to rule over an important Islamic territory since the beginnings of Islam. Their system of government was avowedly non-Islamic—based on the so-called *Yasa* of Jenghiz Khan. This seems to have been a complex of Mongol rules and customs; it was held to be binding on the Khans themselves as well as on their subjects, both Mongols and others. Even after the conversion of the Il-Khans of Persia to Islam, the Mongol laws remained effective, and Mongol practices were only gradually and partially modified under the influence of Muslim administrative and legal traditions.

The Mongol influence was of course strongest in those areas where the rule of the Mongol Khans persisted—in Central Asia, in Persia, and in the territories of the Golden Horde in Russia. It was, however, by no means limited to these areas. The Syro-Egyptian Empire of the Mamlūks, though it escaped Mongol conquest, was profoundly influenced by the Mongol example and by the Mongol deserters and refugees who migrated to Egypt. During the thirteenth and fourteenth centuries the Mongols enjoyed the immense prestige of victory and conquest; they were in consequence imitated in warfare, even in dress—as Europe was imitated in the nineteenth and twentieth centuries. The Mamlūk amīr of thirteenth-century Egypt wore his Tatar coat and hat in much the same way and for much the same reasons as his modern equivalents wear fitted tunics and peaked caps. Both are alien to Islam—but both were the symbols of power and victory.

Far stronger than in Egypt was the Mongol influence in Turkish Anatolia. After conquering Persia, the Mongol horsemen had swept on to Mesopotamia and Anatolia, where they had dealt the Seljuk Sultanate of Rūm a blow from which it never recovered. After dragging out an attenuated existence for some fifty years, it finally disappeared at the beginning of the fourteenth century. Most of eastern and central Anatolia became subject to the Il-Khans of Persia and was ruled either by Mongol governors or by Turkish vassals. Even after the decline of Il-Khan power had permitted the development of local autonomies, the administrative and financial system which the Il-Khans had impressed on the country continued to function. It was still working under the Anatolian princes and survived to exercise a formative influence on the institutions of the Ottoman state.

After the death of the Il-Khan Abū Saʿīd in 1336, the Mongol dominions in the Middle East broke up, and a number of smaller states, ruled by Mongol or Turkish dynasties, appeared in Persia, Mesopotamia, and Anatolia. Those of Persia were of short duration. Farther east, Timur had succeeded in making himself ruler of the Mongol successor state in Central Asia. In 1380, already master of Transoxania, he invaded Persia and in the next seven years overran the whole of it. He twice defeated the Khan of the Golden Horde, raided India, annexed Iraq, and then overran Syria and exacted homage from the Mamlūk Sultan. In 1394 and 1400 he invaded Anatolia and in 1402 inflicted a crushing defeat on the Ottomans at the battle of Ankara, capturing the Ottoman Sultan Bayezid. He died in 1405 while preparing an invasion of China.

Timur was a Muslim from a Turcicized tribe—but he was proud to relate himself to the Mongol Imperial house by marrying a princess of the line of Jenghiz Khan. He led mixed Mongol and Turkish armies, in which the former were the dominant element but the latter the great majority. His career has been variously represented as a reaction of Islam against the Shamanism of the Mongol Khans and as the last convulsion of the Altaic invasion. Unlike the Khans of the earlier conquests Timur was, or claimed to be, a pious Muslim, and amid the enormous destruction he wrought he was careful to show deference to the places and personnel of the Islamic faith. But despite the noticeable Islamizing tendency, his system of government was still in the Mongol tradition. With his death, the great movement of the steppe peoples that had begun in the tenth century seems to have come to an end—though the infiltration of tribes continued and, what was more important, the penetration of nomads already in the Middle East into the structure of urban life and civilization.

Of the great changes that can be discerned in Islamic government and society during and after the invasions of the steppe peoples, how much can be attributed to the influence of the invaders? The question is by no means easy to answer. The Turks, after their conversion to Islam, had surrendered themselves to their new religion almost completely. Partly because of the simple intensity of the faith as they encountered it on the frontiers of Islam and heathendom, partly perhaps because their conversion to Islam at once involved them in Holy War against their own unconverted kinsmen beyond the borders, the Muslim Turks sank their national identity in Islam as the Arabs and Persians had never done.

Yet something of the Turkish past survived. The Turkish language, brought from Central Asia by the first migrants and invaders, lived on and emerged triumphant in a new Muslim dress. Turkish rulers, even in lands of old Islamic traditions, used titles and symbols of authority that go back to pre-Islamic Turkish antiquity. Even in the Ottoman Empire, the symbols of the bow and the arrow and the horsetail remain to commemorate the mounted archers from the steppe that had first crossed the rivers from Central Asia into the lands of Islam; the Altaic titles of Khan and Beg were used or conferred by a sovereign whose roots of power led back to the Mongol Khans as well as to the Sultans of Islam.

The persistence of these old Turkish titles and emblems, long after the Islamization of the Turks, symbolizes the survival, at a deeper level, of habits, practices, and beliefs inherited from an earlier age. The identification and evaluation of these survivals is however a task of no small difficulty. The evolution of Islamic and Persian notions and practices of government is well documented and has been fairly well studied. Those of the Turks, however, are still little known and have formed the subject of some dubious theorizing.

The attempt has been made by some historians to explain the whole structure of Ottoman administration in the Imperial age by reference to the nomadic herdsmen who invaded Anatolia in the eleventh century—rather as at one time a school of historians in Britain tried to trace the British parliamentary system to the alleged practices of primitive Germanic tribes. In avoiding fanciful and exaggerated hypotheses on steppe origins, we should not however fall into the opposite error of underrating them. Both the Turkish and the Mongolian dynasties that ruled over Islam during the formative period between the eleventh and fourteenth centuries were of steppe origin, and even when they had been long assimilated in the cities and river valleys of the Middle East, new waves of nomadic invaders from the steppe were still breaking into the lands of Islam and seeping into the apparatus of government. When the Mongol victories had brought a new aristocracy and a new law from the steppe, the Turks rediscovered their pride in their ancestors and in their ancestral way of life and sought more self-consciously after the emblems and prerogatives of a specifically Turkish sovereignty.

The cultural and political baggage of the steppe peoples when they entered the world of Islam was not limited to their own native inheritance. They had for long been in contact with other sedentary civilizations—for example, with the ancient, little-known but highly important Iranian cultures of Central Asia, the influence of which can be traced through pre-historic Iranian borrowings in the Turkic languages. Easier to observe, and more relevant to our present inquiry, is the influence of China—clearly visible on both the pre-Islamic Turks and the Mongols. It is from Chinese sources that we first hear of the Turks, as a tributary people among the barbarians beyond the northwest frontier of the Chinese Empire. The earliest Turkish records—the eighth-century Orkhon inscriptions—reveal profound Chinese influence and in a sense express a kind of Turkish national revolt after a long period of subjugation to China.

Several of the later Turkish tribes and peoples which entered the Islamic world were still strongly affected by Chinese civilization. Still more so were the Mongols and their kin. The first important group of these to become known to the Muslims were the Kara Khitay, who appeared on the northeastern frontiers of the Empire of the Great Seljuks. Of Mongol or Tunguz stock, they had conquered Northern

China in the tenth century and founded a Chinese dynasty. The name "Cathay" commemorates their period of rule. In the early twelfth century they were driven out of China by another related people and began to move westwards. Towards the middle of the twelfth century they conquered Transoxania from the Karakhanids and set up a vast empire stretching from the Oxus to the Yenissei and the border of China. The Seljuk Sultan Sanjar, trying in vain to stem their advance, suffered a humiliating defeat at the battle of the Katvan steppe in 1141.

This little-known engagement must rank among the decisive battles of Asian history. In Persia, it accelerated the decline of Seljuk power and the break-up of the Seljuk Great Sultanate into a number of small states. In Central Asia it confirmed the domination, over what was now old Muslim territory, of a dynasty of Far Eastern origin, with Chinese Imperial experience. Their language of government, we are told, was Chinese, and they introduced many elements of the Chinese administrative and fiscal system.

With the great Mongol conquests, Muslim Southwest Asia passed under the control of a people of East Asian origin, dominated since the childhood of their race by the vast majesty of China. Jenghiz Khan himself leaned heavily on Chinese precedent and advice; in his first expedition in 1219 across the Jaxartes into the lands of Islam, he was accompanied by his Chinese counsellor, Ye-lu Ch'u ts'ai, a high Chinese official and, incidentally, a descendant of the former Kara Khitay ruling house. By the time Jenghiz Khan's grandson, Hülegü Khan, advanced across the Oxus on a new campaign of westward conquest, the Mongols had conquered China itself—and the subjugated lands of Islam were incorporated in an Empire that, from 1267, had its capital in Peking.

Far to the west, the Khan of the Golden Horde in South Russia and the Il-Khan in Persia were autonomous territorial rulers, but they were subject to the supreme authority of the Great Khan, the head of their family and overlord of their Empire. In time, the Khanates of the West became independent and Islamic—but by that time the oriental civilization of the united Mongol Empire had profoundly affected them.

In the period following the destruction of the Caliphate, a fundamental division becomes apparent in the Middle East, between two great cultural zones. In the north was the zone of Perso-Turkish civilization with its center in the plateau of Iran, extending westwards into Anatolia and beyond into the lands conquered by the Ottomans in Europe, eastwards into Central Asia and the new Muslim Empire of India. In these countries Arabic survived only as the language of religion and the religious sciences; culturally it was supplanted by Persian and Turkish, which became the media of a new form of Islamic civilization. To the south lay the countries where Arabic was spoken—the derelict province of Iraq and the new center in Egypt, with its Syrian and Arabian dependencies and its African hinterland. Here, behind the defenses of a Mamlūk Byzantium, the older Arabic culture survived and entered on its long-drawn-out Silver Age. Persian was not known and, except in art and rather more in architecture, the new cultural developments in the north had little effect.

Politically, however, the Turk and the Mongol were everywhere dominant. Mongol or Turkish dynasties ruled all the countries from the Mediterranean to Central Asia and India, and even the Syro-Egyptian Empire of the Mamlūks was governed and defended by a ruling class of imported slaves of Turkish speech, mainly from the Kipchak country north of the Black Sea.

In the fourteenth century the greatest of Arab historians, the Tunisian Ibn Khaldūn, observed the almost universal supremacy of the Turks and saw in their coming a proof of God's continuing concern for the welfare of Islam and the Muslims. At a time when the Muslim Caliphate had become weak and degenerate, incapable of resisting its enemies, God in His wisdom and benevolence had brought new rulers and defenders from among the great and numerous tribes of the Turks to revive the dying breath of Islam and restore the unity of the Muslims. By the providential dispensation of the Mamlūk system, he affirms, they were constantly reinforced by new importations from the steppe, who embraced Islam with enthusiasm yet retained their nomadic virtues unspoilt by the corrupting influences of civilization.[13]

In this interpretation of events, Ibn Khaldūn is applying his own well-known version of the myth of the noble savage. His praise of the steppe peoples as the saviors of Muslim power is however by no means without foundation. The military prowess of the Turks and Mongols has never been questioned; their political contribution to the recovery, stability, and, for a while, expansion of the Muslim world deserves more attention.

It is perhaps in the forms and functioning of government that the great transformation wrought by the invaders from the steppe can most clearly be seen. In the Mongol kingdom of the Il-Khans and in the states which followed it in Persia and Anatolia, new patterns appear that differ sharply from those of the old Caliphate. The extent of the change may be measured against those countries which knew Turkish but not Mongol rule (as Egypt and India) and those that knew neither (as Morocco).

The first and most striking feature of the new era is the reinforcement of political power. The states of the post-Mongol era are stronger, more stable, and more enduring than those of the past—and the states of the plateaux of Anatolia and Iran are stronger than those of the countries less directly affected by Turco-Mongol rule. In the six centuries before the Mongol invasions, few states in Islam had lasted for much more than three or four generations. The patriarchal Caliphate had perished within forty years of the Hijra; the kingdom of the Umayyads had lasted for less than a century; even the ʿAbbāsid Caliphs, though they reigned in name for five centuries, wielded effective power for little more than the first of them and were thereafter forced to yield it to an unending series of dynasties, some of them great and powerful but all of them ephemeral in the form, the extension, and the duration of their dominion. Even in the periods of their greatness the authority they wielded, though vast, was fragile. Institutions, regimes, realms—all were shifting and impermanent, liable to sudden and total upheaval.

In the Turco-Mongol age all this is changed. In Egypt, the Mamlūks, recruited for the most part from the Khanate of the Golden Horde and deeply influenced by the statecraft of their Mongol neighbors, established a state and a government that lasted for two and a half centuries—certainly the most stable and powerful regime that Egypt had known since the Muslim conquest. In Persia, lying on the main high road of invasion, things were more difficult—but even there the heirs of Timur and the various dynasties that followed them succeeded in maintaining the stability and continuity of government—out of which, in time, the territorially and administratively coherent modern state of Persia emerged. And in Anatolia these same traditions of government helped to maintain the various Turkish principalities and the Ottoman state which eventually swallowed them all.

An important contribution of the steppe peoples to this stability was a workable principle of dynastic succession. The juristic doctrine of Islam was that the headship of the state was elective. In fact the elective principle remained purely theoretical, and Islam was ruled by a succession of dynasties, ranging from those of the Caliphs themselves to the petty hereditary autonomies of the provincial governors. But the elective principle remained strong enough to prevent the establishment of any regular and accepted rule of succession. With the Caliphate, the fiction of election was maintained on each accession, and beyond the general principle that the Caliph should be chosen among the members of the reigning family, there was no restriction of choice. In the secular dynasties which held the real power, authority was personal and military—and rarely survived the grandson of the founder. Besides Islamic influences, Persian influences were also powerful—but they came from the late, degenerate phase of the Sāsānid Empire of Persia, just before its collapse under the shock of Arab invasion. The example it offered was of a personal absolutism, unrestrained—and therefore unsupported—by any entrenched rights or interests, depending on fear rather than on loyalty. In the classical manuals of statecraft the possibility of loyalty—by family, faith, or estate—seems to be discounted altogether, and kingship is based unashamedly on punishment and reward.

The Turks introduced a new conception. Already in the Orkhon inscriptions we find the notion clearly expressed of a family singled out by God to rule over the Turks, and, more vaguely, other peoples and lands beyond them. The same idea reappears in an Islamic form in the correspondence of the Great Seljuks, with their claim to an inherited and divinely sanctioned imperial sovereignty, and again, in a pagan form, in the chancery protocol of the Mongol Khans. For the Persians, the sovereign was the sole autocrat; for the Turks and Mongols, sovereignty was a family possession, and the whole family of the Khan or Sultan had a right to share in it. In the kingdoms of the Karakhānids and Seljuks we see the principle at work, whereby the brothers and cousins of the sovereign are admitted to a share of sovereignty. Under the Mongols, the whole vast Empire won by the conquests was divided up into family appanages, each of which was given to a son or grandson of Jenghiz Khan. We see it again among the Anatolian principalities, and perhaps also in the Seljuk and early Ottoman practice of appointing the sons of the Sultan to provincial governorships, in which they held miniature courts.[14]

A ruling family, held together and sustained by strong ties of tribal loyalty; a divine grant of authority, so sacrosanct that defaulting members of the family were put to death by strangling with a bow-string, to avoid the sacrilege of shedding their blood—these were no small advantages in setting up a regime that was secure and accepted. But to make it permanent, in lands of ancient culture and jaded loyalty, more was needed.

It was found. In the Turkish kingdoms there was a clarity and cohesion in the institutional structure of state and society that is in marked contrast with the looseness and vagueness of classical Islamic times. The power of the state rests on and is exercised through well-established and well-organized institutions and social orders—army, bureaucracy, judiciary, and men of religion, with well-defined powers and functions, with regular recruitment and hierarchic promotion. The emergence of these new features has been variously attributed—to the steadiness and sobriety of the new ruling groups, to changes in the system of land tenure, to the transformation of Islamic belief and attitudes through the new orthodoxy, to the influence of Chinese—and Byzantine—imperial administration, to the introduction and acceptance of fire-arms; all no doubt played their part, though the determining of their relative importance is very much a matter of argument. What is clear is that in these states, and notably in the Ottoman Empire, land ownership and taxation, justice and religion, government and war were better organized and better correlated than ever before in Islam and gave to the Turkish rulers an assurance, a competence, and above all a permanence that were new to the Islamic world.

With the consolidation of the Turkish states came an important change in the nature of the realms over which they ruled. Their territories were wider, their frontiers more permanent. The constant rise and fall of petty principalities—regional or personal, military or tribal, forming and reforming in ever different shapes—had come to an end.

After the Mongol invasions, three great states, based on Egypt, Persia, and Turkey, with more or less stable frontiers, divided the Middle East between them. With the Ottoman conquest of the Mamlūk sultanate in 1517 their number was reduced to two—two great dynastic monarchies, which confronted one another from the Caucasus to the Persian Gulf, as the Sāsānid and Byzantine Empires had done a thousand years earlier. One of them, Persia, has survived to our own day; the disappearance of the other has left many uncertainties that are not yet resolved.

Ottoman Observers of Ottoman Decline

16

In May 1541 the Grand Vizier Lûtfi Pasha, after a brief but successful term of office, was dismissed by Sultan Süleyman the Magnificent, apparently because of a dispute arising in the harem. He retired with a pension to his estate in Dimotika, where he died a number of years later. In his enforced leisure he occupied himself with scholarship and especially history and composed various works, one of which was a history of the Ottoman Empire up to his own day. Another of his writings was a booklet called the *Āṣafnāme*—the Book of Asaph, after the Biblical figure who in Muslim legend was the vizier of King Solomon and the ideal model of the wise and loyal minister.[1]

Lûtfi Pasha's book, however, is more than a Mirror of Ministers, of the kind common in Muslim literature since early times. When he became Grand Vizier, he tells us, he found the High Divan in great disorder and many things contrary to the fundamental laws of the Empire. He, therefore, felt it his duty to set down the results of his own experience, for the guidance of those who, after him, would be called upon to fill this great office beyond which there is nothing to which a subject can aspire and to give both practical advice and ethical principles for the conduct of the affairs of state, while he himself sought peace in retirement. "The Kingdom of this mortal world is swift in passing and full of death. It is better to find wise but not heedless repose in the corner of leisure and the enjoyment of gardens and meadows. May God, from Whom we seek aid, and in Whom we trust, secure the laws and foundations of the House of ʿOsman from the fear and peril of fate and the evil eye of the foe."[2]

It was with these premonitions of mortality that Lûtfi Pasha set down his rules of what Grand Viziers should do and—more urgently—of what they should avoid. First and foremost, the Grand Vizier should be disinterested, without any private aim or spite. "Everything he does should be for God and in God and for the sake of God."[3] This should be possible for the holder of an office that is the peak of ambition. He should not make free with requisitions for the support of couriers but should limit them to those occasions when their absence would be harmful to the affairs of state, for "in the Ottoman realms there is no such inequitable exaction as the courier service."[4] He should preserve the sovereign from love of money and from its evil consequences and see that the property rights of the subjects are respected, "for the summary annexation of the property of the people to the property of the sovereign is a sign of decay in the state."[5] The Grand Vizier should be frank and honest in his dealings with the Sultan and without fear of dismissal. "It is better to be dismissed and admired among men than to render dishonest service."[6] He should observe the five daily prayers in his house; he should be accessible and try to give satisfaction. Above all, he must beware of gifts from tainted sources. "For officers of the state, corruption is a disease without remedy . . . beware, beware of corruption; O God! save us from it."[7] After this sudden note of passion Lûtfi Pasha observes, rather more practically, that the emoluments of the Grand Vizier amount to about 2½ million aspers—"which, thank God, is, in the Ottoman state, a sufficient bounty."[8] When Lûtfi Pasha himself was Grand Vizier, he says, he spent 1½ million on the expenses of his kitchen and his suite, and half a million on charity, leaving half a million in his personal treasury.

Lûtfi Pasha was also concerned about the cost of living. "The control of prices is an important public responsibility, and the Grand Vizier must devote special care to it. It is not right if one high official is a rice merchant or if the house of another is a drug-store. The fixing of prices is in the interests of the poor."[9]

Lûtfi Pasha returns again and again to the question of government appointments. The Grand Vizier should make appointments and promotions solely on the basis of merit and competence, without favoritism or interest. He should give only few and small fiefs to his own followers. He should maintain discipline and respect the order of precedence and seniority. He should submit to no influence or pressure in making appointments but follow his own judgment. He should investigate complaints against minor officials and judges and, when necessary, reprimand or even dismiss them.

The final responsibility, however, belongs to the Sultan, who must from time to time be reminded of this fact: "The Grand Vizier in speaking to the world-protecting Sovereign should repeatedly say: 'My Sovereign, I have cast the yoke off my neck. On the Day of Judgment henceforth thou wilt answer'."[10]

In the second chapter, on the military function of the Grand Vizier, Lûtfi Pasha draws special attention to the need to strengthen the navy. He quotes with approval a remark of Kemalpashazade (*d.* 1533–34) to Selim I: "My Lord, you dwell in a city whose benefactor is the sea. If the sea is not safe no ships will come, and if no ship comes Istanbul perishes." He himself had said to Sultan Süleyman, "Under the previous Sultans there were many who ruled the land, but few who ruled the sea. In the conduct of naval warfare the infidels are ahead of us. We must overcome them."[11]

The third and fourth chapters deal with finance and with the peasants: "The Sultanate stands on its treasury. The treasury stands by good management. By injustice (*ẓulm*) it falls."[12] The Grand Vizier must see that revenue is greater than expenditure and must beware of inflating his own staff. The army should be good rather than large, and the army pay-lists should be kept accurate and up-to-date. A standing paid army of 15,000 men is quite sufficient—and to pay it regularly no mean achievement. Tax-revenues should be assigned to government commissioners rather than to tax-farmers and the amounts fixed by the Chief Treasurer. The extraordinary taxes levied from the peasantry should be neither too heavy nor too frequent, and steps should be taken to prevent the depopulation of the countryside.

Thus, in the middle of the sixteenth century, when the Ottoman Empire was at the very peak of its power and glory, a perceptive Turkish statesman was already deeply concerned about its fate and welfare and was able to lay his fingers unerringly on what became, in the years to follow, the characteristic signs of Ottoman decline. Inflation and speculation, venality and incompetence; the multiplication of a useless and wasteful army and bureaucracy; the vicious circle of financial stringency, fiscal rapacity, and economic strangulation; the decay of integrity and loyalty; and beyond them all, the growing, menacing shadow of the maritime states of the West—all these were already seen by Lûtfi Pasha as he cultivated his garden in Dimotika.

The long debate on the reasons for the decline of the Roman Empire began, we are told, when the sack of Rome by Alaric and his Visigoths first made plain the weakness of the Roman state. The debate on the decline of the Ottoman Empire began when the Empire was at its zenith—and it began among the Ottoman Turks themselves. The percipience of Lûtfi Pasha, his ability to perceive and relate cause and effect in the historical process of which he was a part, his anxious awareness of weakness and decay in the body politic find clear expression in his manual for ministers where, in contrast to the normal euphory of oriental historiography, he points not merely to the errors and failings of his ministerial colleagues and successors—which is fairly common—but also to the cracks that have appeared in the pillars of state and society.

This awareness of process and capacity for analysis were by no means unique in Ottoman annals. On the contrary, Lûtfi Pasha's work was the first of a long series of similar writings, in which the urgent and hopeful demand for reform gives way to a profoundly pessimistic longing for a lost Golden Age, as the faith of the Turks in their ability to restore the greatness of the past faded.

Not all these writings had the form of statesmanly memoranda. One of the most remarkable is in the form of a poem by an obscure poet called Veysi, written in about 1608. The poet gives a stark picture of Turkish government and society, in a manner more reminiscent of an Old Testament Prophet than of an Ottoman office-holder. The poet threatens the judgment of God on a tyranny worse than that of Pharaoh. The Law of God is disregarded, and its professed exponents are hypocritical and self-seeking—"were no pay given for it, the word of God would not be read". The Qāḍīs and Qāḍī-ʿaskers are corrupt and oppressive, the age is dominated by women or young boys; the great are interested only in money; the feudal cavalry are neglected and fiefs given to favorites of the Vizier or of the harem; the Janissaries and their commanders have become a cause of disorder and sedition; the high officers of state are all corrupt and tyrannical; in fine "'the fish stinks from the head', they say; the head of this evil is known."[13]

The crises of the late sixteenth and early seventeenth centuries gave rise to a number of political and ethical tracts and treatises, the most famous of which is the memorandum of Kochu Bey, an Ottoman official of Macedonian or Albanian birth. After being recruited by the *devshirme*, he followed a career in the Saray. He became the intimate adviser of Sultan Murad IV (1623–1640) and in 1630 composed for him the treatise on the state and prospects of the Ottoman Empire which has led scholars to call him the Turkish Montesquieu.[14] In this Kochu Bey analyzes, with courage and penetration, the defects that had led to the decline of Ottoman power since the time of Süleyman the Magnificent and advises the Sultan on how to remedy them. "It is a long time since the high-chambered household of the lofty Sultanate (may it remain under the protection of eternal grace) was served by solicitous, well-intentioned, worthy ulema and by obedient, self-effacing, willing slaves. Today the state of affairs having changed, and evil, upheaval, sedition and dissension having passed all bounds, I have sought occasion to observe the causes and reasons of these changes, and bring them to the Imperial and august ear."[15]

Kochu Bey paints a glowing picture of the golden age of the Ottoman past, which reached its summit under Süleyman the Magnificent. It was, however, during his reign that the deterioration began; it advanced rapidly under his immediate successors. In nineteen chapters, Kochu Bey describes, with somber detail and astonishing frankness, the causes and processes of Ottoman enfeeblement and impoverishment, of material and moral decline.

He attributes the decay of Ottoman power and integrity to four principal, interrelated causes. The first of these is the withdrawal of the Sultans, from the time of Süleyman, from the direct supervision of the affairs of state. In former times the Sultans were present at meetings of the Imperial Council and interested themselves actively in the state of the people and the provinces. After Süleyman the Sultans secluded themselves in the harem and thus broke off the indispensable intimacy between the sources of power and those entrusted with its exercise.

At the same time the office of Grand Vizier, the keystone of the edifice of Ottoman government, was debased and debilitated. In former times the Grand Vizier was the supreme administrator. He rose to his high office through the ladder of administrative employment and experience and was promoted for his competence and merit. Once appointed, he enjoyed absolute discretion and power and was free from any kind of illicit pressure or influence. His tenure was virtually permanent, and he was dismissed only for grave dereliction of duty. The trouble began when Sultan Süleyman in 929/1523 made Ibrahim Pasha, a palace favorite, Grand Vizier in defiance of the old system. Thereafter it became normal for Sultans to advance their personal favorites to this office. Such Grand Viziers had neither experience nor competence and brought the office into disrepute. After 992/1584 the Grand Viziers lost both their powers and their security. They were subject to all kinds of interference by palace favorites and liable at any moment to summary dismissal, confiscation, and even execution. This degradation of the highest office of state adversely affected the morale and the efficiency of both the civilian and the military servants of the Ottoman House.

The withdrawal of the Sultan and the degradation of the Grand Vizier left the way open to the pernicious regime of palace favorites—of women, eunuchs, hangers-on, speculators, intriguers, and self-seekers, men of every religion and none, without loyalty, integrity, or virtue of any kind. Both the imperial household and the corps of Janissaries had been overrun with outsiders and interlopers, the former with "Turks, Gypsies, Jews, people without religion or faith, cutpurses and city riff-raff", the latter with "townsmen, Turks, Gypsies, Tats, Lazes, muleteers and camel-drivers, porters, footpads, and cutpurses."[16] And these in turn had opened the way to corruption, the blight which, if unchecked, would destroy every branch of the civil, military, economic, social, political, and religious life of the Empire.

Kochu Bey demonstrates point by point how palace intrigue and venality were corroding the pillars of the Ottoman state. The Imperial household had been corrupted and had become a source of contamination to the rest of the apparatus of government. The military fief system, which once provided the backbone both of the army and of the countryside, was being undermined and destroyed. The feudal *sipahis* were being crushed out of existence and their fiefs given to courtiers and harem women, who sometimes accumulated as many as fifty of them in a single holding. The result was both military and agrarian breakdown.

If the army's feudal cavalry was disintegrating, its paid infantry and artillery were in no better shape. The corps of Janisseries, once a select *corps d'élite,* had swollen in size beyond all reason by enrolling any riff-raff willing to pay a bribe. They had become a useless and destructive nuisance, terrorizing and exploiting the civil population and performing no military duty other than drawing their pay. With the army in such poor shape, it was not surprising that the Empire had lost nineteen provinces since 1591 and was unable to maintain order in those that remained.

Appointment to office by purchase or favor had become general—even in religious offices such as judgeships. No dynasty in Islam had been as loyal to the Holy Law and as respectful to its representatives as the House of ʿOsman. The chief Mufti of the capital, the Sheykh al-Islam, had been chosen as the wisest, best, and most pious of the ulema and usually held his office for life. Other judges were pious, conscientious, and modest and held office for many years. Dismissals were rare and only for good cause. Now, appointments and promotions among the ulema were made without reference to merit, scholarship, or seniority. All went by favor. Tenure of office was brief and insecure, the holders unworthy and grasping. The judges were hated and despised by the people.

The treasury was empty. Taxes, instead of being collected by trustworthy government commissioners, were leased to tax-farmers. Even the revenues of crown estates were squandered and dissipated. Kochu Bey cites as an example the crown lands on the eastern borders, which formerly brought an income of 48,400,000 aspers. "Part had been lost to the enemy; part given away, contrary to law, as freehold (*temlik*), pious foundation (*vakif*), or slipper-money;[17] part has simply gone to rack and ruin; part has gone into the appanage of the Viziers."[18]

To meet the deficiency the government had sharply raised both the rate and the frequency of the special taxes on the peasantry. The poll-tax on non-Muslims, for example, had been raised from 40-50 aspers per house to 240 aspers per head, as well as many other imposts.[19] How could the peasants bear this? "In fine," says Kochu Bey, "the like of the present oppression and maltreatment of the poor peasantry has never been at any time, in any clime, or in the realm of any king. If in any of the lands of Islam an atom of injustice is done to any individual, then on the Day of Judgment not ministers, but kings will be asked for a reckoning, and it will be no answer for them to say to the Lord of the Worlds, 'I delegated this duty'. . . . The world can go on with irreligion, but not with injustice."[20] Such sentiments are commonplace in Islamic manuals of ethics and politics. It is not however usual to find them coupled with so clear a denunciation of the existing state of affairs—or expressed in a memorandum from an official to a sovereign.

With this note of passion Kochu Bey's careful restraint breaks down, and the profound feelings that inspired his book come to the surface. He remains however practical and specific and prescribes a remedy besides diagnosing the disease. Despite his gloomy picture, Kochu Bey is basically optimistic. He believes that by swift and resolute action the Sultan can stop the rot and restore the old order to its perfection. "And then the enemies of the faith, seeing the good order and stability . . . will say, in helpless fear and envy: 'The House of 'Osman lay for sixty years in neglectful sleep, but now they are wide-awake, and have begun to make good the shortcomings of past days'."[21]

Writing in 1630, Kochu Bey, the loyal servant of the state, could still think of the previous sixty years as an evil interlude to be ended by a resolute Sultan and look forward to the renovation of an Empire which, by its extent, its mineral and other resources, and its masses of valiant men, was without equal in the world. Only twenty-three years later, in 1653, another Ottoman writer, of very different formation, surveyed the state of the Empire in a somewhat different spirit.

Mustafā ibn Abdüllah, variously known as Kâtib Chelebi and as Ḥājjī Khalifa (1608–1657), was also an officer in the Ottoman service and served in various capacities in the Finance Department. Unlike Kochu Bey, he was not a slave of the Porte recruited by *devshirme* but a free Muslim, born in Constantinople, to a father who himself held a palace appointment. His vast and miscellaneous learning, his far-ranging intellectual curiosity, and his versatile and unconventional mind made him one of the outstanding figures in Turkish cultural and intellectual history. He was, incidentally, one of the first Ottoman scholars to show an interest in Western learning.

In 1063/1653, we are told, the Sultan Mehmed IV called a meeting of high dignitaries to discuss the reasons for the persistent deficit in the state finances. "Under the rule of my late father," said the Sultan, "as also earlier, the revenue was sufficient to cover expenditure or even exceeded it. My expenditure is not as great as that of my father, and the revenues are the same. What then is the reason that the income of the state no longer suffices to cover the expenditure, and why is it that money cannot be raised for the fleet and other important matters?" Each present gave his answer, beginning with the Grand Vizier, who replied that in fact the expenditure of the state had increased considerably and that this was why the revenues no longer sufficed. After this meeting some inconclusive investigations of the state finances were made and some ineffective palliatives adopted. Kâtib Chelebi, as a finance official, was present at some of the discussions and set down his own views on the causes and remedies of the chronic financial crisis, in an essay entitled *The Rule of Action for the Rectification of Defects*.[22]

Kâtib Chelebi begins with a brief account of the circumstances that had led him to compose his essay and then sets forth a theory, clearly derived from the *Muqaddima* of Ibn Khaldūn, of the rise and fall of human societies. States and societies, like individuals, are organic and are subject to the laws of growth and decay. The life-span of a state, like that of an individual, falls into three phases; the first of growth, the second of stasis, the third of decline.[23] With states, again as with individuals, the relative lengths of these three phases vary according to the health and strength of any one state. The Ottoman Empire, thanks to the strength of its constitution and the soundness of its limbs, had lived for a long time, and the phase of stasis had passed slowly. The approach of the third stage was indicated by certain symptoms, which could be recognized and treated in individuals by physicians and in states by statesmen.[24]

Kâtib Chelebi then goes on to give his own diagnosis and suggested treatment of the ills of the Ottoman state in three chapters, dealing with the peasantry, the army, and the treasury. The peasantry corresponds to the black bile in the body and is disordered by undernourishment. The Sultans of the first phase were careful to protect the peasantry from oppression and extortion, and not a single village fell into ruin. During the second phase some peasants lost their livelihood through risings and disturbances and fled from the villages to the towns. Now Constantinople was packed with people. In twelve years of travel through the Empire, from 1622 to 1634, he had found most villages deserted. On a visit to Persia, on the other hand, he had traveled fifteen to twenty stages without seeing a single deserted village, since the Persian state was then still at the end of its phase of stasis. The ruin of the Ottoman countryside was well-known. One cause was fiscal extortion, but the basic cause was the sale of offices, which had lowered the standard of loyalty and integrity in the public services and which forced the purchasers to practise extortion in order to recoup themselves. In former times officials were dismissed, dispossessed, or even executed on charges of corruption; but now this damnable practice, contrary both to common sense and to religion, and outlawed even by the kings of the infidels, had become the very axis of the affairs of state. At one time it had at least been disguised and surreptitious. Now it was open and universal. The treasury had been impoverished and the army demoralized, and while formerly the infidels fled before the soldiers of Islam the reverse now happened. "So that, if the tyrannical excess of taxation and the deleterious sale of offices are not abandoned; if by return to justice that which was lost is not recovered and penance is not done; then it is certain that the curse of disobedience to the law and the burden of injustice and violence will ruin the Empire. From God we come and to Him we return (Qur'ān ii, 151)."[25]

After this terrible warning Kâtib Chelebi goes on to discuss the army, which, he says, corresponds in the social body to the phlegm in the physical body. It performs a useful and necessary function but is harmful in excess. Excess of phlegm is a characteristic disorder in old men, and so is an excessive army in ageing states. This is a natural development of old age, and it is wasted effort to try and keep the phlegm—or the army—down. It will inevitably grow back. The most one can hope for is to keep it under control and reasonably harmless. Under Süleyman the Magnificent in 970/1562–63 the total number of paid troops was 41,479 men with an annual pay of 122,300,000 aspers; in 974/1566–67 it had risen to 48,316 men for 126,400,000 aspers; in 997/1588–89 to 64,425 men for 178,200,000 aspers; in 1004/1595–96 to 81,870 men for 251,200,000 aspers; in 1018/1609–10 to 91,202 men for 310,800,000 aspers; and under Osman II (1618–22) and Mustafa I (1617–18) the troops rose to 100,000 men. Thereafter a vigorous attempt was made to reduce their numbers, which fell by 1050/1640–41 to 59,257, at a cost of 263,100,000 aspers, but they soon rose again and reached and surpassed the previous level. It would be useless to try and keep their numbers down to the level at which they were under Süleyman, but efforts should be made to keep the cost within limits.[26]

The treasury, says Kâtib Chelebi, is the stomach of the social body, and all classes of society are affected, directly or indirectly, by its intake and maintenance. When the peasantry are oppressed, the treasury becomes empty, and the whole social body suffers. The signs of old age are lethargy and digestive disorders. Just as in the physical body the hair and beard turn white, so in the social body the phase of decline produces luxury and ostentation. Titles and honors are spread ever wider, more and more classes ape the clothing and household furnishings of the sovereign, so that the expenditure both of the individual and of the community becomes larger and larger. Kâtib Chelebi illustrates this with some figures of the income and expenditure of the Ottoman treasury, of which the following are examples:

Date	*Income*	*Expenditure*
972/1564–65	183,000,000	189,600,000
1000/1591–92	293,400,000	363,400,000
1006/1597–98	300,000,000	900,000,000[*sic*]
1058/1648	361,800,000	500,500,000
1060/1650	532,900,000	687,200,000

To preserve a permanent balance by reducing expenditure and increasing income is very difficult and is regarded by financial experts as impossible. It may, however, be possible to procure an interval of stability and recuperation.[27]

Kâtib Chelebi then sums up his conclusions and recommendations. There are four ways in which the state might be saved and restored to health: by a man of the sword *(sahib-i sayf);* by the dignitaries *(a 'yan-i devlet);* by the army commanders; or by high officers of state *(vükela-i devlet).* The three last are unlikely, since in all three groups loyal and just men are but few; most are concerned only with their personal satisfactions. The solution must, therefore, come from a man of the sword.

The immediate tasks of this military dictator would be to remedy the deficit in the treasury, the excessive size of the army, the increase in expenditure, and the poverty of the peasants. Here Kâtib Chelebi makes some suggestions for fiscal reform, military and budgetary economy, the abolition of the sale of offices, and the restoration of the rule of law.[28]

Despite the pious formulae with which Kâtib Chelebi ends his essay, it is clear that he had little hope of success. Indeed, in another of his works, he remarks of this essay: "As I knew that my conclusions would be difficult to apply, I took no further trouble about it. But a Sultan of some future time will become aware of it, and put that into operation, which will bring him the best results."[29]

The same note of pessimism may be heard in the memoranda of Hüseyn Hezarfen,[30] written in 1669, and of Sarı Mehmed Pasha,[31] written in 1703. Like Kâtib Chelebi, Hezarfen showed some interest in the West and had read European history. He was acquainted with such Western visitors to Istanbul as Marsigli and Antoine Galland and may have provided some of the material for Prince Kantemir's *History of the Ottoman Empire*.[32] His analysis is along the same lines as those of his predecessors, with discussions of the seclusion and incompetence of the later Sultans, the weakness of the Grand Vizier, the sale of offices and resulting evils. He lays rather more stress than Kochu Bey and Kâtib Chelebi on the need for good and conscientious provincial governors and is more inclined than they are to insist on force. The Sultan should maintain a staff of spies to watch his servants as well as his enemies and should not hesitate to use fear as law to maintain his authority. "The Sultans must submit to the noble Sharīʿa, and must not kill anyone except by judgment according to the Sharīʿa . . . but let them not abolish discretionary bodily punishment altogether, for punishment is a condition of kingship. If the fear of such punishment were to pass away from people's hearts, this would make the evildoers more numerous and more insolent. The right thing is that there should be fear among the bad and trust among the good people. Permanent fear and permanent trust are both harmful. While the people are between fear and hope, let the Sultanate be well-ordered and let the Sultan be generous."[33] In the same spirit Hezarfen insists strongly on the investigation and punishment of delinquent officials, officers, and ulema. He lays great stress on the moral responsibility of the Sheykh al-Islām and the corps of ulema for the welfare of the state and the people and urges them to live up to their high calling.

Sarı Mehmed Pasha was a high official of the Ottoman state who no less than seven times was appointed to—and dismissed from—the high office of Defterdar, or chief of the treasury. His lifelong experience of the intimacies of government in his time gives added point to his strictures on corruption and incompetence and his urgent yet hopeless demand for a strong hand at the helm and for a civil service with competence, integrity, and security of tenure. Though he does not differ in essentials from his predecessors, he adds to them the fruits of his own personal experience.

The modern reader of these sixteenth- and seventeenth-century memorialists, while respecting their perspicacity and their integrity, will no longer be entirely satisfied with their historical interpretations, and even while accepting their facts and some of their judgments will question the stress and value they lay upon them. To quote but two examples: in reading Kochu Bey's strictures on Ottoman fiscal rapacity, we shall be less impressed by the rise of the poll-tax from 40 to 240 aspers when we remember that the rate of exchange of the asper to the gold ducat had fallen in about the same proportion. We may also ask whether corruption can really be considered as a major cause of the decay of the Empire and whether it is not rather a pervasive and corrosive manifestation of a deeper ill. For Kochu Bey and his successors, corruption and favoritism, rapacity and oppression were the root causes of Ottoman decline. The different philosophic presuppositions and historical methods of our time may lead us to regard these as symptoms rather than as causes and to seek their origins in deeper and vaster changes.

Our present concern, however, is not with the decline of the Ottoman Empire but with the interpretations of it propounded by contemporary Ottoman observers.[34] In reading their works, we cannot but be astonished at the clarity with which they saw and the lucidity with which they described the decline and stagnation of the Empire whose loyal and devoted subjects they were. With a degree of self-knowledge rare in any society and with a moral courage the more striking in an autocratic monarchy, they did not hesitate to describe and condemn the faults and crimes of those who, so they believed, were responsible for the ruin of the country and the state. The fundamental analysis of Ottoman decline was that of Kochu Bey, whose diagnosis and prescriptions were reproduced, with varying sophistication of exposition, by most of his Ottoman successors in the seventeenth and eighteenth centuries.[35]

Ottoman statesmanship was still looking backward to the golden age in the past, and earnest reformers saw the only hope of salvation in a restoration of Islam and of the pure and ancient traditions of the House of ʿOsman. In 1792, when Selim III asked a score of eminent Ottomans for their advice on how to run the Empire, there were many who still gave the same answer. There were some, however, who had found another way.[36]

The Ottoman Empire and Its Aftermath

17

During the last decades of the Ottoman Empire three different unifying ideologies competed for the loyalty of Ottoman subjects. They may be designated as the Islamic, the Ottoman, and the Turkish principles of identity.

Islam was the traditional basis of the Ottoman state as of virtually all other states in the classical Islamic world. It provided the principle of authority, of identity, and of political and social cohesion and loyalty. The polity was conceived as the Community of Muslims, its head as the successor of the Sultans and Caliphs of the glorious past and as the holder of an Islamic sovereignty dedicated to the maintenance of Islam and the extension of its domain. Characteristically, when Ottoman Muslims observed the role of Prussia and Sardinia in the unification of the German and Italian peoples in the nineteenth century and considered a possible parallel role for themselves, they saw it in terms not of Turks but of Islam—of a greater Islamic unity, embracing all Muslims, with Ottoman Turkey as its leader. In this sense the Empire was conceived not as a domination of Turks over non-Turks, since all Muslims were theoretically equal irrespective of language or origin, but as a domination of Muslims over non-Muslims. The task of the Muslim Empire was to preserve the heritage of the Prophet, to uphold and enforce the law of Islam and bring it ultimately to all mankind. Non-Muslims were at least to be subjugated and preferably converted. Those who accepted the faith of the masters of the Empire could aspire to full equality with them and access to all positions, even the highest. Those who preferred to adhere to their old religions were permitted to do so but were required to recognize the primacy of Islam and submit to the supremacy of the Muslims.

Even during the Turkish War of Independence 1919–1922, the Islamic component in Turkish identity was still very strong, and many of Kemal's supporters certainly saw themselves as fighting for Islam against the unbeliever rather than for Turkey against the foreigner. But the influence of Islam was much weakened by the defection of the Islamic establishment, which in the eyes of many Turks was guilty of collaboration with the occupying powers. This greatly facilitated Kemal's subsequent task in secularizing the Turkish state, disestablishing the Islamic religion and replacing the Islamic codes by modern laws. With the abolition of the Caliphate in 1924, the Turkish state formally renounced the Islamic religious leadership which had been embodied in that office. In the debate on the subject which took place in the Turkish parliament and elsewhere, the question whether to retain or abandon Turkey's role as the leading Islamic power was discussed at length, and the renunciation of Islamic empire expressed in the abolition of the office was conscious and explicit.

Since then, there has been no indication whatever of any desire on the part of any significant body of Turks to resume that role. It is noteworthy that even in recent years, when Islamic revivalism has become something of a force in Turkish domestic politics, there has been no suggestion that Turkey should seek to resume her erstwhile role as the champion and leader of Islam. On the contrary, the Turkish revivalists have been content—no doubt for good practical as well as ideological reasons—to fall in behind the leadership of other Islamic claimants.

The Ottoman dynasty and state lasted for five hundred years. Allegiance to the Ottoman house was the main political loyalty, not only of the Muslim subjects of the empire, but even, to a degree which is not always appreciated, of the non-Muslim subject peoples. The ideal of Ottomanism, however, as a nationality in the European sense is a product of nineteenth-century liberal reformism. This was the concept of an Ottoman identity and loyalty embracing all Ottoman subjects irrespective of religion or of ethnic origin in a single Ottoman nation inhabiting the Ottoman fatherland.

Such an idea was a chimera. It won only limited support among Ottoman Muslims and even less among the Christian peoples of the Empire. It was undermined both by the traditional Islamic supremacism of the rulers of the Empire and at the same time by the growing nationalism and separatism of the subject peoples. Finally, even the Turks themselves embraced nationalism, while the role of the last Sultan in cooperating with the victorious allies and opposing the nationalist rebels discredited the monarchy and ultimately the dynasty in the eyes of many Turks. The loss of the Arab provinces—the only significant non-Turkish (albeit Muslim) areas which had remained under Turkish rule—removed the last justification for the imperial institution. The Ottoman Sultanate was abolished in 1923, the Ottoman Caliphate in 1924. Since then, there has been no attempt to restore the Ottoman dynasty or revive the territorial and other claims associated with it.

The third and latest of the competing ideologies was Turkism, a new notion owing much to external influences especially from the Turkish-speaking subject populations of the Russian Empire, many of whom came to Turkey as refugees from Russian oppression. In Russia, they had encountered militant pan-Slavism and reacted against it with a nationalist ideology of their own. This ideology was concerned not just with Turkey—the very word was still alien to a people who were not yet accustomed to define and name their country in this way—but with all the Turks, *i.e.* pan-Turkism (sometimes called pan-Turanianism) rather than Turkism, involving the vaster community of Turkish peoples extending across Eastern Europe and Asia from the Aegean to the China Sea and embracing large populations in Iran, Afghanistan, China, and, above all, the Russian Empire. In this larger scheme of pan-Turkish unification, Ottoman and later republican Turkey, the only part of the Turkish world that still retained political independence, was cast for a role of leadership. This role too had something of an imperial quality.

The years of defeat, surrender, and occupation, the conduct of the Sultan's government, the rift with the Arab subjects of the Empire, the indifference of the Muslim world to Turkey's fate—all combined to bring about radical changes in the Turks' perception of themselves and of their place in the world. Ottomanism was dead; Islamism gravely weakened. The way was open for a new identity and loyalty based not on community and empire but on nation and country. The change, and in particular the relationship between these two—between nationalism and patriotism—raised new questions and evoked new answers.

The most striking evidence of the change in Turkish attitudes can be seen in the situation in 1923. The newly established Turkish republic was triumphant. The Greeks had been driven from Anatolia; the Allied powers, the former victors over the Ottoman Empire, were divided, in disarray, and unable to offer any effective resistance to the Turkish recovery. The great Russian Empire, once Turkey's most dangerous enemy, was rent by revolution and civil war, and, far from constituting a threat, seemed instead to offer a tempting opportunity. Syria and Iraq, deeply disappointed with the results of the war, now found themselves under French and British rule and might well have been ready to listen to the blandishments of the victorious Turkish leader.

But Kemal was interested in none of these. In 1922, after the capture of Izmir, he made it clear to his more enthusiastic followers that he was not going, as some of them hoped, to advance on Salonica. Instead, he affirmed his recognition of the pre-1914 frontier in Europe. Others, who urged him to lead his victorious armies into Syria and Iraq and recover the lost Ottoman provinces in Asia, were similarly disappointed. An Ottoman claim on Mosul was in due course renounced, and Ottoman claims on the Sanjak of Alexandretta and the island of Cyprus, both with substantial Turkish populations, were left in abeyance as long as the western powers remained.

Perhaps the greatest temptation of all was the liberation of the Turkish subject peoples of the Russian Empire, for which the fall of the Tsars seemed at last to offer a real possibility. But here again Kemal resisted the temptation. Renouncing all adventures beyond the newly defined borders of the Turkish republic, he directed his own energies and those of his people to the difficult and unglamourous task of development at home. He makes the point quite clearly in a speech delivered as early as 1 December 1921:

> Every one of our compatriots and co-religionists may nourish a high ideal in his mind; he is free to do so, and no one will interfere. The government of the

> Grand National Assembly of Turkey has a firm, positive, material policy, and that, gentlemen, is directed to the preservation of life and independence . . . within defined national frontiers. The Grand National Assembly and government of Turkey, in the name of the nation they represent, are very modest, very far from fantasies, and completely realistic. . . .
>
> Gentlemen, we are not men who run after great fantasies and present a fraudulent appearance of doing things which in fact we cannot do. Gentlemen, by looking as though we were doing great and fantastic things, without actually doing them, we have brought the hatred, rancour, and malice of the whole world on this country and this people. We did not serve pan-Islamism. We said that we had and we would, but we didn't, and our enemies said: 'let us kill them at once before they do!' We did not serve pan-Turanianism. We said that we could and we would, and again they said: 'let us kill them!' There you have the whole problem. . . . Rather than run after ideas which we did not and could not realize and thus increase the number of our enemies and the pressure upon us, let us return to our natural, legitimate limits. And let us know our limits. Gentlemen, we are a nation desiring life and independence. For that and that alone may we give our lives.[1]

In another speech delivered in 1923, his renunciation of old style military empire is still more explicit:

> My friends, those who conquer by the sword are doomed to be overcome by those who conquer with the plough, and finally to give place to them. That is what happened to the Ottoman Empire. . . . The arm that wields the sword grows weary and in the end puts it back in the scabbard, where perhaps it is doomed to rust and moulder; but the arm that holds the plough grows daily stronger, and in growing stronger becomes yet more the master and owner of the soil.[2]

One of the more remarkable features of the decline of the Ottoman Empire is the extent to which the Turks were conscious of the process and discussed it among themselves. The long debate on the question 'what is wrong with the Empire?' began during the reign of Süleyman the Magnificent, when the Empire was still at its height. It continued during the seventeenth century when the succession of Ottoman victories in Europe gave way to a stalemate and was resumed with added urgency when the stalemate in turn was ended by a series of defeats from the late seventeenth century onwards. In 1822, an Ottoman official called Akif

Efendi drafted a memorandum discussing the dangers confronting the Empire and the different ways of dealing with them.

> The Muslims must choose between three resolutions: either, faithful to the command of God and the law of Muhammad, we must, regardless of our property and our lives, defend to the last what provinces we still retain; or we must leave them and withdraw to Anatolia; or finally—which God forbid—we shall follow the example of the peoples of Crimea, India and Kazan and be reduced to slavery. In fine, what I have to say can be reduced to this: in the name of the faith of Muhammad . . . let us proclaim the Holy War and let us not cede an inch of our territories.[3]

For Akif, the danger—certainly a real one—was that Turkey, like other parts of the Muslim world, would fall under colonial rule. There were, as he saw it, three choices: to try at all costs to maintain the Empire, to submit to foreign rule, or to retreat to the Anatolian heartland from which the Turks had first entered Europe. During the century and a half that followed, the Turks failed in the first, avoided the second, and finally succeeded in the third.

The Ottoman retreat from empire was a long, slow, and hard-fought process beginning in the suburbs of Vienna in the seventeenth century and ending in the highlands of Anatolia in the twentieth. In its final stages it involved an endless succession of wars: the Balkan wars, in which most of the remaining European provinces of the Empire were lost; the Italo-Turkish war, in which the last footholds in Northern Africa were abandoned; the Yemen war, in which countless, hapless Turkish soldiers died in a futile attempt to maintain Turkish sovereignty at the southern end of the Red Sea; the First World War, in which the Ottoman Empire, after a long and bitter struggle, lost virtually all its territories—and then, in refreshing contrast, the War of Independence, the first major victory for centuries, which enabled the Turks to restore their national life in the Anatolian heartland in a Turkish national state. It was not surprising that for most Turks, Empire meant endless defeat, retreat, and suffering; nationalism and the national state meant success, victory, and the beginning of a new life.

After the establishment of the Turkish Republic there was not only a renunciation of empire; there was a positive revulsion. Not only the Imperial house and the Imperial provinces but even the Imperial capital was abandoned. The center of the new Turkish Republic was not in the ancient city of Istanbul with its immemorial traditions of empire and more recent taint of decadence; instead it was moved to the hill city of Ankara, high on the Anatolian plateau, typifying and symbolizing the replacement of the cosmopolitan Ottoman Empire by a national Turkish state based on the Turkish homeland. Istanbul was deliberately neglected and starved of resources which were lavished on the new capital. And for some years, the fallen Ottoman dynasty and everything connected with it were accorded the same treatment in Turkish school histories as was formerly accorded to the Tsars in Soviet Russia. It was only gradually that Kemalist Turkey began to find it possible to come to terms with the Ottoman past, now presented as a part of the greater Turkish heritage, with the Ottomans merely as one in the succession of Turkish dynasties.

The Turkish rejection of their imperial past was at once an ideology, a policy, and a mood—yet, inescapably, much of it remained, for better or for worse. One example may be seen in the relatively large numbers of civil and military officials who had served in the lost provinces and who now returned to the homeland. Thanks to these, the Turkish Republic in its early formative years was able to draw on much larger cadres of trained and experienced administrators than were available to many other peoples embarking on a new life as nation states. They served Turkey well and enabled the fledgling republic to survive many early difficulties.

Another inheritance not less important was the habit of responsibility. One of the main problems in newly independent states is the legacy of a past in which responsibility for all that went wrong could—often rightly—be ascribed to foreign rule or intervention; this would sometimes breed a habit of irresponsibility which survived into the new era. The Turks did not at any stage—except perhaps briefly during the Kemalist war of independence—have their political life bedeviled by foreign domination and the struggle to end it. The Turks were always masters in their own house—and indeed for long periods in other houses, too; they had retained the habit of calm and practical assessment of situations, of making decisions, and of accepting responsibility for the consequences of those decisions. This may have helped the Turks—alone in the Muslim world—to create and maintain, despite many difficulties, a working parliamentary democracy. It may also explain a quality observable in the policies of the Turkish Republic, more particularly in its foreign policy—a kind of practicality and of realism lacking in other parts. In this may be seen the legacy if not of empire then at least of many centuries of sovereign independence.

A more negative consequence of the Imperial past was a certain contempt for commerce and industry and those engaged in them. In the Empire the Turks had been peasants and artisans at the lower level or part of the apparatus of power—civil, military, or religious—at the higher level. Industry, commerce, and finance were left very largely to non-Turks and in the central lands even to non-Muslims, mostly Greeks, Armenians, and Jews. The rivalries and vicissitudes of these competing non-Muslim communities form an important and somewhat neglected chapter in Ottoman history. In the Republic the non-Muslim communities were greatly reduced in numbers and would probably have been unable, even if expected, to fulfil the economic role of their immediate forebears. Instead, Muslim Turks now took it upon themselves to produce a commercial, technical, and managerial middle class, only the merest rudiments of which had come into being under the Empire. It was a difficult task, and there can be little doubt that the social and cultural attitudes inherited from the Imperial past hindered and delayed its accomplishment.

There are other more subtle legacies of empire—for example a certain attitude to former subject peoples which made it difficult for a while to accept and treat them as equals. This has now passed. Dealings with the former Ottoman successor states are as between one nation and another even where, as with Greece, there is an adversary relationship. Sometimes, indeed, former subjects are treated not only with respect but even with deference.

A certain Imperial pride which persisted long after the fall of the Empire made Turks unwilling to plead or argue in their own cause, especially with those whom they felt entitled to regard as friends. This habit of mind often placed the Turks at some disadvantage as against their rivals or opponents and impeded the presentation of the Turkish case abroad. It was, in part, this disdain for the arts of propaganda and public relations which led to the striking isolation of Turkey at the United Nations. Even now, dignified reticence rather than persuasive eloquence is the quality which the Turks seem most to admire and therefore cultivate.

In one important respect the Turks seem to have fared rather better than some other post-imperial socieites, and that is in accepting and accommodating themselves to their new place in the world. Turkish statemen and diplomats do not take the view that since their decisions and actions no longer determine the course of world events there is no point in bothering at all. On the contrary, they have adjusted themselves to their position as a middle ranking power and have adapted their perceptions and policies accordingly. The decline of the Ottoman Empire was slow and was resisted step by step; its end was clear and unequivocal. This double quality of sustained struggle and final clarity, as contrasted with the swift disintegration and blurred ending of the colonial empires, may have helped to prepare the Turks for their new role.

Something of the feelings of a Turk of the last generation of empire may be seen in the writings of a journalist called Falih Rıfkı Atay who visited London in 1934 to cover the World Economic Conference. In a book which he wrote at the time entitled *The Banks of the Thames,* he gives the text of a speech which he would have liked to deliver to an English audience in Hyde Park "if only I had known enough English":

> I too am the child of a great empire. We came to it in the last days of its decline, as to the leavings of a banquet. I don't know if you can imagine the geography of this Sultanate as it still was in the time of our grandfathers. Let me explain what happened to us taking your own geography as an example. We began to fight in Bombay. Fighting all the way across the continent we fell back upon London and made our last stand in Glasgow. Now our borders are at Dover.
>
> When the Ottoman Empire was already a hundred years old England without Scotland or Ireland was a little country of three million inhabitants and London a town of 40,000. Like Bulgaria they sold sheep to the Europeans; like India they sold raw materials to the manufacturing Flemings.

Because our empire was founded by conquerors its end was epic. Because yours was founded by merchants you are making a liquidation. . . . We left the Danube to the tune of "fair Buda," Africa to the "Algerian march," the Arabian Sea to the dirge "O Gazis" and we returned weeping to the soil of Anatolia. You are driven back to your island by downward turned graphs.

Because I was born and grew up in the atmosphere and the morality of an empire I feel from afar, in the atmosphere and morality of London, with the sensitivity of a seismograph, the tremours of impending collapse.

The great tree, rotted within, is awaiting a thunderbolt or a severe storm to hurl it to the ground.[4]

Ibn Khaldūn in Turkey

18

It has by now become a commonplace of Middle Eastern studies that the discovery, evaluation, and appreciation of the *Muqaddima* of Ibn Khaldūn is an achievement of European scholarship. The Arabic text was first printed in the edition of Etienne Quatremère, published in Paris in 1858; the first complete translation into a European language, the French version of Baron William MacGuckin de Slane, was published in Paris between 1862 and 1868 and for the first time made this masterpiece of historical and sociological thought available to the modern world.

Even before these major publications, Ibn Khaldūn was not unknown to European scholarship. During the first quarter of the nineteenth century, a number of articles appeared in learned journals and elsewhere, containing excerpts and translations from the *Muqaddima* and the History of Ibn Khaldūn, as well as some discussion of these works.[1] Among them are studies by Silvestre de Sacy, who included some excerpts from the *Muqaddima* in his Arabic chrestomathy,[2] and others by Joseph von Hammer, the great Austrian historian of the Ottoman empire. Besides his articles, Hammer refers a number of times in his Ottoman history to Ibn Khaldūn, whom he calls "the Arab Montesquieu."[3]

The facts of the awakening and rapid development of European interest in Ibn Khaldūn, as the epoch-making character of his work was recognized, are clear and well known. What is much less known is the earlier interest and appreciation of his work among the Ottomans. It has often been said that Ibn Khaldūn was neglected and forgotten by his own people, until he was again brought to their notice by Western scholarship. It is doubtful if this is true for North Africa; it is certainly not true for the Ottoman East, where Ibn Khaldūn was known and read, exercising considerable influence.[4]

The Ottoman conquest of the Mamlūk Sultanate of Egypt and Syria touched off a new interest among the Turks in these newly acquired territories and particularly in Egypt. Books were written or adapted into Turkish dealing with the history and geography of Egypt and neighboring countries; the quantity and the variety of Arabic manuscripts of Egyptian provenance preserved in Turkish libraries attest to the widespread interest among Ottoman scholars in the literary heritage of the defunct Mamlūk Sultanate. These holdings include manuscripts of the history and of the *Muqaddima* of Ibn Khaldūn.

These manuscripts were not only available in Istanbul; they were read, and by the seventeenth century there are clear indications of their impact and influence. Three important Turkish authors of the time are particularly revealing. The great scholar, bibliographer, geographer, historian, and polymath Ḥājjī Khalīfa, known as Kâtib Chelebi (1609–1657) names Ibn Khaldūn several times and shows clear signs of his intellectual influence. In his historical writings he cites both the name and ideas of Ibn Khaldūn; in his great bibliography of Arabic books, the *Kashf al-Ẓunūn*, he has entries to Ibn Khaldūn's work under both *Tārīkh* and *'Ibar*, with a cross-reference under *Muqaddima*. Under the first two headings he gives a description of the book and an appreciation of the *Muqaddima* as a comprehensive study of the nature of human history and society.[5] Kâtib Chelebi was also the author of a little treatise entitled "The Rule of Action for the Rectification of Defects" in which he discussed the vexed problem of what was wrong with the Ottoman Empire and what could be done to put it right. Kâtib Chelebi begins his essay, after a brief note on the circumstances which had led him to write it, with a theory on the growth, decline, and death of states that is clearly derived from the *Muqaddima*.[6]

A second Ottoman author of the time to cite Ibn Khaldūn was the Aleppo-born historian Na'īmā (?–1716), a disciple incidentally of Kâtib Chelebi. Na'īmā's chronicle begins with an introduction discussing the nature of history and the rise and fall of human societies, again clearly influenced by Ibn Khaldūn, to whom indeed he refers explicitly. Naming a number of Arabic histories which he had found useful, such as the

Khiṭaṭ and *Sulūk* of Maqrīzī, he goes on to say: "Above all there is the Arabic history of the Maghribī Ibn Khaldūn, *'Unwān al-'ibar fī dīwān al-mubtada' wa'l-khabar,* a work of which the introduction (*Muqaddima*) alone is a whole volume and which is a treasure house filled with gems of learning and rarities of wisdom. Its author is the greatest of all historians. His book is concerned with the history of the Maghrib but its introduction embraces the whole of knowledge."[7]

A third seventeenth-century Ottoman historian who shows clear traces of Ibn Khaldūn's influence is Aḥmed ibn Luṭfullah (?–1702), known as Münejjimbashi, the chief astrologer, after the office which he held. His universal history, written in Arabic but published in a Turkish translation by the early eighteenth-century poet Nedīm, includes an introduction on the nature of history and historiography, clearly based on the *Muqaddima* and often following it verbatim.[8]

By the following century interest was sufficient to evoke a translation. The translator was Meḥmed Ṣāḥib, usually known as Pīrīzāde (1674–1749). Pīrīzāde, the son of a janissary officer, joined the ulema profession and in due course rose to become Sheykh ul-Islam. He began his translation of Ibn Khaldūn into Turkish in 1725 and abandoned it five years later, when he had completed about two thirds of the *Muqaddima.*[9] The remaining third was translated in the following century by the historian Jevdet Pasha, who also arranged for its publication.[10]

Though unfinished and unpublished, Pīrīzāde's translation seems to have had some impact on Turkish readers, even outside the narrow circle of scholars and literati. At least two Turkish ambassadors to Europe in the eighteenth century found an analytical tool in the *Muqaddima* with which to explain recent events in Europe. One was Resmī Efendi, who went as ambassador to Vienna in 1757 and to Berlin in 1763. Discussing the changes in the European situation following the diplomatic revolution, the rise of the new power in Prussia and the victories of King Frederick over his enemies, he remarks: "In the words of Ibn Khaldūn, the complete victory of a newly created state over an old established state depends on the length of time and the recurring sequence of events."[11] A little later, in 1790, another Ottoman ambassador, 'Aẓmī Efendi, who represented the Sultan in Berlin, speaks of the love of comfort and tranquility prevailing among Europeans and ascribes this to "the loss of virility" which, he says, Ibn Khaldūn had seen as a characteristic of the period of decline of a society.[12]

Such allusions, in the writings not only of scholars but also of officials on diplomatic missions, make it clear that Ibn Khaldūn's notions had become part of the intellectual atmosphere in the Ottoman capital—perhaps not surprisingly, at a time when the Ottomans were increasingly conscious of the decline in their own power relative to that of Europe. A reading knowledge of Arabic would have been widespread among educated Ottomans, and in any case by that time the greater part of the *Muqaddima* was available in a Turkish translation. Its popularity is indicated by the number of manuscripts in which it survives.

One cannot say with certainty that the European interest in the *Muqaddima* of Ibn Khaldūn goes back to a Turkish source, but it seems a likely hypothesis. Hammer was obviously familiar with Turkish written sources and personally acquainted with Ottoman diplomats and other officials. Sacy remarks of the work of Ibn Khaldūn that "it enjoys great celebrity in the Levant, and indeed deserves this renown."[13] In any case, it is clear that the Turkish discovery of Ibn Khaldūn, if it did not inspire that of Europe, undoubtedly preceded it. David Ayalon has shown how Ibn Khaldūn recognized and appreciated the role and importance of the Turks in Islamic history. In this small contribution in his honor, I have tried to show how the Turks appreciated the role and importance of Ibn Khaldūn in Islamic historiography.

PART V

IN BLACK AND WHITE

Corsairs in Iceland

19

For many centuries the Barbary corsairs had operated principally in galleys. These vessels required hundreds of rowers, who were expensive both to obtain and to maintain, and were in any case becoming more difficult to find. The cruising range of the galley was limited by the need to carry great quantities of food and water for the rowers, while its construction, designed for the calmer waters of the Mediterranean, made it unfit to withstand the heavier strains of the open ocean.

At the beginning of the seventeenth century, however, an important development took place which enabled the corsairs greatly to extend the scope and scale of their enterprises. After the death of Queen Elizabeth of England in 1603, the new king, James I, at last made peace with Spain, and by the treaty of 1604 the long maritime war between the two countries came to an end. At about the same time the long Spanish struggle with the Netherlands ended, and in 1609 Spain was finally compelled to recognize the independence of the Dutch. The many English and Dutch sea-rovers, who had played an important part in the struggle against Spain, now became not only unnecessary but a nuisance, and the English and other western governments began to adopt measures of increasing severity against their own pirates for the protection of international trade. Many of these pirates, finding conditions in their own countries less and less favorable to the exercise of their profession, fled to the states of the North African littoral, where they received a ready welcome. English and Dutch pirates, accustomed to navigating the oceans of the world on square-rigged sailing ships with their armament disposed along their sides, introduced these vessels to their hosts and instructed them in their construction and use. The corsairs, quick to realize the advantages of the broadside sailing-ship over the galley, mastered the arts of navigation and warfare with these new vessels with remarkable speed, and before long fleets from North Africa were sailing beyond the Strait of Gibraltar and ravaging as far away as Madeira, England, and Ireland. Certainly their boldest venture was their raid on Iceland in the year 1627.[1]

The first published account of this expedition is that of the French priest Pierre Dan, who visited North Africa in 1634 to arrange for the redemption of Christian captives. In his history of the Barbary corsairs published in Paris in 1637, he tells briefly of an Algerian corsair raid on Iceland in 1627. It was carried out, he says, by three ships and was led by a renegade of German origin known as Come Murat. The corsairs raided a number of different places on the Icelandic coast and carried off 400 captives.[2]

A second French account dates from the year 1642. In that year Sieur Emanuel d'Aranda, about to leave Algiers on being ransomed from captivity, was approached by a young "Turk" who asked him to carry a letter to the Danish minister in Madrid. D'Aranda, puzzled by so odd a request, questioned the man, who turned out to be an Icelander converted to Islam. "Some years earlier," the man told him, "an Icelandic renegade, having for long sailed with the corsairs of this city without making any prize, suggested to the captain that they should sail to Iceland." The raid was made and produced 800 captives, many of whom were still awaiting ransom.[3]

These two brief and contradictory accounts are all that, to my knowledge, is to be found in general Western sources of the time on the expedition to Iceland of the Algerian corsairs. So extraordinary an event, however, was not passed over in silence by the Icelanders themselves, nor by the Danes, to whose king Iceland was at that time subject. In both Icelandic and in Danish there is a considerable volume of material on the raid, and even a prayer in the Icelandic liturgy asking God for protection against "the cunning of the Pope and the terror of the Turk."

The first account to be published was the narrative of Olafur Egilsson, an Icelandic priest from Heimaey, in the Vestmann Islands, who was captured by the corsairs and taken to Algiers. After a short stay, he was sent by his captors to Copenhagen to negotiate with the Danish authorities for the ransom of the captives. His account of his adventures, from his capture to his return home on 6 July 1628, was first published in a Danish translation in 1641.[4] The Icelandic original was not printed until 1852, when it appeared in Reykjavík together with another brief and contemporary account by Klaus Eyjolfsson.[5] Another important contemporary source, the *Tyrkjarânssaga* of Björn Jónsson of Skardsà (1574–1655) was printed in 1866.[6] It was written in 1643 and based on the two above mentioned texts, supplemented by letters from captives in Algiers, oral information from ransomed captives, and a number of other written sources that are no longer extant. A critical study of the whole episode was published in Danish in 1899 by the Icelandic scholar Sigfús Blöndal.[7] It was based not only on the printed sources then available but also on a number of narratives and records then still in manuscript, including many letters from Icelandic and Danish captives preserved in various collections. Finally, in 1906–9, another Icelandic scholar, Jón Thorkelsson, published a volume of texts containing all the known sources on the expedition. After a detailed historical introduction on the raid, its origin, course, and results, he gives critical texts of twelve different accounts of the expedition. These are followed by a collection of letters and other documents, including letters from prisoners, negotiations about ransoms, reports on the Icelandic captives in Algiers, accounts and correspondence on the collection of money and the arranging of ransoms. The volume ends with a collection of poems and ballads in Icelandic relating to the raid.[8]

The story begins on 20 June 1627, when an Algerian ship entered the little port of Grindavík, on the south coast of Reykjanes, the southernmost promontory on the west coast of Iceland. The origins of the raid are uncertain. Returned Icelandic captives said that the originator of the raid was a Danish captive in Algiers, whom they name only as Paul. In return for a promise of freedom he gave the corsairs information about the Northern Seas, which he knew well, and accompanied them on the raid. This man is probably identical with the Icelandic renegade mentioned by d'Aranda.

According to Icelandic reports twelve ships set out on the expedition, of which only four actually reached Iceland. The others probably went to England. The leader of the expedition was one Murad Reis, variously described as a German or Flemish (= Dutch) renegade. The rest of the expedition was, as usual, of mixed origin—some Turks, some Western converts, as well as a number of Western captives employed as slaves. This is how Olafur Egilsson describes his captors (the reader will note Olaf's naive astonishment that the dreaded corsairs looked "just like other people," and his remark that it was the converts who behaved worst):

> Now I will say something about how these wicked people looked, both as regards their faces and their clothing, namely, that they were exactly like other people, unequal of height, some white, some with darker faces; some were not Turks, but people of other countries, such as Norwegians, Danes, Germans and English; of these, those who had not left their religion still wore their old clothes in which they had been captured, and had to do the most dangerous work that arose, and received blows as wages. But the Turks (*i.e.*, Muslims) all had tall red caps, some cocked, with gold galloons, some with silk and others with braid; they wore long robes, bound round with sashes, as their robes were very wide; they wore tight canvas breeches, and many went barefoot, with iron heels under their feet; they had black hair, and were shaved except over the mouth, where they had moustaches. The real Turks in their behaviour were just like other nations, if one may say so; those who had been Christians and abandoned their faith followed in clothes, beards and other things the same usage as the Turks, and it was just these that killed people, cursed and beat them, and did all that is evil.[9]

When the corsair fleet arrived off Iceland, it was split up by a severe storm. One ship, separated from the others, entered Grindavík alone on 20 June. In the harbor lay a Danish merchant ship. The corsairs pretended to be whale-fishers and thanks to this disguise were able to seize the cargo of the Danish ship without any difficulty. After a raid ashore they sailed out with booty and prisoners. On their way out they met another Danish merchant ship, which they boarded and captured, putting a corsair crew on board. One of the captured ships was sent back to Algiers with the booty; the other two ships sailed round the west coast of Iceland in the direction of Faxa Bay.

News of the raid spread rapidly, causing great alarm. A system of signal warnings was arranged, and both people and ships assembled at Bessastadir. This town, lying in a small bay called Seila, a few miles south of Reykjavík, was the residence of the Danish governor of Iceland and the center of administration throughout the seventeenth century. It so happened that at this time the famous Jon Olafsson, the Icelandic traveller who is remembered for his journey to India, was in Bessastadir on a visit, accompanied by some Frenchmen. His biography, written by his son Olafur Jónsson, gives the following account of the coming of the corsairs to Bessastadir:

> Jon Olafsson's journey was deferred, and he received orders to stay until he should know for certain how matters stood. The Governor ordered all to be ready to take up their positions for defence, and Jon Olafsson and the Frenchmen were commanded to repair to the fort and be ready to fire the cannon when needed. But the Governor with his servants and a great number of Icelanders in large brass-bound saddles rode about keeping watch with long staves in their hands, so that it was as if one saw armoured men, when the sun shone on their saddle-bows.
>
> And when they were all prepared for defence on land, the pirate ships began to sail into the harbour. When those on the ships and in the fort perceived this, they fired some salvos at them, and the pirates replied by firing on them on shore. But just this moment, by God's appointed plan, one of the two robber vessels ran aground and stuck fast, for the tide was far out. This was the vessel which had the captive people on board and most of the goods. When the other pirates saw this, both vessels lowered their boats to remove the people and goods from the stranded vessel to the other, in order to lighten it, and they also threw overboard many barrels of goods, meal, oil and other liquids, which were heaviest, and which they had taken on Danish ships. The most part drifted ashore, and on these were the mark of the merchant Bogi Nielsson, merchant at Skutilsfjörd. This Jon Olafsson recognized and so knew that a vessel from the Skutilsfjörd port must have been captured by the pirates. While the pirates were splashing about and conveying men and goods from one ship to the other, the Danes left off firing at them, both from the Danish ships, and (alas!) from the fort, but the Icelanders desired to fire at them as much as possible while they were in these difficulties. But in this they did not have their way,[10] and so the pirate ship floated off with the rising tide, and both left Seila, and sailed back along the south coast, and were seen no more until they came to the Vestmann Islands and plundered there in the month of June. These ships came to Seila shortly before the time of the Althing (Icelandic Parliament), and therefore neither the Governor, nor any of those then at Bessastadir, rode to the Althing that summer, by reason of the general terror.[11]

The vessels that later visited the Vestmann Islands were not in fact the same as those that had come to Bessastadir. These latter sailed home, without waiting for the others, and carried with them fifteen Icelandic and an unknown number of Danish captives.

Meanwhile two other ships sailed up the east coast. On 5 July they landed with four boats at the Herutsfjörd, and left again on 13 July with booty and captives. After several other small raids they sailed south with 110 captives. Off the south coast they met the fourth ship and together sailed to the Vestmann Islands. On their way they met an English fishing boat and forced the captain to give them pilots for the dangerous passage into Kaupstad harbor.

The Vestmann Islands are a group of small islands four miles south of Iceland, of which only the largest, Heimaey, was inhabited. It had been raided several times earlier in the century by Spanish and English pirates. News of the approach of the corsairs reached the islanders, and the Icelandic sources tell of wild rumors of "Turks with claws instead of nails, spitting fire and sulphur, with knives growing out of their breasts, elbows, and knees." The islanders hastily prepared defenses around the Danish trading house.

On the morning of 16 July three ships were sighted approaching the island. Despite the preparations no serious resistance was offered, and the corsairs were able to land three large forces. Much booty and many captives were taken, and a Danish merchant ship, the *Krabbe,* was seized in the port, filled with captives and manned by a corsair crew. The corsair flotilla fired nine shots from their cannon as a parting salute and sailed away with 242 captives.

The return journey to Algiers is vividly described by Olafur Egilsson, the captured priest from Heimaey. The weather was very bad, and for a week the *Krabbe* was separated from the other ships. The prisoners on the *Krabbe* outnumbered the corsairs several times and planned to revolt and seize the ship. The plan, however, was betrayed and frustrated. One of the prisoners was a Dane who got into conversation with the Danish renegade Paul and, no doubt with the idea of making himself important, asked him how many mice were needed to kill a cat. Paul understood what was in his mind and warned the other corsairs. The prisoners were put in irons until the *Krabbe* was able to rejoin the rest of the flotilla.

Olafur Egilsson remarks that the prisoners were quite well treated on the journey and notes with surprise that the Turks gave them beer, mead, and brandy to drink while they themselves drank only water.

The captives were confined below decks, and, says Olafur Egilsson:

> Since it was dark there, they had lamps burning both night and day, and every evening food was prepared for us, and we were given the same dishes as the officers got in their cabin; as long as the two tuns of beer and mead, which they seized in the merchants' house in Vestmann Island, lasted, we were given drink from them. They destroyed all the drink in the merchants' houses. Brandy they only gave us in the morning; the Turks never drink anything but water.[12]

The ships returned to Algiers on 17 August, and the captives were sold. Olaf was sent to Copenhagen to arrange ransom, and considerable efforts were made to collect money for this purpose. A document of 1635 lists thirty-one men and thirty-nine women as remaining in captivity, while another of the following year records the redemption of thirty-four. The testimony of d'Aranda shows that some were still in Africa in 1642. At least two of the captives stayed voluntarily and made a career among the corsairs. One of them, Jón Asbjarnarson, obtained a high post at the court of the Dey, while the other, Jón Jónsson Vestmann, became a sea captain in the corsair service. After many adventures he finally returned to Europe and died in Copenhagen.[13]

The Crows of the Arabs

20

Aghribat al-ʿArab, "crows or ravens of the Arabs," was the name given to a group of early Arabic poets who were of African or partly African parentage. Of very early origin, the term was commonly used by classical Arabic writers on poetics and literary history. Its use is well attested in the ninth century and was probably current in the eighth century, if not earlier. The term was used with some variation. Originally, it apparently designated a small group of poets in pre-Islamic Arabia whose fathers were free and sometimes noble Arabs and whose mothers were African, probably Ethiopian, slaves. As the sons of slave women, they were, by Arab customary law, themselves slaves unless and until their fathers chose to recognize and liberate them. As the sons of African women, their complexions were darker than was normal among the Arabs of the peninsula.

Both themes—servitude and blackness—occur in some of the verses ascribed to these poets and, in a sense, define their identity as a group. Professor ʿAbduh Badawī of Khartoum begins his book on the black Arab poets—the first serious and extensive study devoted to the topic—with this definition:

> This name [the crows of the Arabs] was applied to those [Arabic] poets to whom blackness was transmitted by their slave mothers, and whom at the same time their Arab fathers did not recognize, or recognized only under constraint from them.[1]

The term commonly used by the ancient Arabs for the offspring of mixed unions was *hajīn,* a word which, like the English "mongrel" and "half-breed," was used both of animals and of human beings. For example, *hajīn* would indicate a horse whose sire was a thoroughbred Arab and whose dam was not. It had much the same meaning when applied to human beings, denoting a person whose father was Arab and free and whose mother was a slave. The term *hajīn* in itself is social rather than racial in content, expressing the contempt of the highborn for the baseborn, without attributing any specific racial identity to the latter. Non-Arabs, of whatever racial origin, were of course baseborn, but so too were many Arabs who, for one reason or another, were not full and free members of a tribe. Full Arabs—those born of two free Arab parents—ranked above half-Arabs, the children of Arab fathers and non-Arab mothers (the opposite case was inadmissible). In turn, half-Arabs ranked above non-Arabs, who were, so to speak, outside the system.

Among the ancient Arabs there was an elaborate system of social gradations. A man's status was determined by his parentage, family, clan, sept, and tribe, and the rank assigned to them in the Arab social order. All this is richly documented in poetry, tradition, and a vast genealogical literature. A more difficult question is how far the ancient Arabs recognized and observed social distinctions among the various non-Arab peoples and races who supplied much, though not all, of the slave population of Arabia. According to Badawī, "there was a consensus that the most unfortunate of the *hajīns* and the lowest in social status were those to whom blackness had passed from their mothers" (*S*, p. 21).

At his discretion, the free father of a slave child could recognize and liberate him and thus confer membership of the tribe. Under the Islamic dispensation such recognition became mandatory. In pre-Islamic custom, however, the father retained the option; according to Badawī and the sources cited by him, Arab fathers at that time were reluctant to recognize the sons of black mothers. The alleged reason for this reluctance was their color, since

> the Arabs despised the black color as much as they loved the white color; they described everything that they admired, material or moral, as white. A theme in both eulogy and boasting was the whiteness of a man, just as one of the signs of beauty in a woman was also whiteness. It was also a proof of her nobility. In the

same way a man could be eulogized as 'the son of a white woman'. Similarly they would boast that they had taken white women as captives. [*S*, p. 21]

This is probably an accurate description of the social attitudes of the Bedouin aristocracy of conquest that emerged after the great expansion of the Arabs in the seventh century and for a while dominated the new Islamic empire which they created in the lands of the Middle East and North Africa. There may be some doubt, however, as to whether such attitudes prevailed before all this happened. Apart from some inscriptions, there is no contemporary internal historical evidence on life in Arabia on the eve of the birth of the Prophet Muḥammad. There is a great deal of poetry and narrative, which was however not committed to writing until much later, in Islamic times. Although very detailed and informative, it needs careful critical scrutiny, since it often projects back into the pre-Islamic Arabian past the situations and attitudes of the very different later age in which the texts were collected and written. This consideration applies with particular force to the poems and traditions relating to blacks, whose situation changed radically after the great Arab conquests, as did the attitude of the Arabs toward them.

The normal fate of captives in antiquity was enslavement, and Ethiopians appear, together with Persians, Greeks, and others, among the foreign slave population of Arabia. The proportion of black slaves is unknown, but, from such evidence as we have (for example, the lists of slaves and freedmen of the Prophet and of some of his companions), it would seem that they formed a minority. These slaves included a proportion of women, who were normally and lawfully used as concubines.

Arabic poetry and legend have preserved the names of several famous figures in ancient Arabia—notably, three poets said to have been born to Ethiopian mothers and, consequently, of dark complexion. The most famous of these was the poet and warrior ʿAntara, whose father was of the Arab tribe of ʿAbs and whose mother was an Ethiopian slave woman called Zabība. One of the greatest Arabic poets of the pre-Islamic period, he is by far the most important of the "crows of the Arabs." Of the twenty-four black Arabic poets studied by Badawī, ʿAntara alone ranks as a major figure in general Arabic literature. His poems, both authentic and ascribed, were collected in a *Dīwān,* and one of them is included among the seven *Muʿallaqāt,* the so-called Suspended Odes, which are regarded as the supreme achievement of pre-Islamic Arabic poetry. A famous warrior, ʿAntara is especially admired for his descriptions of battles. Some of the verses attributed to him speak of his unrequited passion for his paternal cousin ʿAbla, who scorned his love and whose father refused to give her in marriage to ʿAntara despite the Arab custom by which male cousins had first claim.

Already in early times ʿAntara had become the subject of a whole cycle of tales and legends. As the son of a slave mother, he was himself a slave; his father refused to recognize him. A relatively early narrative tells how he gained his freedom. One day his tribe, the ʿAbs, were attacked by raiders from a hostile tribe, who drove off their camels. "The ʿAbs pursued and fought them, and ʿAntara, who was present, was called on by his father to charge. 'ʿAntara is a slave,' he replied, 'he does not know how to charge—only to milk camels and bind their udders.' 'Charge!' cried his father, 'and you are free.' And ʿAntara charged."[2] If we are to accept as authentic certain verses ascribed to him, even ʿAntara, once free, despised those who were still slaves, and, proud of his half-Arab descent, looked down on the "jabbering barbarians" and "skin-clad, crop-eared slaves" who lacked this advantage. Later, as ʿAntar (the shortened form of his name), he became the hero of a famous Arab romance of chivalry that celebrated the wars against Persia, Byzantium, the Crusaders, and many other enemies. In one campaign, against the blacks in Africa, the hero penetrates farther and farther south until he reaches the empire of Ethiopia and discovers, in true fairy-tale style, that his mother, the slave girl Zabība, was the granddaughter of the emperor.

All this is clearly fiction, but even the early historical accounts of ʿAntara are questionable, and only a very small part of the poetry extant in his name can be ascribed to him with any certainty. The greater part, and especially the verses in which he complains of the insult and abuse that he suffered because of his blackness, is probably of later composition, some of it perhaps the work of other black poets. Some of these verses do indeed recur in various collections and are ascribed by name to later poets of African or part-African birth. The same verses are at times attributed to more than one of these poets. A famous verse ascribed only to ʿAntara runs:

> I am a man, of whom one half ranks with the best of ʿAbs
> The other half I defend with my sword.[3]

This may mean no more than that his mother was a slave, without reference to race or color. Other verses ascribed to ʿAntara, however, indicate that his African blood and dark skin marked him as socially inferior and exposed him to insult and abuse. In one poem he is even quoted as insulting his own mother:

> I am the son of a black-browed woman
> like the hyena that thrives on an abandoned camping ground
> Her leg is like the leg of an ostrich, and her
> hair like peppercorns
> Her front teeth gleam behind her veil like lightning
> in curtained darkness.[4]

In another poem he sounds a note that was unconsciously echoed centuries later:

> Enemies revile me for the blackness of my skin
> But the whiteness of my character effaces the blackness.[5]

Similar complaints are ascribed to other figures of the pre-Islamic and early Islamic period. Also named among the "crows of the Arabs" was a certain Khufāf, a contemporary of the Prophet. He was known as Ibn Nadba, after his mother. Khufāf, like the other original "crows of the Arabs," was the son of an Arab father and a black slave woman. He was, however, a man of high social position and was chosen to be chief of his tribe. A verse ascribed to him remarks that his tribe had made him chief "despite this dark pedigree."[6]

The third of the original trio of "crows of the Arabs" was Sulayk ibn al-Sulāka, another pre-Islamic poet whose father was an Arab of the tribe of Tamīm and whose mother was a black slave woman, according to most sources an Ethiopian. Sulayk found a different solution to his problems

—he became celebrated as a brigand. He was one of a number of brigand poets whose exploits form the subject of heroic narratives and whose verses are cited, usually together, in the early anthologies. By a confusion between the two groups—the "crows of the Arabs" and the brigand poets—several of the latter are described by some early sources as having been black, though this is not supported by the main tradition.

The best indication that the stories and verses about ʿAntara and Khufāf belong to a later period is their content, reflecting a situation which did not yet exist in pre-Islamic Arabia. This is shown by the very fact that men of such mixed social and racial parentage could attain a high position, something which would have been much more difficult, if not impossible, a century later. In pre-Islamic and early Islamic Arabia, Arabs had no reason whatever to regard Ethiopians as inferior or to consider Ethiopian ancestry as a mark of base origin. On the contrary, there is a good deal of evidence to show that the Ethiopians were regarded with respect, as a people on a level of civilization substantially higher than that of the Arabs themselves. A slave as such was of course inferior, but a black slave was no worse than a white slave; the sons of black slave women seem to have suffered no particular impediment. Many prominent figures in the earliest Islamic period had Ethiopian women among their ancestresses. They include no less a person than the caliph ʿUmar himself, whose father, al-Khaṭṭāb, had an Ethiopian mother. Another was the great general ʿAmr ibn al-ʿAṣ, conqueror of Egypt and one of the architects of the Arab empire.

The great change in the position of blacks and in the attitude of the Arabs toward them came after the creation of the empire. Conquest resulted in new sets of relationships, the most important of which was the transformation and enormous extension of the institution of slavery. In antiquity, most slaves had been of local provenance—enslaved for crime, debt, or money. From time to time the suppression of a rebellion or a war on the frontier flooded the market with slaves from far away. Otherwise, local sources of supply provided for local needs. Islam created a new situation by prohibiting the enslavement not only of freeborn Muslims but even of freeborn non-Muslims living under the protection of the Muslim state. The children of slaves were born slaves, but, for a number of reasons, this source of recruitment was not adequate.

The growing need for slaves had to be met, therefore, by importation from beyond the Islamic frontier. This gave rise to a vast expansion of slave raiding and slave trading in the Eurasian steppe to the north and in tropical Africa to the south of the Islamic lands. It is for this reason, no doubt, that the massive development of the slave trade in black Africa and the large scale importation of black Africans for use in the Mediterranean and Middle Eastern countries date from the Arab period. In one of the sad paradoxes of history, this resulted from one of the most important of the liberalizing and humanizing changes that the Islamic dispensation brought to the ancient world.

At first, there seems to have been no particular discrimination among the various nations and races of non-Arabs who made up the vast majority of the subject as well as the servile population. But in time, differences of color began to matter, and this is clearly indicated by the literary, pictorial, and even lexical evidence. One of the commonest Arabic words for slave, *ʿabd* (from a verb meaning "to serve"), mirrors these changes. In early classical usage, it means "slave," irrespective of race or color; by the High Middle Ages, its use is restricted to black slaves only; in later colloquial Arabic, it is used to mean blacks, whether slave or free. One reason for the change is surely that those who were of black or partly black origin were more visible. As Islam spread by conversion, the races of the Middle East and North Africa intermingled rapidly through polygamy and concubinage. As a result, the difference between the Arab conquerors and the kindred peoples of the region became less and less important. Only those of African origin showed visible and unmistakable evidence of their non-Arab ancestry. Slaves of white origin, from the Eurasian steppe and from Europe, could mingle into the population; this was much more difficult for Africans.

These changes are clearly reflected in the poetry ascribed to some of the poets of the seventh and eighth centuries, whom later Arab anthologists and literary historians of the classical period do not normally include among the "crows of the Arabs." Some of them are not the sons of Arab fathers and black mothers but are of purely African origin.

One of these latter was Suḥaym (who died in 660). His name is the diminutive form of a word meaning "black" and might be rendered as "little blackie." He was born and lived a slave and, indeed, was commonly known in literary histories as "the slave of the Banū'l-Ḥasḥās," after the family to which he belonged later in his life.

Suḥaym was of course a nickname; his real name is said to have been Ḥabba. According to one story, his owner offered him to the caliph ʿUthmān saying, "I can sell you an Ethiopian slave poet." The caliph, in this version, refused, remarking that he did not need a slave who treated his owners as did Suḥaym: "When he is sated he directs love-verses at their women, and when he is hungry he directs satires at them." Later Suḥaym passed into the hands of the Banū'l-Ḥasḥās, a clan of the tribe of Asad. He is variously described as an Ethiopian and as a Nubian. According to an early source he was branded on his face, a detail which suggests a Nubian rather than an Ethiopian origin. He is said to have angered the men of the tribe by flirting with their women, a practice for which he was eventually killed and burned by his owners.

In some of his poems, Suḥaym speaks of his love affairs and of the troubles they caused him:

> Though I hate servitude, I would gladly serve
>   as camelherd to Ibn Ayman
> provided that I am not sold, and that they tell me, "Slave! Take the
>   maiden her evening drink!"
> And I may prop a languorous lady,
>   sleep stripping her garment, baring her breast,
>   for even a slave may find an assignation.
> And if she refuse me, I hold her tight, she cannot break free,
>   so that her beauty and her charm are manifest.
>
> [*D*, pp. 56–57]

Such adventures were punished, and Suḥaym was condemned to imprisonment and flogging. He bore them with fortitude:

> If you imprison me, you imprison the son of a slavewoman,
>   if you free me, you free a tawny lion.
> Prison is no more than the shadow of the house where I live,
>   and a whipping no more than hide meeting hide.
>
> [*D*, p. 57]

But Suḥaym's amours did not always go well. In one poem he laments:

She points with her comb and says to her companion,
"Is that the slave of Banū'l-Ḥasḥās, the slick rhymester?
She saw a threadbare saddlebag, a worn cloak,
a naked negro such as men own.
These girls excite other men and turn away from my shock of hair,
despising me as I can clearly see.
If I were pink of color, these women would love me,
but my Lord has shamed me with blackness.
Yet it does not diminish me that my mother was a slavewoman
who tended the udders of she-camels.

[*D*, p. 26]

In another poem he defends himself in words which strikingly anticipate a famous poem of William Blake:

My verses serve me on the day of boasting
in place of birth and coin;
though I am a slave, my soul is nobly free;
though I am black of color, my nature is white.

[*D*, p. 55][8]

The same theme is expressed in several poems, often attributed to more than one of these black poets. Here are two examples:

Blackness does not degrade a whole man
nor a young man of discernment and breeding
If blackness has fallen to me as my lot
so has the whiteness of my character.

[*D*, pp. 54–55]

My blackness does not harm my habit, for I am like musk; who tastes
it does not forget.
I am covered with a black garment, but under it there is a lustrous
garment with white tails.

[*D*, p. 69]

Perhaps the most gifted of these black poets was Nuṣayb ibn Rabāḥ, who died in 726. The Arab literary historians have preserved some fragments of biographical information about him. From these and from his surviving poems, it is clear that he was very conscious of his slave birth and black color and that he endured many insults because of them. In one story, Nuṣayb was asked by his friends to reply in kind to an Arab poet who had composed some insulting verses alluding to his blackness. Nuṣayb refused. God, he said, had given him the gift of poetry to use for good; he would not abuse it by turning it into satire. And in any case, Nuṣayb responded, "all he has done is call me black—and he speaks truth." In a striking poem, Nuṣayb says of his own color:

> Blackness does not diminish me, as long
> as I have this tongue and a stout heart,
> Some are raised up by their lineage;
> the verses of my poems are my lineage.
> How much better is a black, eloquent and keen-minded,
> than a mute white.
> For this merit the nobleman envies me from his heights
> and no one gloats over me.

But in spite of this note of pride, Nuṣayb had his moments of desperation. Like other early black poets writing in Arabic, he cites the example of musk as something which is black but rare, precious and highly esteemed:

> If I am jet-black, musk is blacker,
> and there is no medicine for the blackness of my skin;
> I have a nobility that towers over their depravity
> like the sky over the earth.
> There are few of my like among your menfolk;
> there is no lack of your kind among the women.
> If you accept my advances, you respond to one who is compliant;
> if you refuse, then we are equal.[9]

Nuṣayb was able to make a career as a court poet, with the Umayyad caliph ʿAbd al-Malik. He is sometimes confused with another poet of the same name, known as Nuṣayb the Younger, who died in 791. By this time, the worsening condition of blacks in Islamic society brought a change of tone to this poetry—dignified self-respect turned to desperate self-deprecation. In a panegyric ode addressed to the caliph Hārūn al-Rashīd, Nuṣayb the Younger says of himself:

Black man, what have you to do with love?
Give over chasing white girls if you have any sense!
An Ethiop black like you can have no way to reach them.[10]

After the eighth century, blackness as a poetic theme almost disappears from Arabic literature. A few poets composed in Arabic in the black lands converted to Islam, but most black African Muslims preferred to use Arabic for scholarship and their own languages for poetry. In the central lands, though the flow of black as of other slaves continued, the school of self-consciously black poets came to an end. Few of the slaves were sufficiently assimilated to compose poetry in Arabic; while the few Arabic poets of African or part African ancestry were too assimilated to see themselves as black and therefore Other.

PART VI

HISTORY AND REVOLUTION

State and Society under Islam

21

Christendom and Islam are in many ways sister civilizations, both drawing on the shared heritage of Jewish revelation and prophecy and Greek philosophy and science, and both nourished by the immemorial traditions of Middle Eastern antiquity. For most of their joint history, they have been locked in combat, in an endless series of attacks and counter-attacks, jihads and crusades, conquests and reconquests. But even in struggle and polemic they reveal their essential kinship and the common features which link them to each other and set them apart from the remoter civilizations of Asia.

As well as resemblances, there are, of course, profound disparities between the two, and these go beyond the obvious differences in dogma and worship. Nowhere are these differences more profound—and more obvious—than in the attitudes of these two religions, and of their authorized exponents, to the relations among government, religion, and society. The founder of Christianity bade his followers "render unto Caesar the things which are Caesar's; and unto God the things which are God's"—and for centuries Christianity grew and developed as a religion of the downtrodden, until Caesar himself became a Christian and inaugurated a series of changes by which the new faith captured the Roman Empire and—some would add—was captured by it.

The founder of Islam was his own Constantine and founded his own empire. He did not therefore create—or need to create—a church. The dichotomy of *regnum* and *sacerdotium*, so crucial in the history of Western Christendom, had no equivalent in Islam. During Muḥammad's lifetime, the Muslims became at once a political and a religious community, with the Prophet as head of state. As such, he governed a place and a people, dispensed justice, collected taxes, commanded armies, waged war, and made peace. For the first generation of Muslims, whose adventures are the sacred and salvation history of Islam, there was no protracted testing by persecution, no tradition of resistance to a hostile state power. On the contrary, the state that ruled them was that of Islam, and God's approval of their cause was made clear to them in the form of victory and empire in this world.

In pagan Rome, Caesar was God. For Christians, there is a choice between God and Caesar, and endless generations of Christians have been ensnared in that choice. In Islam, there was no such choice. In the universal Islamic polity as conceived by Muslims, there is no Caesar, but only God, who is the sole sovereign and the sole source of law. Muḥammad was his Prophet, who during his lifetime both taught and ruled on God's behalf. When Muḥammad died in A.D. 632, his spiritual and prophetic mission, to bring God's book to man, was completed. What remained was the religious mission of spreading God's revelation until finally all the world accepted it. This was to be achieved by extending the authority and thus also the membership of the community which embraced the true faith and upheld God's law. To provide the necessary cohesion and leadership for this task, a deputy or successor of the Prophet was required. The Arabic word *khalīfa,* the title by which that successor came to be known, combines the two meanings. This was the title adopted by the Prophet's father-in-law and first successor, Abū Bakr, whose accession to the leadership of the Islamic community marked the foundation of the great historic institution of the caliphate.

Under the caliphs, the community of Medina, where the Prophet had held sway, grew in a century into a vast empire, and Islam became a world religion. In the experience of the first Muslims, as preserved and recorded for later generations, religious belief and political power were indissolubly associated: the first sanctified the second; the second sustained the first. The late Ayatollah Khomeini once remarked that "Islam is politics or it is nothing." Not all Muslims would go that far, but most would agree that God is concerned with politics, and this belief is confirmed and sustained by the Sharīʿa, the Holy Law, which deals extensively with the acquisition and exercise of power, the nature of authority, the duties of ruler and subject—in a word, with what we in the West would call constitutional law and political philosophy.

In the Islamic state, as ideally conceived and as it indeed existed from medieval through to Ottoman times almost into the nineteenth century, there could be no conflict between Pope and Emperor; in classical Middle Eastern Islam, the two mighty powers which these two represented were one and the same, and the caliph was the embodiment of both. As a building, a place of public worship, the Muslim equivalent of the church is the mosque; as an institution, a corporate body with its own hierarchy and laws, there is no church in Islam. For the same reason, there is no priesthood in the true sense of the term, and therefore no prelates or hierarchy, no councils or synods, to define orthodoxy and thus condemn heterodoxy. The ulema, the professional men of religion in the Islamic world, may perhaps be called a clergy in the sociological but certainly not in the theological sense. They receive no ordination, have no parishes, perform no sacraments. There is no priestly mediation between the worshiper and his God, and in early Islam there was no constituted ecclesiastical authority of any kind.

The primary function of the ulema—from a word meaning "knowledge"—is to uphold and interpret the Holy Law. From late medieval times, something like a parish clergy emerged, ministering to the needs of ordinary people in cities and villages, but these were usually separate from and mistrusted by the ulema and owed much more to mystical than to dogmatic Islam. In the later Islamic monarchies, in Turkey and Iran, a kind of ecclesiastical hierarchy appeared, but this had no roots in the classical Muslim tradition, and members of these hierarchies never claimed and still less exercised the powers of Christian prelates.

If one may speak of a clergy only in a limited sociological sense in the Islamic world, there is no sense at all in which one can speak of a laity. The very notion of something that is separate or even separable from religious authority, expressed in Christian languages by such terms as lay, temporal, or secular, is totally alien to Islamic thought and practice. It was not until relatively modern times that equivalents for these terms were used in Arabic. They were borrowed from the usage of Arabic-speaking Christians.

Yet, from the days of the Prophet, the Islamic society had a dual character. On the one hand it was a polity—a chieftaincy which successively became a state and an empire. At the same time, it was a religious community, founded by a Prophet and ruled by his deputies who were also his successors.

Christ was crucified, Moses died without entering the Promised Land, and the beliefs and attitudes of their religious followers are still profoundly influenced by the memory of these facts. Muḥammad triumphed during his lifetime and died a conqueror and a sovereign. The resulting Muslim attitudes can only have been confirmed by the subsequent history of their religion.

In the West, barbarian but teachable invaders came to an existing state and religion, the Roman empire and the Christian church. The invaders recognized both and tried to serve their own aims and needs within the existing structures of Roman polity and Christian religion, both using the Latin language. The Muslim Arab invaders who conquered the Middle East and North Africa brought their own faith, with their own scriptures in their own language; they created their own polity, with a new set of laws, a new imperial language, and a new imperial structure, with the caliph as supreme head. This state was defined by Islam, and full membership belonged, alone, to those who professed the dominant faith.

The career of the Prophet Muḥammad, in this as in all else the model which all good Muslims seek to emulate, falls into two parts. In the first, during his years in his birthplace Mecca (?570–622), he was an opponent of the reigning pagan oligarchy. In the second, after his migration from Mecca to Medina (622–632), he was the head of a state. These two phases in the Prophet's career, the one of resistance, the other of rule, are both reflected in the Qur'ān, where, in different chapters, the believers are enjoined to obey God's representative and to disobey Pharaoh, the paradigm of the unjust and tyrannical ruler. These two aspects of the Prophet's life and work inspired two traditions in Islam, the one authoritarian and quietist, the other radical and activist. Both are amply reflected, on the one hand in the development of the tradition, on the other in the unfolding of events. It was not always easy to determine who was God's representative and who was Pharaoh; many books were written, and many battles fought, in the attempt. Both traditions can be seen very clearly in the polemics and struggles of our own times.

Between the extremes of quietism and radicalism, there is a pervasive, widely expressed attitude of reserve, even of mistrust, of government. An example is the sharp difference, in medieval times, of popular attitudes towards the qadi, a judge, and the mufti, a jurisconsult in the Holy Law. The qadi, who was appointed by the ruler, is presented in literature and folklore as a venal, even a ridiculous figure; the mufti, established by the recognition of his colleagues and the general population, enjoyed esteem and respect. A recurring theme in biographies of pious men—of which we have hundreds of thousands—is that the hero was offered a government appointment and refused. The offer establishes his learning and reputation, the refusal his integrity.

Under the Ottoman sultans there was an important change. The qadi gained greatly in power and authority, and even the mufti was integrated into the public chain of authority. But the old attitude of mistrust of government persisted and is frequently expressed in proverbs, folk tales, and even high literature.

For more than a thousand years, Islam provided the only universally acceptable set of rules and principles for the regulation of public and social life. Even during the period of maximum European influence, in the countries ruled or dominated by European imperial powers as well as in those that remained independent, Islamic political notions and attitudes remained a profound and pervasive influence.

In recent years there have been many signs that these notions and attitudes may be returning, albeit in much modified forms, to their previous dominance. There are therefore good reasons to devote a serious study to these ideas, and in particular to how they deal with the relations among government, religion, and society.

The term "civil society" has become very popular in recent years and is used in a number of different—sometimes overlapping, sometimes conflicting—senses. It may therefore be useful to examine Islamic perceptions of civility, according to various definitions of that term.

Perhaps the primary meaning of civil, in the Middle East today, is as the converse of military; it is in this sense that civility must begin, before any other is conceivable. This has a special relevance in a place and at a time when the professional officer corps is often both the source and the instrument of power. Understood this way, Islamic society, at the time of its inception and in its early formative years, was unequivocally civil. The Prophet and the early caliphs that followed employed no professional soldiers but relied for military duties on a kind of armed, mostly voluntary militia.

It is not until the second century of the Islamic era (A.D. eighth century) that one can speak, with certitude, of a professional army. The caliph, who in early though not in later times occasionally commanded his armies, was nevertheless a civilian. So too was the *wazīr,* who, under the caliph's authority, was in charge of all branches of the government, both civil and military. The wazīr's emblem of office was an inkpot, which was carried before him on ceremonial public occasions. During the later Middle Ages, internal upheavals and external invasions brought about changes which resulted in the militarization of most Islamic regimes. This has persisted to modern times. During the late nineteenth and early twentieth centuries, there was an interlude of civilian, more or less constitutional government, mostly on Western models. During the 1950s and after, these civilian regimes, for the most part, came to an end and were replaced by authoritarian governments under ultimate military control.

This is, however, by no means universal. In some countries, including, for example, Saudi Arabia and Morocco, traditional monarchies still maintain a traditional civilian order; in others, such as Turkey and, later, Egypt and Pakistan, the military themselves have prepared the way for a return to civilian legality. On the whole, the prospects for civilianization at the present time seem to be reasonably good.

In the more generally accepted interpretation of the term civil society, civil is opposed not to religious or to military but to government as such. So construed, the civil society is one in which the mainsprings of organization, initiative, and action come from within the society rather than from above, from the holders of authority, the wielders of power. Islamic precept, as presented by the jurists and theologians, and Islamic practice, as reflected by the historians, offer a variety of sometimes contradictory precedents.

The tradition of private charity, for example, is old and deeply rooted in Islam and is given legal expression in the institution of *waqf.* A *waqf* is a pious endowment in mortmain, consisting of some income-producing property, the proceeds of which are dedicated to a pious purpose—the upkeep of a place of worship, a school, a bathhouse, a soup kitchen, a water fountain, and the like. The donor might be a ruler or government official; he might equally be, and very often was, a private person. Women, who in Islamic law had the right to own and dispose of property, figure prominently among founders of *waqfs,* sometimes reaching almost half the number. This is perhaps the only area in the traditional Muslim society in which they approach equality with men. By means of the institution of *waqf,* many services, which in other systems are the principal or sole responsibility of the state, are provided by private initiative. One of the major changes brought by modernizing autocrats in the nineteenth century was to bring the *waqfs* under state control. (Several present-day Muslim states, including Egypt, have departments or ministries of *waqfs.*)

Islamic law, unlike Roman law and its derivatives, does not recognize corporate legal persons, and there are therefore no Islamic equivalents to such Western corporate entities as the city, the monastery, or the college. Cities were mostly governed by royal officers, while convents and colleges relied on royal or private *waqfs.* There are, however, other groupings of considerable importance in traditional Muslim society. Such, for example, are the kin group—family, clan, tribe; the faith group, often linked together by common membership of a sufi fraternity; the craft group, joined in a guild; the ward or neighborhood within a city. Very often these groups overlap or even coincide, and much of the life of a Muslim city is determined by their interaction.

In the Islamic context, the independence and initiative of the civil society may best be measured not in relation to the state but in relation to religion, of which, in the Muslim perception, the state itself is a manifestation and an instrument. In this sense, the primary meaning of civil is nonreligious, and the civil society is one in which the organizing principle is something other than religion, that being a private affair of the individual. This idea received its first classical formulation in the *Letter Concerning Toleration* by the English philosopher John Locke, published in 1689. Locke's conclusion is that "neither Pagan, nor

Mahometan, nor Jew, ought to be excluded from the civil rights of the commonwealth because of his religion."

The first European country which actually accorded civil rights to non-Christians was Holland, followed within a short time by England and the English colonies in North America, where extensive though not as yet equal rights were granted to nonconformist Christians and to Jews. These examples were followed by others, and the libertarian ideas which they expressed contributed significantly to the ideologies of both the American and French Revolutions.

In time, these ideas were almost universally accepted in Western Christendom. Though few nations, other than France and the United States, accepted a formal constitutional separation of religion and the state, most of them in fact accepted secular principles. This virtually ended the earlier situation which the Danish scholar Vilhelm Grønbech spoke of as "a religion which is the soul of society, the obverse of the practical, a living and real religion, the practical relationship of the people to God, soul and eternity, that manifests itself in worship and works as a life-giving power in politics and economics, in crafts and commerce, in ethics as in law. In this sense," he concludes, "the modern state has no religion."

Despite the personal devoutness of great and growing numbers of people, Grønbech is right—the Western democratic state has no religion, and most, even among the devout, see this as a merit, not a defect. They are encouraged in this belief by the example of some states in Central and Eastern Europe, yesterday and today, where the principle of unity and direction was retained but with a shift of stress—religion replaced by ideology, and the church by the single ruling party, with its own hierarchy, synods, inquisition, dogmas, and heresies. In such countries, it was not the state that withered away but the civil society.

In the Islamic world, the dethronement of religion as the organizing principle of society was not attempted until much later and resulted entirely from European influences. It was never really completed and is perhaps now being reversed. Certainly in Iran, organized religion has returned to something like the status which it enjoyed in the medieval world, both Christian and Islamic. Indeed, in some ways—notably in the power of the priesthood and the emergence of a political prelacy—the

Iranian theocracy is closer to the Christian than to the classical Islamic model.

During the fourteen centuries of Islamic history, there have been many changes. In particular, the long association, sometimes in coexistence but more often in confrontation, with Christendom led to the acceptance, in the later Islamic monarchies in Iran and Turkey and their successor states, of patterns of religious organization that might suggest a probably unconscious imitation of Christian ecclesiastical usage. Certainly there is nothing in the classical Islamic past that resembles the more recent offices of the chief mufti of the Ottoman empire or the grand ayatollah of Iran.

These Western influences became more powerful and more important after the French Revolution—the first great movement of ideas in Christendom which was not Christian but was even, in a sense, anti-Christian and could therefore be considered by Muslim observers with relative detachment. Such earlier movements of ideas in Europe as the Renaissance, the Reformation, or the Enlightenment had no impact whatsoever on the Muslim world and are virtually unnoticed in contemporary Muslim philosophical and even historical writings. The initial response to the French Revolution was much the same, and the first Muslim comments dismiss it as an internal affair of Christendom, of no interest or concern to Muslims and, more important, offering them no threat.

It was on this last point that they were soon obliged to change their minds. The dissemination of French revolutionary ideas in the Islamic world was not left to chance but was actively promoted by successive French regimes, both by force of arms, and, much more effectively, by translation and publication. The penetration of Western ideas into the Islamic world was greatly accelerated when, from the early nineteenth century, Muslim students in increasing numbers were sent to institutions of higher education in France, Italy, and Britain, and later also in other countries. Many of these, on their return home, became carriers of infectious new ideas.

The revolutionaries in France had summarized their ideology in a formula of classical terseness—liberty, equality, fraternity. Some time was to pass before they, and ultimately their disciples elsewhere, came to realize that the first two were mutually exclusive and the third meaningless. Of far greater effect, in the impact of Western ideas on Islam, were two related notions—neither of them originating with the French Revolution but both of them classically formulated and actively disseminated by its leaders: namely, secularism and nationalism. The one sought to displace religion as the ultimate basis of identity, loyalty, and authority in society; the other provided an alternative.

In the new dispensation, God was to be doubly replaced, both as the source of authority and as the object of worship, by the Nation. Secularism as such had no appeal to Muslims, but an ideology of change and progress, free—as it seemed then—from any taint of a rival religion, offered attractions to nineteenth-century Muslims who were increasingly aware of the relatively backward and impoverished state of their own society, as contrasted with the wealth and power of Europe. Liberalism and patriotism seemed to be part of the same progressive ideology and were eagerly adopted by young Muslim intellectuals seeking arguments to criticize and methods to change their own societies. The West European civic patriotism proved to have limited relevance or appeal, but the ethnic nationalism of Central and Eastern Europe had greater relevance to Middle Eastern conditions and evoked a much more powerful response. According to the old view, the Muslims are one community, subdivided into such nations as the Turks, the Arabs, the Persians, and so forth. But according to the new, the Arabs are a nation, subdivided into Muslims and Christians, to which some were, for a while, willing to add Jews.

For a time the idea of the secular nation, defined by country, language, culture, and descent, was dominant among the more or less Westernized minority of political activists. Beginning with the decline and fall of the old Westernized elites in the mid-twentieth century and the entry into political life of more authentically popular elements, the ideal of the secular nation came under challenge and in some areas has been decisively defeated.

Nowadays, for the first time in many years, even nationalism itself is under attack and has been denounced by some Muslim writers as divisive and un-Islamic. When Arab nationalists complain that the religious fundamentalists are creating divisions between Muslim and Christian

Arabs, the fundamentalists respond that the secular nationalists are creating divisions between Arabs and other Muslims and that theirs is the larger and greater offense.

The attack on secularism—seen as an attempt to undermine and supplant the Islamic way of life—has been gathering force and is now a major element in the writings of religious fundamentalists and other similar groups. For these, all the modernizing leaders—Kemal Atatürk in Turkey, the Shah in Iran, Fārūq, Nasser, and Sadat alike in Egypt, the Baʿthist rulers of Syria and Iraq, and their equivalents elsewhere—are tarred with the same brush. They are all apostates who have renounced Islam and are trying to impose neo-pagan doctrines and institutions on the Muslim world. Of all the Muslim states, only one, the Turkish republic, has formally declared itself a secular state and legislated, in its constitution, the separation of religion and government. Indonesia, by far the largest Islamic state, includes belief in one God among the basic constitutional principles but does not formally establish Islam. Virtually all the others either proclaim Islam as the state religion or lay down that the laws of the state shall be based on, or inspired by, the holy law of Islam. In fact, many of them had adopted secular legislation, mostly inspired by European models, over a wide range of civil and criminal matters, and it is these laws that are now under strong attack.

This is of particular concern to the two groups which had, in law at least, benefited most from the reforms, namely women and non-Muslims. Hence the phenomenon, paradoxical in Western but not in Muslim eyes, that such conventionally liberal causes as equal rights for women have hitherto been espoused and enforced only by autocratic rulers like Kemal Atatürk in Turkey and Mohamed Reza Shah in Iran. For the latter, this was indeed one of the main grievances of the revolutionaries who overthrew him. It has been remedied under their rule.

Until the recent impact of Western secularist ideas, the idea of a non-religious society as something desirable or even permissible was totally alien to Islam. Other religious dispensations, namely Christianity and Judaism, were tolerable because they were earlier and superseded versions of God's revelation, of which Islam itself was the final and perfect version, and therefore lived by a form—albeit incomplete and perhaps debased—of God's law. Those who lacked even this measure of religious guidance were pagans and idolaters, and their society was evil. Any Muslim who sought to join them or imitate them was an apostate.

Some medieval Muslim jurists, confronting a new problem posed by the Christian reconquest, asked whether it was lawful for Muslims to live under non-Muslim rule and found different answers. According to one view, they might stay, provided that the non-Muslim government allowed them to observe the Muslim religion in all its aspects and to live a full Muslim life; according to another school, no such thing was possible, and Muslims whose homeland was conquered by a non-Muslim ruler were obliged to migrate, as the Prophet did from pagan Mecca to Medina, and seek a haven in Muslim lands, until in God's good time they were able to return and restore the rule of Islam.

One of the tests of civility is surely tolerance—a willingness to coexist with those who hold and practice other beliefs. John Locke, and most other Westerners, believed that the best way to ensure this was to sever or at least to weaken the bonds between religion and state power. In the past, Muslims never professed any such belief. They did however see a certain form of tolerance as an obligation of the dominant Islamic religion. "There is no compulsion in religion" runs a much quoted verse in the Qur'ān, and this was generally interpreted by Muslim jurists and rulers to authorize a limited measure of tolerance for certain specified other religious beliefs, though of course without questioning or compromising the primacy of Islam and the supremacy of the Muslims.

Does this mean that the classical Islamic state was a theocracy? In the sense that Britain today is a monarchy, the answer is certainly yes. That is to say that, in the Muslim conception, God is the true sovereign of the community, the ultimate source of authority, the sole source of legislation. In the first extant Muslim account of the British House of Commons, written by a visitor who went to England at the end of the eighteenth century, the writer expresses his astonishment at the fate of a people who, unlike the Muslims, did not have a divinely revealed law and were therefore reduced to the pitiable expedient of enacting their own laws. But in the sense of a state ruled by the church or by priests, Islam was not and indeed could not be a theocracy. Classical Islam had no priesthood, no prelates who might rule or even decisively influence those who did. The caliph, who was head of a governing institution that was state and church in one, was himself neither a jurist nor a theologian but a practitioner of the arts of politics and sometimes of war. There are no popes in Islamic history and no political cardinals like Wolsey or Richelieu or Alberoni. The office of ayatollah is a creation of the nineteenth century, the rule of Khomeini an innovation of the twentieth.

In most tests of tolerance, Islam, both in theory and in practice, compares unfavorably with the Western democracies as they have developed during the last two or three centuries but very favorably with most other Christian and post-Christian societies and regimes. There is nothing in Islamic history to compare with the emancipation, acceptance, and integration of other-believers and non-believers in the West. But equally, there is nothing in Islamic history to compare with the Spanish expulsion of Jews and Muslims, the Inquisition, the autos-da-fé, the wars of religion, not to speak of more recent crimes of commission and acquiescence. There were occasional persecutions, but they were rare and atypical, and usually of brief duration, related to local and specific circumstances.

Within certain limits and subject to certain restrictions, Islamic governments were willing to tolerate the practice, though not the dissemination, of other revealed, monotheistic religions. They were able to pass an even severer test by tolerating divergent forms of their own. Even polytheists, though condemned by the strict letter of the law to a choice between conversion and enslavement, were in fact tolerated, as Islamic rule spread to most of India. Only the total unbeliever—the agnostic or atheist—was beyond the pale of tolerance, and even this exclusion was usually enforced only when the offense became public and scandalous. The same standard was applied to the tolerance of deviant forms of Islam.

In modern times Islamic tolerance has been somewhat diminished. After the second Turkish siege of Vienna in 1683, Islam was a retreating force in the world, and Muslims began to feel threatened by the rise and expansion of the great Christian empires of Eastern and Western Europe. The old easy-going tolerance, resting on an assumption not only of superior religion but also of superior power, was becoming difficult for Muslims to maintain. The threat which Christendom now seemed to be offering to Islam was no longer merely military and political; it was beginning to shake the very structure of Muslim society. Western rulers and, to a far greater extent, their enthusiastic Muslim disciples and imitators brought in a whole series of reforms, almost all of them of Western origin or inspiration. These reforms increasingly affected the way Muslims lived in their countries, their cities and villages, and finally in their own homes.

These changes were rightly seen as being of Western origin or inspiration; the non-Muslim minorities, mostly Christian but also Jewish, were often seen, sometimes also rightly, as agents or instruments of these changes. The old pluralistic order, multi-denominational and polyethnic, was breaking down, and the tacit social contract on which it was based was violated on both sides. The Christian minorities, inspired by Western ideas of self-determination, were no longer prepared to accept the tolerated but inferior status accorded to them by the old order and made new demands—sometimes for equal rights within the nation, sometimes for separate nationhood, sometimes for both at the same time. Muslim majorities, feeling threatened, became unwilling to accord even the traditional measure of tolerance.

By a sad paradox, in some of the semi-secularized nation-states of modern times, the non-Muslim minorities, while enjoying complete equality on paper, in fact have fewer opportunities and face greater dangers than under the old Islamic yet pluralistic order. The present regime in Iran, with its ruling clerics, its executions for blasphemy, its consecrated assassins, represents a new departure in Islamic history. In the present mood, a triumph of militant Islam would be unlikely to bring a return to traditional Islamic tolerance—and even that would no longer be acceptable to minority elements schooled on modern ideas of human, civil, and political rights. The emergence of some form of civil society would therefore seem to offer the best hope for decent coexistence based on mutual respect.

The Significance of Heresy in Islam

22

For the medieval Muslim, the significance of heresy was religious: it was related, that is to say, to differences of belief, opinion, or practice concerning divinity, revelation, prophecy, and matters deriving from these. These matters, in Islam, extended to include the whole range of public and political life, and any further explanation, beyond the religious one, was unnecessary, even absurd, for what could be added to the greatest and most important of all the issues confronting mankind? The grounds and terms of argument between opposing religious factions were almost invariably theological. That is not to say that Muslim polemicists always accepted the good faith of their opponents. Very often they accuse those whose doctrines they dislike of pursuing ulterior motives—but usually these ulterior motives are themselves religious. The commonest of them is the recurring theme of a plot to undermine Islam from within in favor of some other faith. This is usually connected with some more or less fabulous figure, of superlative malignity and perversity, who functions as a *diabolus ex machina,* to explain dissension and heresy in the community. This is in part due to the general tendency of Islamic historical tradition to attribute to the limitless cunning and multifarious activity of an individual the results of a long development of thought and action; in part also to the tactic, familiar in other times and places, of discrediting critics within the community by associating them with enemies outside the community. The two classical examples are ʿAbdallāh ibn Sabaʾ and ʿAbdallāh ibn Maymūn al-Qaddāḥ. The first, a convert from Judaism and a contemporary of the Caliph ʿAlī (reigned

656–661), is credited with devising most of the beliefs and policies of the extremist Shīʿa in the first centuries of Islam. On the second, an associate of Ismāʿīl ibn Jaʿfar al-Ṣādiq (disappeared ca. 755–762), is fathered the whole complex development of the Ismāʿīlī religion and organization up to Fāṭimid times. He is variously described as a Jew, as a follower of the Mesopotamian Christian heretic Bardaisan, and, most commonly, as an Iranian dualist; like his predecessor, he is alleged to have sought to destroy Islam from within in the interests of his previous religion. Modern criticism has shown that the roles attributed to these two, together with many of the doctrines ascribed to them, are exaggerated, distorted, and in many respects fictitious.

The medieval European, who shared the fundamental assumptions of his Muslim contemporary, would have agreed with him in ascribing religious movements to religious causes and would have sought no further for an explanation. But when Europeans ceased to accord first place to religion in their thoughts, sentiments, interests, and loyalties, they also ceased to admit that other men, in other times and places, could have done so. To a rationalistic and materialistic generation, it was inconceivable that such great debates and mighty conflicts could have involved no more than "merely" religious issues. And so historians, once they had passed the stage of amused contempt, devised a series of explanations, setting forth what they described as the "real" or "ultimate" significance "underlying" religious movements and differences. The clashes and squabbles of the early churches, the great Schism, the Reformation, all were reinterpreted in terms of motives and interests reasonable by the standards of the day—and for the religious movements of Islam too explanations were found that tallied with the outlook and interests of the finders.

To the nineteenth century, obsessed with the problems of liberalism and nationality, only a struggle for national liberation could adequately explain the religious cleavage in Islam, the bitter controversies between doctrine and doctrine, the armed clash of sect with sect. The intuition of Gobineau and Renan, the insight of Dozy and Darmesteter helped to create a picture of Shiʿism as a liberal revival of the Persian national genius, as a resurgence of the Aryanism of Iran in generous revolt against the alien and constricting Semitism of Arabian Islam. Increased knowledge among scholars of Shīʿa literature and close acquaintance by travellers with Shīʿa practice soon exploded the legend of a liberal reformation. But the identification of Shiʿism with Iran was more persistent and derived some support from the adoption of Shiʿism as the state religion of Persia from the sixteenth century onwards, as well as from the frequent statements by early authors attributing Shiʿite doctrines and activities to Persian converts.

Nevertheless this hypothesis is now generally abandoned. Wellhausen, Goldziher, Barthold and others have shown that the main centers of early Shiʿism were among the mixed, predominantly Semitic-speaking population of southern Iraq; that Shiʿism was first carried to Persia by the Arabs themselves and for long found some of its most enthusiastic supporters there among the Arab soldiers and settlers, and in such places as the Arab garrison city of Qum—even today one of the most vigorous centers of Shiʿite religion in Persia. Though ethnic antagonisms played their part in these struggles—and the nineteenth-century scholars made a lasting contribution in discerning them—they were not the sole or even the most potent factor. The accusations of the early polemicists are directed against the old Persian religion, not against the Persian nation—and the charges of Iranian dualist infiltration can be paralleled by similar tales of Jewish and Christian attempts to insinuate their own doctrines into Islam under the cover of Islamic heresy. It was in North Africa, Egypt, and Arabia that Shiʿism won its earliest and most resounding political successes. Only two of the important independent dynasties of Muslim Persia professed the Shiʿite religion. The first, the tenth-century Būyids, came from the peripheral and untypical Persian province of Dailam, by the Caspian Sea. Despite their Shiʿism they were willing to preserve the Sunnī, Arab Caliphate, and their fall was followed by an effortless Sunnī restoration. The second, the sixteenth-century Safavids, were a Turkish-speaking family from the northwest, relying on Turkish support and professing doctrines that derive from the religious ideas of Turkish Anatolia and Azerbaijan, not from the Persians. Their success in forcibly imposing these doctrines on a country that was still predominantly Sunnī must be explained in terms of the moral and political condition of Iran in the sixteenth century. It has little bearing on the schisms and conflicts of earlier times.

The advance of knowledge and of understanding thus brought the abandonment of a theory which in any case had ceased wholly to satisfy. For the twentieth century, in the West at least, the problems of nationality and national liberation were no longer the main themes of the historic process. The expansion and contraction of societies, the clash of interests and classes, economic change and social upheaval, class war and cataclysm—these were the basic truths which the twentieth-century historian saw in the mirror of history. Kharijism, Shiʿism, and the other movements in Islam were now interpreted in terms not of national but of social categories, not of race but of class. In the first quarter of the twentieth century, the Russian progressive Barthold, the German conservative Becker, the Italian positivist Caetani, the French Catholic Massignon looked around them and achieved a new understanding of the revolutions of early Islam—both of those that succeeded and of those that failed.

At this point it may be useful to describe briefly the picture that Orientalist scholarship at the mid century offered of the causes and phases of heresy in Islam. While there were certainly differences of opinion or interpretation on many specific issues, the current pattern of thought was broadly as follows.

During the period between the death of the Prophet in 632 and the fall of the Umayyad Caliphate in 750 two main heretical groups developed, expressing in religious terms the opposition of certain parties to the existing social and political order and to the orthodox faith that was its moral and public expression. One of these, the Kharijites, drew on largely Bedouin support and expressed the resentment of the untamed nomads against the encroaching state—not so much against the Umayyad state specifically, as against the very fact and notion of the state, of a constituted authority exercising constraint and even coercion and curtailing the total freedom of tribal society. The Kharijite theory of the Caliphate carries the doctrine of consent to the point of anarchy, and the Kharijites have indeed been described as the anarchist wing of the revolutionary opposition.

The second and far more important opposition group was the *Shīʿat ʿAlī*, the party of ʿAlī, commonly known as the Shīʿa. This began as a political group supporting the claims of ʿAlī to the Caliphate but rapidly developed into a religious sect. As such, it reflected the outlook and aspirations of an important social class—the *mawālī* (singular *mawlā*)—those Muslims who were not full members by birth of an Arab tribe. The greater part of these were the non-Arab converts to Islam. These were to be found especially in the industrial and commercial quarters which grew up around the garrison cities planted by the Arabs in the conquered provinces. Around the cantonments where the Arab warriors were stationed, new cities appeared, full of *mawlā* craftsmen and merchants, purveying to the growing and diverse needs of the conquerors and thriving on the flow of gold brought by the conquests. Soon *mawlā* soldiers themselves took part in the wars of conquest, while their superior skill and experience gave them a predominant place in the day-to-day administration of the Empire. Conscious of their growing importance, they became increasingly resentful of the economic and social disabilities imposed upon them by the Arab aristocratic regime and rallied readily to a form of Islam that challenged the legitimacy of the existing Arab aristocratic state. Their aspiration was for an order in which all Muslims would be equal and Arab birth would no longer carry privileges. Their religious doctrines were adapted from their previous faiths. Judaeo-Christian and Persian messianism and legitimism prepared them to accept the claims of the descendants of the Prophet, who promised to overthrow the Empire of tyranny and injustice and establish an Empire of equity and justice.

Within the Shīʿa camp there were two main trends—a moderate one, with much Arab support and limited political objectives; and an extremist one, with mainly *mawlā* support, and with radical policies and tactics. The existing regime was Arab; Persians were prominent among the radicals, and some elements of ethnic conflict were injected into the struggle. But the *mawālī* were by no means exclusively Persian; many of them, including their leaders, were Arab, and the conflict was basically social rather than national.

The ʿAbbāsids rode to power on the crest of one of these religious opposition movements, and their victory was a social as well as a political revolution. In the first century of ʿAbbāsid rule the exclusive hegemony of the Arab aristocracy was ended, and men of many races found equal opportunity in a new social and political order. Renouncing their disreputable revolutionary antecedents, the ʿAbbāsids strove to formulate and inculcate a new orthodoxy, no longer the tribal cult of a race of alien conquerors but the universal religion of a universal empire. After some early and unsuccessful experiments with other religious ideas, the ʿAbbāsids eventually adopted the consensus of the theologians, which in time became orthodox, Sunnī Islam. Orthodoxy was once more the religion of the state and the existing order—and new heresies arose to meet the spiritual needs and material aspirations of the dissatisfied.

The first to oppose the ʿAbbāsids, their state, and their faith was the disappointed extremist wing of the movement that had brought them to power. Later, the great economic and social changes of the eighth and ninth centuries created new centers of discontent, especially among the artisans and workpeople of the swarming cities and among the dethroned and dispossessed Arab tribes of the desert borderlands. These discontents found expression in a welter of small radical sects, each with its own local and sectional support. Most of these sects accepted in one form or another the claims of the house of ʿAlī and are thus loosely classified as Shīʿite. By the beginning of the tenth century most of them had coalesced about one of two main groups. One of them, the Ithnāʿasharī or Twelver Shīʿa, continued the moderate, limited opposition of the early Arab Shīʿa; the other, the Ismāʿīlī sect, resumed the interrupted development of the earlier extremist *mawlā* Shīʿa. This second group carried through a successful uprising and established the Fāṭimid Caliphate, which reigned in Egypt for two centuries.

By the eleventh century social and political change in the East had once more created a revolutionary situation. The growth of feudal and military rule, accelerated and consolidated by the Seljuk invasions, brought massive upheavals. Arab and Persian landowners, dispossessed or subjugated by Turkish feudal lords, merchants ruined by the shortage of minted money and the decline of trade, bureaucrats chafing under the bridle of foreign military masters, all helped to swell the ranks of the discontented and rebellious. To these Ismaʿilism, in a revived and modified form, brought a seductive doctrine of moral and political revolution, now associated with a new and effective strategy of attack.

For a time the activities of the Ismāʿīlī Assassins were subordinate to the Fāṭimid capital in Cairo, but soon, as the Fāṭimids themselves fell under the domination of their Turkish military commanders, relations between Cairo and the Assassins were broken off, and the latter were free to pursue their radical ideas and policies uncontaminated by any links with state or empire. The Seljuks were well aware of the danger and endeavored to meet it. As their soldiers guarded the bodies of their servants from Assassin daggers, so their theologians and teachers guarded the minds of their subjects from Ismāʿīlī ideas. It is in this period that the *madrasa* appears—the theological seminary, founded as a center for the formulation and dissemination of orthodox doctrine, to meet the Ismāʿīlī challenge that came first from the colleges and mission-schools of Fāṭimid Egypt, later from the Assassins' castles in the mountains. At the same time the religious genius of al-Ghazālī (*d.* 1111) evolved a new form of orthodoxy, in which the cold, flat dogmas of the theologians drew warmth and contour from the intuitive and mystical faith of the Ṣūfīs. The tide of popular piety, given new channels and new impulses, began to flow towards and not away from the schools and the dynasty—the nearest Muslim equivalents of Church and State.

By the time of the great Mongol invasions of the thirteenth century, extremist Shiʿism had ceased to be a vital force in Islam. Here and there, in remote fastnesses of mountain and desert or isolated and immobilized amid alien surroundings, it dragged on an attenuated and fossilized existence. But in the main Islamic centers of the Middle East, the theologians and the people, driven towards one another by the double shock of Christian and Mongol invasion, henceforth professed the same orthodox Sunnī religion; the same, that is, in its essential central doctrines, though still varying greatly in belief and still more in practice and organization, from place to place and from group to group.

Since the thirteenth century the religious history of Middle Eastern Islam has been chiefly concerned with the interplay of dogmatic religion and popular piety. Though the great synthesis of al-Ghazālī and his successors brought the two into communion, they remained distinct—sometimes in alliance, sometimes in conflict, always modifying and influencing one another by alternate clash and compromise. For the people—as distinct from the State, the schools, and the hierarchy—the characteristic expression of religious life has remained, until our own time, the Ṣūfī brotherhood, with its mystical and ecstatic faith, its dervish saints and leaders, its latent hostility to the established theological and political order. Though the Ṣūfī orders in time became formally Sunnī and politically quietist, many of them remained suspect in the eyes of sultans and ulema—and occasionally, as in the great revolt of the Ottoman dervishes in the early fifteenth century, the buried embers of discontent burst into conflagration.

The above summary of the genesis and evolution of Islamic heresy is obviously incomplete and necessarily schematic and personal. But it reflects broadly the findings of modern scholarship; and indeed, as truth is dealt with by historians, it is in all probability substantially true—that is to say, it represents as much as can be seen in the evidence at present available by the present generation of observers, though in the future new sources may yield greater knowledge, new experience bring deeper insight.

But what after all do we really mean when we say that such-and-such an interest or motive "underlies" a religious movement—or, approaching the problem from the opposite angle, that one or another sect or doctrine "represents" or "expresses" a social group or aspiration? Does it mean, as the cruder disciples of our time would have it, that scheming men made unscrupulous use of religion as a mask or cloak behind which they hid their real purposes from their deluded followers? Does it mean, in Marxist terms, that the sect was the ideological exponent of the economic conditions and interests of a class—or, in the subtler language of Max Weber, that once an appropriate form of religion appeared in a certain stratum, the conditions of that stratum gave it the maximum chance of survival in the selective struggle for existence against other, less appropriate forms? The problem is of more than purely historical interest, since in our own day, in Iran, in Egypt, and in other Islamic countries, new religious movements are stirring beneath the secularized surface; brotherhoods and creeds are replacing the wrecked parties and programs that have never really responded to the needs and passions of the peoples of Islam.

It may bring us closer to an understanding of the meaning of heresy in Islam if we look at what the classical Islamic authors themselves said on the subject and in particular examine the precise import of the various technical terms used.

It is curious, even astonishing, that among the very few loan-words of European or Christian origin used in modern literary Arabic are the words *hartaqa*—"heresy" and *hurtūqī* (or *hartīqī*)—"heretic." This word first appears in the Christian Arabic literature of Syria, as far back as medieval times, and no doubt came by way of Syriac and the Eastern Churches. During the nineteenth century it began to pass into common Arabic usage. At first it appeared chiefly in translations of Western books and in Western Christian or non-religious contexts. But in our own day it is used by Muslim writers on Muslim history—not, admittedly, by those brought up on traditional theological lines, but by western-trained historians seeking to apply to their own history the principles and methods learnt elsewhere. Can it be that Islam, with its seventy-two and more named heresies, has no name for "heresy" and is thus in the position of the Red Indian tribe which, we are told, has a score of verbs for different ways of cutting but no verb "to cut"? Or is the notion of heresy in the Christian sense so alien to Islam that a loan-word was needed to describe it?

There are in fact several Islamic terms which are tendered as "heresy" by western scholars. They are by no means synonyms. Each has its own meaning, and none of them, as modern Arabic writers have found, can properly express that which in the Christian Churches is called heresy.

The first of these in order of appearance is *bid'a,* meaning "innovation," and more specifically any doctrine or practice not attested in the time of the Prophet. The term is thus the converse of *Sunna.* It is used commonly by the early theologians and even appears in the traditions attributed to the Prophet, who is quoted as saying that "the worst things are those that are novelties; every novelty is an innovation, every innovation is an error and every error leads to hell-fire." In its extreme form this principle meant the rejection of every idea and amenity not known in Western Arabia in the time of Muḥammad and his companions, and it has indeed been used by successive generations of ultra-conservatives to oppose tables, sieves, coffee and tobacco, printing-presses and artillery, telephones, wireless, and votes for women. It soon became necessary to distinguish between "good" or licit innovations and "bad" or illicit innovations, the latter being such as were contrary to the Qur'ān, the Traditions, or to the *ijmāʿ*, the consensus of the Muslim community. This last meant in effect that the acceptance or rejection of an innovation was determined by what in modern parlance would be called "the climate of opinion" among the learned and the powerful, and that, since the climate of opinion changes, the *bidʿa* of today may become the *sunna* of tomorrow, opposition to which is itself a *bidʿa*. Moreover, since no machinery exists for the consultation or formulation of a universal *ijmāʿ* for all Islam, there may be differing *ijmāʿ*s influenced by different traditions and circumstances in different parts of the Islamic world, and the dividing-line between *sunna* and *bidʿa* may thus vary with place as well as time. Islam has in fact absorbed a great deal that was foreign to the religion of the Companions, sometimes in concession to new ideas, sometimes by way of compromise with the existing practices of the peoples to which it came. But these innovations of doctrine and practice were always restrained and modified by the action of *ijmāʿ* and from time to time drastically curtailed by a wave of religious conservatism. The gravamen of the charge of *bidʿa* levelled against a doctrine was not primarily that it was false or bad but that it was new—a breach of habit, custom, and tradition, respect for which is rooted deep in the pre-Islamic tribal past, and reinforced by the belief in the finality and perfection of the Muslim revelation.

It will readily be seen that there are many contexts in which the word *bidʿa* can reasonably be translated as heresy, but the two terms are far from being exact equivalents. Theological polemicists are ready enough to hurl accusations at those whose doctrines they disapprove of, but they are often reluctant to pursue their charges to their logical conclusion. Even so fanatical an opponent of all innovations as the Syrian jurist Ibn Taymiyya (d. 1328) prefers a sort of quarantining of suspect groups and individuals, followed where necessary by admonition and even coercive action. Only when a *bidʿa* is excessive, persistent, and aggressive are its followers to be put beyond the pale of the community of Islam.

The idea of excess is also expressed in another theological term—*ghuluww*, from an Arabic root meaning "to overshoot, to go beyond the limit." Underlying this is the notion, deep-rooted in Islam, that a certain measure of diversity of opinion is harmless and even beneficial. "Difference of opinion in my community is an act of divine mercy," says a tradition attributed to the Prophet. The Holy Law of Islam is expounded in four versions, by four schools of jurisprudence, each with its own principles, text-books, and judiciary. All four are different, yet all are valid and live in mutual toleration. Even Shiʿism was in its origin a *tashayyuʿ ḥasan*—a lawful partisanship, one not exceeding the limits of permitted disagreement—and only later left the common ground of orthodoxy. This almost parliamentary doctrine of limited disagreement and common basic assumptions, despite periods of lapse, survives right through the history of Islam, and explains the mutual toleration of Twelver Shīʿī and Sunnī in ʿAbbāsid Iraq, of dervish and ulema in post-Mongol Islam. The followers of the four schools, and of some others that have disappeared, are all considered orthodox. Even the Shiʿites, the Kharijites, and others, though held to be in manifest error on important points of doctrine and Holy Law, were still Muslims and enjoyed the privileges of such in this world and the next. Only certain groups, who carried their divergence to excess *(ghuluww)* are excluded from Islam. Such are the exaggerators *(ghulāt*—singular *ghālī)* among the Shīʿa, who in their veneration for ʿAlī and his descendants ascribe divine powers to them and are thus guilty of polytheism. Such too are the other groups of extremists among the Shiʿites, Kharijites, Murji'ites, Muʿtazilites, even among the Sunnīs, who deny prophecy, revelation, or Holy Law, or preach such doctrines as reincarnation, metempsychosis, or antinomianism. These, in the view of the majority of the theologians, are to be excluded from Islam—though, characteristically, opinions differ as to where the line should be drawn.

The term most commonly translated as heresy is *zandaqa*—the faith of the *zandīq* or, more commonly, *zindīq*. This word is of Iranian origin and apparently denoted those who adopted a deviant interpretation of the Zoroastrian scripture, the *Zand Avesta*. In Sāsānid times it seems to have been applied to Manichaeans and more generally to followers of ascetic and unorthodox forms of Iranian religion. In Islamic times too the word was at first applied to Manichaeans and related groups, more especially to those who held dualist doctrines while making nominal profession of Islam. Later it was generalized to cover all holders of unorthodox, unpopular, and suspect beliefs, particularly those considered dangerous to the social order and the state. At the same time it was applied loosely to materialists, atheists, agnostics, and the like and came to have the general meaning of free-thinker and libertine.

Despite this vagueness of usage, the word *zindīq* had, in another respect, a terrible precision. For unlike the other terms discussed, it belonged to administrative rather than theoretical usage. A charge of *bid ʿa* or *ghuluww,* uncomplicated by any act of overt rebellion, meant no more than being consigned by some theologian to hell-fire. A charge of *zandaqa* meant being taken by a policeman to prison, to interrogation, perhaps to execution. The first recorded prosecution is that of Jaʿd ibn Dirham, a forerunner of the Muʿtazila, who in 742, during the reign of the Umayyad Caliph Hishām, was condemned, mutilated, and crucified on a charge of *zandaqa.* Generally speaking, however, the Umayyads repressed only those doctrines that openly challenged their own title to the Caliphate. They were not greatly concerned with deviations from dogma as such, the less so since orthodox dogma was still in process of formulation.

The ʿAbbāsids were more keenly aware of the potentialities of seditious religious teachings. The repression of *zindīqs* began during the reign of al-Manṣūr (754–775), and some were condemned to death. The Caliph attached sufficient importance to this question to include an injunction to extirpate *zandaqa* in his political testament to his successor, al-Mahdī (775–785), under whom the really serious repression began. In 779, while passing through Aleppo, the Caliph ordered a *zindīq*-hunt, in which many were caught, condemned, beheaded, and quartered. Thereafter the repression proceeded with vigor, and a kind of inquisition was established, under the control of a Grand Inquisitor called *ʿArīf* or *Ṣāḥib al-Zanādiqa.* There seems little doubt that among the many victims claimed by the inquisition under al-Mahdī and al-Hādī (785–786) the Manichaeans provided the main bulk. But, as one would expect, the inquisitorial net caught other fish, too. Some, like the poets Bashshār ibn Burd and Ṣāliḥ ibn ʿAbd al-Quddūs—both executed for *zandaqa* in 783—were hardly more than earnest enquirers with inadequate respect for authority. Others, too numerous to mention, were good Muslims whose removal, for political or personal reasons, was deemed opportune by the Caliph, his ministers, or his inquisitors.

After the time of al-Hādī the direct threat of Manichaeism seems to have subsided, and the persecutions of the *zindīqs*, though they continue, are intermittent and on a smaller scale. At the same time the word *zindīq* loses its connotation of Manichaeism and dualism and comes to be applied to any extreme or seditious doctrine—to some forms of Ṣūfī belief—or no belief at all. In legal parlance the *zindīq* is the criminal dissident—the professing Muslim who holds beliefs or follows practices contrary to the central dogmas of Islam and is therefore to be regarded as an apostate and an infidel. The jurists differ as to the theoretical formulation of the point of exclusion, but in fact usually adopt the practical criterion of open rebellion.

More or less synonymous with *zandaqa* in its later, generalized application is the word *ilḥād,* originally meaning "deviation from the path." The word appears in this general sense in the Qur'ān but was not part of the technical vocabulary of the earliest jurists and theologians. In the first few centuries of Islam the *mulḥid*—deviator—is the man who rejects all religion, the atheist, materialist, or rationalist of the type of the notorious Ibn al-Rāwandī (ninth–tenth centuries). In this sense the word was misapplied by orthodox theologians as a term of abuse to a number of sects and especially to the Assassins in Persia. By Mongol times it had become the common appellation of the Assassins, so that both Chinese and European visitors to Persia call them by it. In post-Mongol times, and especially in Ottoman usage, *mulḥid* and *ilḥād* tend to replace *zindīq* and *zandaqa* as the common terms for subversive doctrines among the Shīʿīs, the Ṣūfīs, and elsewhere. In the nineteenth century an Ottoman historian used both *ilḥād* and *zandaqa* to describe the ideas disseminated in Turkey by the emissaries of the French Revolution.[1]

From the days when the seeds of Islam were first flung by the Arab hurricane onto the soil of many lands, strange flowers have often appeared in the garden of the faith—doctrines and practices that were aberrant, discordant, incongruous. Some of them were perhaps native growths in Arabian Islam—weeds and tares brought by the self-same wind of conquest. Others, the majority, were grafts and hybrids from alien stocks—beliefs and customs from pre-existing cults, foreign teachings from Plotinus, Mazdak, and Mani, later from Voltaire, Rousseau, and Marx. These were duly recognized and condemned by the guardians of the faith as innovatory, exaggerated, intrusive, and erroneous. Though they brought some modifications to the main stock and local sub-varieties of Islam, most of them were in the course of time quietly extruded by the action of the slowly evolving consensus of the Islamic community.

But how far do these amount to heresy in the strict, technical sense of the word? The Greek word *αἵρεσις* originally meant "choice," then a school or sect that represents the "choice" of its adherents. Finally, in the Christian Church, it is specialized to mean a religious error, contrary to the truth as authoritatively defined and promulgated by the Church and condemned as such by a competent ecclesiastical authority. By this definition, there has been and can be no heresy in Islam. As Goldziher says:

> The role of dogma in Islam cannot be compared with that which it plays in the religious life of any of the Christian Churches. There are no Councils and Synods which, after lively controversy, lay down the formulae, which henceforth shall be deemed to embrace the whole of the true faith. There is no ecclesiastical institution, which serves as the measure of orthodoxy; no single authorized interpretation of the holy scriptures, on which the doctrine and exegesis of the Church might be built. The Consensus, the supreme authority in all questions of religious practice, exercises an elastic, in a certain sense barely definable jurisdiction, the very conception of which is moreover variously explained. Particularly in questions of dogma, it is difficult to determine in unanimity what shall have effect as undisputed Consensus. What is accepted as Consensus by one party, is far from being accepted as such by another.[2]

In the absence of an apostolic tradition and of a supreme pontiff, orthodoxy and heterodoxy in Islam could at first sight be determined only by making the teachings of one school the touchstone for the rejection of the others. The difficulties and absurdities of such a standard are well summarized by al-Ghazālī. Is al-Bāqillānī a heretic for disagreeing with al-Ashʿarī, or al-Ashʿarī for disagreeing with al-Bāqillānī? Why should truth be the prerogative of one rather than the other? Does truth go by precedence? Then do not the Muʿtazilites take precedence of al-Ashʿarī? Because of greater virtue and knowledge? In what scales and with what measures shall the degrees of virtue be measured, so that the superiority of one or another theologian may be established? . . . "If you are fair, you will soon realise that whoever makes truth the preserve of any one theologian is himself nearest to heresy . . . because he gives his master a rank that belongs only to the Prophet, considering him immune from error, so that orthodoxy consists in following him and heresy only in opposing him."[3]

In this passage, the Arabic words translated as heretic and heresy are not any of those discussed above, but *Kāfir* and *Kufr,* "unbeliever" and "unbelief." And with these terrible and unequivocal words we perhaps come nearest to an Islamic equivalent of heresy. The sectarian, though some of his doctrines may in time be excluded by the cumulative force of the Consensus from the mainstream of Islam, is still a Muslim. In the eyes of the jurists, he is still entitled to the status and privileges of a Muslim in society—property, marriage, testimony, the holding of public office, even to treatment as a believer, though a rebel, in insurrection and war. In the eyes of the theologians, he is a Muslim though a sinner and may aspire to salvation in the life to come. The vital barrier lies not between Sunnī and sectarian but between sectarian and unbeliever. And unbelief, as al-Ghazālī observes, is a legal question, like slavery and freedom, to be determined by legal rules and processes and involving legal consequences.[4] The excommunicated unbeliever is not only damned in the world beyond; he is outlawed in this world. He is deprived of all legal rights and barred from all religious offices; his very life and property are forfeit. If he is born a Muslim, his position is that of an apostate, a dead limb that must be ruthlessly excised.

In this as in so many other respects the practice of Islam was less severe than its theory. In theological circles, it is true, charges of unbelief were readily bandied about, and the word *kāfir* was part of the small change of religious polemic. "The piety of theologians," observes al-Jāḥiẓ, "consists of hastening to denounce dissidents as unbelievers."[5] Al-Ghazālī speaks with withering contempt of those "who would constrict the vast mercy of God to His servants and make paradise the preserve of a small clique of theologians."[6] But in fact these loose accusations had no practical effect. The victims were for the most part unmolested, and many held high office—even legal office—in the Muslim state.

As the rules and penalties of Muslim law were codified and brought into application, charges of *kufr* became rarer and rarer. There are two versions of the last words of al-Ashʿarī (d. 935–36), one of the greatest of Muslim dogmatists. According to the one, he died cursing the Muʿtazila. According to the other, his last words were: "I testify that I do not consider any who pray towards Mecca as infidels. All turn their minds in prayer towards the same object. They differ only in expression."[7] This statement, even if it be apocryphal, is a true expression of the attitude of Sunnī Islam to the problem of *takfīr*—the denunciation or excommunication of the unbeliever. Many definitions were attempted of the basic minimum of belief—but most inclined, in practice if not always in theory, to accept as Muslims any who testify to the unity of God and the apostolate of Muḥammad. This standard was the more acceptable to jurists, since the only religious transgressions for which the *Sunna* of Muḥammad prescribes the death-penalty are polytheism and the reviling of the Prophet. Outward performance is sufficient, according to a tradition of the Prophet, since God alone can judge a man's sincerity. Thinkers as diverse as the tolerant and mystical al-Ghazālī and the fanatical and puritanical Ibn Taymiyya agree in stretching the limits of Islam to the utmost.

A dictum of the jurists lays down that in a trial for apostasy, any legal rule or precedent, even a weak one, which would give an acquittal must be followed. Even open rebellion did not automatically involve *takfīr*. In 923 the chief Qadi Ibn Buhlūl refused to denounce the Carmathian rebels as unbelievers, since they began their letters with invocations to God and the Prophet and were therefore *prima facie* Muslims. The Shāfiʿī law insists that the sectarian, even in revolt, is entitled to be treated as a Muslim; that is to say, that his family and property are respected and that he cannot be summarily despatched or sold into slavery once he becomes a prisoner. Only the most persistent and outrageous error or misconduct was condemned as *kufr* or as the more or less equivalent crimes of *zandaqa* and *ilḥād*. The accused was then summoned to recant and repent, and, if he failed to do so, was put to death. Some jurists refused the opportunity to recant, since the good faith of a *zindīq* could not be accepted.

All this does not of course mean that persecution of heresy was unknown in Islam. From time to time heretics were tried and condemned, with or without *takfīr,* and punished by imprisonment, whipping, decapitation, hanging, burning, and crucifixion. Inquisitions were rare, but the ordinary Islamic judiciary could be empowered to deal with the discovery and punishment of religious error. The suppression of *zindīqs* by the early ʿAbbāsids has already been mentioned. Under al-Ma'mūn a new inquisition, known as the *miḥna,* was used to impose the official Muʿtazilite doctrine; with the restoration of Sunnī orthodoxy under al-Mutawakkil (847–861), the same means were used against the Muʿtazila themselves and against the Shīʿa.

Repression of dangerous doctrine continued sporadically under the ʿAbbāsids, the most striking being that of the extremist Shīʿa. At the same time mystical teachings, the menace of which to the state was less immediately obvious, were kept under surveillance. In 922 the God-intoxicated Ṣūfī al-Ḥusayn ibn Manṣūr al-Ḥallāj suffered martyrdom in Baghdad for proclaiming his union with God and thus endangering the established order in heaven and on earth. Two and a half centuries later the illuminist al-Suhrawardī suffered a similar fate in Aleppo. The Seljuks used all possible means to meet the threat of the Assassins—Saladin stamped on the embers of the Ismāʿīlī Fāṭimid Caliphate and compulsorily restored Sunnism in Egypt. In post-Mongol times the threat of Shiʿism had for a while subsided, and mystic and dogmatist were drawn closer by adversity. A few executions of individual Shiʿites are recorded in Syria under the Mamlūks—most of them seem to be due to the deliberate provocations of would-be martyrs.[8]

In Turkey the growth of the Ottoman principality to statehood and empire constricted the erstwhile religious freedom and eclecticism of the frontier and provoked the armed resistance of groups on or beyond the limits of orthodox tolerance. The Bekṭāshīs, strongest among the mixed populations of Western Anatolia and Rumelia, made their peace with the Empire and received tolerance and even favor. The Shīʿa were mostly to be found among the Turcomans in Central and Eastern Anatolia and had close affinities with the Shīʿa Safavids who ruled Persia from the beginning of the sixteenth century. The Anatolian Shiʿites were thus potential or actual enemies of the state, and the Ottoman Sultans used both repression and re-education to render them harmless. At the same time a far more effective repression was carried out in Persia, this time of Sunnism, resulting in its virtual extinction in that country.

The one constant criterion was subversion. The followers of doctrines and practices which threatened the state, the dynasty, or the fabric of society were outlawed and repressed. Others—be they as remote from Islam as the Nuṣayrīs, Druze, and Yazīdīs—were accorded tolerance and even allowed the name and status of Muslims.

In our own time the concept of *takfīr* has acquired a new and radically different significance, as part of the intellectual armory and technical vocabulary of the militant Islamic fundamentalist movements. As used by them, *takfīr*, denunciation as a *kāfir*, is not an accusation levelled by the authorities against the subject but by the subject against the authorities. For the militant Muslim opposition movements in Egypt, in imperial Iran, and elsewhere, the governments of those countries, though they call themselves Muslim, do not deserve that name in any true sense of the word. By abandoning the law of God, the *Sharīʿa,* and replacing it with imported foreign laws and customs, they ceased to be Muslims, and the states and societies over which they rule are no longer part of the House of Islam. Such rulers and those who carry out their orders are therefore apostates and infidels and as such are not entitled to the obedience of the believers. Such regimes represent a return to the *jāhiliyya,* the age of ignorance and barbarism which preceded the advent of the Prophet Muḥammad. Far from obeying such rulers, it is the duty of the true Muslim to disobey and indeed remove them, in order to bring about a restoration of true Islam through the enforcement of the Holy Law. The name given to one of the militant Islamic groups in Egypt, *al-takfīr wa'l-hijra,* accurately symbolizes this Islamic doctrine of revolution: *takfīr,* recognizing and denouncing the apostate, means the formal condemnation of the existing regime and society; *hijra,* evoking the migration of the Prophet from pagan Mecca to found his own Islamic society and polity in Medina, means the departure of the true Muslims from the existing society, not in a territorial but in a social and political sense, in order to create a new one that is truly Islamic. This Islamic doctrine of revolution has proved extraordinarily powerful.

It has been observed as a curiosity that the word "religion" does not occur in the Old Testament. This is not because the ancient Hebrews had no religion but because they did not distinguish a separate part or compartment of their personal and public lives for which they might require this special term. Religion embraced the whole of life—man's dealings with his fellow men, with society and with the state, as well as his dealings with God. Even the simple, basic acts of working and resting, eating, drinking, and procreation were sanctified as the fulfillment of a divine command and a divine purpose. Islam too has no words to distinguish between sacred and profane, spiritual and temporal, for it does not accept or even know the dichotomy that these pairs of antonyms express—the cleavage and clash of Church and State, of Pope and Emperor, of God and Caesar. The Islamic state is in theory and in the popular conception a theocracy, in which God is the sole source of both power and law and the sovereign His viceregent on earth. The faith was the official credo of constituted state and society, the cult the external and visible symbol of their identity and cohesion, and conformity to them, however perfunctory, the token and pledge of loyalty. Orthodoxy meant the acceptance of the existing order; heresy or apostasy, its criticism or rejection. The same sacred law, coming from the same source and administered through the same jurisdiction, embraced civil, criminal, and constitutional as well as ritual and doctrinal rules. The sovereign was the supreme embodiment of the Holy Law, maintained by it and maintaining it. Where Church and State are inextricably interwoven, so too are religion and politics, and religion provided the only possible expression, in public and social terms, of sustained opposition. Whenever a group of men sought to challenge and to change the existing order, they made their teachings a theology and their instrument a sect, as naturally and as inevitably as their modern western counterparts make ideologies and political parties.

Yet even this explanation, based on the local characteristics of Semitic law and faith, cannot be more than partial. Beyond it lies a profounder relationship between heresy and revolt, one that is bound up with the ultimate meaning of religion in human life.

The Revolutions in Early Islam

23

In a sense, the advent of Islam itself was a revolution. The new faith, hot from Arabia, overwhelmed existing doctrines and churches; the new masters who brought it overthrew an old order and created a new one. In Islam there was to be neither church nor priest, neither orthodoxy nor hierarchy, neither kingship nor aristocracy. There were to be no castes or estates to flaw the unity of the believers; no privileges, save the self-evident superiority of those who accept to those who willfully reject the true faith—and of course such obvious natural and social facts as the superiority of man to woman and of master to slave. Even these inferiorities were softened by the new dispensation. The slave was no longer a chattel but a human being, with recognized legal and moral rights; woman, though still subject to polygamy and concubinage, acquired property rights not equalled in the West until modern times; and even the non-Muslim enjoyed a tolerance and security in sharp contrast with the lot of non-Christians in medieval—and sometimes modern—Christendom.

In the Roman world, neither the advent of Christianity nor the coming of the barbarians brought any sudden revolutionary impact comparable with that of Islam. Both movements were slower and more gradual than the Arab-Islamic conquests. Christianity, after more than three centuries of opposition, captured the Roman Emperor and itself became enmeshed with the Roman Empire and government; the Germanic barbarians accepted and took over both the Christian faith and the Roman state and adapted both to their own ways and purposes. The Arab conquerors brought their own religion and created their own state; much of the conflict of early Islamic times arises from the clash between the two.

All the Arab warriors shared—though not equally—in the tribute of the conquered lands. Many of them sought further—sometimes conflicting—advantages. There were tribesmen in search of pasturage, oasis-dwellers looking for estates, and Meccan merchants avid to exploit the rich commerce of great cities. To many it seemed that the government of the Caliphs, especially the third Caliph ʿUthmān, was more responsive to their needs than to those of Islam.

The needs of Islam were variously understood and interpreted. For the nomads, deprived of the free use of the lands they had conquered and subjected to the irksome and unfamiliar control of organized authority, the wealth and power of the Meccans were an affront, a betrayal of the cause for which they had fought. Islam meant the brotherhood and equality of the believers, limited only by their freely given and revocable loyalty to their chosen leader. Wealth and the status which it gave, power and the authority which it conferred, were regarded as a derogation from the authentic message of Islam, and charges of robbery and tyranny evoked a ready response.

Achievement rarely accords with aspiration. The Islamic Caliphate was established to serve the cause and spread the message of Islam. Instead, it seemed to serve the interests of a small group of rich and powerful men, who maintained it by methods that approximated, to an increasing and disquieting extent, to those of the ancient Empires that Islam had superseded. Pious and earnest men denounced the Caliphs as worldlings, usurpers, and tyrants; angry and ambitious men joined them in seeking to overthrow this tyranny, and the state and community of Islam were convulsed by a series of bitter civil wars. The declared issues were the Caliphate—who should rule, and how—and the restoration of authentic Islam. Each victory, whether of the rebels or of the defenders, ended with a reinforcement of the sovereign power and a further step in the direction of a centralized autocracy in the old Middle Eastern style. By a tragic paradox, only the strengthening of the Islamic state could save the identity and cohesion of the Islamic community—and the Islamic state, as it grew stronger, moved further and further away from the social and ethical ideals of Islam. Resistance to this process of change was constant and vigorous, sometimes successful, but always unavailing—and out of this resistance emerged a series of religious sects, different in their ideologies and their support but alike in seeking to restore the radical dynamism that was being lost. At first, when Arab and Muslim were still virtually synonymous terms, the religious struggle was a civil war of the Arabs; later, as Islam spread among the conquered peoples, converts began to play an increasing and sometimes a dominant role. It is a striking testimony to the universalist appeal and surviving revolutionary power of Islam that the great revolutionary movements in the Islamic Empire were all movements within Islam and not against it.

The first civil war ended in 661 with the victory of Muʿāwiya and the establishment of a new Caliphate, in his own family, that lasted for ninety years. The discipline and order of Muʿāwiya's regime, in contrast to the anarchic factionalism of many of ʿAlī's supporters, seemed to offer a better prospect for the unity and survival of Islam and its protection against the forces of disruption, and many even of the pious transferred their allegiance to the less attractive but more effective Umayyad. The Umayyad Caliphate, in its successive phases, represented a series of compromises—of interim arrangements which preserved the unity of the Islamic polity, at the cost of establishing a predominance of the Arab aristocracy and an imperial system that gradually borrowed more and more of the structure and methods of the defeated empires.

The process was not unresisted. One group of ʿAlī's supporters, the Kharijites, had turned against him during his lifetime and continued to oppose the Umayyads and after them the ʿAbbāsids. The Shīʿa, or party of ʿAlī, transferred their allegiance after his death to other members of the Prophet's family, not necessarily his descendants, and followed a series of rebels and pretenders who attempted to overthrow the Umayyads and take their place.

The dramatic martyrdom of the kin of the Prophet at Karbalā' in 680, more than any other single event of the time, helped to transform the Shīʿa from a political faction—the supporters of a candidate for office—to a religious sect with strong messianic overtones. Another contribution came from the new converts, who brought with them from their Judaeo-Christian and Iranian backgrounds many religious ideas alien to primitive Islam. These new converts became Muslims; they did not become Arabs, still less aristocrats, and the expectations aroused in them by their new faith made them deeply resentful of the inferior social and economic status accorded to them by the dominant Arab aristocracy. These feelings were shared by both pious and discontented Arabs, especially those who suffered from the sharper economic and social differentiation that came with conquest and riches. Many of the new converts were familiar with both political and religious legitimism. They were readily attracted by the claims of the house of the Prophet, which seemed to offer an end to the injustices of the existing order and a fulfillment of the promise of Islam.

The early history of Shīʿism is still very obscure. Most of the expositions that have come down to us are the work of theologians, both Sunnī and Shīʿite, and are presented according to a theological, not an historical classification, determined by types of doctrine rather than by the sequence of events. They were all written at later dates and often read back into the past the ideas and conflicts of later times. In doing so, they tend to systematize and stabilize much that was shifting and chaotic. In time, the Shīʿa crystallized into a sect or group of sects with clearly defined doctrines, marking them off from Sunnī Islam on the one hand and from other sects on the other. In early times this had not yet happened. The Muslims were still a single community, in which various groups formed and broke up, following different doctrines and leaders and changing them with bewildering ease.

It was during this early and obscure period that certain doctrines, which came to be characteristically Shīʿite, were gradually formed. One was the belief in an *Imām*—a divinely chosen leader, of the house of the Prophet, who was the sole rightful head of the Islamic community. Another, closely linked with it, was the belief in a *Mahdī,* a messianic *Imām* who, in God's good time, would overthrow the rule of the impious usurpers who held sway and would "fill the earth with justice and equity as it is now filled with tyranny and oppression."

Behind the luxuriant myths, the exotic doctrines, the passionate and violent outbursts, powerful forces were at work. Their nature has been variously interpreted, and the attempt to explain them, first in national and then in socio-economic terms, has encountered many obstacles.

One difficulty has arisen from the terms and categories used by

Western scholars, and derived from Western experience—that is, from Christian theology and European society. Explanations of Muslim "sects" by means of Muslim "classes" tend to be explanations of an analogy by means of another analogy—with results that are highly abstract and remote from reality. Another, more practical problem is the lack of hard, factual knowledge concerning economic and social developments in early Islam. It is difficult enough to relate religious movements to social conditions when both are well documented and thoroughly explored; very much more so when one is trying to relate the little-known to the unknown—and with intellectual tools forged for another purpose.

Nevertheless some progress can be recorded. Explanations in terms of a simple conflict between rich and poor, between the possessors and the dispossessed, are seen to be as inadequate in themselves as the purely ethnic explanations which preceded them. The class structure of medieval Islamic society was of bewildering complexity. There were, for example, nomads, countrymen, and townsmen—but with countless sub-divisions and cross-classifications. The nomads included powerful and weak tribes, noble and base tribes, Northern and Southern, rich and poor. Within the tribe, too, there were important distinctions of birth, wealth, and status. In the countryside there were gentry and peasantry, large and small landowners, free peasants, sharecroppers, and serfs. In the towns there were freemen, freedmen, and slaves; notables and populace; courtiers, government officials, tax-farmers, soldiers, scholars, men of religion, merchants great and small, artisans, and the mass of the urban poor. Occupations were by no means clearly differentiated—governors and soldiers drew profits from commerce as well as pay from the state, while merchants might qualify for salaries and pensions. In addition there were social distinctions and disputes—gentilic, tribal, and so forth—which were deeply felt and bitterly contested, yet to which it would be very difficult to assign any clear economic origins or consequences; similarly the effect of religious and ethnic divisions should not be discounted and cannot be fully explained. Finally there were very important regional variations and divisions, between the cities and provinces of a newly assembled Empire, with vast differences both in their previous history and subsequent development.

The sources are rich in references to economic and still more to social conflict—often between interest groups that are relatively small and locally defined. Some are manifestations of wider conflicts. Tribesmen complain of an unfair distribution of land and other booty, in which their tribe has not received its proper share; nomads object to the use of conquered lands for cultivation instead of grazing. Bedouin debtors speak bitterly of merchants and moneylenders, both Arab and Persian; Iranian gentlemen retain their well-born contempt for commerce and those who engage in it. There is general resentment of taxation, unfamiliar to the nomads, demeaning to the conquerors—but becoming more effective and more onerous as the Islamic state establishes itself. That resentment is intensified by inequalities in assessment, and the emergence of fiscally privileged elements. Much is said of the grievances of the *mawālī*, who adopt the faith of the conquerors and join the brotherhood of Islam but are denied the fiscal and some other privileges of Muslims.

The *mawālī* are to be found especially in the new cities, the rapid growth of which is one of the most important developments of the Arab Caliphate. In the former Byzantine provinces, where city life was old and familiar, the change was relatively slight; in the former Sāsānid lands, where urbanization was much less advanced, the swift and sudden development of the Muslim cities brought tension and conflict.

The economic and social history of the early Islamic Empire is still little known or explored, but certain significant developments can be perceived or reasonably inferred. The Arab conquests displaced important possessing and dominating groups; the impact of this change must have been far greater in the Eastern than in the Western provinces. From Syria and Egypt the defeated and dispossessed Byzantine magnates could withdraw to what was left of the Byzantine Empire, leaving their former subject provinces to new masters. No such escape was open to the magnates of the fallen Persian Empire, who had to remain where they were, endure the new domination, and find their place in it as best they could. It is not surprising that these elements, with their reserves of skill and experience and their recent memories of lost greatness, should have played a more decisive role in the development of Islamic society and government than the inert residue of population in the long-subject Byzantine cities. At first they seem to have made their accommodation with the Arab conqueror and retained something of their functions and privileges under his rule. But with the consolidation of Arab power, the massive settlement of Arab tribes in Iran, and the growth of cities, new conflicts and new alignments can be discerned.

The conquests also restored to circulation great accumulated riches which had been frozen in private, public, and church possession. The sources are full of stories of rich booty, wide distribution, and lavish expenditure. They also tell of great new fortunes, built up by members of the Arab aristocracy.

> On the day ʿUthmān was killed [says al-Masʿūdī] he possessed, in the hands of his treasurer, 100,000 dinars and a million dirhams. The value of his estates in Wādī 'l-Qurā, Ḥunayn and elsewhere was 100,000 dinars, and he also left many horses and camels. In the time of ʿUthmān a number of the Companions of the Prophet acquired houses and estates. Al-Zubayr ibn al-ʿAwwām built his house in Basra, where it is well known at the present time, the year 332 of the Hijra [= A.D. 943–44], and provides lodgings for merchants, sea-going traders and the like. He also built houses in Kūfa, Fusṭāṭ and Alexandria. These houses and estates are well known to the present day. The value of al-Zubayr's property at his death was 50,000 dinars. He also left a thousand horses, a thousand slaves, male and female, and lands in the cities we have mentioned. Similarly, Ṭalḥa ibn ʿUbaydallah al-Taymī built a house in the Kunāsa quarter in Kūfa, which is well known at the present time as "the house of the Ṭalḥīs." His income from his estates in Iraq amounted to a thousand dinars a day, and some say more; from his estates in the region of al-Sharāh he received more than that. He built himself a house in Madīna, made with plaster, bricks and teakwood. Similarly, ʿAbd al-Raḥmān ibn ʿAwf al-Zuhrī built a house and made it wide. In his stables were tethered 100 horses, and he owned 1,000 camels and 10,000 sheep. At his death, a quarter of his property was worth 84,000 dinars. Saʿd ibn Abī Waqqāṣ built his house in al-ʿAqīq. He made it high and spacious, and put balconies around the upper part. Saʿīd ibn al-Musayyab said that when Zayd ibn Thābit died he left ingots of gold and silver that were broken up with axes, in addition to property and estates to the value of 100,000 dinars. Al-Miqdād built his house at the place called al-Jurf, a few miles from Madīna. He put balconies round the upper part, and plastered it inside and outside. When Yaʿlā ibn Munya died, he left half a million dinars, as well as debts owed to him by people, landed property and other assets, to the value of 300,000 dinars.[1]

With their share of the spoils, their generous endowment in lands and revenues, their monopoly of military commands and their indirect control of administration, the Arab aristocracy of conquest acquired immense riches; amid the opportunities and delights of the advanced countries in which they found themselves, they spent their wealth with abandon. Among the conquered peoples, and before that among their own Arab compatriots, there were growing murmurs of discontent. There must, however, also have been others who profited.

The Arab conquests finally ended the Perso-Byzantine conflict across the Middle Eastern trade routes and, for the first time since Alexander, joined the whole region from Central Asia to the Mediterranean in a single imperial system. It seems likely that these changes favored the growth of trade and industry, for which the newly rich *conquistadores* provided markets. Like the Vikings in medieval Europe, the wealthy Arabs in the Middle East spent money on high grade textiles, in which the Umayyad court and aristocracy showed a particular interest. The textile industry may well have been the most important single factor leading to the growth of a commercial and industrial society. The construction of royal and private palaces and other buildings and the manifold needs of the well-paid Arab soldiers and settlers in the garrison cities will also have encouraged this development.

These new, rapidly growing cities became centers of discontent, which seems to have been due to dislocation and frustration more than to actual hardship. Among the wealthy, the arrogance of the conqueror aristocracy and the disabilities imposed on those who did not belong to it became increasingly irksome; among the poor, ripped from their protective village systems and adrift in the cities, the unaccustomed spectacle of wealth aroused new desires which could not be satisfied. If, as in both earlier and later times, the population of cities grew more rapidly than was justified by their economic development, there will also have been an unstable, disoriented, precariously surviving populace of unskilled laborers, runaway peasants, vagabonds, paupers, and beggars—uprooted, frustrated, and resentful.

In the pious and sectarian opposition to the Umayyad system, various gradations can be discerned; in the degree of their sophistication, their extremism, their radicalism—their divergence from Islamic norms, and their readiness to use violence. Many attempts have been made to relate these gradations to ethnic and social groups, and some conclusions may, very tentatively, be accepted. Northern Arabs tend to be less radical than Southern Arabs, Southern Arabs less than *mawālī*. From the time of Mukhtār (d. 686) the radical Shīʿa tend to draw increasingly on *mawlā* support, though their leaders remain Arab, usually from Southern or from assimilated border-tribes. Ethnic identifications are relatively easy, since the sources express themselves more readily in ethnic terms; this does not necessarily mean that they are more important.

Among early exponents of *ghuluww*, extremist doctrines, the sources mention a weaver, a seller of barley, and a dealer in straw. These and a few other references to artisans and shopkeepers among the *ghulāt* hardly suffice to document any statement of the social composition of their support. A better indication may be obtained from their teachings and aspirations—what they wanted, and what they opposed. They were against aristocracy—against the system of privileged exclusiveness, which distinguished even between two sons of the same father, where one was born of a free Arab mother and the other of a slave-woman. There were many such sons of concubines, whose families added to the numbers of the discontented. They were against autocracy and the growing power of the state, especially in the imposition and collection of taxes. God had sent His Prophet to reveal the truth, not to collect taxes, and merit lay in the observance of God's command, not in noble birth. If there was to be an order of priority, it should be by precedence in Islam, not by descent, by wealth, or by power.

Their political program usually consisted of the overthrow of the existing Caliphate and the installation of their chosen Imām. It is more difficult to speak of any social or economic program, though their activities—and such successes as they managed to achieve—are clearly related to social and economic discontents, antagonisms, and aspirations. There are scattered references to the promises made by agitators and rebel leaders—to defend those who are not noble, to distribute the booty fairly, to give grants to those who are deprived, even to liberate slaves who rally to the cause. Some idea of the hopes that were aroused may be gathered from the messianic traditions telling of what the Mahdī would do when he revealed himself. Apart from a variety of picturesque personal, topographical, and military details, these traditions give a fairly accurate idea of what needs the Mahdī was expected to meet. Part of his task was Islamic—to bring men back to true Islam, spread the faith to the eastern and western limits of the earth, and conquer the Christian city of Constantinople. More urgently and more insistently, he was to establish justice—"to fill the world with justice and equity as it is now filled with tyranny and oppression." Some versions are more specific; he would establish equality between the weak and the powerful, bring plentitude and security, and a prosperity so great that money would be unconsidered and uncounted—"like that which is left on the ground to be trampled on"; the heavens would not withhold rain; the earth would give bountiful crops and surrender her precious metals. In that time a man would say "O Mahdī, give!" and the Mahdī would say "Take," and would pour into his garment as much as he could carry.

To a growing extent these political, religious, and social aspirations were focused about the claims of the kin of the Prophet, the Hashimids, to an inheritance which, so it seemed, had been misappropriated and misused by the representatives of the nobility of Quraysh. After many failures, this inheritance was successfully claimed by the house of ʿAbbās.

With the fall of the Umayyads, the old order had been overthrown. A new order had been established, with the kin of the Prophet at its head. The victory had been won by a brotherhood of dedicated religious revolutionaries, working, preaching, and growing for more than thirty years. Great hopes and great expectations had been aroused. Their fulfillment was now due.

It was not long before the new masters of the Empire confronted the dilemma which, sooner or later, faces all successful rebels—the conflict between the responsibilities of power and the expectations of those who brought them to it. For a while the ʿAbbāsids did indeed try to persuade the Muslims that their accession really represented the achievement of the promised millennium. The adoption of black flags and then black robes as the emblems of the dynasty were one attempt to comply with the pattern of the coming of the righteous ruler, as depicted in the prophecies. Another was the adoption of regnal titles of messianic import. The Umayyads had used no honorific or other titles, being known simply by their personal names. The first ʿAbbāsid too was known in his own day simply as Abu'l-ʿAbbās, without a title—but the second was called al-Manṣūr, the appellation of the awaited redeemer of the Southern Arabs, and his son and grandson bore the still more obviously messianic titles of al-Mahdī and al-Hādī. Only with the fifth ʿAbbāsid Caliph, Hārūn al-Rashīd, does this messianic note disappear from the official nomenclature of the dynasty.[2]

There was more to show for the successful revolution than a variation in royal titulature. An immediate and striking change was the abandonment of the aristocratic principle of descent. All but the last of the Umayyad Caliphs had been the sons of free Arab mothers, as well as of Umayyad fathers; the son of a slave woman, however able, was not even considered as a possible candidate for the succession. Abu'l-ʿAbbās too was the son of a free and noble mother, and it was for this reason that he had been preferred to his brother Abū Jaʿfar, the son of a Berber slave-girl, as Imām and then Caliph. But on his death it was Abū Jaʿfar who, despite reproaches from some of his followers, succeeded as Caliph with the title al-Manṣūr. Al-Mahdī's mother was, appropriately, a Southern Arabian woman, said to be a descendant of the ancient kings of Ḥimyar; but his successors al-Hādī and Hārūn al-Rashīd were the sons of a slave-girl of uncertain origin. Of Hārūn's two sons who warred for the succession, al-Amīn, the loser, was born to an ʿAbbāsid princess, al-Ma'mūn, the winner, to a Persian concubine. Thereafter most of the ʿAbbāsid caliphs were the sons of slave mothers, usually foreign, and such parentage ceased to be an obstacle to worldly success or social prestige.

The Arab aristocracy and the aristocratic principle suffered other defeats. During the first half-century of ʿAbbāsid rule, noble birth and tribal prestige ceased to be the main titles to positions of power and profit, and the Arab tribes gradually withdrew into insignificance. Instead, the favor of the Caliph was now the passport to success, and more and more it was given to men of humble and even of foreign origin. The *mawālī* were at last acquiring the equality that they had craved, and with their success the very name and status of *mawlā* lost their significance. A new multi-national ruling elite emerged, of officials, soldiers, landowners, merchants, and men of religion. Their common characteristic was Islam, which replaced Arabism as the first-class citizenship of the Empire.

The ʿAbbāsids laid great stress on the Islamic character of their rule and purpose. The impious and worldly Umayyads had gone, and in their place had come the pious kin of the Prophet, to restore and preserve the equality and brotherhood of the believers. Though their own personal way of life was rarely if ever better than that of the Umayyads, the ʿAbbāsid Caliphs were careful to preserve the outward decencies of religion—a due show of respect for the cult, the law, and above all the personnel of the Muslim faith.

To maintain this posture required a position much closer to the central Sunnī consensus than was afforded by the Hāshimiyya sect, which had been the main instrument of the ʿAbbāsid bid for power. The militant missionaries and leaders who had contributed so greatly to the ʿAbbāsid victory were, in one way or another, removed, and a religious group which hailed the Caliph as divine was ruthlessly crushed by the Caliph's troops. The disavowal by the ʿAbbāsids of origins which they now regarded as disreputable was completed by the Caliph al-Mahdī, who abandoned the claim to the Imāmate derived from Muḥammad b. al-Ḥanafiyya and Abū Hāshim and instead announced that the Prophet had appointed his uncle al-ʿAbbās as successor, thus conferring a hereditary right on his descendants and, incidentally, excluding the ʿAlids.

The conversion of the ʿAbbāsids to empire and to orthodoxy inevitably disappointed the hopes of some who had followed them. There were also other sources of resentment. The changes in Islamic society that were taking place generated new tensions and gave rise to new discontents, which sought an outlet. Several such changes can be discerned, beginning before the ʿAbbāsid accession and continuing for a long time after it. As with other revolutions, the change of regime did not mean a sudden, immediate, and total transformation in the order of society, in the vulgar sense of the term revolutionary; rather did it mark the point when a new political order emerged as part of the profound and extensive changes that were already taking place, and then itself helped to carry these changes further.

One of these changes is the growth of commerce and the rise, in wealth, power, and status, of the merchants—the bourgeoisie of the growing Muslim cities. The prosperous and respected merchant was not a new figure. Unlike other conquering aristocracies, the Arab nobility did not despise trade; on the contrary, many of them engaged in it, to great advantage—though most of them found government and war more lucrative and more attractive. The merchant community, however, continued to grow and was reinforced by *mawālī* and even by non-Muslims. In ʿAbbāsid times the merchants became an important class—wealthy, confident, and self-reliant; they were proud of their membership in an honorable profession and were even inclined to look down on the servants of the state as engaged in tasks that were morally inferior and as recipients of moneys that were morally tainted. To no small extent, the theologians and jurists who were formulating the rules of Islamic orthodoxy were drawn from the merchant class, and their writings often tend to reflect the ethos and the needs of the Muslim bourgeoisie. Numerous traditions were cited or invented to show that commerce is an occupation pleasing in God's eyes, and wealth a sign of God's favor. Even conspicuous consumption enjoyed divine approval, for "when God gives riches to a man, He wants it to be seen on him." This and similar traditions are cited to justify the wearing of fine clothes and the building and furnishing of luxurious dwellings. One dictum, improbably attributed to the Prophet, even asserts that "poverty is almost like apostasy." Under the early ʿAbbāsids, the role of the merchants is limited, and they are overshadowed by the bureaucrats, many of them Iranians with an aristocratic tradition of contempt for commerce. By the ninth century, however, they appear among powerful figures at the court, on terms of intimacy with the rulers themselves.

Agriculture and stockraising remained the source of livelihood of the overwhelming majority of the population and the main source of revenue of the state. The techniques of industrial production showed little improvement on those of antiquity; the organization and extent of production, however, show considerable development, while commerce, both within and beyond the far-flung Muslim Empire, expanded vastly in scope and scale. A stable and internationally accepted specie coinage and an elaborate system of credit facilitated trade and encouraged the growth of large-scale commercial and financial enterprises. This emergent capitalism affected other layers of society. Not only merchants and financiers, but also officials, landowners, literati, generals, and even princes ventured their capital in commercial undertakings—while merchants for their part sometimes invested part of their savings in landed estates and in tax-farms.

In contrast to Europe in the same period, there was a great development of cities, which became larger, more numerous, and more sophisticated. The main center of town life shifted from the citadel and cantonments, which had been the core of the early cities, to the residential and commercial suburbs. There were artisans, apprentices, and journeymen, often organized in large-scale enterprises under public or private ownership, laborers, shopkeepers and itinerant vendors, and a floating population of uprooted and unemployed. Slavery was of limited economic importance—slaves appear mainly in domestic functions, as craftsmen or as agents or stewards of landowners and entrepreneurs.

Our sources are of urban origin and tell us little about the countryside. The impression they leave is that, by and large, the changes of the times had little effect on the lot of the peasant and nomad. Agricultural techniques remained substantially unchanged, though new crops and new methods of irrigation were sometimes introduced from one region to another. The country supplied food and raw materials to the cities, but the return seems to have gone in the main to city-dwelling landowners and tax-farmers. Trade was between cities; there is little evidence of the movement of goods or services from the city to the countryside, which supplied its own simple needs. The concentration of ownership in the hands of rich merchants and military chiefs brought larger estates and stricter control and a harder life for the peasants. In earlier ʿAbbāsid times there were still peasant smallholders and more or less independent lessee sharecroppers. There even seems to have been some attempt to amend the system of tax assessment to their advantage. In later times, however, they were compelled by fiscal and other pressures to make over their holdings to large landowners and remain on them as tenants. Islamic law did not recognize serfdom, but the debtor could pay his debt only by personal labor and was pursued if he fled. Some found a refuge in banditry, which became rife. Others joined the rabble of the cities.

The eastern provinces, taken from the former Persian monarchy, had special problems. Here city life was relatively new, and the tensions resulting from the growth of new urban centers more keenly felt. The old Iranian gentry had survived the Arab conquest with much of their power and influence in local affairs intact and with a proud memory of the recently fallen Sāsānid Empire. Under the early ʿAbbāsids, men of this class, converted to Islam, were able to play a role of some importance in the administration of the Muslim state. Later, when discontents arose, they could provide a coherent and competent leadership lacking in the socially fragmented western provinces.

The changes which prepared, accompanied, and followed the ʿAbbāsid revolution brought release and opportunity to some, hardship and disappointment to others. In some respects, the aims of the radical sectarians were fulfilled. The privilege of birth and, to a large extent, of race was gradually abolished, and the road to preferment opened to all—or almost all—Muslims. Despite the inevitable and recurring tendency to the formation of aristocracies, this social egalitarianism has remained characteristic of Islam to the present day. True, the non-Muslim was still subject to certain disabilities, but this was felt to be reasonable; the disabilities were not oppressive, and submission to them was in a sense by choice, since the brotherhood of Islam was now open to all who chose to join it. In theory and to no small extent even in practice, Islam was the common citizenship of the community, the source of its ethos and its law, the ultimate determinant of identity, loyalty, and status.

Despite these improvements, old discontents survived and new ones appeared. In general, the millennium had failed to materialize; more specifically, rapid economic and social development had brought distress to many. Socially the revolution had achieved notable successes, though these were often uneven in their effect in different regions and among different classes. Politically, things were worse then before. The aristocratic Umayyad state had been limited by the need to gain and retain the loyalty of the great Arab aristocrats—powerful and influential men whose power and influence derived from sources independent of the Caliph and to a large extent beyond his reach. The bureaucratic ʿAbbāsid state, with its well-ordered civil service and its professional army, suffered no such limitation. Despite the trappings of Islamic piety with which the ʿAbbāsids adorned themselves and their court, their government was in effect more distant from Islamic political ideals than was that of the Umayyads—and far closer to the imperial polity of ancient Iran. The sovereign was no longer a first among equals but a remote and inaccessible autocrat, wielding immense power over his subjects through an apparatus of government that was becoming more complex and more oppressive. Small wonder that a poet exclaimed:

> *Would that the tyranny of the sons of Marwān would return to us,*
> *would that the justice of the sons of ʿAbbās were in hell!*[3]

Islamic Concepts of Revolution

24

In the middle of the eighth century the Umayyad Caliphate was overthrown and the ʿAbbāsid Caliphate established in its place. Among modern scholars it has become customary, when speaking both of the actions which brought about this change and of the results which followed from it, to use the term *revolution*. Among contemporaries, the term commonly used to denote the ʿAbbāsid victory was the Arabic world *dawla*, which in later times came to mean "dynasty" and then simply "state." This was not however its original meaning. The basic meaning of the root *d-w-l*, which also occurs in other Semitic languages, is "to turn" or "to alternate"—as for example in the Qur'anic verses "These [happy and unhappy] days, we cause them to alternate *(nudāwiluhā)* among men" (Qur'ān, iii, 134/140), and "what God has assigned as booty to His Prophet, from the people of the cities, belongs to God and the Prophet and the kinsmen, the orphans, the poor, and the wayfarer, that it may not become a perquisite circulating *(dūlatan)* among those of you who are rich" (lix, 7). Other early texts confirm the meaning of "turn"—the time of success, power, office, or ownership enjoyed by an individual or a group. Sometimes the word is used in the context of the vicissitudes of fortune. *"Al-dunyā duwal"* says an early author—roughly, the world is full of ups and downs—and continues: "What is for you will come to you in spite of your weakness; what is against you, you cannot prevent by your strength."[1] In an essay by Ibn al-Muqaffaʿ (ca. 720–ca. 756), the Persian adviser of the first ʿAbbāsid caliphs, he urges caution on a ruler whose power is newly established and uses the phrase *"Idhā kāna sulṭānuka ʿinda jiddati dawla"*—if your rule is at the beginning of a turn.[2] It is in this sense that Ibn al-Muqaffaʿ, speaking of the accession of the

ʿAbbāsids, says: "Then came this *dawla*" and that the first ʿAbbāsid Caliph al-Saffāḥ, addressing the people of Kūfa after his accession, says to them, "You have reached our time, and God has brought you our *dawla.*"[3] In another passage, al-Saffāḥ is quoted as speaking of the *dawla,* that is, the time of power and success, of Abū Muslim[4]—a servant and not a member of the dynasty. In time, the term *dawla* came to be used more particularly of the reigning ʿAbbāsid house and thus acquired the meaning of dynasty and ultimately of state.

It is possible that cyclical theories of politics, derived from Greek or Persian sources, may have contributed to this use of the word *dawla.* Though no early statements of such theories in Arabic have so far come to light, they appear in slightly later writings, as for example in an astrological essay by the ninth-century philosopher al-Kindī and, more extensively, in the tenth-century encyclopaedic work called *Rasā'il Ikhwān al-Ṣafāʾ (Epistles of the Sincere Brethren).* According to these, *dawla,* which is associated with *mulk,* "kingship," passes from nation to nation, from country to country, from dynasty to dynasty. Such a change occurs at intervals of 240 years. Significantly, the *Rasā'il* were composed about 240 years after the accession of the ʿAbbāsids, and their authors were connected with the Ismāʿīlīs, an activist Shīʿite group which aimed at the overthrow of the ʿAbbāsids and their replacement by a new line of Imām-Caliphs, descended from the Prophet through his daughter Fāṭima.[5] Cyclical interpretations of history are central to the doctrines of the Ismāʿīlīs and related sects and are often adduced to support the claims of Messianic pretenders and rebels.

The troubles of the ʿAbbāsids did not end with the defeat of the Umayyads and their own enthronement as supreme sovereigns of Islam. They still had to face a series of opposition movements and even armed rebellions by groups which challenged their right to rule and sought to install others in their place. The most active and best known among them were those who felt that the change had not gone far enough—that the ʿAbbāsid regime too closely resembled that which it had replaced and should give way to one which would bring a more radical transformation of the political and social order. Some of them, loosely designated by the general name of Shīʿa, hoped to achieve this result by transferring power to the kin of the Prophet; others, the Kharijites, rejected all forms of legitimism and sought to establish a truly elective caliphate based on the voluntary and revocable consent of the ruled.

A quite different point of view was represented by the group who are sometimes called al-Nābita, roughly "the young upstarts." Politically, these were supporters of the deposed Umayyads—that is, legitimists who believed in the rights of the old caliphal dynasty and questioned the arguments adduced by the 'Abbāsids and their spokesmen to justify their violent supersession. In an essay written in about 840, the great Arabic prose-writer al-Jāḥiẓ briefly reviews the political history of Islam to his own time and attempts to justify, on religious grounds, the action of the 'Abbāsids in overthrowing the reigning Caliph. He specifically rejects the doctrine of unconditional obedience which, he claims, is implicit in the arguments of the Nābita:

> The wrong-doer is accursed, and whoever forbids the cursing of the wrong-doer is himself accursed. But the Nābita of our time and innovators of our age allege that to abuse bad rulers is sedition *(fitna)* and to curse tyrants is an innovation *(bid 'a)*, even if these rulers . . . terrorize the good and encourage the bad, and rule by favoritism and wilfulness, the flaunting of power, contempt for the people, repression of the subjects, and accusations without restraint or discretion. If this misconduct reaches the degree of unbelief, if it passes beyond error to irreligion, then it becomes a greater error even than that of whoever refrains from condemning them and dissociating himself from them. . . . The Nābita agree that anyone who kills a believer, whether with clear intent or with specious pretexts, is accursed; but if the killer is a tyrannical ruler or a fractious amir, they do not consider it lawful to curse him or depose him or banish him or denounce him, even if he has terrorized the good, murdered the learned, starved the poor, oppressed the weak, neglected the frontiers and marches, drunk fermented drinks and flaunted his depravity.[6]

Al-Jāḥiẓ's position in this essay is clear. The sovereign is a human being and may be guilty of some human error and sin while retaining his right to rule and his claim on the obedience of his subjects. But if his error reaches the point when he is neglecting his duties and abusing his powers as sovereign, then the duty of obedience lapses, and his subjects have the right—or rather the duty, since it is with duties, not rights, that

Islamic jurisprudence and politics are concerned—to denounce him and if possible to depose and replace him.

The Western doctrine of the right to resist bad government is alien to Islamic thought. Instead, there is an Islamic doctrine of the duty to resist impious government, which in early times was of crucial historical significance. This doctrine is enshrined in the traditions of the Prophet, particularly in two sayings: "There is no [duty of] obedience in sin," and "Do not obey a creature against his Creator." The intention of these two oft-quoted sayings and of other similar dicta[7] is fairly obvious. Normally, the subject owes a duty of complete and unquestioning obedience to the Imām, the head of the Islamic state and community. If, however, the Imām commands something that is contrary to God's law, then the duty of obedience lapses, and instead it is the duty of the subject to disobey—and resist—such a command.

At first sight this principle looks like a basis for doctrines both of limited government and of justified revolution. Its effectiveness, however, was reduced by two fatal flaws. In the first place, the jurists never explained how the lawfulness or sinfulness of a command was to be determined; in the second place no legal procedure or apparatus was ever devised or set up for enforcing the law against the ruler. In fact, social and political pressures were usually sufficient to enforce formal respect for the basic precepts of Islamic observance—and for little more. This interpretation is expressed in a number of sayings ascribed to the Prophet. According to one undoubtedly spurious tradition, the Prophet adjured his followers: "If you have rulers over you who ordain prayer, the alms-tax, and the Holy War, then God forbids you to revile them and allows you to pray behind them." Another tradition, equally spurious, conveys the message of quietism—and its limits—in a more vivid form: "The Imāms are of Quraysh [the Arabian tribe to which the Prophet belonged] . . . if Quraysh gives a crop-nosed Ethiopian slave authority over you, hear him and obey him, as long as he does not force any of you to choose between his Islam and his neck. And if he does force anyone to choose between his Islam and his neck, let him offer his neck."[8]

In time, the duty of disobedience was hedged around with restrictions and qualifications and was in effect forgotten in the general acceptance, in theory as well as in practice, of the most complete quietism. A fourteenth century qāḍī, al-Ījī, still mentions, somewhat obliquely, the duty of resistance to sin; it only applies, however, if two conditions are met. First, a man must be satisfied that his action will not stir up sedition *(thawarān fitna)* and that it will achieve its purpose. (If he thinks it will not achieve its purpose, then resistance is meritorious, but not obligatory.) Second, there must be no snooping *(tajassus)*.[9] In other words, don't look for trouble; if you meet it, try to avoid it; and do not resist until success is a foregone conclusion.

In earlier times, when this defeatist and quietist attitude had not yet been adopted, the duty of disobedience was still a political and religious factor of importance. It was of particular concern to the early ʿAbbāsids, who felt the need to justify, in Islamic terms, both their acquisition of power by revolution and their retention of it against any further challenge. The question was discussed by Ibn al-Muqaffaʿ in an essay addressed to the Caliph al-Manṣūr, ca. 757–58. There are some people, he says, who cite the saying that a creature should not be obeyed against his Creator and who give it a false and distorted interpretation. According to them, if the Imām commands us to disobey God, he must be disobeyed; if he commands us to obey God, he must be obeyed. But if the Imām is to be disobeyed in disobedience, and others beside the Imām are to be obeyed if they command what God commands, then there is no difference between the Imām and anyone else in the right to obedience. This doctrine, says Ibn al-Muqaffaʿ, is a device of the devil to subvert obedience and disrupt order, so that men may be equal *(naẓāʾir)* and leaderless and defenseless against their enemy. Another group, he says, go to the opposite extreme. According to them, we must obey the Imāms in all their commands, without inquiring whether these commands are in obedience or disobedience to God. None of us can call them to account, for they are the masters of power and knowledge, and we are their subjects, bound to obey and submit. This doctrine, says Ibn al-Muqaffaʿ, is as harmful as the first in degrading authority and undermining obedience, since it leads to foul wickedness in rule and to clear and public licence for sin. The truth lies between the two. It is right to say that there should be no obedience in sin; it is wrong to undermine the authority of the Imām by giving licence to disobey him. The limitation of the duty of obedience applies only to the major precepts of religion. If the Imām forbids fasting, prayer, and pilgrimage, prevents the fulfilment of God's commands, and permits what God has forbidden, then he has no authority to do this. He has however the right—moreover the exclusive right—to be obeyed in all matters of governmental judgment, discretion, and administration, such as beginning and ending military campaigns, collecting and expending moneys, appointing and dismissing subordinates, discretionary decisions, based on Qur'ān and Sunna, in matters where there is no binding precedent, making war and peace, and so forth.[10] Most later writers agreed in limiting the duty of disobedience to clear violations of major prescriptions of the ritual law; many go further and specify that this does not apply to the personal conduct of the ruler, who presumably may violate the law with impunity, but only to the orders which he issues to his subjects.

A recurring theme in discussions of the duty of disobedience is the imperative need to avoid *fitna*—the term normally used for a movement which tends to disrupt the religious, social, and political order. The word has an interesting history. The basic meaning of the root is "a test" or "proving," hence by extension a temptation, which tests a man's faith and his loyalty to the community. The word occurs frequently in the Qur'ān in the sense of temptation or trial of faith, against which the believer is warned to be on his guard. Often, the context indicates that the danger is public and social rather than private and personal—a temptation to disaffection as much as to unbelief. "Expel them [the Meccans] from whence they have expelled you, for *fitna* is worse than killing . . . fight them until there is no more *fitna,* and the religion of God prevails" (Qur'ān, ii, 191, 193).

It is this meaning—of disturbance or disaffection—that predominates in post-Qur'anic usage and is reflected back in some of the apocryphal sayings attributed to the Prophet. The Islamic conception of *fitna* is a natural consequence of the Islamic conception of conformity. Orthodoxy, in Christianity, means in the first instance belief in an officially defined creed and submission to ecclesiastical authority. Sunnism, in Islam, basically implies loyalty to the community and acceptance of its traditions—and, since religion and politics in Islam are inextricably intermingled, this in turn involves obedience to the Caliph as the accredited head of both state and community. Religious dissent is a private matter as long as it is concerned only with theological beliefs; it becomes a *fitna*, dangerous and punishable, when it involves a rupture of social and political bonds—separation from the community *(mufāraqat al-jamā'a)*, and the withholding of allegiance from the Caliph.

The archetypal *fitna*, often called the "great *fitna*," arose in connection with the murder of the Caliph 'Uthmān in A.D. 656 and the civil war which followed it. The Caliph had been murdered by Muslim mutineers, and another was installed in his place. He in turn was challenged by others, who denied his right to his office and accused him of condoning a crime. According to one side, 'Uthmān was the rightful Caliph; those who killed him were rebels and murderers whose crime must be punished; those who condoned their offense were themselves offenders. According to the other side 'Uthmān had violated the law of God and forfeited his right to rule; his death was an execution, not a murder, an act of justice, not a crime. The civil war was a time of great trial and temptation, in which the faith and loyalty of all the Muslims was put to the test.

Thereafter *fitna* became the normal term for seditious dissent or violent opposition to established authority. It is for example the term used by al-Kindī in his astrological epistle for the troubles and upheavals that bring a cycle of power to an end. It is used of religious groups whose deviation from tradition goes beyond the permitted limits of difference—particularly of such militant groups as the Kharijites and the Ismā'īlīs. In this context, it is often associated with the idea of *bid'a*—innovation, which is a departure from or violation of the *Sunna*. Later it is applied to almost any outbreak of violence—military mutinies, city riots, provincial rebellions. It is invariably a term of abuse, used of other groups, never of one's own. It was the term used by the first Muslim writers to speak of the French Revolution of 1798.[11]

Classical Arabic has a number of words to denote rebellion or insurrection. The commonest verbs are *kharaja*, literally "to go out,"[12] *qāma*, "to rise or stand up," and *nazā*, "to leap, leap out," hence break loose, escape. In the derived form *intazā* this root is used, especially in western (that is, North African and Spanish) texts, in the sense of "to revolt against one's sovereign, to make oneself independent." The tenth-century Spanish author Ibn Faraj of Jaen is said to have written, while in prison, a history of rebels and insurgents in Muslim Spain *(Ta'rīkh al-muntazīn wa'l-qā'imīn bi'l-Andalus wa-akhbāruhum).* This book is unfortunately—but not surprisingly—lost.[13]

A word with a rather different history is *baghā* (active participle *bāghī*, plural *bughāt*). Starting from the basic root-meaning of "excess, abuse," the *bāghī* comes to be a law-breaker, a violator of legal, social, religious, or moral standards. As well as a rebel, he may be a tyrannical ruler who abuses his power; he may also be a sexual debauchee or pervert. Inevitably, the word can also be used of a high-spirited or refractory camel. In the technical language of the Muslim law, *bughāt* is the normal term for rebels.

The jurists give careful consideration to the legal problems of rebellion—the regulation of warfare against rebels, their rights as belligerents and as prisoners, the sanctity of their property, the validity of legal judgments made under their jurisdiction.[14]

As so often, the terminology and argumentation of the jurists cloak a purpose other than the apparent one. In the strict theory of the Muslim law, there could be only one Muslim state, the universal *Dār al-Islām* (House of Islam), and only one Muslim sovereign, the Caliph. Juristic discussions of international law—of warfare, diplomacy, and so forth—could therefore only deal with relations between the Muslim state and a non-Muslim state or states. In fact of course the Muslim world was divided into many autonomous or independent states, and it was necessary to regulate, legally, the relations between them. This was achieved by the legal fiction that a state other than the Caliphate was an established group of rebels. The *bughāt* of juristic literature are assumed to be Muslims; they have at their disposition organized armed forces and control a territory in which they maintain (Muslim) law and order. Their rebellion consists of withholding obedience from the Caliph. From all this, it is clear that what the jurists have in mind is not an attempt to overthrow the regime but merely to withdraw from it and establish an independent state within a certain territory. In a word, their concern is not with revolution, but with secession.

During the nineteenth and twentieth centuries the need to discuss European revolutions, and later also domestic revolutions, brought three more terms into use. *Ikhtilāl*, though Arabic in origin, is mainly confined to Turkish usage. Originally meaning disorder or upheaval, it is commonly used by Turkish authors of the eighteenth century for revolts, riots, mutinies, and disturbances of public order of any kind.[15] It was the term used by contemporary Turkish writers to designate the great French Revolution.[16] Since then, it has been specialized in modern Turkish usage to denote revolutionary upheavals which lack the user's respect or approval. Thus, it is never used of the Young Turk or Kemalist revolutions, occasionally but not frequently used of the Russian Revolution, and almost invariably used of the anti-Young Turk rising of 1909. It is also used by the nineteenth-century Turkish historian Jevdet, in what must be one of the earliest Muslim accounts of the American Revolution.[17]

In the Arabic-speaking countries a different word was used for revolution—*thawra.* The root *th-w-r* in classical Arabic meant "to rise up (for example, of a camel), to be stirred or excited," and hence, especially in Maghribī usage, to rebel. Already in medieval times the word occurs in political contexts. Thus al-Saffāḥ, the first ʿAbbāsid Caliph, using the active participle, calls himself *al-Thā'ir* in his address to the people of Kufa, and an Alid leader in tenth-century Persia even adopts it in his title—*al-Thā'ir fi'llāh,* the *thā'ir* in God. Certainly in the first and in probably the second the significance of *thā'ir* is one who brings disturbance and upheaval. In a negative sense it is used by Saladin's biographer to denote a plot to overthrow him and restore the deposed Fatimids.[18] Often, it connotes the establishment of a petty independent sovereignty; thus, for example, the so-called party kings who ruled in eleventh-century Spain after the break-up of the Caliphate of Cordova, are called *thuwwār* (sing. *thā'ir*). The noun *thawra* at first means excitement, as in the phrase, cited in the *Ṣiḥāḥ,* a standard medieval Arabic dictionary, "*intaẓir ḥattā taskun hadhihi 'l-thawra*" (wait till this excitement dies down)—a very apt recommendation. The verb is used by al-Ījī, in the form *thawarān* or *ithārat fitna,* stirring up sedition, as one of the dangers which should discourage a man from practicing the duty of resistance to bad government. *Thawra* is the term used by Arabic writers in the nineteenth century for the French Revolution[19] and by their successors for the approved revolutions, domestic and foreign, of our own time.

In current Arabic usage, the noun *thawra* and the adjective *thawrī* are the terms accepted by the revolutionary socialist regimes in Egypt, Syria, Iraq, and elsewhere to describe their own actions, intentions, and ideologies. Apart from the rejection of hereditary monarchy and the assertion of a form of socialism, these terms are not identified with any specific political system. The converse of *thawrī* is *raj'ī*, a neologism[20] meaning "reactionary" and used especially of monarchical, conservative, and liberal regimes in Arab countries. The specialization of the term *thawra* to denote governments, their ruling groups, and their aulic ideologists has opened new lines of semantic development. For some, the antithesis *thawra/raj'iyya* (revolution/reaction) replaces the earlier antithesis Islam/Unbelief, with the same suggestion of perpetual conflict and inevitable ultimate victory. For others, *thawra* has simply become a synonym for authority and is thus repeating the semantic evolution of the medieval word *dawla*.

One last term remains to be considered. The classical Arabic root *q-l-b* means "to turn or revert." The seventh form, *inqalaba,* usually means "to be altered, changed, or turned upside down" and occurs in a famous verse of the Qur'ān (xxvi, 227) *"Wa-saya'lamu'l-ladhīna ẓalamū ayya munqalibin yanqalibūn"*—"Those who have done wrong will know to what end they will revert." Al-Kindī in his astrological writings[21] uses it of the predetermined cyclical turn of power, *inqilāb al-dawla.* The use of the verbal noun *inqilāb* as the equivalent of the European term revolution seems to have been introduced by the Young Ottoman exiles, notably by the radicals Mehmed Bey and Vasfi Bey, who published a journal called *Inqilāb* in Geneva in 1870. Thereafter this became the accepted Turkish and later also Persian word for revolution and was applied to the political changes of 1908 and 1919–23 in Turkey and of 1979 in Iran. Its use in Arabic is rare, and when it occurs it is usually derogatory.

PART VII

NEW IDEAS

The Idea of Freedom in Modern Islamic Political Thought

25

In traditional Islamic usage freedom was a legal, not a political concept. The Arabic terms *ḥurr,* "free," and *ḥurriyya,* "freedom," with their derivatives and equivalents in the other languages of Islam, denoted the status of the free man in law as opposed to the slave. In some periods and places, words meaning free were applied to certain privileged social groups which were exempt from taxes and other burdens to which common people were subject. This social usage is however exceptional and untypical, and the term *ḥurr* was normally used only in a juridical sense, with little social and no political content. When Muslim writers discussed, as they often did, the problems of good and bad government and denounced the latter as tyranny, they were distinguishing between just and unjust, lawful and wilful rule. Good government was a duty of the ruler, not a right of the subject, whose only recourse against bad government was patience, counsel, and prayer. The converse of tyranny was justice, not freedom; the converse of freedom was not tyranny but legal and personal slavery.[1]

The first examples in Islamic lands of the use of the term freedom in a clearly defined political sense come from the Ottoman Empire in the eighteenth and early nineteenth centuries and are patently due to European influence, sometimes to direct translations from European texts. Significantly, the word chosen by the Turkish translators to render this unfamiliar notion was not the legal term for non-servile status, but a quite different term, previously used mainly in fiscal and administrative contexts. *Serbestiyet* (later also *Serbestī*) is an abstract formed from *serbest,* which in Ottoman official usage denoted "the absence of certain limitations or restrictions." Thus, in the Ottoman military feudal system, a special kind of *timar* (a form of grant or fief) was called *serbest*. This meant that all the revenues of the *timar* went to the holder, as against an ordinary *timar* in which certain revenues were reserved to the imperial exchequer.

In its first known appearance in an official political document, the word *serbestiyet* denotes collective rather than personal freedom—that is, independence rather than liberty in the classical liberal sense. This is in the third article of the Russo-Turkish treaty of Küchük Kaynarja (1774), which ended Ottoman suzerainty over the Khan of the Crimean Tatars and recognized their independence from both Turkey and Russia (as a preliminary to their absorption into the Russian Empire in 1783). The two states agree to recognize the Tatars as "free and entirely independent of any foreign power"; the Sultan is regarded as their religious head, "but without thereby compromising their political and civil liberty as established." The forms of words in the Italian original of the treaty for these two phrases are *"liberi, immediati, ed independenti assolutamente da qualunque straniera Potenza"* and *"senza pero mettere in compromesso la stabilita libertà loro politica e civile."* The language and content of these clauses, so reminiscent of the free cities of the Holy Roman Empire, must have presented some difficulty to the dragomans of the Sublime Porte, who at that time were Phanariot Greeks. The Turkish text, containing concepts and expressions new to Ottoman usage, reveals their ingenuity.[2]

The French Revolution gave the word *serbestiyet* a new meaning. Moralı El-Sayyid Ali Efendi, the Ottoman ambassador in Paris under the *Directoire*, uses it several times in his report on his embassy to translate *liberté*, chiefly in relation to symbols and ceremonies.[3] The Chief Secretary Atıf Efendi, in his memorandum of 1798 on the political situation resulting from the activities of revolutionary France, shows a clearer understanding of the new political content of the term and of the danger which it represented to the established order, in the Ottoman Empire as elsewhere. In his introductory account of the Revolution, he tells how the revolutionaries had enticed the common people to follow them with promises of equality and freedom as a means of obtaining complete happiness in this world. More specifically, he is alarmed by the actions of the French in the former Venetian possessions which they had acquired, the Ionian islands and four towns on the Greek mainland. By evoking the forms of the government of the ancient Greeks and installing "a form of liberty," he said, the French had made clear their hostile intentions.[4]

Before the end of the year the French had landed in Egypt, where General Bonaparte, on arrival, addressed the Egyptians on behalf of the French Republic, "founded on the basis of freedom and equality."[5] The word used for freedom is *ḥurriyya* which, however, was still far from being a commonly accepted equivalent to the European term in its political sense. Ruphy's French-Arabic word-list, printed in 1802,[6] renders *liberté* by *ḥurriyya* but with the restriction *"opposé à l'esclavage"*; in the sense of *"pouvoir d'agir"* he prefers *sarāḥ*, from an Arabic root meaning "to roam or graze freely." In classical usage it also denoted the dismissal of a wife by divorcement.

Early references to freedom in works of Muslim authorship are hostile and equate it with libertinism, licentiousness, and anarchy. A significant change can, however, be seen in a passage in which the Ottoman chronicler Shanizade (d. 1826), under the year 1230/1815, discusses the nature of council meetings, which became frequent at this time. Neither Islamic tradition nor Ottoman policy favored the assertion of new political ideas, and Shanizade is careful to base the holdings of such consultations on Islamic precedent and "ancient Ottoman practice" and to give warning against its misuse; at the same time he points out that such consultations are normally held, with beneficial effects, in "certain well-organized states"—a striking euphemism for the states of Europe—and attributes to the members attending the councils a representative quality entirely new to Islamic political thought. The members of the councils consist of two groups, "servants of the state" and "representatives of the subjects"; they discuss and argue freely (*ber vejh-i serbestiyet*) and thus arrive at a decision.[7] In this indirect and unobtrusive way Shanizade was able to introduce to his readers such radical and alien ideas as popular representation, free debate, and corporate decision.

In the decades that followed, the notion of political freedom became more familiar through discussions of European affairs and translations of

European works, as for example the Turkish version of Carlo Botta's *Storia d'Italia,*[8] which abounds in references to liberal principles and institutions. It was also discussed and developed by several Muslim writers, who were influenced more especially by the rather conservative constitutionalism of the post-Napoleonic era—the idea of the *Rechtsstaat,* or state based on the rule of law, in contrast to both the unbridled absolutism of Napoleon and the license of the Revolution.

One of the most important of these was the Egyptian Shaykh Rifā'a Rāfi' al-Ṭahṭāwī (1801–1873), a graduate of al-Azhar who lived in Paris from 1826 to 1831 as religious preceptor to the Egyptian student mission. His account of what he saw and learnt was first published in Egypt in Arabic in 1834 and in a Turkish version in 1839; it includes a translation with commentary of the French constitution and a description of parliamentary institutions, the purpose of which is to secure government under law and "the protection of the subject from tyranny." What the French call freedom (*ḥurriyya*) says Shaykh Rifā'a, is the same as what the Muslims call justice and equity (*al-'adl wa'l-inṣāf*)—that is, the maintenance of equality before the law, government according to law, and the abstention of the ruler from arbitrary and illegal acts against the subject.[9]

Shaykh Rifā'a's equation of *ḥurriyya* with the classical Islamic concept of justice helped to relate the new to the old concepts and to fit his own political writings into the long line of Muslim exhortations to the sovereign to rule wisely and justly, with due respect for the law and due care for the interests and welfare of the subjects. What is new and alien to traditional political ideas is the suggestion that the subject has a *right* to be treated justly and that some apparatus should be set up to secure that right.

With remarkable percipience, Shaykh Rifā'a sees and explains the different roles of parliament, the courts, and the press in protecting the subjects from tyranny—or rather, as he points out, in enabling the subjects to protect themselves. What is far from clear is the extent to which he felt these ideas and institutions to be relevant to the needs of his own country. In his later writings there is little suggestion of any such relevance; even his commendation of the Khedive Ismā'īl for setting up a consultative assembly in 1866 shows a traditional concern with the duties of the ruler—justice and consultation—rather than a liberal concern with the rights of the ruled. In his book *al-Murshid al-amīn* (*The Faithful Guide*)[10] he defines freedom under five sub-headings, the last two of which are civic (*madanī*) and political (*siyāsī*). Both are defined in relation to social, economic, and legal rights, without any specific reference to *political* rights in the liberal sense. The first three sub-headings are natural, social (that is, freedom of "conduct"), and religious. Political freedom is the assurance of the state to the individual of the enjoyment of his property and the exercise of his "natural" freedom—that is, the basic innate power of all living creatures to eat, drink, move, and so forth, limited by the need to avoid injury to himself or to others.[11]

Shaykh Rifā'a's Turkish contemporary Sadık Rıfat Pasha (1807–1856), though vaguer in his theoretical notions of the meaning of freedom, is more specific on its immediate application at home. In an essay first drafted while he was Ottoman ambassador in Vienna in 1837—and in close touch with Metternich—he discusses the essential differences between Turkey and Europe and those respects in which Turkey might profitably seek to imitate Europe. Sadık Rıfat is deeply impressed by European wealth, industry, and science, in which he sees the best means of regenerating Turkey. European progress and prosperity, he explains, are the result of certain political conditions, of stability and tranquillity, which in turn depend on "the attainment of complete security for the life, property, honor and reputation of each nation and people, that is to say, on the proper application of the necessary rights of freedom." For Sadık Rıfat, as for Shaykh Rifā'a, freedom is an extension of the classical Islamic idea of justice—an obligation of the ruler to act justly and in accordance with the law; but it is also one of the "*rights* of the nation," and the establishment of these rights in Turkey is a matter of "the most urgent necessity."[12] Similar ideas are expressed by another Turkish writer, Mustafa Sami, a former Embassy secretary in Paris, who in an essay published in 1840 speaks with admiration of the political and religious liberties of the French.

Such ideas find official expression in the first of the great Ottoman reforming edicts—the Rescript of the Rose Chamber (*Gülhane*) of 1839, which recognizes and seeks to establish the rights of the subject to security of life, honor, and property, and to government under law.

There are two specific references to freedom—in the clause guaranteeing that "everyone shall dispose of his property in all freedom (*serbestiyet*)," and in the clause concerning the Councils, in which everyone present "shall express his ideas and observations freely (*serbestçe*) and without hesitation."[13]

These ideas of freedom are still very cautious and conservative; one would expect no other from Shaykh Rifāʿa, the loyal servant of the rulers of Egypt, or from Sadık Rıfat, the disciple of Metternich and coadjutor of the reforming minister Mustafa Reshid Pasha. The subjects were to be treated justly, and laws should be promulgated to secure such treatment. But there is still no idea that the subjects have any right to share in the formation or conduct of government—to political freedom, or citizenship, in the sense which underlies the development of liberal political thought and institutions in the West.

While conservative reformers talked of freedom under law, and some Muslim monarchs even experimented with councils and assemblies, government was in fact becoming more and not less arbitrary and oppressive. The modernization of government and the abrogation of intermediate powers at once strengthened the autocracy of the state and removed or weakened the traditional limitations on its functioning. More authoritarian government provoked more radical criticism; the newly created and rapidly expanding press provided a medium for its expression; nineteenth-century Europe offered a wide range of inspiration and example.

The suggestion has been made that some of the Lebanese movements of the periods 1820–21 and 1840 may have been inspired or influenced by French Revolutionary ideologies of national liberation and political democracy. The documents on which these suggestions rest[14] are few and uncertain and may reflect the activities of French agitators more than any genuine local movement. A more definite expression of libertarian ideas occurs in an account of the revolt of the Maronites of Kisrawān in 1858–59, led by Ṭanyūs Shāhīn; he is said to have aimed at "republican government" *(ḥukūma jumhūriyya)*, probably meaning some form of representative government.[15]

The intensification of Western influence during and after the Crimean War on the one hand and the growing internal political and economic pressures on the other both helped to bring a revival of libertarian thought and activities in the 1860s. The press provided a platform of a kind previously unknown. The first privately owned newspaper produced by a Turk, the *Terjüman-i Ahval*, began publication in 1860 and was followed in 1862 by the better-known *Tasvīr-i Efkâr*. The poet and journalist Ibrahim Shinasi, in his introductory editorials to the first issues of both newspapers, laid great stress on the importance of freedom of expression.

The topic was by no means academic. As far back as 1824, a Frenchman had established a French-language monthly in Izmir which, despite some difficulties with the authorities, grew into a weekly and played a role of some importance in the affairs of the Empire. Its vigorous comments sometimes got the editor into trouble—with foreign powers rather than with the Turkish authorities. A contemporary Turkish historian quotes an intervention by the Russian ambassador:

> Indeed, he said, in France and England journalists can express themselves freely, even against their kings, so that on several occasions, in former times, wars broke out between France and England because of these journalists. Praise be to God, the divinely-guarded realms [i.e. the Ottoman Empire] were protected from such things, until a little while ago that man appeared in Izmir and began to publish his paper. It would be well to prevent him. . . .[16]

Official regulation of books and pamphlets was introduced in 1857; the first press law was promulgated in 1864. There was reason, for libertarian ideas were in the air. In Syria in 1866 the Christian author Francis Fatḥ Allāh al-Marrāsh wrote an Arabic allegorical dialogue[17] which includes a philosophic and political discussion of freedom and of the conditions which are required to maintain it. More directly political in content was the work of a Muslim writer, the famous Khayr al-Dīn Pasha, one of the authors of the Tunisian constitutional enactment of 1861.[18] In this rather conservative programme of reform, Khayr al-Dīn examines the sources of European wealth and power and finds them in the political institutions of Europe, which secure justice and freedom. Identifying the two, he makes some cautious and rather obscure recommendations on how to secure them in the Islamic state without violating or departing from Islamic traditions and institutions, by reliance on "consultation," since the consultation of ministers, ulema, and notables is the authentic Islamic equivalent of the European system of representative and constitutional government. It may be noted that neither as chief minister in Tunisia in the years 1873–77, nor as Grand Vizier in Turkey in 1878–79, did he do anything to restore the constitutions which had been suspended in both countries.

Already in 1856, in an ode addressed to Reshid Pasha on the occasion of the Reform Edict of that year, Shinasi tells the reforming Pasha: "You have made us free, who were slaves to oppression," and continues: "Your law is an act of manumission for me, your law informs the Sultan of his limits."[19]

The radical implications of these words—the replacement of justice by freedom as the antithesis of tyranny and the suggestion of a constitutional restriction of the sovereign's powers—were developed and made clear in the late sixties and seventies by the group of liberal patriots known as the Young (strictly "new") Ottomans. The political ideas of the Young Ottomans, though couched in Islamic terms and related, sometimes with visible effort, to Islamic traditions, are of European origin and express an Ottoman-Islamic adaptation of the liberal patriotism current in Europe at that time. Their ideal was the British parliament at Westminster, their ideology was drawn from the liberal teachings of the French enlightenment and revolution, their organization and tactics were modelled on the patriotic secret societies of Italy and Poland.

In the political writings of the Young Ottomans the two key words are *Vatan*—"fatherland," and *Hürriyyet*—"freedom." The latter was the name of the weekly journal which they published in exile (London, June 1868–April 1870; Geneva, April–June 1870). In this journal and in other writings, the Young Ottoman ideologists, above all Namık Kemal (1840–1888), expounded their interpretation of liberty—the sovereignty of the people, to be secured by constitutional and representative government.[20] For Kemal as for earlier Muslim writers, the primary duty of the state is still to act justly—but justice means not only care for the welfare of the subject but respect for his political rights. These rights must be safeguarded by appropriate institutions:

> To keep the government within the limits of justice, there are two basic devices. The first of them is that the fundamental rules by which it operates should no longer be implicit or tacit, but should be published to the world. . . . The second principle is consultation, whereby the legislative power is taken away from the government.[21]

Like his predecessors, Namık Kemal tries to present these imported ideas as natural developments from traditional Islamic notions; in this way justice grows into freedom and consultation into representation.

Thus far, Namık Kemal and his associates had been anticipated by earlier nineteenth-century writers, and even to some extent by rulers, who had summoned councils and issued edicts. But the Young Ottomans, in both thought and action, went far beyond their cautious forerunners. For Namık Kemal, a consultative assembly, even an elected one, is not enough. The essence of the matter is that this assembly be the exclusive possessor of the legislative power, of which the government would thus be deprived. This doctrine of the separation of powers, to be expressed in and maintained by a written constitution, is supported by the even more radical idea of the sovereignty of the people, which Namık Kemal identifies with the classical *bayʿa,* the juridical term for the process by which the accession of a Caliph, according to Islamic law, was proclaimed and recognized.[22]

> The sovereignty of the people, which means that the powers of the government derive from the people, and which in the language of the Holy Law is called *bayʿa* . . . is a right necessarily arising from the personal independence that each individual by nature possesses.[23]

He was not deceived by the apparently liberal and constitutional aspects of the Ottoman reforms. The reform edict of 1839 was not, as some had claimed, a fundamental constitutional charter, but a measure of administrative westernization.

> Had the Rescript not confined the general precepts of law set forth in its preamble to personal freedom alone, which it interpreted as security of life, property and honor, but also proclaimed such other basic principles as freedom of thought, sovereignty of the people, and the system of government by

consultation [*i.e.* representative and responsible government], then only could it have taken the character of a fundamental charter. . . .[24]

In 1876, with the promulgation of the first Ottoman constitution, the liberal and parliamentary program of the Young Ottomans seemed to be on the point of realization. Article 10 of the constitution lays down that personal freedom is inviolable, and subsequent articles deal with freedom of worship, the press, association, education, and so on, as well as with freedom from arbitrary violations of the rights of the person, residence, and property. In its political provisions, however, the constitution is less libertarian. It derives not from the sovereignty of the people but from the will of the sovereign, who retains important prerogatives and all residual powers; it gives only perfunctory recognition to the principle of the separation of powers. Its effective life was in any case brief. In February 1878 Parliament was dissolved; it did not meet again for thirty years.

Under Sultan Abdülhamid II freedom was a proscribed word, and the ideals which it connoted became all the more precious. For Turkish modernists of that generation, the fountainhead was the West, which provided both material examples of the benefits of freedom and intellectual guidance on the means of attaining it. "When you look upon this fascinating display of human progress," wrote a young Turkish diplomat from the Paris Exhibition of 1878, "do not forget that all these achievements are the work of freedom. It is under the protection of freedom that peoples and nations attain happiness. Without freedom, there can be no security; without security, no endeavour; without endeavour, no prosperity; without prosperity, no happiness. . . ."[25] As an earlier generation had turned to Voltaire, Rousseau, and Montesquieu, so the new generation read the writings of Haeckel, Büchner, Gustave Le Bon (specially favored because of his sympathy for Islam), Spencer, Mill, and many others.

If there are today [wrote Hüseyn Rahmi in 1908], men who can think, can write, and can defend freedom, they are those whose minds were enlightened by these sparks [of European culture]. In those dark and melancholy days, our friends, our guides were those intellectual treasures of the West. We learned the love for thinking, the love for freedom, from those treasures.[26]

In more practical political terms, freedom meant constitutional and representative government—the ending of autocracy, the restoration of the constitution, and the safeguarding of the rights of the citizen by free elections and parliaments.

But freedom was no longer a purely political matter. For some, the exponents of materialist and secularist ideas, it involved an intellectual liberation from what they saw as the shackles of religious obscurantism. Perhaps the first to conceive of liberation in social and economic terms was Prince Sabaheddin (*c.* 1877–1948), who sought to lead Turkey from a collectivist to an individualist social order by a policy of federalism and decentralization and by the encouragement of private enterprise. In 1902 he founded a society dedicated to the achievement of these purposes. Similar ideas inspired the Liberal Entente, which appeared in 1911 as a rival to the Young Turk Union and Progress Party. An interesting example of the use of the word in a social and individualist connotation is in the Egyptian author Qāsim Amīn's famous book *Taḥrīr al-mar'a (The Liberation*—that is, emancipation—*of Woman).*[27]

After the Young Turk revolution of 1908 the establishment, for a while, of effective freedom of thought and expression initiated a period of vigorous debate, in which the problem of freedom, with others, was examined, analyzed, and discussed from many points of view; political, social, economic, and religious freedom all found their exponents and defenders. But as the bonds of autocracy and censorship were wound tighter by the Young Turks, the debate dwindled into insignificance. In the new Turkey that emerged under the first and second republics, the discussion of freedom does not differ significantly from that of Europe and is not expressed in Islamic terms.

Ottoman subjects from the Arab lands played a certain role in the libertarian movement almost from the beginning. On 24 March 1867, the Egyptian prince Muṣṭafā Fāḍil Pasha published in the French newspaper *Liberté* an open letter to the Sultan, advising him to grant a constitution to the Empire.[28] Besides endowing them with their first manifesto, the Pasha also helped the Young Ottoman exiles financially and was later succeeded in this by his brother the Khedive Ismāʿīl, who saw in them a useful instrument of his political purposes.

In Hamidian times, one of the first libertarian journals published in exile was started by Salīm Fāris, a son of the Sultan's Arabic journalist Aḥmad Fāris al-Shidyāq. Published in London in January 1894, it was entitled *Hürriyet*—a significant evocation of the earlier Young Ottoman weekly. He was later induced by agents of the Sultan to cease publication. Other exiles included the Lebanese amir Amīn Arslān, who published an Arabic journal in Paris in 1895, and a former Syrian deputy in the Ottoman parliament of 1876, Khalīl Ghānim, who became active in Young Turk circles. The ideas and arguments of the Young Ottomans and of the Young Turks found their echoes also in Arabic publications, which at this period tend to offer a provincial adaptation of ideas circulating among the Turkish ruling groups.

In Egypt, under Khedivial and then British rule, political thought evolved along different lines, more directly influenced by Europe and less directly affected by events and movements in the Ottoman Empire—though even here these had their effect. Many of the leaders of thought were Arabic-speaking émigrés from the Ottoman lands; the occasional presence and activity in Egypt of such Turkish personalities as Prince Sabaheddin and Abdüllah Jevdet (1869–1932) cannot have passed unnoticed. Walī al-Dīn Yakan (1873–1931), of Turkish origin and a participant in Young Turk politics, wrote extensively in Arabic on political and social problems. A work of some influence was Abdüllah Jevdet's Turkish translation of Vittorio Alfieri's *Della Tirannide*. Entitled simply *Istibdād* (Despotism), it was first printed in Geneva in 1898 and reprinted in Cairo in 1909. This translation appears to underlie the famous Arabic adaptation of Alfieri's book by the Aleppine exile in Egypt, ʿAbd al-Raḥmān al-Kawākibī (1849–1902), entitled *Ṭabāʾiʿ al-istibdād (The Characteristics of Despotism)*.[29]

One of the earliest discussions—little noticed at the time—of freedom in Egypt, after Shaykh Rifāʿa, is that of the Azharī Shaykh Ḥusayn al-Marṣafī. In his *Risālat al-kalim al-thamān (Essay on Eight Words)*,[30] he examines and interprets, for the benefit of "the intelligent young men of these times," eight political terms "current on the tongues of men."[31] One of them is *ḥurriyya*[32] which the Shaykh explains in natural and social terms—the difference between men and beasts, the human habit of social specialization and association, and hence the need for social cooperation and the mutual recognition of rights. The Shaykh recognizes the necessity of freedom in its natural and social sense but rather obscurely warns his young readers against untoward extension of the concept into the realm of politics.

Despite such warnings, the influence of European liberal political thought continued to grow and found frequent expression in Arabic as well as Turkish writings. The merits of freedom are variously presented and defended. For some, a vaguely understood freedom is still the secret talisman of Western prosperity and power; its adoption is therefore desirable in order to achieve the same results. For others, freedom means the overthrow of tyranny, usually identified with Sultan Abdülhamid, and the establishment of a constitutional regime in its place.

Perhaps the last and most cogent exposition of the classical liberal position in Arabic is that of the Egyptian Aḥmad Luṭfī al-Sayyid (1872–1963). A declared disciple of John Stuart Mill and other nineteenth-century liberals, Luṭfī al-Sayyid gives a central position to the problem of liberty in his political thought. Freedom, basically, means the rights of the individual—his inalienable natural freedom, defined and safeguarded by civil rights, which in turn are secured by political and legal arrangements and institutions. The action and interference of the State must be kept at the minimum; the freedom of the individual and of the nation must be secured by a free press, an independent judiciary, and a constitutional regime guaranteeing the separation of powers.

Luṭfī al-Sayyid is concerned not only with the freedom of the individual but also with that of the nation, which has corporate natural rights distinct from and additional to the aggregate of the rights of the individuals composing it. Rejecting pan-Islamism and disapproving of Arab nationalism, he sees the nation as Egypt and argues for her liberation from both foreign rule and native authoritarianism.[33]

The liberal interpretation of freedom continued to find exponents, particularly after the Young Turk revolution of 1908 and again after the military victory of the democracies ten years later. But in the meantime a new interpretation of freedom was gaining ground, resulting from the spread of imperialism and the rise of nationalism. In nationalist usage, freedom is a synonym for independence—the sovereignty of the nation state untrammeled by any superior, alien authority. In the absence of any such subordination to aliens, a nation is called free, irrespective of the political, social, and economic conditions prevailing within it. This interpretation of freedom had less impact among the Turks, whose independence though threatened was never lost, than among the Arab peoples for whom the main theme of political life was the ending of alien rule.

During the period of British and French domination, individual freedom was never much of an issue. Though often limited and sometimes suspended, it was on the whole more extensive and better protected than either before or after. The imperial regimes conceded freedom but withheld independence; it was natural that the anti-imperialist struggle should concentrate on the latter and neglect the former.

In the general revulsion against the West, Western democracy too was rejected as a fraud and a delusion, of no value to Muslims. The words liberty *(ḥurriyya)* and liberation *(taḥrīr)* retained their magic but were emptied of that liberal individualist content which had first attracted Muslim attention in the nineteenth century. A few voices still spoke of personal individual rights, and some writers used a word from the same root, *taḥarrur*, to denote psychological self-liberation or emancipation (from the shackles of tradition and the like). But for most users of the word, freedom was a collective, not an individual attribute; it was first interpreted politically, as independence, and then, when this by itself proved inadequate, reinterpreted in quasi-economic terms, as the absence of private or foreign exploitation. In the 1950s and 1960s the idea of political freedom in the classical liberal sense seemed to be dead in most Arab countries and dying elsewhere in the world of Islam. The beginning of the 1970s saw signs of a revival of interest, linked with a growing disillusionment with the other interpretations of freedom which had been imposed on them.[34] This interest increased in the late 1980s and early 1990s, when many saw in liberal democracy the only alternative to religious fundamentalism in the worsening crises of their societies.

On Modern Arabic Political Terms

26

During the past hundred years the Arabs, like many other peoples in Asia and Africa, have had to find new words for a series of political concepts and institutions alien to their own traditions and imposed or imported from outside. Drawn from European history and expressed in terms of European thought, the new political language was strange and difficult and remained so even when the structures themselves began to change. Arab history offered no precedents for the new facts and ideas; the wealth of the Arabic language seemed to lack words to denote or even adequately to describe them.

In devising its vocabulary of modern politics, Arabic has resorted to four main methods—borrowing, neologism, semantic rejuvenation, and loan-translation.

Of these, borrowing is the least important. In contrast to other languages such as Turkish and even colloquial Arabic, modern literary Arabic has accepted very few loanwords, and even these, while remaining lexically foreign, have usually been grammatically assimilated. Political loanwords came in the main with identifiably foreign referents. These may be institutions, like *barlamān,* parliament, presumably via French; functions, like *qunṣul,* consul (with *qunṣuliyya,* consulate); political movements or ideologies, like *balshafī,* Bolshevik, and *fāsh*[*ist*]*ī,* fascist. The former is now of rare occurrence; the latter is very extensively used, usually in a standardized collocation with *nāzī,* as a non-specific term of abuse for political and national opponents. Two loanwords of more general application are *diktātūrī* (also *dīktātūrī*), dictatorial, and *dīmūqrāṭī,* democratic, each with its corresponding abstract noun ending in *iyya. Diktātūrī,* a pejorative term for authoritarian government, is of limited usefulness in the Arab countries at the present time. *Dīmūqrātī* on the other hand is widely used with a very variable range of meaning, including elements derived from Eastern and Western Europe and from North and South America, as well as from indigenous tradition and experience.[1]

At first sight it may seem surprising that Arabic should have borrowed the word *dīmūqrātī*. The notion was not altogether new and could have been known to scholars through the Arabic versions and adaptations of Greek political writings, in which "democratic polity" is rendered *madīna jamāʿiyya*. This literature was however little read in the nineteenth and early twentieth centuries, and those who did read it may be excused for failing to perceive the connection between the systems described by ancient and medieval philosophers and the ideas and practices which were called democratic in their own day.

The same observations can be made of such neologisms as *jumhūriyya*, republic. In classical Arabic, the usual equivalent of the Greek *polīteía* or Latin *res publica* was *madīna*, a word of Aramaic provenance which originally meant a jurisdiction, then a country or district, and finally a city. This word was obviously too vague for precise political description. When, in late medieval times, the Arabic-speaking countries encountered functioning republics in Venice and elsewhere, they seem to have felt no need to devise any special term for them. It was not until the French Revolution that the Muslims, recognizing the emergence of a new political phenomenon, coined a new word to denote it.

This term, like many of the Arabic neologisms of the nineteenth century, was an Ottoman rather than an Arab creation. The Turks were the first Muslim ruling group to encounter the facts and read the literature of modern politics and therefore to feel the need for a new vocabulary for both discussion and administration. Turkish was the dominant language in the Ottoman Empire, in Central Asia and for a while even in Egypt and part of North Africa. When it gave way, it was usually to European languages—French, Russian, English, or Italian. Modern Arabic was thus a comparative latecomer and was able to make use of an important new vocabulary coined by Ottoman scholars, officials, and journalists. For educated Turks, Arabic was a classical language, on which they drew in the same way as West Europeans drew on Latin and Greek. Lexically, metaphysics and telephone are both Greek loanwords in English—but the historical and cultural difference between the two cases is obvious. Both have their equivalents among the Arabic words in Ottoman Turkish. Many, like metaphysics in English, are words borrowed from an earlier culture along with the ideas and objects which they denote. Others, like telephone, are new coinages for new referents. When such words are adopted back into their languages of etymological origin, they are lexical natives but semantic intruders. Such are *têlephônon* and *têlegraphima* in modern Greek; such too are a wide range of new terms in modern Arabic.

These repossessed neologisms comprise an important part of the modern Arabic political vocabulary. *Jumhūriyya,* at first republicanism and then simply republic, is an Ottoman coinage of the late eighteenth century. An Arabic term for republic produced at the time of the French occupation of Egypt, *mashyakha,* was not accepted into common usage and soon disappeared in this sense. Today *jumhūriyya* is the universally recognized word for republic in all the Arab lands.[2]

Two other Ottoman neologisms of great popularity at the present time are *qawmiyya,* nationalism, and *ishtirākiyya,* socialism. Both date from the nineteenth century and appear to be products of Turkish journalism. *Kavım* (from Arabic *Qawm*) is used in Turkish in the sense of tribe or people, often with a somewhat derogatory implication, rather like the French *peuplade. Kavmiyet* was at first used in a pejorative sense to mean tribalism, and thence factional, particularistic, or disruptive nationalism. Thus in 1870 Ali Suavi uses it when arguing against nationalism. For Muslims, he says, only religious identity is important. Religion unites them; nationalism would divide them.[3] The same line of argument is pursued by other anti-nationalist Turkish writers, of both pan-Islamic and Ottomanist opinions, and in 1913 Mehmet Akif gave it vigorous poetic expression.[4] In the same year Ahmed Naim published a book denouncing nationalism *(kavmiyet)* as "a foreign innovation as deadly to the body of Islam as cancer is to man."[5] Even the theoretician of Turkish nationalism, Ziya Gökalp, used *kavım* and *kavmiyet* to denote identity and solidarity based on ethnic affinity and thus at a more primitive level than nationality based on religion *(ümmet)* or culture *(millet)*.[6]

In Turkish *kavmiyet* remained on the whole derogatory and gradually fell into disuse. In Arabic, however, the word entered on a new phase of development. It appears in the proclamation published by the Sharīf Ḥusayn of the Hijāz in 1916[7] and thereafter becomes standard Arabic usage. More recently, it has been specialized to denote pan-Arab nationalism as against the national or rather patriotic loyalties of the individual Arab countries.

Socialism in nineteenth-century Turkish was *ishtirāk-i emvāl*, literally "sharing of property," whence *ishtirakjı*, a socialist, and *ishtiraki*, socialistic. In Turkish the term fell into disuse and was replaced by *Sosyalist*. Adopted in Arabic, it soon gained universal acceptance.

Other Ottoman Arabic neologisms include learned expressions, such as *iqtiṣādī*, economic, and a wide range of public administrative terms, such as *khārijiyya*, foreign affairs; *dākhiliyya*, home affairs; and *baladiyya*, municipality.

Apart from Ottoman usage, Arabic neologisms come from two main sources—Egypt and the Arabic-speaking Christians, especially the Maronites in Lebanon and elsewhere. They include such terms as *ʿilmāni*, from *ʿalamānī* (earlier *ʿālamānī*), secular (from *ʿālam*, world, whence worldly); *shuyūʿī*, communist (from *shuyūʿ* or *shiyāʿ*, a legal term for community of property ownership); *duwalī*, international (derived, contrary to accepted grammatical usage, from the broken plural of *dawla*, state); *iqṭāʿī*, feudal (from *iqṭāʿ*, a grant of revenue to an officer or functionary in medieval Islamic states); *rajʿī*, reactionary (from *rajaʿa*, to return or turn back); *diʿāya*, propaganda (from *daʿā*, to call or summon, a term technically applied to the preaching of certain sectarian missionaries in medieval Islam). Most of these words date from the late nineteenth or early twentieth century.

Another method of devising new terms is by a process of semantic rejuvenation or resemanticization. This occurs where an old word, which may or may not be obsolete, is given, more or less arbitrarily, a new meaning different from those which it previously expressed. Two examples, both from the nineteenth century, are *ḥukūma*, government, and *dustūr*, constitution.[8] In classical Arabic *ḥukūma* was a noun of action, meaning the act, later also the function, of adjudicating, of dispensing justice, whether by an arbitrator, a judge, or a ruler. After some semantic development, it was adopted in early nineteenth-century Turkish to express the European notion of government, that is, the group of men exercising the authority of the state, as distinct from the abstraction of the state on the one hand and the person of the sovereign on the other. In this sense it passed into Arabic and became common usage in the late nineteenth century.

Dustūr comes from a Persian word, originally meaning a person exercising authority, more particularly a member of the Zoroastrian priesthood. In classical Arabic usage, it had several meanings but commonly meant a rule or set of rules, especially in the craft-guilds. Its modern use in the sense of constitution is no doubt a development of this last meaning.

Other more recent refurbishments of old words include *shuʿūbiyya,* local (in other words, not pan-Arab) particularism (originally an anti-Arab faction in medieval times); *fidāʾī,* guerrilla or commando (literally one who offers his life as ransom, especially used of the terrorists sent out by the medieval Islamic sect known as the Assassins); *thawra,* revolution, originally rising, from the verb *thāra,* to rise, at first in the physical sense, for example—to quote examples given by classical lexicographers—a camel rising to its feet, a swarm of locusts rising into the air, and thence by extension an insurrection.

It is tempting to include such words as *umma,* nation, and *shaʿb,* people, in this category, since their content at the present time differs radically from classical and even early modern Arabic usage. They might however more properly be placed in the fourth category, of loan-translation or calque.

This is, at the present time, by far the most usual method of procuring new terms and accounts for the greater part of the modern Arabic technical vocabulary, of politics as of other fields of activity and themes of discussion. Briefly, loan-translation means that an Arabic word is given a change of meaning or an extension of range of reference, borrowed from the historical development of the equivalent word in another language. Loan-translations occur even in classical Arabic—for example, in the terms *umm al-qurā,* "mother of towns," from the Greek *mêtropolis,* and *tadbīr al-manzil,* "management of the house," economy, from the Greek *oikonomía.* In modern times they have hitherto usually been drawn from English or French. One or two simple examples may suffice to explain the process. *Kahrabā'* in classical Arabic means amber, in modern Arabic electricity. This reproduces the development of the western word, which comes from the ancient Greek *êlektros*—amber. *Adhā'a* in classical Arabic means to spread or disseminate news or information, that is, to broadcast in the pre-technical English sense of the word. In modern Arabic it has imitated the development of the English word and acquired the meaning of public radio transmission.

Loan-translation of political terms takes several forms. The earliest examples are common Islamic political terms, used with a change of meaning of which the users were probably unaware. Thus, according to the dictionaries, *malik* means king and *wazīr* means minister—but the use of these words for nineteenth-century European or European-style monarchs and the members of their governments represented a substantial modification of the hitherto accepted connotation of these terms among Arabic-speakers. The same is true of such other terms as *umma,* religio-political community, nation; *dawla,* dynasty, government, state; *ra'īs,* head, chief, president; *ḥizb,* faction, group, party; *istiqlāl,* unrestricted rule, independence; *za'īm,* surety, pretender, leader.

The last of these is particularly interesting. In early classical Arabic *za'īm* had the meanings of leader, spokesman, or surety. In medieval practice it was used chiefly of rulers or claimants whose claims the user did not recognize. It was thus applied by Sunnī authors to the chiefs of the Ismā'īlī sectaries in Persia and Syria and to the head of the Jewish community in Baghdad; it was also used by scribes in the service of the Egyptian Mamlūk Sultanate to designate the Zaydī and Almohade "Caliphs" in the Yemen and North Africa, whose title to the Caliphate was not admitted. This meaning of pretender or false claimant is confirmed by an Arabic-Spanish vocabulary of 1505, which explains *za'īm* as *"hablador de sobervias, vanaglorioso."*[9] The word *za'īm* came into general use in the 1930s, when an Arabic equivalent for *Duce* or *Führer* was required.

In all these, the new meaning is an extension rather than a replacement of the old political content, which still remains and can affect the use and understanding of these terms in Arab political life, often to the confusion of outside observers. In another type of loan-translation, the political meaning is wholly new. Thus, the word *inqilāb,* in classical Arabic, means revolution in the literal sense—that is, revolving, turning round. In Turkish, it became and for long remained the "good" word for revolution, used of revolutions of which the user approves; in Arabic on the other hand it has acquired a pejorative meaning and is used in a sense which might be translated by the French *coup* or German *Putsch*—English experience happily provides no suitable equivalent.[10]

There are many other words, previously non-political, which have acquired a new political significance, drawn from panoccidental usage. They include such terms as *ḥurriyya,* freedom;[11] *al-ra'y al-ʿāmm,* public opinion; *majlis nuwwāb,* chamber of deputies; *majlis shuyūkh,* Senate; *istiʿmār,* colonization; *muḥāfiz,* conservative; *waṭan,* country, *patrie; intikhāb,* election; *taʿāyush,* co-existence; and *taṣāʿud,* escalation.

The emergence of the modern Arabic political vocabulary is an important aspect of the political and cultural life of the Islamic world. A careful study of its development is essential to the evaluation of texts and documents; an appreciation of the layers of content of the current language of politics can contribute greatly to the decipherment of political symbols and kennings and thus to the better understanding of political thought, purpose, and process.

Islam and Development: The Revaluation of Values

27

The term "developing countries" is at the present time applied, by polite convention, to a large group of countries in Asia, Africa, and elsewhere, which differ very widely among themselves in culture, background, social and political structure, and degree of development, but have this in common—that they are classified as undeveloped or under-developed in relation to the societies of Europe and the lands of European settlement overseas. In addition, they have shared the traumatic experience of the impact, influence, and, sometimes, domination of the alien civilization of the West, which brought immense and irreversible changes on every level of social existence. Some of these changes were the work of Western rulers and administrators. Such foreigners, however, tended on the whole to be cautiously conservative in their policies; while they brought many great changes in practical and material things, their influence on institutions and ideas was far less radical than that of the native Westernizers. These were of many kinds—rulers who sought to acquire and master the Western apparatus of power; men of affairs, anxious to adopt Western methods and techniques for the creation or acquisition of wealth; men of letters and of action, fascinated by the potency and efficacy of Western knowledge and ideas.

The acceptance of modern civilization by a developing country may involve the installation of a modern-style political and administrative structure, the adoption of modern social and cultural patterns and institutions, the acquisition of modern economic and technical methods and skills. But in addition to these and other borrowings and as an essential concomitant to their successful assimilation, it must involve the acceptance, implicitly or explicitly, of the modern values and standards that underlie and accompany the growth and functioning of these things.

The revaluation of values was, and has remained, a problem at every stage of development in the West itself. The process of borrowing values from another society poses additional difficulties, especially when the borrower is itself a society of ancient civilization, with cherished and deep-rooted values and standards, sustained by high achievement, of its own. There are some values that are no doubt common to all mankind—such as truth, wisdom, valor, and loyalty; but the social application and interpretation of these values may vary greatly from one society to another and even present the appearance of a contradiction. Such a conflict—between the traditional values assumed in the family, the community, the home, and social surrounding and the new values proclaimed in the public life of the school, college, university, and government—may set up dangerous tensions in the individual and in society. Officially, the old values are abandoned, even discredited and derided, and are replaced by the values and standards of the modern West; in fact they survive, with sufficient power and vitality to exact submission, even from the most modernized of citizens. When a society adopts a new religion, the gods of the old faith sometimes survive as devils in the new theology. In the same way, when a society adopts new values, the old values may survive in a vestigial and surreptitious form as vices in the new order. The citizen, while obeying his instincts and traditions, will nevertheless feel guilt at flouting the new values on which the new order rests, and thus imperilling its success; he will also feel shame vis-à-vis the outside world, which he feels will despise him for failing to live up to its—now also his—standards.

A good example of this is the value of loyalty—a social virtue prized by all mankind and essential to the survival of any kind of society. But the basis of identity and cohesion may vary greatly from society to society. In the Muslim Middle East the two strongest claims on loyalty were those of kinship and religion. These were displaced, in the official scale of values, by new public, civic, and legal loyalties—to political principles and ideals, to nation and country, and, on a different level, to specific obligations, codes, and institutions. The old loyalties to kin and faith lived on; but instead of being virtues, they were often condemned, in the new political morality, as vices. The old virtue of family loyalty has become the vice of nepotism; the old virtue of religious loyalty has become the vice of fanaticism—and both are despised, sometimes even by those who obey them, as retrograde and uncivilized. There is no ascertainable moral difference here—the protection of one's political associates is not notably superior to the patronage of one's cousins; blind and unreasoning nationalism is not markedly more attractive than fanatical religious zeal—but the former are considered modern and progressive, the latter backward and barbarous, out of accord with the needs and purposes of the modern state; and indeed there is no doubt that religious fanaticism often divides the nation, which is the modern political unit, and delays development, or that the vague but potent loyalties of kinship lead to the fragmentation of capital and the limitation and diffusion of effort and thus inhibit economic growth. Their persistence, in the modern state, creates grave problems of adjustment and even survival.

Even some of the old, high religious ideals have been condemned as hostile to development. Such for example is asceticism, which tends to reduce and limit human needs instead of satisfying them and thus discourages effort; the virtue of renunciation leads too easily to the vice of indolence. Similarly, the great importance attached to the virtue of charity—in the sense of alms-giving—in the traditional Islamic scale of values has been criticized, in that it gives an accepted—even an honorable—place to the beggar in society and thus discredits and discourages honest toil. The charge that the Islamic religion is innately hostile to economic development is difficult to sustain; the social and cultural causes of economic backwardness in Muslim countries must be sought in a complex of factors, of which historic Islam is a part and, to some extent, an expression. In the Middle Ages, the Muslim Empires achieved a real flowering of economic life; in more recent times, as Becker remarked, Christian Ethiopia has been at least as handicapped as the Muslim lands.[1] There is nothing in Islamic doctrine to oppose economic progress, though there is much in the social and legal practices of Muslims that needs careful reconsideration from this point of view.

While the old virtues have become vices, some of the old vices are becoming virtues—and moreover virtues which are necessary for the growth of a modern society. An example of this may be found in the traditional and modern—or bourgeois—views of generosity and meanness. In the old scale of values generosity is a great personal and social virtue; meanness a low and contemptible vice. Anecdote, historiography, and social comment unite in extolling the open-hearted and open-handed individual or ruler, who bestows his largess freely and unstintingly without inquiring too closely into the claims and merits of the beneficiary or the purposes of the benefaction. To withhold such largess or to make such inquiries brings charges of meanness—even of avarice. The modern world, reared on the bourgeois virtues of thrift and industry, takes a different view. The ʿAbbāsid Caliph al-Manṣūr, whom the Muslim tradition condemned for his miserliness and nicknamed Abu'l-Dawāniq—the father of farthings—is praised by modern historians for his careful and provident economic policies. Other rulers, famous for their generosity, are now condemned as reckless and ruinous spendthrifts. It would be easy to multiply examples of the same process, from both public and private life, in our own time.

Associated with the traditional contempt for thrift is an attitude towards the acquisition of wealth in general and certain occupations in particular. In the Muslim Middle East a number of crafts and professions were originally followed, in the main, by members of religious or ethnic groups regarded as social inferiors. The stigma of inferiority remained even after this specialization had ceased to operate. Trade and finance came to be despised and those engaged in them suspect; thrift was confused with avarice and enterprise with greed. The worthiest occupations were the service of God and the State; the most esteemed persons were the ulema, the military, and the civil servants. These alone, according to the traditional scale of values, were engaged in noble pursuits, which were honorable and dignified even if not always very remunerative. All others were either vile mechanics or grasping hucksters. To work with one's hands, in particular, was contemptible, and the possession of manual skills, outside the artisan classes, carried no prestige or esteem. This had a harmful effect on the development of science and technology, in which progress often depends on a combination of intellectual training and manual—even, in a sense, artisanal—dexterity. Muslim landowners in the old days might be cultivated gentlemen or working farmers. They were rarely both and were therefore unable to produce anything resembling the technical and agrarian improvements introduced by the gentlemen-farmers of England in the seventeenth and eighteenth centuries. The same attitude is noticeable in the time of the nineteenth-century Turkish and Egyptian reforms, when graduates of the new schools of agronomy and medicine preferred to work in offices rather than soil their hands with earth or with patients. Of the first classes of graduates of the medical schools established in the early nineteenth century, it was in the main only the failures who actually became doctors. The successes became administrators, officers, officials, and statesmen. Even today, economic and technical progress can be held back by the survival of traditional evaluations of attainment and achievement and traditional definitions of prestige, honor, and dignity. Such, for example, is the old and deep-rooted attitude to work, power, and status which often makes the Middle Eastern motorist a bold and resourceful driver but a reluctant and unpredictable mechanic.

Development and progress are the basic needs of the developing countries—the needs in relation to which they are so defined and classified; yet development requires certain qualities—of enterprise, experiment, and originality—which are condemned as vices and defects in the old scale of values. In traditional societies the very concepts of development and progress are lacking. Improvement, according to traditional ideas, is achieved by trying to conform to a model or pattern—the perfect man, the perfect city, the perfect state. This model is, so to speak, external and given, and the effort towards improvement is thus basically an attempt at imitation: the more successful and sustained the imitation, the better. The modern idea of development—of a process of growth and maturing, whereby the innate qualities and aptitudes of an individual or a society are fostered and cultivated and brought to a higher level—is usually absent.

In the self-view of traditional society there is no progress and no development; there can, however, be change, and change is usually for the worse. The ideal model is usually situated in the past, in terms of a mythology, a revelation or master-philosophy, or a semi-historical golden age. Given this original perfection, all change is deterioration—a falling-away from the sanctified past. Virtue, in society, means the acceptance and observance of tradition; departure from it is the major social offense. The true path is the doctrine and practice of the ancestors, as preserved and recorded by tradition—in a word, the Sunna. Departure from it is *bid 'a*—innovation, the Islamic theological term which is the nearest equivalent to the Christian concept of heresy.[2] A *bid 'a* can be good and can be admitted as such by the religious authorities—but this is the exception rather than the rule. Normally, an innovation is assumed to be bad unless specifically accepted as good or permissible. There could be no more striking contrast with the attitude of modern society—the insistent and often fatuous pursuit of novelty as something necessarily and intrinsically good for its own sake. In the modern world, political and ideological as well as commercial salesmen try to market old wares by disguising them as new. In traditional society, on the contrary, new ideas and doctrines can only be made acceptable, if at all, by presenting them as a return to the pure and ancient tradition.

This tendency springs in part, of course, from a kind of cultural or communal nationalism—from a desire to soften the humiliation of accepting an alien practice or doctrine by disguising its alien provenance and ascribing it to long-lost, newly-discovered indigenous origins. But such nationalism, though widespread, is by no means the sole or even the main source of this historical romanticism. Another derives from the conscious attempts of would-be innovators to make their innovations more palatable by relating them to familiar and accepted things. Thus, when constitutional and representative government was in fashion in the Middle East, a series of attempts were made to relate it to Islamic origins, culminating in the speech from the throne at the opening of the Ottoman parliament on 14 November 1909, which referred to the "parliamentary form of government prescribed by the Holy Law." In the same spirit, when socialism became popular in the Arab lands, and official in Egypt, a shaykh of al-Azhar was found to proclaim that Islam is the true socialism and that Muḥammad was the first socialist. The purpose of this, of course, was not to convert socialists to Islam but to make socialism acceptable to Muslims. In the socialist states of today as in the parliamentary democracies of yesterday, official ideologists are not lacking to prove that what the government does is right—*i.e.*, conforms to the inherited tradition. That too, after all, is part of the tradition.

This raises the question of authority and freedom, with which that of tradition is closely linked. It is often said that Islam is an authoritarian religion, which inculcates an attitude of fatalism in man's relations with God and the world and of quietism in his relations with the state and society. This judgment of Islam might be difficult to maintain in abstract theological terms; it would, however, derive much support from the historic practice of Muslim states and communities, as recorded for the greater part of Muslim history.

Even here, some traces of another attitude remain. Not long ago it was fashionable for both Turks and Arabs to complain of the loss of their pristine freedom and to accuse one another of responsibility for that loss. Both complaints are true; both accusations are false. The Arabs among whom Islam was born were a people just emerging from nomadism and retained much of the anarchic freedom of the nomad. This freedom, it may be noted in passing, has nothing to do with democracy—a term relating to the manner in which authority is acquired, organized, and exercised in the state, and therefore irrelevant to a society in which there is neither authority nor state. Like other peoples at the same stage of development, they had a simple, rudimentary political system, with a chieftain ruling—or rather leading—by consent according to custom. The advent of the Islamic theocracy transferred the ultimate source of authority from the people to God, thus removing the consensual and revocable element in sovereignty and immensely strengthening the prestige and authority of the sovereign. Within a few generations of the death of the Prophet the Islamic state was transformed under the influence of the absolutist traditions of the old oriental Empires. The Arabs from Arabia—as later the Turks from Central Asia—forgot the nomadic freedom of the desert and the steppe and became part of the immemorial city and peasant civilization of the Middle East. The memories of ancient freedom are enshrined in the classical formulations of constitutional principles by the early Muslim jurists, with their insistence on the subordination of the sovereign to the law and the duty—duty, not right—of the subject to disobey an unlawful command.

These principles, however, were theoretical rather than practical and soon lost all real meaning. As restrictions on the sovereign's absolutism they were not very serious. For one thing, the law itself concedes him virtually absolute power, in all but religious matters. For another, the law—and the lawyers—never answered or even asked the question of how one would test the lawfulness of a command or deal with a sovereign who gave unlawful commands. Before very long, even the jurists accepted the view that the subject owed the sovereign a duty of absolute and unquestioning obedience—a religious duty, failure in which was a sin as well as a crime.

At first, this duty of obedience was claimed only for the legitimate or rightful sovereign ruling according to Holy Law. Later, the logic of events and the deductions of jurists from them extended it to any ruler irrespective of how he obtained power and of how he exercised it. *"Man ishtaddat waṭ'atuhu wajabat ṭā'atuhu,"* "whose power prevails must be obeyed" say the jurists—meaning that the religious duty of obedience relates to any holder of effective power. The same point is made in such oft repeated dicta as that "tyranny is better than anarchy" or "sixty years of tyranny are better than an hour of civil strife." Islamic political literature is full of exhortations to the sovereign to be generous and to be just, both in his own interest and as a religious obligation. But—and here is the fundamental point—this is a duty of the sovereign, not a right of the subject. The subject may have needs and hopes; he has no rights. The very idea of such rights is alien, appearing for the first time in the nineteenth century when writers in Turkey and Egypt begin to use such expressions as the "rights of freedom" and the "rights of the citizen." The source of these new ideas is obvious. The traditional attitude is well expressed in the old Arabic dictum: "If the Caliph is just he will be rewarded and you must be thankful. If he is unjust he will be punished and you must be patient."

Such a system gives great privileges to the holders of power; it also imposes great duties on them, which in the main they have discharged conscientiously and diligently, if not always effectively. However great these burdens, the ruling groups have rarely been willing to share them with others. The nineteenth century, on the whole, strengthened rather than weakened the power of the state, as social changes enfeebled or removed the classes and interests which had formerly limited it, and technical changes reinforced its means of surveillance and coercion. There was even some ideological reinforcement, as the ideas of the central European Enlightenment were brought to the notice of Turkish and other statesmen. For authoritarian reformers such ideas were welcome and familiar; they too knew what was best for the people and did not wish to be distracted by so-called popular government from the business of applying it. This view still commands some support at the present time in various countries and is frequently expressed in terms of socialism. As the bourgeois liberal revolution was introduced in the nineteenth century, without a bourgeoisie and without liberalism, by decision and action of the governing elite, so the socialist revolution was to be introduced in the twentieth century, without a proletariat or a working class movement, by the military and political elite of the nation. It has not been more successful.

There was, however, another view, drawing its inspiration from the political and, to a lesser extent, the economic liberalism of Western Europe. For Namık Kemal (1840–1888) and the Young Ottoman liberal patriots, the people had rights, and these must be secured, together with the progress of the country, by representative and constitutional government. And that is not all:

> If there is anything we want [Namık Kemal complained in 1872] we first wait for the government to provide it, and then for God. There must be no doubt that the government is neither the father nor the teacher, neither the tutor nor the nursemaid of the people. . . . What right have we to compel the government to act as our nursemaid? And for that matter, it is not God's duty to improve the world, nor are the prosperity of a country or the education of a nation necessary to Him.[3]

The battle was joined—between those on the one hand who believed in self-help, self-government, and the effective sovereignty of the people and those on the other who believed that the inert masses, accustomed by age-old tradition to follow and to obey, cannot yet be entrusted with their own fate but must be taught and commanded by those whose historic function it is to teach and to command—the intellectuals and the soldiers. So far the second school of thought has prevailed in most developing countries. It will probably continue to prevail until such qualities as initiative, enterprise, and self-reliance are accorded the same honors in the popular scale of values as are at present given to discipline, endurance, and obedience.

These military virtues are necessary in the armed forces and public services and more widely in times of war or national emergency. But for economic growth, intellectual progress, and political liberalization, other and somewhat different values and qualities must be added.

One of the more important methods of achieving this is education, and much effort is expended in developing countries on educational reform and expansion. But there are difficulties. Social change and political reform brought great changes in education; the new-style officials and officers of the post-reform period, and still more so the followers of such new professions as journalism and secular law, required a new type of education, different from the traditional religious and literary learning of the old schools and colleges. There was need, too, for new conceptions of knowledge and learning. For the old-style teachers and scholars, knowledge consisted of a finite number of pieces of information; learning consisted of acquiring them. Neither the scientists and philosophers of Islam on the one hand nor the mystics on the other would have accepted this view of knowledge and education. The schoolmasters and professors and their pupils did, however, and they applied it in the schools. The new intelligentsia required new pabulum—Western languages and literatures, history, geography, and law, to which were later added the economic, social, and political sciences. Most of these subjects were at first new and strange, but they were familiar in that they were all literary in form. They could be learnt in words, from books or lectures, and then memorized. That is to say, they could be assimilated to traditional methods of education, relying chiefly on the authority of the teacher and the memory of the pupil. There were not a few teachers who saw that this was not enough and told their pupils that they must use their own judgment, exercise their critical faculties, and decide things for themselves. The pupils accepted this because their teachers said so, and they learnt this lesson also by heart. It is not easy to impose freedom by authority.

The literary and authoritarian character of traditional pedagogy, as well as the attitudes of traditional society, made it very difficult to assimilate either the physical and natural sciences or the practical and technical skills associated with them. Society despised manual skills and rejected as inferior those who taught, acquired, or exercised them. A good illustration of this is the low rating and limited attention given to artists in traditional Islamic society, as contrasted with the high respect accorded to poets and scholars—artists of the word, not the hand. The only exception to this rule was the architect who, as an officer concerned with bridges and fortifications and as a director of building operations rather than a mere builder, qualified as a gentleman.

The position of the scientist was somewhat higher than that of the artist but, in post-classical times, with little justification. The once-great Muslim tradition of scientific research and experiment had long since withered and died, leaving a society strongly resistant to the scientific spirit. In the words of the late Dr. Adnan Adıvar: "The scientific current that arose in the time of Mehmet the Conqueror broke against the dykes of literature and jurisprudence."[4] The new literary, legal, and even social sciences could be assimilated without great difficulty by societies with rich and varied experience of all three; the natural and physical sciences could not. In many countries the scientific schools remained alien and exotic growths, in constant need of renewed transplants from the West. In a few non-Western countries there has been a real development of original scientific work, making important contributions to the common stock of modern knowledge; in most there has been little or none, and each generation of students must draw again from the sources in the West, which has meanwhile itself been making immense progress.

A century and a half ago, when the movement of Westernization began in Turkey and Egypt, its main purpose was to achieve military parity with the advancing West. There is bitter irony in the fact that the disparity in scientific knowledge, technological capacity, and, therefore, of military power between the Middle East and the advanced countries of the West is greater now than it was then, before the whole process of Westernization began. The result is certainly disappointing; the disappointment can be only slightly diminished by the realization that the disparity would have been infinitely greater—and the consequences far more deadly—had the attempt never been made.

The authority of the word, and of those who wield it professionally, has not infrequently been a major obstacle to progress—not a medium but a barrier in education, not a guide to reality but a shield against it. This danger is especially great where the written language of the learned is a complex and artificial idiom, divorced from the living speech of the common people. In Turkey and Persia this gap has substantially been closed, and the divergence between the written and spoken forms of the national language is hardly greater than in the countries of Europe. In the Arab world, the gap remains very wide, and the written and spoken forms of Arabic are in effect different languages.

In education and afterwards in life, the word, written or even spoken, has a magic and potency of its own, independent of, even transcending, both meaning and reality. There is a sense in which assent is more important than compliance, promise than fulfilment, law than observance, project than execution. The Turks, long accustomed to the exercise of power and responsibility, are relatively—though not wholly—free from this tendency. Among other peoples, long deprived of any power of determining or even influencing the course of events, there is a vast hiatus between expression and reality which must be closed before either serious discussion or effective action becomes possible. The difference between the practical, factual view of the West and the eastern concern with words and status is illustrated in the contrast between two proverbs, one English and one Turkish. "Sticks and stones may break my bones but words can never harm me" says the one; "the hurt of a blow passes but the hurt of a word endures" says the other.

But perhaps the most important single obstacle to progress, in the world of values and attitudes, remains the deep-rooted feeling that what is old is good, that change is bad, and that progress, or, to be more precise, improvement, consists in restoring what existed before the change. This feeling manifests itself in a variety of ways. A good example from Turkey may be found in the analyses and recommendations of the long series of writers and observers who examined the causes of the decline of Ottoman power and propounded remedies.[5] They were men of both vision and courage who, within the limitations of their time and place, saw in detail what was wrong and wrote in detail of what they saw. It is the more striking that for centuries all of them, without exception, saw the basic fault as a falling-away from the high standards and good practices of the Islamic and Ottoman past and the basic remedy as a restoration of those standards and practices. By the eighteenth century it was becoming clear to some at least that the return to the past was a mirage and that the path of progress lay in another direction. But even they, with greater or lesser sincerity, disguised their recommendations as a return to a past which they reinterpreted to suit their own ideas.

A similar tendency has already been noted in the writings of the liberals and reformers of the nineteenth century and after, who, despite their subjection to Western influences and adoption of Western views, still sought to relate these, even to identify them, with tradition—not in the existing form but in one allegedly more ancient. They revolt against today and yesterday—not in the name of tomorrow but of the day before yesterday. Thus, Namık Kemal identifies constitutional government with old Islamic principles of jurisprudence, sees a chamber of deputies in the assembly of mutinous janissaries, and equates the "natural law" of Montesquieu with the Holy Law of Islam—since the "natural law" comes from the "nature of things," the Holy Law comes from God, and God, after all, *is* the nature of things. It is not surprising that neither the radicals nor the conservatives were wholly convinced. But the same kind of argument continued to be advanced, with national and ethnic instead of (or as well as) religious loyalties behind them.

It has been claimed that such reinterpretation of the past does no harm—that indeed it does good, since it prepares deeply conservative peoples to accept novel and foreign ideas which they would otherwise reject, by concealing their novelty and foreignness—the sugar-coating on the pill, so to speak.

There is some truth in this. Tradition should not lightly be cast aside or abandoned, and progress will be surer and healthier if it can be related to the deeper sentiments, loyalties, and aspirations which a people has inherited from its past. Particularly in a tradition as rich and diversified as that of Islam, there is enough to support, by changes of selection, emphasis, and interpretation, most of the desired variation in attitudes and values. But the changes must be of interpretation and presentation, not of content—a reappraisal, not a perversion of the past.

PART VIII

NEW EVENTS

Behind the Rushdie Affair

28

On 14 February 1989, the Ayatollah Khomeini, the highest Islamic religious authority in Iran, issued a *fatwā* "to inform all the zealous Muslims of the world that the blood of the author of the book entitled *The Satanic Verses,* which has been compiled, printed, and published in opposition to Islam, the Prophet, and the Qur'ān, as also of those involved in its publication who were aware of its contents, is hereby declared forfeit. I call on all zealous Muslims to dispatch them quickly, wherever they may be found, so that no one will dare to insult Islamic sanctities again. Anyone who is himself killed in this path will be deemed a martyr." Shortly after, the head of an Islamic charitable trust in Tehran offered a bounty to anyone who carried out this sentence—twenty million tumans (about three million dollars at the official rate, about $170,000 at the open-market rate) for an Iranian, one million dollars for a foreigner. In 1992 the bounty, still unclaimed, was increased by the trust.

Strictly speaking, a *fatwā* is a responsum, a legal opinion or ruling given in answer to a question and is not in itself a judicial verdict or sentence. Khomeini's *fatwā* has, however, been treated, by its defenders and opponents alike, as combining both characters, and an enormous literature has appeared, in many languages, discussing the merits of the case. This discussion has been concerned almost exclusively, on the Western side, with the literary and political issues raised by the condemnation; on the Iranian side, with considerable but not universal Islamic support, with the alleged insult to Islam. Remarkably little attention has been given to the Islamic legal and historical issues raised by Khomeini's *fatwā* and the Muslim responses to it: What offense against Muslim law is Rushdie alleged to have committed? What jurisdiction can be claimed for Muslim law and judges over persons in non-Muslim countries? And how valid are the historical precedents from the life of the Prophet, cited by Iranian spokesmen in support of Khomeini's action? It is with these issues only that I shall be concerned.

I do not therefore intend to discuss the literary merit or lack of merit of the book. Good books enjoy no immunities from the law, bad books are subject to no penalties from the law, merely because they are good or bad. To condemn the one or privilege the other on the basis of literary merit would give to literary critics the right to determine not only the publication or suppression of a book but the life or death of its author, and that might seem excessive even by present-day norms of literary criticism. The literary quality of the book is irrelevant to what I have to say, and I shall at no point touch on it.

A second theme that I do not intend to discuss is freedom of speech. I do not by any means wish to suggest that this is unimportant or that it is irrelevant to the Rushdie affair, but it is not the aspect with which I am concerned. Let me just say that I am a firm believer in freedom of speech. I do not believe that this freedom should be completely without limits. I do believe that such limits should be defined and enforced by due process of law.

A third question that I prefer not to discuss is whether or not *The Satanic Verses* is insulting to Islam. For one thing, I am not quite sure what the phrase "insulting to Islam" really means. For another, insofar as it means anything, it is for Muslims and only for Muslims to decide whether the book is insulting to Islam or not. And since there are approximately a billion Muslims in the world, there are some further questions that must be answered, such as how that decision is made on their behalf and by whom, how that decision is to be made known and how put into effect. These, too, are matters for Muslims alone to decide, except insofar as their decisions may run counter to the laws of the United States, the United Kingdom, or other non-Muslim countries in which they may live.

One other literary point that I would like to mention only in passing is the argument sometimes made that *The Satanic Verses* is a novel and that Muslims don't understand novels because they have none in their literatures. There are by now a great number of novels in Arabic, Persian, and Turkish, and other Muslim languages, but the novel as such is indeed a Western importation to the Islamic world. Dating back little more than a century, it may not yet have reached the Mullahs and their flocks. There is, however, an old and indigenous literary tradition of satire and parody. Both are well represented in classical literature, sometimes on very sacred themes.

Before turning to the Islamic legal and historical implications of the Rushdie affair, it may be useful to look very briefly at the chronology of events. In September 1988, *The Satanic Verses* was first published in the United Kingdom. In the following months there were rumblings of dissatisfaction and protest among Muslims in the United Kingdom and in their countries of origin, in India and Pakistan. In November 1988, the book was reviewed in the literary supplement of a Tehran daily paper. Rushdie the novelist was already at that time known in Iran, and a Persian translation of one of his previous novels had a little earlier been awarded a major Iranian literary prize for best translated novel of the year. The review of *The Satanic Verses* was deadly, but only in the figurative sense. Rushdie and his literary work may have been unknown to the Ayatollahs —it is unlikely that they follow the literary journals, but some of their advisers must surely have done so.

On 12 February 1989, the book was published in the United States. There is normally an interval of several months between the publication of an American book in England or of an English book in America. It is rather remarkable that, although the book was published in England in September 1988 and reviewed in Iran in November 1988, the major crisis broke when it was published in the United States, in February 1989. The Khomeini *fatwā* was issued two days later. One may wonder why it was the delayed American publication, not the original British publication, that constituted the offense calling for a sentence of death.

The *fatwā* evoked a variety of responses in the Muslim world. In Islamabad, the capital of Pakistan, the American Cultural Center was attacked by a mob of enraged literary critics bent on deconstruction. Again, one wonders, why American? This was not an American book, not by an American author, but the work of a Muslim author of Indian birth, a citizen and resident of Britain.

On 16 March 1989 a group of Islamic foreign ministers, at a meeting of the Organization of Islamic States in Saudi Arabia, issued a statement denouncing the book and condemning its author as an apostate, *murtadd.* A Saudi official spokesman, commenting on this decision, pointed out that this was a resolution of a congress and not the decision of a court of law—a rather significant distinction. He further pointed out that even the resolution of the congress made no allusion to any death sentence.

What precisely was the offense of which Rushdie was accused? The charge is what in English we would call blasphemy. Specifically, it was the offense of insulting or abusing the Prophet, variously known as *sabb* and *shatm,* about which there is an extensive discussion in Muslim law books. Muslim law is based primarily on the Qur'ān and the Traditions of the Prophet *(ḥadīth)*—that is to say, narratives handed down concerning the actions and utterances of the Prophet on various occasions. Where there is a clear and unequivocal ruling in the Qur'ān or a generally accepted and unambiguous tradition, there is little if any room for difference of opinion. But in the course of time many differences of opinion arose among Muslims. There are some who accept, others who reject, a particular tradition, and even a generally accepted tradition may be differently interpreted. The major division is between Sunnis and Shī'a, who, though their theological differences are minimal, often diverge considerably on points of law. Even among the Sunnī Muslims, there are different schools of law that recognize each other as orthodox and valid but nevertheless sometimes take up different positions on important legal issues.

The law books cite a number of rulings and statements concerning the offense of abusing or insulting the Prophet. Normally, these discussions consider the case of a *dhimmī*—that is, a non-Muslim subject of the Muslim state, who insults the Prophet. On this the schools differ somewhat. The Ḥanafī school, which was followed in the Ottoman Empire and among a vast number of Muslims in Central Asia, South Asia, and elsewhere, generally took the position that if a *dhimmī* insulted the Prophet, he was to be punished by flogging or imprisonment or death or any combination of these, depending on the severity of the offense. There is some discussion about the severity of the offense—what made it severe and in what circumstances it constituted an offense. The general view among the Ḥanafī jurists was that it only constituted an offense if it was scandalous, public, and persistent. A chance remark thrown out in anger or in a moment of drunkenness did not count, or counted for very little. A prosecution for *sabb* was a very serious matter, involving major penalties, and according to the Ḥanafī jurists was not to be undertaken lightly. Some of them also insist that there must be witnesses who are free from malice or hostile intent. For Ḥanafī jurists it goes without saying that before anyone can be punished for this offense, he must be brought to trial, accused, and given the opportunity to defend himself.

The Mālikī school, followed principally in Africa—in medieval times also in Muslim Spain and Sicily—takes a more severe view and would normally regard any such offense as capital. A *dhimmī* who insults the Prophet must be put to death. There is an interesting case that occurred in Tunis in 1857 of a Jewish *dhimmī* who insulted the Prophet while drunk. Normally, since Tunisia then had Ḥanafī law as its official code, he would have been brought before a Ḥanafī qāḍī and given a light sentence. In fact, the ruler insisted on sending him before a Mālikī qāḍī, thus ensuring a death sentence. The reason was that a Muslim soldier had not long before been executed for robbing and murdering a Jew, and the ruler could not afford to be seen as more lenient to a Jewish blasphemer against the Prophet than to a Muslim.

What constitutes the offense of insulting the Prophet? Here again the jurists try to define carefully. The Ḥanafī jurists say, and the others do not disagree with them seriously on this point, that the unbeliever is not to be punished for "that which constitutes his unbelief." The *dhimmī* is known to be an unbeliever; he is allowed to live in the Muslim state as an unbeliever; he is not therefore punished for being an unbeliever. If the unbeliever says, "Muḥammad is not a prophet," this does not constitute blasphemy or *sabb*. That is his belief; so much is known and accepted. If he abuses the Prophet—that is to say, applies dishonorable epithets to him—that is another matter.

The case of a Muslim who insults the Prophet is of course much more serious. From a non-Muslim, such an offense is a breach of the *dhimma* and is dealt with accordingly. But a Muslim who insults the Prophet is seen as an apostate, and apostasy is a capital offense in all schools of Muslim law. A Muslim who renounces Islam, whether for another religion or for none, or a convert to Islam who reverts to his previous religion, is to be sentenced to death. Some allow the possibility of remission of sentence after recantation, others do not allow even that. Recantation may save the apostate in the next world, but not in this.

I turn now to the question of jurisdiction. How is the case to be adjudicated, and who has authority over the accused, to bring him to trial or to pronounce sentence? This raises the very important issue of the Muslim in a non-Muslim land. The world, according to Islamic law, is divided between the *Dār al-Islam* and the *Dār al-Ḥarb*, the *Dār al-Islām*—the house of Islam—being that part of the world in which a Muslim government rules and Muslim law prevails. The rest of the world is the *Dār al-Ḥarb*, the house of war. There is an intermediate category, which need not detain us now, as it has no bearing on this point. What is the legal position in Muslim law of a Muslim who is living outside the Islamic lands?

The first question is whether there should be Muslims living outside Islamic lands. On this the authorities have differed. Muslim law books devote a great deal of attention and discuss in very great detail the problems of the non-Muslim subject of the Muslim state. They devote only minimal attention and sometimes no attention at all to the problems of the Muslim subject of the non-Muslim state.

The reason for this is obvious. During the early centuries of Islamic history—that is, the formative period when the basic principles and norms of Islamic law were accepted, formulated, and committed to writing—the second question did not arise. The Islamic state was in a process of almost continuous expansion. Vast numbers of non-Muslims were being brought under Muslim rule, and there was no non-Muslim advance into Muslim territory. There were occasional, minor, temporary, tactical retreats, frontier adjustments and the like, but nothing of any great consequence. The problem of the non-Muslim ruler over Muslim subjects did not arise and was therefore not discussed, and probably would have been regarded as inconceivable and absurd at a time when it was generally assumed that the rapid expansion of Islam would continue without interruption until all the world was brought into the *Dār al-Islām*.

The problem of a Muslim in a non-Muslim land appears to have been first posed, theoretically, in the case of an unbeliever in the land of the unbelievers, who sees the light and embraces Islam. May he stay where he is, or must he go to a Muslim country? The Sunnī answer is unequivocal —he must leave home and go to a country under Muslim authority and law. If he stays at home, he is failing in his duty. If his country is subsequently conquered by the advancing Muslims, his property may be treated as booty, like that of his unbelieving compatriots. The Shīʿa view is the exact opposite. He should stay where he is to spread the light of Islam, and even if he fails and remains alone, then on the Day of Resurrection he will rank as a community all by himself.

A more frequent question was whether it is lawful for a Muslim to visit a non-Muslim land. Here the jurists differ somewhat. Most of them dislike the idea and regard it as bad but are prepared to tolerate it in certain circumstances. Most or all allow a Muslim to visit a non-Muslim state in order to arrange the ransom or exchange of captives or prisoners. And so, for example, virtually every Moroccan ambassador's report from Europe, from the earliest times until at least the eighteenth century, is headed: "Report on a Mission for the Ransoming of Captives." This ensured that the mission was lawful and protected both the envoy and the sovereign who sent him from possible charges.

There was some discussion among Mālikī jurists in North Africa on whether it was permissible to go to Europe to buy foodstuffs in a time of shortage. Some said that in a time of real shortage, when the infidels have food and the Muslims do not, it is permissible to go. Others held that even then it was not permissible to go, because spending money in the land of the infidels meant strengthening them for the wars that they would certainly wage against the Muslims.

There was also the question, east rather than west of Islam, of small groups of merchants who went to settle for short periods for trade purposes in China, in India, in Central Asia, in Southeast Asia, where they were not subject to the rule of a rival religion, but in a sort of religiously neutral area. There is some discussion, again very brief, among Muslim jurists on this question.

The issue became urgent, and in a new form, with the advance of the reconquest in Europe—the recovery for Christianity, first of southern Italy and Sicily, and then of Spain and Portugal, which for the first time brought significant Muslim populations under the rule of Christian states. Now, the question that was asked was, "May they stay or must they go?" The virtually unanimous opinion of the Mālikī jurists—and they were the only ones who faced this question since this was happening in the far west of Islam—was that they must go. It is not permissible for Muslims to remain under non-Muslim rule, and if their homeland is conquered by infidels, they must do what the Prophet did when he left Mecca and went to Medina. This migration—in Arabic *hijra,* commonly misspelled *hegira*—marks the beginning of the Muslim calendar. There is a basic Muslim principle of seeing the Prophet as what we would nowadays call a role model. The phrase used in the Qur'ān, *uswa ḥasana,* might reasonably be thus translated. Muslims must emulate the Prophet in all things, and just as the Prophet left his home in pagan Mecca and faced the risks, dangers, and difficulties of going to another and a strange place, so Muslims finding themselves under a non-Muslim ruler must pack their bags and go. Al-Wansharīsī, a Moroccan jurist who in 1485 wrote a major *fatwā* on this question, lays down that migration from the land of unbelief to the land of Islam is an obligation until the Day of Resurrection. For a Muslim to remain under infidel rule is as bad as eating carrion or blood or pork, or committing murder. The questions and answers speak specifically of Christians, because that was the challenge they faced. The question was asked, "But if the Christian ruler is just and tolerant, what then?" According to al-Wansharīsī, even if the Christians are just and tolerant, the Muslims must leave.

By his day this had become a largely hypothetical question, since the Christians were neither just nor tolerant in the countries that had been reconquered. During the centuries of the Spanish Reconquest, communities of Muslim subjects, known as *Mudejar,* probably from an Arabic term denoting tamed or domesticated animals, remained under Christian rule. The completion of the Reconquest in 1492 was followed, after an interval, by their enforced departure. An earlier—twelfth century—jurist, al-Māzarī, a Tunisian of Sicilian origin, as his name indicates, from Mazara in Sicily, agrees in principle that when the non-Muslims have conquered their homeland—he is speaking of Sicily not of Spain—they must leave, but nevertheless finds a number of excuses to enable them to stay for the time being: if they are allowed to practice their religion without impediment; if they have reasonable hope of converting their new masters to Islam; even, if they are not aware of the law that requires them to go. Al-Māzarī is obviously trying to be helpful, and indeed Muslims did stay for quite a while in Sicily under the relatively tolerant rule of the Normans, before they went and mostly relocated in North Africa. One finds similar, though less systematic, discussions in the East, in the areas of the Levant that were conquered and for a while held by the Crusaders.

Why did this matter? A reason sometimes cited is the repeated Qur'anic obligation imposed on Muslims "to enjoin good and forbid evil"—*al-amr bi'l-ma'rūf wa'l-nahy 'an al-munkar.* A Muslim is required not merely to do good and avoid evil—personal choices that can be made anywhere. He is required to enjoin good and forbid evil, and that requires the exercise of authority. It is on that basis that some jurists argue that one can only be a good Muslim under a Muslim state. Others disagree.

The question of stay or go became more urgent and more frequent in the early modern centuries, first with the retreat of Ottoman power in Eastern Europe and then with the expansion of the European empires. The first stage of the Ottoman retreat posed an agonizing choice for great numbers of Muslims, some of them Turkish-speaking, some of them speaking the local languages, in the lands north of the Black Sea that were annexed by Russia during the eighteenth century and in the Balkan Peninsula where province after province, country after country, was lost by the Ottomans and therefore lost to Islamic rule. Many left and were resettled in what is now Turkey and what are now the Arab states of the Fertile Crescent. There are many families in Turkey and in the former Arab provinces of the Ottoman Empire today whose origins can be traced to places in what are now Romania, Hungary, Bulgaria, Yugoslavia, and Greece. Others came from the countries conquered by the Russians: from the Caucasian lands, from the Crimea and Central Asia.

Interestingly, the term that was applied to them was *muhājir.* A *muhājir* is one who performs a *hijra* and thus emulates the action of the Prophet. The term *refugee* was used in the Ottoman Empire for Christians or Jews who had fled from persecution in Europe and found refuge in the Ottoman lands. It was not used of Muslims who came from the lost provinces. They were not seen as refugees or as immigrants but as fellow Muslims who had performed the religious obligation of *hijra.*

Much more recently, the term has been applied to Muslims who left secular India to relocate in Islamic Pakistan.

The jurists discuss the plight of a Muslim among non-Muslims under several headings—the lone convert, the reluctant visitor, the unhappy victim of infidel conquest. The possibility of a Muslim who voluntarily goes to a non-Muslim land and stays there of his own free will was never considered by the classical jurists and was quite obviously unimaginable. Usāma ibn Munqidh, a fascinating Syrian writer in the period of the Crusades, struck up a friendly relationship with a Frankish knight who was his neighbor. The knight one day offered to take Usāma's fourteen-year-old son to Europe to "live among the knights and learn wisdom and chivalry." The suggestion was no doubt kindly meant, but Usāma was shocked: "Words struck my ears such as would never come out of the head of a man of sense. If my son were taken captive no greater misfortune could befall him from his captivity than being taken to the land of the Franks." Voluntary migration was not an acceptable idea and did not take place until very recently.

By now there are very considerable numbers of Muslims who have migrated and settled in countries outside Muslim control—that is to say, where non-Muslim governments rule and where the Muslim law, the *sharī'a,* is not enforced. The argument sometimes adduced in defense of such migration is that the Prophet himself, while still in Mecca, permitted some of his companions to seek refuge in Christian Ethiopia from the persecution of the pagan Meccans. The weakness of this argument—as others have pointed out—is that there was no Muslim state in existence at that time, and that the Companions were fleeing from pagan to Christian rule, a clear improvement, and entirely unlike a migration to Christian from Muslim rule, which is the reverse.

Does the jurisdiction of Islamic law extend into countries where non-Muslim governments rule? Here again there is a clear difference between the juristic schools. The Ḥanafī school says no: the enforcement of Islamic law, the jurisdiction of an Islamic court are limited to the *Dār al-Islām*. Sarakhsī, one of the major Ḥanafī jurists of the medieval period, even gives an extreme formulation to emphasize his point. He says: If a Muslim traveling in the lands of the unbelievers commits robbery and murder and returns with his loot to the lands of Islam, he cannot be prosecuted for murder, nor can the property be touched, since this offense was committed outside the jurisdiction of Islam, and it is for the judicial authorities of the unbelievers to take action if they judge it appropriate and are able to do so. Muslim law and the Muslim judges are not concerned with what happens outside the realm of Islam. The Shīʿa position is the exact opposite: that the jurisdiction of the Islamic law and of an Islamic legal authority is universal. Wherever there are Muslims, they are subject to Muslim law; they are bound to obey Muslim law; they may be punished for disobeying Muslim law. The other schools—that is to say, the other Sunnī schools other than the Ḥanafīs—vary, some inclining more to the Shīʿa, some inclining more to the Ḥanafī view, some with various compromise positions between them. Some jurists, for example, say that a Muslim may be tried and punished for an offense that he commits in the land of the unbelievers but only when he returns to the lands of Islam, not while he is still in the lands of the unbelievers. Khomeini's *fatwā* goes beyond even the most extreme of earlier Shiʿite rulings in that it also condemns those involved in the publication of the book; that is to say, it extends the jurisdiction of Islamic law, and the execution of its penalties, to infidels living in the lands of the infidels.

The Rushdie sentence raises another juridical question, that of trial and sentence. An offense is alleged to have been committed. A person is accused of having committed that offense. What is the legal position regarding prosecution and sentence? On this there are considerable differences among the juridical schools. The majority of Sunnī jurists and a minority of Shīʿa jurists consider that arraignment and trial are necessary. Anyone who is accused of an offense must be brought to trial, told of the charges against him, confronted with the witnesses to his offense, and given the opportunity to defend himself, after which the judge will give a verdict, and, if appropriate, pronounce sentence. There is, however, another view, held by a majority of Shīʿa and a minority of Sunnī jurists, that the offense of insulting the Prophet, particularly by a Muslim, is so utterly heinous that in the case of that offense one may, indeed one must, dispense with the formalities of trial and conviction and proceed directly to the execution.

This view, though primarily Shiʿite, is also held by a minority among the Sunnis, including the eastern Ḥanafīs in Trans-Oxania and Central

Asia. They cite texts and traditions, according to which the Prophet said, "If anyone insults me, then any Muslim who hears this must kill him immediately." And, some versions add, there is no need to refer to the imām or the sultan, meaning no need to obtain the approval of a higher authority, whether religious or political. Others take exactly the opposite view and say that such an action constitutes murder and should be punished as such, to which the more rigorist school replies: if a man carries out the sentence in this way and kills a blasphemer and then is himself killed, he will receive a martyr's reward in paradise. According to this view, then, summary and immediate execution is not only lawful but is obligatory, and those who do not do this are themselves committing an offense, which in English legal language might be called misprision of felony. A similar view is expressed in some legal texts, which require a Muslim actively to prevent the public commission of offenses such as drinking and revelry. On this point also Khomeini's *fatwā* and sentence go far beyond even the most rigorous jurists, who only require a Muslim to kill anyone who insults the Prophet in his hearing and in his presence. They say nothing about an arranged killing for a reported insult in a far place.

So much for the law. In the juridical and theological discussions of the case during the last year or so, principally in Iran, a number of historical precedents have been quoted. The Prophet is seen by Muslims as their guide and mentor, not only through revelation but also through his own actions and utterances. The difficulty is that some of the material purporting to relate to the Prophet's life is of questionable authenticity. Most of the biography is accepted by Muslims without question; but parts are regarded as legendary or problematic, with a rather vague and uncertain area between the two.

Perhaps the most astonishing and extraordinary aspect of the whole controversy over the Rushdie affair during the last year is the effort that has been made by Iranian spokesmen, by searching through biographies of the Prophet, to prove by historical precedent that the Prophet both condoned and rewarded assassination, or even instigated it. After the battle of Badr in 624, between the Prophet and the Muslims on the one hand and the unbelievers on the other, it is told that two pagan Arab poets who had lampooned the Prophet were killed by their own kinsmen, hoping thereby to prove their loyalty to the Prophet. One of them, according to the narrative, was a very old man, said to be a hundred years old; the other was a young woman, indeed a nursing mother. No punishment was imposed, and no blood feud was incurred as a result of these killings. This is adduced as prophetic authorization for the sentence against Rushdie. Another case occurred after the capture of Mecca in 630, when a certain ʿAbdallah ibn Hilāl ibn al-Khatal composed satirical poems attacking the Prophet, which were sung in public by two singing girls who were his slaves. One of the girls was executed, the other was pardoned.

A better-known example is Kaʿb ibn al-Ashraf, a poet and opponent of the Prophet, who was apparently the author of some widely circulated anti-Muslim verses. According to a narrative, the Prophet had let it be known that he would gladly be rid of Kaʿb ibn al-Ashraf, who was duly murdered. These particular cases have been repeated again and again, not to besmirch the Prophet by proving that he was an instigator of assassination but to prove that instigating assassination is a good thing, because the Prophet did it. One is reminded of the famous story of the destruction of the library of Alexandria, which according to legend was destroyed by order of the caliph ʿUmar. There is ample evidence that nothing of the kind happened. This story was not, as has sometimes been suggested, a Christian invention to show that ʿUmar was a barbarian who burned libraries. It was a Muslim invention to show that destroying libraries could be a good thing, because ʿUmar did it. This story appears at the time of the dispersion of the heretical Fāṭimid libraries in Egypt, and its purpose was probably to justify something that was in itself unacceptable to a civilized people.

Perhaps the most heartening aspect of the otherwise rather depressing Rushdie affair is the response in many parts of the Islamic world, particularly in some of the Arab countries, to these events. The chief mufti of Egypt, in March 1989, stated quite clearly that, if Rushdie had committed the offense of which he was accused, he was liable to the death penalty, but there could be no execution without arraignment and trial. In many other countries, silence was eloquent. In countries where speech is often extremely dangerous, silence itself could be a very powerful expression of opinion. Possibly most remarkable was the action of a number of Syrian intellectuals living in Syria—not comfortably ensconced in some European or American university—who signed and published a manifesto in a Beirut newspaper denouncing the condemnation of Rushdie and the *fatwā,* the death sentence and the bounty.

The matter is not yet closed. The *fatwā* stands, and since its author is dead there is no one else who can abrogate it. The sentence still stands and has recently been reaffirmed, and it is unlikely that Mr. Rushdie will ever live a normal life again.

The *fatwā* has raised a number of very serious questions, which Muslims must confront. And of course, not only Muslims, since these matters affect many other people, too.

The Egyptian Murder Case

29

During the few moments that passed between the murder of Sadat and the seizure of his murderers, the leader of the four assassins shouted some words that were repeated all over Egypt during the days that followed. According to reports, he cried out: "My name is Khālid al-Islambuli. I have killed Pharaoh. I am not afraid to die."

Of this tripartite declaration, the most significant part is certainly the second. Its meaning is clear—that he had killed a tyrant. The choice of Pharaoh as the prototype of tyranny conveys a religious perception of the offense, the judgment, and the punishment executed.

To anyone brought up in the Judaeo-Christian tradition, and with even a minimal acquaintance with the Book of Exodus, the naming of Pharaoh as a paradigm of the evil ruler seems obvious enough. But Sadat's murderers were neither Jews nor Christians. They were Muslims, and moreover Egyptians. The Old Testament had not formed part of their education, and in modern times they had been taught at school to regard Pharaoh as a symbol of the greatest and most glorious age of Egypt's past, a source of national pride rather than an oppressor of God's servants.

Until the mid-nineteenth century, in Egypt as in other Muslim lands, Pharaoh was known only from the Qur'ān, which presents the Exodus in terms broadly similar to those of the Old Testament. In the Qur'ān, Pharaoh is the villain of a story in which Moses and the children of Israel are the heroes, and in several passages Pharaoh appears as the ultimate

---

A review of *Autumn of Fury: The Assassination of Sadat* by Mohamed Heikal, Random House, from *The New York Review of Books*, 31 May 1984.

example of the irreligious and oppressive ruler whom it is the believer's duty to disobey and if possible to overthrow. From the mid-nineteenth century onward, as the achievements of the European science of Egyptology made the language, literature, and history of pre-Islamic Egypt known for the first time to the Muslim Egyptians, a new sense of identity began to transform their perceptions of themselves, their country, and their place in the world. Their sense of themselves became patriotic and national rather than religious and communal, and they formulated new and different views of the past and hopes for the future.

The resulting tensions and contradictions are at the heart of the problems of political life in Egypt today and, in similar forms, in the other countries of the Arab world. This very use of the term "Pharaoh" encapsulates a central dilemma of modern Arab nationhood. In one significant respect the two images of Pharaoh—the Egyptian hero and the Islamic villain—coincide. No one could accuse him of being "soft on Israel." And this has at times raised troubling questions.

Why was Sadat killed? The immediate response of the Western world, better informed, or rather more extensively informed, about the international than about the internal affairs of the region, found a characteristic answer—simple, clear, and misleading. Everyone had always known that the first Arab leader to make peace with Israel would be murdered by his own people. Sadat had made peace, and Sadat had duly been murdered. What could be more obvious? The overwhelming enthusiasm with which the Egyptian masses had responded to Sadat's peace moves, and the existence of some other grievances against him, were conveniently overlooked. Since then, this oversimplified explanation has been abandoned by most serious students of the region. Even Mohamed Heikal, despite his consistent and unconcealed hostility to the peace with Israel, does not insult readers of his new book by offering it to them as the sole reason. In addition to his condemnation of the peace, he puts forward a series of criticisms of the man, his policies, and above all his personality, which in his view led to the murder and—far more striking—to the lack of grief or even surprise that it occasioned.

During the period of relaxation of central control and repression that followed the death of Nasser and his replacement by Sadat, two major opposition groups appeared in Egypt. Forced underground and subjected to severe repression in Nasser's day, they came to the surface under Sadat, and—despite some difficulties in Sadat's last years—remain active to the present. One of them expresses its criticism of the old order, and its aspiration for change, in Islamic religious terms. Its exponents belong to various wings of the militant Islamic resurgence which, in the English-speaking countries, has come to be known as "fundamentalist," a term from the history of American Protestantism which is at best a loose analogy and can be seriously misleading when applied to something as different as these Islamic movements.

The other opposition group is known, by an equally inaccurate transference of a term derived from another history and another culture, as "leftist." The two forms of opposition overlap at some points—for example in their denunciation of the freewheeling capitalist enterprise favored by Sadat, of Egypt's closer relationship with the United States, and of the peace with Israel. But they differ vastly in the relative emphasis that they give to these and other matters, in the reasons for opposing them, and, most important of all, in the remedies they propose.

Of the two kinds of opposition, that of the "leftists" is by far the better known in the Western world. Many of its leaders are Western educated and can address a Western audience not only in its own language but also by appealing to its own values, or at least to its rhetoric. In fact, it is to these "leftist" circles that most Western academic and journalistic inquirers turn for enlightenment on Egyptian affairs. One of the most enlightening informants—if not on Egypt, then at least on the outward aspect of Egyptian leftism—is Dr. Mohamed Heikal, editor of the great national newspaper *Al-Ahrām* under Nasser and in the early years of Sadat and author of a series of books that were translated into many Western languages. The leftist school is anti-Western and particularly anti-American, and its exponents have acquired considerable skill in detecting, and even directing, the Western taste for self-criticism. They are also anticapitalist and prosocialist, though the socialism of Nasser to which they look back nostalgically probably owes less to either the communism of Eastern Europe or the social democracy of Western Europe than to the bureaucracies of the Pharaohs, the Ptolemies, and the Ottoman Pashas who directed the economic life of Egypt over the past millennia by means of the state apparatus. The leftist school is also opposed to the Camp David agreements and more generally to Israel and Zionism. In its Arabic though not in its Western-language publications, it sometimes goes still further and uses arguments and makes points that are unmistakably anti-Semitic.

The religious, more specifically Islamic, opposition is little known in the West, because it has made no attempt to address itself to a Western public and feels no need to seek any kind of Western support or approval. Its views can be found only in the publications, many of them illegal, of its leaders, and by some occasional windfall such as the reports of the long interrogation of Sadat's murderers. But despite its lack of exposure in the Western press, there can be little doubt that the religious opposition is vastly more important than the opposition of the leftists—both in the extent of its support among the masses and in the magnitude of the threat that it offers to the existing order.

Like the "leftists," the "fundamentalists" are against the West. Unlike the leftists, they are also against the Soviet Union, seeing the two superpowers and the two different ways of life that they embody as equally alien to Islam and equally menacing to the Muslims. Like the leftists, again, they are highly critical of Sadat's capitalism, but for different reasons. They oppose neither profit nor private enterprise, both of which are sanctioned and regulated by the Holy Law. What they reject is the crass materialism and corruption, which they attribute to the particular brand of economic activity stimulated by the Western nations. This however does not make them any more sympathetic to socialism, whether in its Marxist or Nasserist forms. Indeed, while for the leftists Nasser is a great hero and his time of rule a golden age, for the fundamentalists he is one of the major figures in their demonology.

Like the leftists again, they are anti-peace and anti-Israel, but for different reasons and with different priorities. Curiously, the entire Palestine question occupies only a minor place in their writings, and the very words "Palestine" and "Arab" are of infrequent occurrence. In their perception, these are Muslim lands and peoples that have been usurped and dominated by an infidel stranger. In God's good time, the stranger will be evicted and the land restored to the realm of Islam. This is, however, not of immediate concern. The major problem is the domination of the Muslim lands, Egypt and elsewhere, by apostates and secularists who, while pretending to be Muslims, are in fact destroying Islam from within. In their view, the major crime of Sadat, as of the Shah in Iran, Saddam Hussein in Iraq, Assad in Syria, and before them Nasser in Egypt and Atatürk in Turkey, was the abrogation of the Holy Law of Islam and the paganizing of Islamic society by the introduction and imposition of laws and usages imported from the outside world.

This, they assert, is the ultimate crime against God and his Holy Law, for which the penalty is death. Rulers and regimes that have abandoned the Holy Law have thereby forfeited their legitimacy; they have become the enemies of God and therefore of all good Muslims. The duty of *jihād*, usually rendered as "holy war," is incumbent upon all Muslims, but the first task is to destroy the tyrant at home and thus make possible the restoration of a truly Islamic society governed by Islamic law. After that, with God's help, the removal of the external enemy, whose penetration had been made possible by Muslim sinfulness and weakness, would be a relatively simple matter.

That tyrant is Pharaoh. For the secularist, the patriot, even the socialist, Pharaoh may be a hero and a source of pride. But for the religious Muslim, who rejects all these philosophies, Pharaoh is the terrible example, named in God's book, of arbitrary rule and the defiance of God's law. That Pharaoh was not particularly well-disposed to the Jews does not make him any more acceptable. If anything, his persecution of the Jews is a sin, not a merit, since they, not the pagan Egyptians, were at that time the custodians of God's truth. The fundamentalist view on this point is in striking contrast with the secular nationalist viewpoint as expressed for example in speeches by Saddam Hussein, in which he acclaimed Nebuchadnezzar as a hero of ancient Iraq and praised him in particular for his efficient handling of the Zionist problem in his day.

For Sadat's murderers and in general for the religious circles to which they belong, Sadat's crime, for which he deserved the death penalty, was betrayal of Islam and reversion to paganism. His alliance with America and his peace with Israel were only particular manifestations of this larger and deeper evil. The case against Sadat was thus much the same as the case against the Shah. The Iranian fundamentalists were more successful. They destroyed the regime and launched their country on a far-reaching religious revolution. The Egyptians succeeded only in destroying the ruler. The regime survived, and so did the leftist opposition.

If it was the fundamentalists who removed Sadat, it was the leftists who have brought their explanations to the Western world. Heikal's book, subtitled *The Assassination of Sadat,* is not a biography but rather an attempt to explain the events leading up to that single act. It is a sustained attack on Sadat's aims, his manner of accomplishing them, his actions, his associates and friends, his personality, his family, and even—in a traditional local style of invective—his ancestors.

Much has been said in praise and in condemnation of Sadat's innovations. Three major achievements are claimed on his behalf. The first and best known abroad is the peace treaty with Israel; this brought two substantial advantages, the restoration of the territorial integrity of Egypt by the recovery of the Sinai peninsula and the shift of the Egyptian economy from a war- to a peace-footing, thus ending the devastating financial drain of the previous thirty years and the loss of life which led one eminent Egyptian journalist to speak of Egypt as "the blood bank of the Arab world." The price that Egypt paid for this peace—and it was a heavy one—was the break with the Arabs and to some extent also with the Islamic world. This price was paid in particular by those Egyptians—diplomats, writers, and others—who had shared directly in Egyptian leadership in the Arab world. The ending of this phase of Egyptian isolation took several years and was completed by the Gulf crisis of 1991–92. One after another the Arab states tried to improve their relations with Egypt; significantly it was the Arab states that conceded the point at issue, and not Egypt, which retained its peace treaty and its limited but continuing relations with Israel.

The second major achievement was the relaxation of the dictatorship, which, under Nasser, had grown more and more oppressive. While Sadat's reforms fell short of full freedom of expression and political activity, they nevertheless represented an immense improvement on the previous situation and also on those prevailing in most other Arab countries. Not everyone, however, appreciated this change. Nasserists like Dr. Heikal, who had suffered few if any restrictions on their freedom of expression under the previous regime, gained nothing by the change. The same is true, for different reasons, of the impoverished masses, for whom the press and parliament meant very little and whose primary concern was their precarious economic survival. Toward the end of his life Sadat, feeling threatened by the new freedom which he himself had created, began to crack down on his critics and political opponents and sent a number of them, including Dr. Heikal, to jail. His repression at its worst was milder than that of the previous regime but differed from it in that its most prominent victims were men who could command a hearing in the Western world.

The third of Sadat's major innovations was a new economic policy which paralleled his political liberalization. The "opening," as it was called, meant a relaxation of Nasser's Arab socialism and the rapid development of a new capitalism. It is still too early to judge the long-term economic effects of this change or to relate them to other factors, notably the demographic explosion at home and the changes in the international economy. The charge most consistently brought against this aspect of Sadat's policies is that of corruption. This was certainly widespread and is said to have reached even into the president's family circle.

Two points may be made on this matter. One is that corruption is hardly a novelty in the region. It existed before Sadat's accession and no doubt continued after his death. Its rise and fall are to some extent determined by the honesty and severity of government but also—perhaps to a greater extent—by the increase and decrease of economic activity. The second point concerns the contrast between American and Middle Eastern perceptions of the relationship between money and power. In the US it is customary and acceptable to make money and use it to win political power. In the Middle Eastern tradition the sequence has commonly been reversed. There would seem to be no obvious moral superiority in the one way or the other, though there may be economic or political advantages and disadvantages. Under Sadat's presidency, corruption seems to have gone beyond the limits of tolerance. More important, the modern style of life made the conspicuous consumption of its beneficiaries more extensive and more visible and offered a constant affront to both the misery of the poor and the austerity of the pious. And Sadat was seen as a Pharaoh—if not in tyranny, then at least in his remoteness from the needs and feelings of the people.

Heikal has little to say about Sadat's accomplishments; some are denied, some passed over in silence, and some attributed to others. In order to sustain his case, Dr. Heikal makes use of three devices. Wherever possible, he attributes the basest of motives to Sadat and his supporters, while always attributing the highest and most disinterested motives to his opponents. Where this is inadequate, he resorts to a rather high-handed selection and treatment of the historical record. And where both of these methods are insufficient for his purpose he uses personal abuse, sometimes by direct attack, more often by innuendo.

A few examples of these methods may suffice.

In Dr. Heikal's version, Sadat and all his associates, in virtually every political choice, both in domestic and international affairs, were guided by personal, mostly selfish, concerns. Their opponents, in contrast, acted out of the highest patriotic or ideological motives. In his explanation of some of Sadat's decisions, Dr. Heikal hints, sometimes rather strongly, at financial motives and inducements. He does not mention the possibility that the Egyptian Medical Association or the Egyptian journalists, whose opposition to the normalization of relations with Israel wins Dr. Heikal's approval, might have been influenced by concern to retain the prosperous Arab market for their services. In fact, of course, in this as in any similar situation, a ganglion of professional and commercial interests developed rapidly around both the pro-peace and pro-Arab lines of policy. By emphasizing one to the point of absurdity and failing to mention the other at all, Dr. Heikal is playing a rather crude polemical game.

Much more serious is his treatment of past events. Some of his misstatements are due to unpolemical carelessness or ignorance. Thus, there is no propaganda value in asserting that Helmuth von Moltke, who went to Turkey in 1835, was "brought by the Sultan to train the Turkish army before the 1914 war" (p. 170). The statement is even, in a limited sense, correct. Only carelessness can explain the reference to the two German spies with whom Sadat was involved in 1942 as "Hans Eppler and his colleague known only as Sandy" (p. 17). The first spy was in fact called John Eppler, and his colleague, as Eppler explains in his own book on the subject, was called Sandberg. There is perhaps a very minor propaganda point in Heikal's attribution of "the principle that religions other than Islam might be permitted to exist but not to expand" to an "old Ottoman rescript" instead of, correctly, to a basic rule of Islamic Sharī'a law (p. 157).

Where, however, Dr. Heikal really outdoes himself in restructuring and reinterpreting the past is in his treatment of the military outcome and political consequences of the 1973 war. In his version, the Egyptians won a great military victory, the fruits of which were frittered away by Sadat's failure to exploit it politically. No reader with unhampered access to newspapers and books is likely to agree with either judgment. As Heikal tells the story:

> The October War was a strategic victory for the Arabs. It was almost a tactical victory for the Arab armies, Egyptian and Syrian, which fought the war, but this in the end eluded them owing to miscalculations in the field and America's determination to rescue Israel, whatever the cost. (p. 274)

Immediately after the war, "Sadat failed to recognize the magnitude of the victory that was now within his grasp. He held all the trumps" (p. 62). Instead of exploiting this victory, Sadat concluded a treaty which gave the Israelis everything they wanted. "In return what had the Israelis conceded? Virtually nothing" (p. 214). The recovery of Sinai, with its oil and other resources, its communications, and its bases, appears only in a footnote:

> The only "concession" made by Israel under the Camp David agreements related to Sinai, territory over which Israel had never had any historical or theological claims, and which was held onto only as a defensive screen against Egypt. (p. 212)

The opposing view of the relative value of recognition and territory was well stated in an interview in a Beirut Arabic newspaper, discussing the possible acceptance by Israel and her Arab neighbors of Security Council Resolution 242:

> If the Arabs wish to go back on their agreement to the Security Council Resolution, they can easily do so by a single word. But if Israel should wish to go

> back on the implementation of this Resolution, she will have to wage a new war to reconquer the territories she will have evacuated in accordance with this Resolution.

This statement appeared in the newspaper *Al-Nahār* of 2 August 1970 and was made by Dr. Heikal. The point that he made would seem to have some relevance to the Camp David peace treaty, too.

Perhaps the most unpleasant aspect of Dr. Heikal's book is the note of personal spite that colors many of his allusions to Sadat, his associates, and even his family. Dr. Butrus Butrus-Ghali, who as acting foreign minister had an important part in the initiation and negotiation of the peace treaty, "was prepared to take on the job for a number of reasons" (p. 105). Of these reasons, Dr. Heikal names three—that Butrus-Ghali was a Copt, that he had a Jewish wife, and that he bore the same name as a kinsman who had been assassinated by a Muslim nationalist in 1910, after presiding, as judge, in a court which had sentenced some Egyptian villagers after the famous Denshawai incident. For these reasons, in Heikal's view, "Ghali combined ambition with a realistic feeling that there was little prospect for a man like him in the normal context of Egyptian politics. 'What have I to lose?' summed up his attitude" (p. 105).

This is insulting and unfair, both to Egypt and to Dr. Butrus-Ghali. Many Copts have been involved in the political life of modern Egypt and continue to be. Had such "reasons" determined Butrus-Ghali's actions, they would surely have led him to hold back, rather than step forward. After all, he had a great deal to lose, as the previous example of his namesake and the subsequent example of his president demonstrate. But in Butrus-Ghali as in Sadat himself, vision and courage are qualities that Dr. Heikal does not seem to recognize.

Even Sadat's widow is not immune from Dr. Heikal's form of political analysis. One example of his method is a footnote reference to Jihan Sadat's partly English origins: "When she became a President's wife Jihan pursued the idea that her mother's family originated in Sheffield, but exhaustive searches failed to find any trace of them there" (p. 25). Dr. Heikal does not explain who conducted these searches, or in what circumstances.

The attacks on Sadat himself are manifold and constitute the main content of the book. The charges are undocumented, and many are clearly based on malicious gossip. There are enough verifiable errors of fact—Hermann Eilts, the US ambassador in Egypt at the time, found more than a hundred—to throw doubt on the rest. Nothing is too petty to use. According to Heikal, Sadat indulged daily and liberally in vodka, a detail denied by others who knew the late president well. This offense was compounded by his eating "calorie-free toast . . . made from calorie-free flour imported from Switzerland" (p. 171). My own "exhaustive researches" have failed to find any trace of such flour.

But the meanest of all, which caused a wave of revulsion when the contents of the book became known in Egypt, is the disguised attack on Sadat's mother. According to most versions of Sadat's family background, Sadat's mother was a Sudanese, and it was from her that he inherited his swarthy complexion. This is not enough for Dr. Heikal. According to him, Sadat's mother was the daughter of a black slave brought from Africa, called Kheirallah.

> After the British occupation, when pressure to abolish slavery intensified, his master (whose identity is unknown) freed Kheirallah. His daughter . . . was, like her father, completely Negro, and the fact that Sadat inherited her complexion and some of her features was to have a profound effect on him. (pp. 8–9)

Later, according to Heikal, Sadat's father took a second wife, a fair-skinned eighteen-year-old, and Sadat's mother was "reduced to a position of servitude no less harsh than that from which her father . . . was supposed to have been rescued . . . [she], the black wife, became the household drudge" (p. 11).

Heikal returns to this point again and again. Sadat as a young man, he says, "feared his father but could not love him; he could not respect his unfortunate mother, and had come to resent the badge of color which he inherited from her" (p. 12). His marriage to Jihan is presented as a matter of black and white: "Jihan appealed to Sadat not only because she was beautiful and adoring but because she was white. Color had been, and was always to be, almost an obsession with him" (p. 25). Dr. Heikal finds this even in the pictures of the president that were on public display: "Like a pharaoh in a bas-relief he preferred, in the representations of him which were now to be seen in all public places, to be shown in profile—which also had the advantage of not emphasizing the Negroid element in his features" (p. 181).

It was however as a Pharaoh, not as Negroid, that Sadat was condemned and executed by his devout assassins. Heikal devotes some but not a great deal of attention to these men and their intellectual mentors. One of the latter was an electrical engineer called ʿAbd al-Salām Faraj, who in 1980 published a little book called *Al-Farīḍa al-Gha'iba*. Dr. Heikal's translator renders this title as "The Absent Prayer"; "The Hidden Commandment" might perhaps be closer. A passage in this book—not cited by Heikal—gives a clear idea of the outlook of its author and his disciples:

> There are people who say that the occasion for *jihād* today is the liberation of Jerusalem, the Holy Land; certainly this is an obligation in Holy Law and a duty for every Muslim . . . but:
>
> First: The fight against the near enemy takes precedence over the fight against the distant enemy.
>
> Second: Since the blood of the Muslims flows until victory, one may ask one's self, to whose advantage would this victory be? Of the Islamic state, or of the impious power of which it would merely serve to reenforce the foundations? . . .
>
> Third: The cause of the existence of colonialism and imperialism in our Muslim countries arises from these same impious rulers. To begin by attacking imperialism is a useless and inglorious work and a waste of time; we must concentrate on our own Islamic problem, that is to say, the establishment of the law of God in our countries.

From these and other writings of the fundamentalists, it is possible to get a reasonably full and accurate idea of their purposes. Of particular value is the detailed transcript of the interrogation of the accused, conducted by an Egyptian examining magistrate in accordance with the French-style procedures followed by Egyptian criminal justice. A copy of this was obtained by a Lebanese journalist and published *in extenso* in the Beirut daily newspaper *Al-Safīr* between 20 and 28 May 1982. But of all this Dr. Heikal, whose case against Sadat is very different from that of the fundamentalists, has little or nothing to say.

In his introduction, Dr. Heikal observes that he was "very fond of Sadat as a man." Contrary to the popular view, Sadat had not, he says, dismissed him from the editorship of *Al-Ahrām*, and there had not been "a total breach" between the two men. Dr. Heikal had left the editorship by his own decision. "Nor did we suddenly switch from being friends to being enemies." Sadat subsequently offered him various positions of importance, which he refused. It was only later that Sadat began to attack him "regularly by name in public" (pp. ix–x) and in due course sent him to jail. Despite all this, Dr. Heikal insists that the book is in no sense an attack on Sadat, that it is not "the expression of a personal grudge against him," and that there is on his side "no feeling of personal animosity." One is left wondering what kind of book Dr. Heikal would have written had he indeed been inspired by a personal grudge, or felt animosity, or desired to attack the murdered president.

How Khomeini Made It

30

In October 1962, the Shah's government in Iran, as a step toward the extension of representative institutions, promulgated a law which provided for the election of representative local councils throughout the country. The religious leaders opposed the law and raised three main objections. First, it gave women the vote, for the first time in Iran; second, it did not restrict eligibility or even the franchise to Muslims; and third, to show that this was no mere formality, it provided a formula of oath by which elected councilors would swear not on the Qur'ān but on "the holy book," a form of words clearly intended to accommodate elected councilors of other faiths.

The religious leaders were able to mobilize powerful support against the proposed law, which was opposed by preachers and teachers in mosques and seminaries, in petitions bearing thousands of signatures, and in meetings of protest and prayer. The prime minister wished to placate the opposition, first by trying to explain away the clauses that they disliked and offering to postpone the elections, and after that by sending telegrams and letters to the religious leaders informing them that the law had been suspended. Some of the religious leaders were content with this. Others, led by Khomeini, insisted that a private communication of a cabinet decision was insufficient and that a public announcement was required. This was made on 1 December.

Khomeini's arguments foreshadow his later views. Granting the vote

---

A review of *The Reign of the Ayatollahs: Iran and the Islamic Revolution* by Shaul Bakhash, Basic, from *The New York Review of Books*, 17 January 1985.

to women was a violation of Islamic principles and "an attempt to corrupt our chaste women." The proposal to allow non-Moslems to vote or to be elected was part of a larger and deeper plot aimed at Islam and therefore ultimately at the independence of the country. The law, he said in a statement quoted in Shaul Bakhash's book, "was perhaps drawn up by the spies of the Jews and the Zionists. . . . The Koran and Islam are in danger. The independence of the state and the economy are threatened by a takeover by the Zionists, who in Iran have appeared in the guise of the Baha'is."

The incident, as Bakhash shows, was revealing in a number of respects. It revealed the nature of Khomeini's concerns and perceptions; it demonstrated his skill both as a charismatic leader and as a political tactician; it illustrated the willingness of important parts of the Iranian population to respond to religious leadership in opposing the Shah's government. The significance of these events was well understood by Khomeini. It was underestimated by both the Shah's government and the liberal opposition, and it was entirely ignored in the West.

Encouraged by this victory, Khomeini launched a new attack in the following year, when the Shah's government promulgated the land reform law. Khomeini was not impressed by the reform, which he denounced as a fraud. In general, he had little use for the Shah's forced modernization, in which he saw the hidden hand of foreign enemies: "In the interests of the Jews, America and Israel, we must be jailed and killed; we must be sacrificed to the evil intentions of foreigners." This marked the beginning of a series of speeches, sermons, and declarations in which he attacked the Shah in language of increasing violence.

In June 1963 Khomeini was arrested and detained at a military barracks. News of his arrest led to demonstrations and rioting which were suppressed only with considerable bloodshed. At first, the Shah seems to have hoped that he could deal with Khomeini by appeasement. A number of royal emissaries called on him in his place of detention and tried to persuade him not to interfere in politics. Khomeini later related that one of his visitors, no less a person than the chief of the Savak, told him: "Politics is lies, deception, shame and meanness. Leave politics to us." To which, according to his own statement quoted by Bakhash, Khomeini replied: "All of Islam is politics." Ten months after his arrest

Khomeini was released and allowed to return to his home in Qum. The authorities claimed that Khomeini had agreed to keep out of politics; Khomeini himself denied that he had ever given any such understanding.

In either case, he did not observe it. Ten days after his return to Qum he gave a major address, which was followed by several others. Though somewhat more conciliatory in tone than his earlier pronouncements, the note of opposition was unmistakable, and his denunciation of the Shah and of his presumed foreign masters became ever more vehement. When the Iranian parliament in October 1964 passed a law granting extraterritorial status to Amerians in Iran, Khomeini denounced this as "a document for the enslavement of Iran." By this vote, he said, the parliament had "acknowledged that Iran is a colony; it has given America a document attesting that the nation of Muslims is barbarous."

Through this campaign, Khomeini added an important new element to his supporters. In condemning the extension of political rights to women and non-Moslems, he expressed the sentiments of great numbers among the conservative merchant and artisan classes and the devout poor. In denouncing the granting of extraterritorial privileges to Americans, he was expressing feelings and opinions shared by liberals and nationalists, and more generally prevalent among the educated and modernizing classes. In November 1964 he was arrested again, and this time sent into exile, from which he did not return for fourteen years.

For Khomeini, the first step toward home was his removal from Iraq to Paris. Though the distance was far greater, the means of communication were incomparably better. When King Ibn Saud, in 1927, first introduced the telephone to his Arabian kingdom, there was a great theological debate before the ulema were persuaded of the lawfulness of this alien invention. Khomeini and the Islamic fundamentalists suffered from no such compunction. From the first, as Dr. Bakhash points out, they were ready to make the fullest possible use of modern technology, its military weapons, and—in the early stages more importantly—its media of communication. The Islamic revolution of Iran is probably the first revolution in modern history that was inaugurated by telephone, television, and tape recorder.

In Najaf in Iraq, where Khomeini lived for many years, communications were technologically backward and politically censored. In France he enjoyed the full advantage of direct dialing and free speech. By telephone, he could contact and instruct his many followers and disciples in Iran. Through tape recordings, he could bring his ideas, resonantly spoken in his own familiar voice, to far greater numbers than could ever crowd into a mosque. And thanks to television, and the willing compliance of those who operate it, he was able to win at least the acquiescence and often the lively support of important sections of Western public opinion and even of Western governments.

His return in triumph to Iran early in 1979 was the culmination of a long process extending over many years, in the course of which the position of the Shah and his regime was thoroughly undermined both at home and internationally, while the revolutionary forces mobilized the hopes and aspirations of millions of Iranians and enjoyed the sympathetic support of a very large part of the international community. In this he was greatly helped by his three Western-educated, leftist supporters, Yazdi, Qotbzadeh, and Bani-Sadr. In the words of Dr. Bakhash, "They helped produce the bland responses that persuaded a host of foreign journalists, unfamiliar with Khomeini's own writings, that once in power in Tehran, the Ayatollah would withdraw from affairs and preside as the benign father of a liberal democracy."

Since Khomeini's return, Iran has gone through all the classical stages of a major revolution—upheaval and repression, terror and revolutionary justice, intervention and war, ideological debate and political conflict, and vast social transformations. Half a million Iranians, mostly middle class and professional, have left the country and live in exile. Some ten thousand, including women and sometimes even young children, have been put to death in successive waves of public and private executions, while rebellion, intervention, and war have cost half a million casualties and created two million refugees.

The price of revolution is familiar and has been paid at a high rate. The returns are still unknown, and it will be a long time before they can be evaluated. Meanwhile an extensive literature has grown up, most of it dealing with the circumstances of the revolution and the events that led to it and in particular with the international ramifications. Less attention has been given to the sequence and significance of events inside Iran from 1979 onward. It is these events that form the theme of Dr. Bakhash's brilliant and profound book, a model of the difficult discipline of contemporary history.

Dr. Bakhash, who has worked as both journalist and scholar, combines the liveliness and the immediacy of the one with the meticulousness and restraint of the other. He commands a narrative style that is at once lean and elegant, vivid and powerful. His analyses, penetrating and well informed, are lucidly presented. Unlike so much writing on current affairs, both academic and journalistic, this book suffers from neither jargon nor bombast, neither apology nor denunciation—at the most there are some gently ironic contrasts, suggested rather than asserted, between the aims and the achievements of the revolutionary factions. Dr. Bakhash's writing is informed both by intimate personal knowledge of the country, its people, and the events through which they have passed and by a scholarly study of the printed evidence and especially of the extraordinarily informative Iranian press, from which he has been able to enliven his narrative and analysis with many apt and vivid first-hand quotations.

Dr. Bakhash's history covers many aspects of the life of revolutionary Iran, including some that have received little attention in the West. Such for example are the somewhat arcane disputes between different schools of revolutionary theology. Sometimes these differences are formulated in relatively simple terms. Thus, for Rajavi, the Mojahedin leader, "the struggle is over two kinds of Islam, one an Islam of class, which ultimately protects the exploiter; and a pure, authentic and popular Islam, which is against classes and exploitation." A religious judge in Kermanshah put it even more simply: "The Islam that fires the hearts of the feudal elements is an American Islam."

These, together with the more sophisticated debates and with their social implications and political consequences, are examined in some detail in Bakhash's book, but at the same time with due reference to the effect of straightforward violence, both formal and informal, in determining the outcome of these disputes. Some of the more dramatic passages in the book deal with the administration of revolutionary justice, by the courts and the streets, against the successive groups and individuals identified and marked for destruction as enemies of the Islamic revolution.

> Khomeini took the view that the insistence on open trials, defense lawyers, and proper procedures was a reflection of "the Western sickness among us," that those on trial were criminals, and "criminals should not be tried; they should be killed." He also believed that trials were an expression of the popular will. "If the revolutionary courts did not prosecute them," he said of those brought to trial, "the people would have gone on a rampage and killed them all." Radical clerics around Khomeini encouraged this view: "The revolutionary courts were born out of the anger of the Iranian people," said Sadeq Khalkhali, "and these people will not accept any principles outside Islamic principles."

Western criticism made the angry even angrier, and a prosecutor, rebuked and attacked when he showed some concern for legal procedures and the rules of evidence, asked: "Should we dance to the tune of Amnesty International, that asks why we kill and do not grant amnesty, or to the tune of these gentlemen, who ask why we grant amnesty?" The official newspaper of the Islamic Republican party expressed the prevailing view, when it described liberalism as "the bulldozer of colonialism and the steamroller of imperialism."

Dr. Bakhash is particularly enlightening on the constellation of forces supporting different factions and adhering to different schools—the choices that they made and the consequences that followed. Why, for example, did the bazaar merchants, who had benefited so greatly from the Shah's economic modernization, turn against him and give crucial financial and other support to the revolutionaries—and how did they fare afterward? Dr. Bakhash's explanation is worth quoting at length:

> Merchants resented the import licenses and privileges granted to court favorites. Although some of the new industrial families emerged from the bazaar and there existed economic links between industrialists and merchants, the two groups tended increasingly to inhabit different worlds. The bazaar merchants seemed relegated to secondary status by a government which emphasized industrialization and the "modern" sector of the economy; they sensed exclusion from a social world in which Western-educated government ministers and technocrats mixed easily with their counterparts in industry and banking. Moreover, by the mid-1970s, the major industrial families appeared to have developed a powerful grip over the economy by combining interests in industry with interests in banking, insurance, and trade. Several of the largest trading companies developed alongside major industrial enterprises.
>
> These powerful industrial groups, along with dozens of lesser domestic

industrialists, increasingly threatened the role of the traditional merchants. They were not only edging the bazaar merchants out of the wholesale trade; by establishing their own retail network and outlets, they were threatening the bazaar hold on the retail trade as well. Their price policies cut into the profit margins of the bazaar traders. The brunt of the government's 1976 campaign to control high prices and profiteering fell on the smaller merchants and traders, thousands of whom were fined, publicly humiliated, and in some instances jailed.

Dr. Bakhash also has much to say on such questions as the rise and fall of Bani-Sadr, the repression of the left, and the changing economic policies of the revolution, culminating in the economic Thermidor of recent years. Economic realities have already forced the revolutionary regime to reconsider some of its economic doctrines and, more especially, its practices. Political realities are taking somewhat longer.

Dr. Bakhash is not primarily concerned with questions of foreign relations but does pay some attention to these, presenting them—a welcome change—within the setting of internal developments rather than, as most of his predecessors did, the other way around. The war with Iraq, relations with the superpowers, Iranian attitudes toward the Arab world and toward Afghanistan, are seen from the perspective of Iranian domestic politics and in the light of statements made by Iranian leaders to their own people rather than to foreign journalists. On the hostage crisis, Dr. Bakhash notes the importance of this affair in the transfer of power from the moderates to the hard-liners. In discussing the final release of the hostages, he notes four reasons, mentioned by Iranian leaders, which impelled them to take this step—the war against Iraq, the need for access to their frozen financial resources, the belief, in the words of Behzād Nabavī, the chief Iranian negotiator, that "the hostages are like a fruit from which all the juice has been squeezed out," and finally the fear of what the incoming President Reagan might do. Again, to quote Nabavī: Carter, he said, was just "a peanut farmer," but Reagan was a man who came on the scene "with a six-shooter, like a movie cowboy." Alarm at what the man with the six-shooter might do was clearly a factor in bringing the hostage crisis to a conclusion.

During the twentieth century the Middle East has known many movements that called themselves revolutionary and tried, with greater or lesser success, to gain political power and to initiate major changes. The first of these was the Iranian revolution of 1905, which served as the pattern for a series of constitutional movements in the Ottoman empire and, between the two world wars, in its Arab successor states. The first of the interwar revolutions, that led by Mustafa Kemal Atatürk in Turkey, brought a doctrine of nationalism and secularism and inaugurated major changes in Turkey. It was however only the nationalist part of its program that had impact in other Middle Eastern countries. The growing influence of the fascist powers and, after their defeat, of the Soviet Union reduced the appeal of constitutional democracy, which was already somewhat discredited by the failure of its local exponents, and in the years following the Second World War the new revolutions were conducted for the most part by military officers who seized power and then looked around for ideologies and programs.

Iran, for the second time in the twentieth century, has set a new pattern—by carrying through a revolution with long ideological preparation, careful and elaborate planning, and extensive popular participation. Compared with these events, earlier movements which claimed the name of revolutionary in neighboring countries pale into insignificance. It will be a long time before we can assess the meaning and results of this revolution for Iran, for Islam, and for the world. Meanwhile Dr. Bakhash has given us a major book on one of the major events of our time.

The Revolt of Islam

31

Until the latter part of 1978 the discussion of Islam as a factor in politics was subject to certain taboos in the Western world. There was no such taboo in the Middle East and generally in the Muslim world, where the rise of nationalism had touched off a continuing debate on the relationship between patriotic or national and religious loyalties and on the place of Islam in ideology, allegiance, and government.

This debate attracted little attention in the Western world, which in this as in other matters tended to see other societies in its own image. For one thing there was a growing consensus among social scientists that religion was no longer an adequate criterion by which to classify peoples and societies and that to use it could involve grave distortions. In the second place, and perhaps more important, it was felt that to suggest that anybody, especially in other cultures, was influenced or, worse, determined by religion in making political choices was somehow insulting. This was particularly true of those who professed the religion of Islam, the great majority of whom were Asians and Africans and thus part of what had come to be known as the third world.

There were still scholars, in both the first and second worlds, who continued to undertake the academic study of Islam, its history and its culture, and some of these from time to time ventured to publish their findings and offer their opinions of the relationship between Islam and politics in the past and even in the present. For the most part their studies, and the impact they made, remained confined within their own professional circles. The International Congress of Orientalists, which has held meetings every few years since 1873, has always devoted one of its major sections to the study of Islam, alongside other sections concerned with India, China, and the ancient civilizations of the Middle East. The one exception was the Twenty-third International Congress, which met in Moscow in 1960. On that occasion the local organizing committee deleted the section on Islamic studies and reassigned the papers that had been submitted for consideration by this section to other sections, dealing with the history, languages, and literatures of the Arabs, Persians, Turks, and other predominantly Muslim peoples. For the first time, a section on Afghan studies was added.

In subsequent congresses the section on Islam was restored, but in some circles the Islamicist approach, that is, the approach using Islam as the organizing principle of study, was still viewed with some mistrust. Indeed, one angry polemicist came close to implying that Islam itself was an invention of malicious orientalists, who had not only constructed the Orient but had also devised its component parts.

Paradoxically, this curious reluctance to ascribe political significance to Islam sprang from a deep-seated cultural arrogance, which by this time has become rare in most other Western circles. Its judgments rest on the basic assumption that we of the liberal West are the model of progress and enlightenment, the standard by which others must be judged. To be like us is to be good, to be unlike us is to be bad, to become more like us is to improve, to become less like us is to deteriorate. From this it follows that to suggest that any other nation, people, or society is in fact unlike us is to insult them.

Most of us in the Western world have long since outgrown this kind of crude ethnocentrism. On the contrary, we often tend to fall into the opposite extreme. This makes it all the more surprising, even disconcerting, that some non-Westerners still feel insulted at the suggestion that they may be different from us—as if being like us were so wonderful. At one time such attitudes were not uncommon among the old liberals and both the old and new left of the Islamic world. They have become rare, surviving chiefly among expatriates living in the West and addressing a Western audience.

They do not appear among the Muslim militants, who recognize and indeed proudly proclaim the difference, seeing it as the measure of their own moral and religious superiority over the materialistic and decadent infidels of the Western world. The current Islamic revolution—by far the most powerful and significant movement within the Islamic world for more than a century—has no problem in defining itself, through the words of its theorists and the actions of its leaders, by religion, which is seen as the ultimate basis of identity, the final source of authority, the only true loyalty. And the revolution means a return to Islamic ideals, to the mainstream of Islamic history and civilization, after a period of alien-inspired deviation and—to borrow a phrase from another religion—the pursuit of strange gods.

The revolution in Iran in 1979 and the emergence of a charismatic religious figure, the Imām Khomeini, as its leader forced a change in the perceptions of even the most ideologically blinkered Western observers. Some of them indeed went to the opposite extreme and began to see Islamic fundamentalists under every bed. That too is absurd. The Muslim world embraces a billion people, extending across Africa and Asia from Morocco and Senegal to China and Indonesia, as well as several million adherents in Europe—both old, established populations, as in the Balkans, and recent immigrants, as in the countries of the EEC—and in the Americas. In the course of more than fourteen centuries, Muslims have developed a rich, varied, and complex civilization, differing in many significant respects from those of the Christian and post-Christian West. But not in all, and many of their problems—and their responses to these problems—are part of our common humanity. Muslims like others suffer when deprived and are angry when ill-treated. Like others, they express their discontents and their hopes for change in ways that are familiar to them.

In his attack on the old regime and his program for the new, Khomeini was working within the historic and religious traditions of Islam. The Ayatollah was no mere rabble-rouser, though he had considerable skill in this activity; he was a man of learning, a theologian and a jurist and the author of many scholarly works as well as of appeals to popular sentiment. These leave no room for doubt on what he found wrong in the Shah's regime and how he proposed to put it right. To a very large extent, he carried out his declared intentions.

At first there was considerable misunderstanding of the nature of the Khomeini phenomenon, not only among Western observers but even—with less excuse—among the Westernized liberal elite in Iran. He was so outspokenly and vehemently opposed to the Shah, to the United States, to all things Western, that nothing else seemed to matter. The main point, as it seemed to many at the time, was that he was against the old regime and, far more important, offered the first real chance of overthrowing it. Some Iranian leftists assumed, despite extensive evidence to the contrary, that he was as insincere as they were in his use of populist—which in Iran necessarily meant religious—themes and would forget them when the revolution was won. Others, only slightly more realistic, believed that while they needed him and his appeal to rouse the masses, they would be able to dispose of him and the other unworldly mullahs when the moment came.

In this they were sadly mistaken. In fact, it was they who were unworldly and the mullahs who proved adept in handling the affairs both of this world and the next. Khomeini declined the role of Kerensky that had been assigned to him, and instead the mullahs have been steadily and efficiently disposing of the liberal and leftist allies who had given them some help—the extent should not be exaggerated—in achieving power.

With few exceptions Western sympathizers and supporters reacted with indifference to the consequences of the revolution to which, at crucial moments, they gave encouragement and help—not only the general consequences for the Iranian people but the specific imprisonment, torture, and execution of great numbers of their own liberal and leftist friends. Nor did they show much concern at the reversal, by the revolutionary government, of the steps that had been taken under the old regime to give greater rights to women and to religious minorities. In Khomeini's view these steps, inspired by Western secularism, were among the gravest crimes committed by the Shah, and their rectification was a priority of the revolution. Most of Khomeini's former Western admirers chose to turn aside and devote their attention to newer and more rewarding subjects. The popular press, on the rare occasions when it gives some attention to Iran, prefers to regale it readers with lurid accounts of the more picturesque aspects of the Islamic penal code.

Does all this mean that the revolution has gone wrong, that it has been perverted from its original purposes, that—as one participant put it—it has been hijacked by the mullahs? The answer to these questions depends of course on who the authors of the revolution really were and what their intentions were.

There can be no serious doubt that what happened in Iran in the first few years after the fall of the Shah was an authentic revolution—to use this word in the same sense as when we speak of the French Revolution or the Russian Revolution. This is not to speak in praise or blame of the change in Iran; only to say that it is major and significant. For better or for worse—which one still remains to be seen—there were genuine and radical changes, brought about by an authentic mass movement with very wide participation. This was a change of a very different order from the so-called revolutions in other Middle Eastern countries in this century. The earlier ones were largely inspired by European models and programs; the more recent might be more accurately designated by such terms as *coup d'etat* or *putsch*. In Iran a transfer of power took place not just from one group of people to another but from a whole social order to another, comprising a process of profound social transformation. And, as with other major revolutions, this was itself part of a longer, broader, deeper process than the immediate transfer of power that took place at a moment in 1789 in Paris, in 1917 in Petrograd, in 1979 in Tehran.

As in prerevolutionary France and Russia, so too in imperial Iran a major process of change was already taking place under the old regime. These changes had imposed great strains and stresses on traditional Iranian society. The old institutions, the structure of loyalties, the system of values cracked and broke under the impact. The institutions and values that had been imported from the West were still imperfectly assimilated or understood. Not surprisingly, they failed to respond to the needs and aspirations of the people at a time of crisis. The Iranian revolution, like others, was the result and expression of deep resentments, strong convictions, and passionate hopes, and the forces that launched it are still far from spent.

In the meantime, the linking of Islam and politics has now become permissible in both polite and intellectual Western society. Indeed, there is a certain curiosity about the nature of these powerful pent-up forces, which men like Khomeini can release and direct, and a desire for more and better information about Islam, and more particularly about the relationship between religion and the exercise and pursuit of power in the Islamic world.

The Islamic revolution in Iran, followed by such events as the seizure of the Great Mosque in Mecca, the assassination of Sadat, and other ominous signs of mounting religious passions in the Muslim world aroused a new interest in political Islam, which both the media and the academy were quick to gratify. The task was not an easy one. Though the literary output of the Islamic movements is vast and rich, it is mostly in Arabic and other Islamic languages, and there are few scholarly studies based on this literature. Even an appropriate vocabulary seemed to be lacking in Western languages, and writers on the subject had recourse to such words as "revivalism," "fundamentalism," and "integrism." But most of these words have specifically Christian connotations, and their use to denote Islamic religious phenomena depends at best on a very loose analogy. Even the common use of such words as "clergy" and "clergymen," to denote the mullahs of Iran, obscures the profoundly significant difference between the Christian priesthood and ministry and the Muslim doctors of the Holy Law.

There is another reason why such terms as "revivalist" and "fundamentalist" are misleading when applied to current Islamic movements. In Western usage these words have a rather specific connotation; they suggest a certain type of religiosity—emotional, indeed sentimental; not intellectual, perhaps even anti-intellectual; and in general apolitical or even anti-political. Fundamentalists are against liberal theology and biblical criticism and in favor of a return to fundamentals—*i.e.*, to the divine, inerrant text of the scriptures.

For the so-called fundamentalists of Islam these are not and never have been the issues. Liberal theology has not hitherto made much headway in Islam, and the divinity and inerrancy of the Qur'ān are still central dogmas of the faith—sometimes tacitly disregarded, but never challenged. Unlike their Christian namesakes, the Islamic fundamentalists do not set aside but on the contrary embrace much of the post-scriptural scholastic tradition of their faith, in both its theological and its legal aspects. It is indeed with the latter that they are primarily concerned.

For more than a century Muslim theologians have been debating the problems posed to their faith and community by the impact of the modern Western world on traditional Islamic societies, and the replacement, in one Muslim country after another, of the Holy Law of Islam by the laws, norms, and values of the secular West in all but matters of personal status and sometimes even these. These legal changes were accompanied—sometimes preceded, sometimes followed—by major economic and social changes, the discrediting of old values and loyalties, and the imposition—often by force—of new, imperfectly-understood values imported from an alien world and loyalties defined in alien terms. In the eyes of many Muslims, Western-inspired political change brought tyranny, economic change brought poverty, social change brought immorality and corruption.

Traditionalists and modernists have long argued over these matters. The neoconservative radicalism of Khomeini and his disciples springs from a profound conviction that the experiment in modernization—both in deed and in thought—has failed and that the only salvation for Muslims is to return to the divine origins of their faith. All that is worth having from the West is its devices and its appliances, and these can be bought. Its so-called culture is contaminated and dangerous and is doomed—along with all who are foolish enough to join it—to decay and extinction. In contrast to Western sympathizers and Western-influenced modernists who argue that Islam has nothing to do with politics, Khomeini observes that "the Qur'ān contains a hundred times more verses concerning social problems than on devotional subjects. Out of fifty books of Muslim tradition there are perhaps three or four which deal with prayer or with man's duties towards God, a few on morality and all the rest have to do with society, economics, law, politics and the state. . . ." Islam, according to the same authority, "is political or it is nothing." A significant and growing number of Muslims in many countries agree with him.

The Middle East Crisis in Historical Perspective

32

One of the most disquieting features of the Gulf crisis and war was the surge of emotional support for Saddam Hussein among Arabs and to some extent also in the broader Muslim world. This was by no means universal. Most Arab and other Muslim governments supported the UN decisions and the US-led action, but they participated with extreme caution and showed keen awareness of powerful trends of opinion in their own countries, among their own populations, in support of Saddam Hussein and against his opponents—even against his victims. This support was expressed not only in the Arab world but also, more openly because of the greater freedom that they enjoyed, among the Arab and Muslim immigrant communities in Western Europe and North America.

It is at first sight astonishing that anyone should choose so ogreish a hero. To quote two comparisons sometimes made by his critics, Saddam Hussein is like Hitler, but without Hitler's charm, like Stalin, but without Stalin's appeal, however perverted, to noble human ideals. He has appeared on the world stage as a tyrant to his own people, a plunderer to his neighbors, a terrorist to his remoter friends and enemies alike.

Even in specifically Arab and Muslim terms, Saddam would at first sight appear an unlikely candidate for the role of hero. By his elaborate cult of Babylon and the accompanying reassertion of the pre-Arab and pre-Islamic identity of Iraq and by his single-minded pursuit of what he perceived as Iraqi national interests, he has violated one of the basic rules of the pan-Arab canon and committed the sin of regional particularism. Egyptian leaders have from time to time been excoriated in other Arab countries for the equivalent offense and accused of Pharaonism—a crime against Arab unity. His stance in the 1980s as the champion of secular modernism against the religious fanaticism of the Islamic revolution and as the defender of the old order of the Gulf sheikhs against social subversion made him an object of anathema to both religious and social reformers. His armed invasion of Kuwait broke the rules not only of the United Nations but also—perhaps more to the point—of the Arab League pact and violated one of the strongest taboos of inter-Arab politics: that however great and deep their differences, Arab states do not go to war against other Arab states in settlement of disputes. His espousal as role model of the pagan tyrant Nebuchadnezzar—at best an equivocal figure, even in Muslim tradition—aptly symbolized all these policies and actions.

All this did not prevent a significant part of the Arab and Muslim world from accepting and soon acclaiming him as a hero of Arabism, of revolution, and even—*quia absurdum*—of Islam. Some were ready to condone and even approve his invasion, occupation, and annexation of Kuwait. Others, while deploring these actions, were willing to accept the fait accompli and reserved their main indignation for the efforts of the coalition—described by them as an unholy alliance of Western imperialists and their Arab clients—to dislodge him. One is left wondering what logic could have made the heir of Nebuchadnezzar and scourge of Khomeini a warrior in the holy war for Islam; the violator of a peaceful neighboring Arab state, a paladin of Arabism; and the paid defender of the Gulf sheikhs, a revolutionary leader for social change.

A study of the pro-Saddam movement in its various aspects and expressions makes it clear that the ultimate driving force was hostility to the West and hence also to those seen as allies or supporters of the West. This in turn raises the obvious question—why should there be so deep and violent a hostility to the West?

There has been no lack of answers to this question, and there is no difficulty in drawing up a long series of grievances held by the Arab and Muslim world against Western powers. Middle Easterners, discussing this question, will usually lay the main stress on those grievances that concern them directly; Western observers, on the other hand, are inclined to lay the greatest stress on those grievances that can be satisfied at the expense of others. An alarming feature is that the resolution of specific problems, the removal of specific grievances, seems to bring at best a temporary alleviation, and often an aggravation, of this hostility. Imperial rule—British, French, Italian—in Arab countries was once seen as the principal cause of Arab hostility, and it was widely believed, and still more widely asserted, that with the ending of imperial rule, this hostility would disappear. More than forty years have passed since the ending of imperialist rule—indeed, in most Arab countries, more years than that rule itself lasted, and during that time some Arab states have established an imposing financial and physical presence in the Western world. But the hostility remains or recurs and sometimes reaches new heights. To understand what has been happening, it is necessary to look back over a longer period and to explore the deeper levels of the historic process.

Another of Saddam Hussein's heroes was the Egyptian president, Gamāl ʿAbd al-Nasser, who rose from being a local Egyptian ruler to being the loved and acclaimed leader of the Arab world. The circumstances of this transformation are worth a closer look. The key date is September 1955, when the governments of Egypt and Czechoslovakia, the latter at that time a Soviet satellite, announced to the world that they had concluded an agreement for the supply of Czechoslovak arms to Egypt. This incursion of an Eastern-bloc power into what had until then been an exclusively Western preserve was clearly a slap in the face for the West in general and the United States in particular. What is significant is not so much the deal itself as the wave of ecstasy with which it was greeted across the Arab world. The Syrian, Lebanese, and Jordanian parliaments at once adopted, by acclamation, resolutions of congratulation to Nasser, and even Nūrī al-Saʿīd of Iraq, a well-known friend and supporter of the West, was constrained by public opinion in his own country to join the chorus of congratulation. All this enthusiasm, and the rapturous and almost unanimous approval of the Arabic press, were not due to any pro-Soviet or pro-communist sentiment, nor to any desire to bring Soviet power into the Middle Eastern region. The arms deal was welcomed, first and last, as an action against the West—an important step towards breaking the Western monopoly of external influence in the region and a gratifying blow to what was seen as Western arrogance.

One suggestion made at the time was that this action was a protest against the long British occupation of Egypt and a reaction against British imperial domination. But British imperial domination of Egypt had come to an end some time previously, and the last British troops were withdrawn from the Suez Canal on 2 April 1955. One would hardly expect so great a degree of passion over an issue already resolved.

Some later commentators saw this enthusiasm for the Soviets as a reaction to American support for Israel. But this is reading history backwards. The United States and the Soviet Union competed, and in some measure cooperated, in securing the majority of votes that passed the UN resolution for the partition of Palestine in 1947, and the Soviet Union preceded the United States by some time in according *de jure* recognition to the Jewish state. More important, it was the speedy supply of arms from the same Soviet surrogate, Czechoslovakia, which enabled the infant state to survive its first war in 1948. The small quantity of arms smuggled to Israel from the United States at that time was due to private and illegal initiatives in defiance of an otherwise strictly enforced official US arms embargo. American financial and military aid to Israel was on a very small scale and did not reach substantial proportions until the late sixties and the seventies. The American strategic relationship with Israel, which began in 1962 and became significant only after 1967, was a consequence, not a cause, of Soviet penetration and of growing Soviet influence in country after country in the Arab world. And, in the meantime, most of the Arab states have shown a noteworthy indifference to the plight of the Palestinians and appear to have no use for them, except as an occasional distraction for their own downtrodden peoples or as a stick with which to beat the West.

Another of Saddam Hussein's heroes, and an acclaimed figure in present-day Iraq, was Rashīd ʿAlī al-Gaylānī, a politician who with military support seized power in Baghdad in April 1941. He established a pro-Axis regime and sought help from Germany and Italy. The help was too little and too late, and his regime was overthrown by British and British-led forces after six weeks. A committee formed at the time in Vichy-controlled Syria to mobilize support for the Rashīd ʿAlī regime was the nucleus that later developed into the Baʿth party.

Rashīd ʿAlī was by no means the only Axis supporter in the Arab world. One of his closest associates, the Mufti of Jerusalem Ḥājj Amīn al-Ḥusaynī, joined and helped him in Iraq and after the fall of his regime became his companion in exile in Germany. Nasser, Sadat, and several other members of the officers' group that seized power in Egypt in 1952 had at least been sympathizers and some of them active workers for the Axis. The Mufti had declared his support and offered his help immediately after Hitler's accession to power in 1933, and during the war years the rulers of the Third Reich received more offers of help than they found it expedient to accept.

The same questions may be put concerning this earlier support for the enemies of the West, and the same answers have indeed been offered. Israel did not yet exist, but the growth of Jewish settlement in mandatary Palestine was already a cause of concern to Palestinians and to a growing extent to other Arabs. Nazi propaganda was explicitly and to some listeners gratifyingly anti-Jewish. But it was the policies of the Nazis in Germany and their disciples elsewhere that were the principal cause of Jewish migration to Palestine and of the consequent strengthening of the Jewish community in that country. The Nazis not only provoked and permitted this migration; they even encouraged and facilitated it until the outbreak of war, while the British, in the vain hope of winning Arab goodwill, imposed restrictions. In spite of this, significant numbers of Arabs rallied to the Germans, who sent the Jews to Palestine, rather than to the British, who tried to keep them out.

The British, and to a lesser extent French, presence during the thirties and early forties was of course much more of a factor, and during the war years this presence was vastly increased. It is easy to understand why Arab patriots struggling against British domination should have been eager to establish links with the enemy of their enemy. It is more difficult to see why so many of them should have been willing to embrace a younger, hungrier, rival imperialism that was incomparably more brutal and more contemptuous of all the values that they cherished.

Nazi racism as such cannot have had much appeal for a people who in the Nazi pseudo-science were classified as racial inferiors. Marxist atheism must surely have been repellent to the vast majority of believing, practicing Muslims. Nationalism, as distinct from racism, would have been more familiar, and the fervent nationalism of the Germans and Italians was certainly more intelligible to Arabs than the low-key patriotism of the Western allies—the more so since Germany and Italy had long been cited by pan-Arab writers as models of successful unification. Several Arab states unsuccessfully tried to emulate the achievement of Prussia or Sardinia, and there was no lack of candidates for the role of Bismarck or Cavour or of a sadly misunderstood Garibaldi. The authoritarian philosophies and centralized dictatorships of the Axis and later of the Soviets also seemed models more worthy of imitation than the hated, and when no longer hated, despised democracies of the West. Both fascism (in the thirties and forties) and communism (in the fifties and sixties) had a considerable impact on some groups of Arab intellectuals.

But beyond all these there was and unfortunately still is a profound, pervasive, and passionate hatred of the West and all it represents, as a world power, as an ideology, as a way of life, and that hatred is extended to embrace a wide range of local Westernizers and modernizers. It is a hatred so deep that it has led those who feel it to rally to any plausible enemy of the West—even a racist like Hitler who despised Arabs, an atheist like Stalin who suppressed Islam, a gangster like Saddam Hussein who violated every rule of Arab decency and Islamic morality.

The roots of this hatred are old and deep and strong and must be sought in the millennial history of relations between Islam and Christendom—Islam, whose historic center has always been and still is the Middle East, and Christendom, which was for long virtually coterminous with Europe and is so even today with Europe and her daughters.

The first missionary religion with universalist aspirations known to human history was Buddhism. These aspirations were abandoned centuries ago, and Buddhism is now in effect a regional religion, confined to south, southeast, and east Asia. All the other surviving religions, all that is but two, are even more confined, belonging in effect to one country or people or at most one region: Judaism is for Jews, Hinduism for Indians, the religions of China for Chinese. They have on occasion expanded into neighboring areas but claimed no universal mission. These religions may accept recruits but do not seek or encourage them. On the contrary, they are content to allow men and women of other faiths to find their own way to salvation and to God.

The Christian and the Muslim both rejected this view and agreed that there is only one true path to salvation and God. They differed, however, in that each believed that he alone had been shown that path and that he and his fellow believers were the sole custodians of God's final revelation to man. Since the seventh century, Christianity and Islam have faced each other across the Mediterranean and elsewhere—two religions divided less by their differences than by their resemblances. Both claimed the same heritage of prophecy and revelation, though they may have defined it in different terms. Both proclaimed the same duty, to bring the truth to all mankind and induce them to accept it or at least to submit to the authority of those who bring it. Both created rich and versatile civilizations; both also established mighty and far-flung empires. And final irony, both claimed the same human space around the Mediterranean Sea and its hinterland. For some fourteen centuries, two religions, two cultures, two power blocs have lived side by side, in occasional communication and even cooperation, in frequent conflict, in permanent confrontation. Their common origins and parallel aspirations made communication between them possible. They also made it possible for them to exchange insults and abuse meaningfully and effectively. When Christian and Muslim said to each other, "You are an infidel and you will burn in hell" each understood exactly what the other meant and both meant the same thing.

Islam, even more than Christianity, is not only a religion, a system of belief and worship. It is a civilization—an identity and an allegiance, which remain even when belief is lost and worship abandoned. For the first thousand years, from the first irruption of the Arab Muslim armies from Arabia into the lands of eastern Christendom until the second Turkish siege of Vienna in 1683, Christian Europe was under constant threat of invasion, conquest, and conversion. The first great wave of Arab expansion in the seventh and eighth centuries wrested the Levant, Egypt, and North Africa from Christendom and incorporated them permanently in the realm of Islam. The advance continued into Spain, Portugal, and southern Italy, and even into France, where it seemed for a while that the very survival of western Christendom might be at stake. The Arab threat in the West was finally contained, but another Muslim advance, this time from the east, brought the Islamized Tatars to the domination of Muscovy and eastern Europe and the Ottoman Turks to the mastery of

Constantinople and the whole of southeastern Europe. In 1480 Sultan Mehmed II, the conqueror of Constantinople, landed forces on the heel of Italy, and only a civil war at home forced their withdrawal. While a Turkish fleet captured Otranto, Turkish cavalry raided the territories of the Venetian Republic, and Turkish artillery pounded the walls of city after city in central Europe.

The Christian Europeans fought back as best they could. Sometimes they failed, as in the ultimately unsuccessful series of counterattacks known in history as the Crusades. These were not, as some anachronistic modern reinterpretations would have it, an early venture in modern imperialism but rather a Christian attempt to recover former Christian territory lost to the Muslim invader and containing the holy places of Christendom. The war to recover the Holy Land failed; other such wars were more successful, and after a long, hard struggle the Christian peoples of both eastern and southwestern Europe succeeded in overthrowing and expelling their former Muslim masters and restoring Christian rule. The Spaniards and the Portuguese ended almost eight centuries of Moorish domination in the Iberian peninsula; the Russians threw off what is known in their history as "the Tatar yoke." At both ends, the triumphant Christians followed their fallen masters whence they had come—the Portuguese and Spaniards into Africa and beyond, the Russians into Asia.

It was this movement of recovery, reconquest, and counterattack that inaugurated the great expansion of Europe known to Europeans as the Age of Discovery and that resulted in the establishment, for a while, of worldwide European domination. But that domination took some time to achieve and even then was limited in the main to the remote periphery of the Islamic world. At the center, Islam remained a mighty power and, spearheaded by the Ottoman Turks, still seemed to threaten the very heart of Europe. Muslim fleets still dominated much of the Mediterranean. Well into the seventeenth century, Barbary corsairs were still raiding the coasts of the British Isles and once, in 1627, even reached Iceland. Almost to the end of the seventeenth century, Turkish pashas still governed in Buda and Belgrade, while Turkish armies were preparing their second attack on Vienna.

It was their last, and this one, unlike the first, which introduced a century and a half of stalemate, ended in unequivocal defeat. For the first time ever, the hitherto invincible Ottoman armies were driven back in disarray. For the first time ever the Ottoman sultan, accustomed to dictating terms to a defeated foe, was compelled by his victorious Christian enemies to sign a humiliating peace and to relinquish important territories.

This disaster, at once military and political, came as a profound shock to a government and people accustomed to looking down on the rest of the world from a pinnacle of—as they saw it—unassailable religious and military superiority. It was the first of a series of such shocks, growing steadily in magnitude, extent, and force. In the north the Austrian victories opened the way for the far more dangerous Russians. They in turn expanded into the lands of Islam—to the Black Sea, where they annexed the old Tatar Muslim kingdom of the Crimea; to the Caucasus and Transcaucasia, and to central Asia, creating a new empire from which they pressed ever harder on the Ottomans and their Persian neighbors. In south and southeast Asia, the maritime powers of the West no longer came just to trade but also to rule and were establishing what ultimately became the Portuguese, Dutch, and British empires in Asia and Africa. Increasingly, the Islamic Middle East, Turkish, Persian, and Arab alike, was caught in a pincer's grip between the Russians in the north and the West Europeans approaching the south from their new possessions in Asia. At the end of the eighteenth century, with the arrival of General Bonaparte's expedition to Egypt, the Christian attack was reaching to the very heart of the Islamic world. The French occupation of Egypt was of brief duration and seems to have had limited immediate effect. But it was ended by British not by Muslim power and marked the beginning of a period of Anglo-French rivalry for trade, for influence, and ultimately, during a brief period in the twentieth century, for direct control.

The debate among Muslims about what had gone wrong and how to put it right began immediately after the retreat from Vienna and has continued—with increasing anguish and urgency—to the present day. At first and for some time, the debate was limited to the Turks who had borne the main brunt, while the Persians, and to an even greater extent the Arabs, were sheltered from reality behind the barrier of the Ottoman Empire, still, even in its decline, a formidable military power. They were thus able to cherish—as we have all done at one time or another—the illusion of the immeasurable and immutable superiority of their way of life. By the late twentieth century, such illusions were no longer possible, and people even in the remotest fastnesses of the Islamic world were aware of the changed balance of power between Christendom and Islam and were feeling the effects of that change in every aspect of their daily lives.

The impact of the West, which for this purpose includes both America and Russia, on non-Western civilizations affected many besides the Muslims and notably the ancient civilizations of India and China. In the encounter between the West and Islam, there was an element lacking in the parallel encounters between the West and the other Asian civilizations—the element of previous experience, and the memories and attitudes which that experience bequeathed to both sides. The Hindus had never conquered Spain or crossed the Pyrenees; the Chinese had never conquered Constantinople or crossed the Danube, and neither had offered a new revelation and a new scripture to supersede the Bible. Christians and Indians, Christians and Chinese met each other as almost total strangers. Christians and Muslims met each other as old neighbors and, for the most part, adversaries, and each carried a load of prejudices about the other. This made the new Christian ascendancy particularly galling for Muslims. It also made it far more difficult for Muslims to learn about new ways from Christian teachers. There were nevertheless some, at first few, then increasing numbers, who were willing to make the effort.

To begin with, the problem was seen as purely military. The infidels were doing better, the Muslims were doing worse in the battlefield. It was therefore necessary to study and where appropriate to adopt the weapons and methods of the infidel. This raised other problems that were well described by one of the most acute military minds of his time, Count Maurice de Saxe, who defined the Ottoman predicament in these words:

> Among all nations it is difficult to abandon old ways, whether through pride, through indolence or through foolishness. Good ways take an infinite time to penetrate, and sometimes even when everybody is convinced of their usefulness, nevertheless they often abandon them to follow custom and routine. . . . The

> Turks today are in the same case. What they lack is not valor, not numbers, not riches; but rather, order, discipline, and "*la manière de combattre.*"

Before long, the Turks themselves became aware of these and of other problems in their military reforms. A modern army needs modern officers—and this required educational reform. Modern weaponry and logistics involved technological education and change. Most difficult of all, a modern army could no longer be maintained on feudal lines but demanded ever-increasing infusions of cash.

To accomplish these changes, the Ottomans imported European expert advisers and instructors. The first who came were renegades and adventurers. They were followed, with portentous consequences, by military missions sent by their home governments. To benefit from their foreign guides, it became necessary for the first time for Muslims to learn the hitherto despised languages of the Frankish barbarians. This in turn facilitated the next stage—the sending of students to Europe. Learning European languages for such practical needs as might arise had previously been left to foreign or marginal elements—to renegades from Europe or native Christians and Jews with some Western connections. Now the masters of the empire themselves found it necessary to acquire this hitherto despised skill. Some of them learned to speak and also read, first Italian, then French, then other languages, and thus to come into direct contact with European thought and European ways. By the nineteenth century, knowledge of a major European language was becoming increasingly useful, in some areas indispensable for a successful career.

Increased contact with the West opened the way to new knowledge, particularly after the establishment of a lively newspaper press in Turkish, Persian, Arabic, and other languages. With this came a growing awareness of Western strength in the world and an increasing realization that the sources of that strength lay not only in superior weaponry and tactics but also in many other things.

In the course of the nineteenth century, more and more Muslim thinkers identified the principal problems of their own society as ignorance, poverty, and arbitrary rule and tried to understand and adapt the European remedies for these problems—education; economic development, especially through industry; political freedom and the laws by which it is maintained. In the course of the nineteenth and twentieth centuries, far-reaching changes were attempted and some of them accomplished. In the areas under direct imperial rule, change was relatively slow. Imperialist regimes are usually cautious and conservative and try to work with rather than against the old establishments. In independent Muslim states, reforming rulers and ministers carried through a far more rapid and extensive westernization of the legal system and the governmental apparatus and of secondary and higher education. Some also made a valiant effort to modernize the infrastructure and develop the economy. In these reforms they were encouraged and sometimes helped by the European powers, who seized the economic and political opportunities that these changes offered to them. For the more enthusiastic modernizers, officially sponsored change was never fast enough. Already in the late nineteenth century, there were opposition groups, some of them in exile. In the twentieth century, the Persian Revolution of 1906 and the Young Turk Revolution of 1908 were the harbingers of a long series of seizures of power, mostly, though not exclusively, by military officers, the declared purpose of which was to achieve greater freedom and to expedite necessary reforms.

The source of these new ideas and practices was manifestly and almost entirely Western, and when the imported machinery broke down, in either the literal or figurative sense, it was natural and human that the blame should be placed with the original suppliers rather than the local handlers. The Egyptian constitution, for example, was adapted from that of Belgium and provided for a limited parliamentary monarchy. When things went badly wrong, Egyptians very naturally judged parliamentary institutions not by the Belgian or other West European originals, but by the local imitation administered by King Fārūq and the pashas.

In general, the Muslim reaction to the West, and to Western ideas and institutions and aspirations, has fluctuated between response and rejection. Both have always been present among different elements in the population. The interaction and relative strength of the two have differed from country to country and from period to period according to local circumstances. Response has meant a genuine respect and understanding for Western culture and a desire to adopt and adapt selected elements of that culture in a harmonious blend with their own. This does not mean submission to Western rule—on the contrary, the struggle against Western domination was often inspired by such Western notions as personal freedom, human rights, and national self-determination. For the rejectionists, these selfsame Western ideas and institutions were either pagan or Christian and therefore anti-Islamic, and their purpose was to undermine and de-Islamize the Islamic world. The remedy was to return to authentic Islam as seen in an often idealized past and to restore the rule of the God-given holy law. When things go badly—when the political talisman doesn't work and the economic panacea doesn't cure—it is natural that the rejectionists should find a ready audience for their doctrine that the whole Westernizing movement was a disastrous error and that the only salvation for Muslims lies in a return to Islam.

There can be no doubt that things have gone badly in recent years and that modern methods have for the most part not worked. Modern government has brought not freedom but tyranny, far worse than the traditional autocracies in that it is not limited by traditional constraints and has at its disposal all the modern means of surveillance and repression. Modern military methods, introduced and applied at an immense cost in blood and treasure, have with very few exceptions brought not victory but humiliating defeat. Apart from a small elite, modern economic methods have brought not wealth but poverty, and the impoverished masses have been made more numerous by modern science and more aware of their poverty by modern media. Even more powerful than actual harm are the wounded pride and outraged morality of those who see with horror how Western ideas, Western practices, and Western fashions are destroying the very fabric of Muslim government, Muslim society, and even the innermost sanctuary, the Muslim family. It is surely significant that one of the most widely and frequently repeated grievances of the Muslim fundamentalists is the emancipation of women and the consequent damage to propriety and decency.

It is hard to be overshadowed, worse to be dominated by neighbors who flaunt and exploit their superior power, superior wealth, and superior knowledge and intrude themselves into every aspect of your private as well as your public life. It is even harder when these neighbors are old and familiar and, for many centuries, ending not so long ago, were themselves overshadowed in all these and many other respects, in the glorious days when Muslims led mankind in the arts and sciences of civilization. In times of real distress as well as wounded pride, it is hardly surprising that a message of hate and vengeance was eagerly received, even if it came from a Hitler, a Stalin, or a Saddam Hussein.

Very recently there have been signs that, among some at least, the mood of rejection may be passing and giving way to a new mood of acceptance and cooperation. The hatred of America is not due simply to this or that American action or policy but is the consequence—the inevitable consequence—of America's leadership of the hated West. That hatred is now being modified by a new interest in American political institutions and ideas and, in particular, in the notion of freedom secured by law. Khomeini paid unintended tribute to this interest when he called America "the Great Satan"—for Satan is feared, above all, as the Tempter. One of the most helpful signs of this new trend is the emergence of new intellectuals in Arab countries who are willing to look closely and critically at their own societies and to do so without attributing all blame for all failure to some external *diabolus ex machina.*

And there have been many failures—poverty both moral and material, tyranny both political and social, backwardness both cultural and technological, which these new intellectual critics have not feared to call by their names and for which they have tried to find causes and remedies.

In the early days of Western impact on the Islamic world, the question was often put in the form of a direct comparison between Europe and Islam. Why, asked Muslim writers, did the Islamic world remain poor, weak, and backward, while Europe grew richer, stronger, and ever more advanced? Why could not the Muslims, who had once preceded and led Europe in so many fields of human endeavor, keep up with them now? The question proved unanswerable, principally because it was badly put. In general, it is much more difficult to explain why things do not happen than why they do happen. What was remarkable, and in need of explanation, was not the slow pace of Islamic progress, which was much the same as in the rest of the non-Western world, but rather the extraordinarily swift and extensive rise of the West during the last few centuries. Western historians have of course examined the phenomenal rise of the West and attributed it to a variety of causes—the Renaissance, the Reformation, rainfall, readily accessible sources of energy, metals, technology, the discovery of America, the Scientific Revolution, and others. Few of these, and certainly not the combination of all of them, could be found in any non-Western society, and the fate of the Islamic world was not significantly different from that of the other non-Western civilizations of south and east Asia. A similar discrepancy may be seen in the Asian acceptance and Muslim rejection of Western art and music.

Today, however, the question is being asked in a new and more relevant, and therefore more painful, form. Why has the Islamic world not been able to parallel the economic and political modernization of these other non-Western civilizations? The success of Japan is unique, but others are advancing on the same road. Korea is now a major economic power, and the Chinese in Taiwan, Hong Kong, and Singapore have shown what they can do when not hamstrung by Marxist philosophy and communist economics. Even in mainland China, they have made substantial progress in modernization and development. Of the successor states of the British Empire in India, the Indian republic, with a population of daunting religious and ethnic diversity, has managed to maintain democratic institutions, while the two Muslim states, Pakistan and Bangladesh, despite their far greater ethnic and religious homogeneity, have staggered, with at best brief intervals of democratic rule, from dictatorship to dictatorship. Of the forty-six member states of the World Islamic Conference, only those endowed by chance with oil have created wealth and significantly raised the standard of living of their people, and only Turkey can qualify as a democracy, by the simple but effective test of having changed its government several times by due process of election. Japanese, Chinese, Korean, and Indian scientists are now part of the world scientific community, to which they make a significant contribution. That of the Muslim world, with its billion inhabitants, is still embarrassingly small.

The movement for change began with an awareness of weakness and a consequent desire for strength. In time it was realized that to be strong one must be prosperous, and to be prosperous one should be free. The search for strength, for prosperity, and, ultimately, for freedom still goes on. But prosperity—the experience of the oil-rich states notwithstanding—will not be found in Ali Baba's cave or summoned by

Aladdin's lamp, nor will the realm of Islam be made free by some warrior-hero on horseback.

Muslims—especially but not exclusively Western-educated Muslim intellectuals—are well aware of these facts and profoundly concerned about their implications. They are acutely conscious of the contrast between the glorious past and the inglorious present of their society and of the still more painful contrast between the promise and the achievement of the thinkers and leaders, both reformers and reactionaries, who have guided and led them. There is by now a vast and growing literature on the causes of the Muslim malaise and the means of resolving it.

Basically, these writings fall into two groups, whose attitudes are expressed in two questions. The first is "What did we do wrong?" The second is "Who did this to us?" The first leads naturally and inevitably to the follow-up question "How do we put it right?" The second leads to delusions and fantasies and conspiracy theories—indeed, the most dangerous enemies of the Muslim peoples at this time are those who assure them that in all their troubles the fault is not in themselves but in open or occult hostile forces. Such beliefs can only lead to resentment and frustration, to an endless, useless succession of bigots and tyrants and to a role in world history aptly symbolized by the suicide bomber. In the first of these questions, for those who have the courage to ask it, and the vision to answer, lies hope for the future and for a new dawn of Muslim creativity.

NOTES

Chapter 1. The Study of Islam

1. See for example the prayer recited in Egyptian mosques and published on the front pages of the Egyptian papers on 17 March 1959:

   "God is great! God is great! There is no might and no power save in God! May He strengthen the martyrs with His grace and ordain them everlasting life in His mercy and abase their enemies in shame and ignominy! God is great! God is great! There is no victory save in God! Whoever offends, God will crush him; whoever exalts himself by wrongdoing, God will humble him! Consider not those who are killed in the cause of God as dead, but as living, with their Lord who sustains them.

   "O God Almighty, All-powerful! Conquer Thine enemy with Thine omnipotence so that he returns to Thee! O God, Almighty, All-powerful, strengthen the community of Thy Prophet with Thy favor, and ordain defeat for their enemy. O God, O Lord of the Qur'ān, give victory to Thy Qur'ān as Thou gavest victory to ʿAbd al-Muṭṭalib on the Day of the Elephant, when Thou didst send against them flights of birds who pelted them with clay stones, so that they became like consumed chaff [Qur'ān 105]! In faith we worship Thee, in sincerity we call upon Thee, the blood of our martyrs we entrust to Thee, O merciful and compassionate One, Who answers the prayers of him who prays—our innocent martyrs and pure victims for the sake of Thy religion. For the glory of Thy religion they shed their blood and died as martyrs; believing in Thee, they greeted the day of sacrifice blissfully. Therefore place them, O God, as companions with the upright and the martyrs and the righteous—how good these are as companions! [Qur'ān, iv, 69]."
2. W. Cantwell Smith, *Islam in Modern History* (Princeton, N.J., 1957), p. 151.
3. In *Religion in the Middle East,* ed. A. J. Arberry, i (Cambridge, 1969), p. 415.
4. Letter to Isaac da Costa, 11 February 1823, in *Brieven van Mr. Willem Bilderdijk,* iv (Rotterdam, 1837), pp. 75–76; cited by C. F. Pijper, *Islam and the Netherlands* (Leiden, 1957), p. 16.
5. Charles Forster, *Mahometanism Unveiled,* ii (London, 1829), pp. 365, 378. *Cf.* N. Daniel, *Islam, Europe and Empire* (1966), p. 33; Albert Hourani, "Islam and the Philosophers of History," in *Middle Eastern Studies,* iii (1967), pp. 223–25.
6. See below, pp. 127ff.
7. François Bernier, *Histoire de la dernière révolution des états du Grand Mogol* (4 vols., Paris, 1670–71). There are numerous later editions and translations of Bernier's travels, correspondence, and other writings. A revised English translation of the travels was edited by V. A. Smith (Oxford, 1914).

8. Volney, *Voyage en Egypte et en Syrie* (1787, English tr. 1787); ed. Jean Gaulmier (Paris and The Hague, 1959); *Les Ruines, ou Méditations sur les révolutions des Empires* (Paris, 1791).
9. A. Slade, *Turkey and the Crimean War* (London, 1867), pp. 31–32. See further pp. 31–38 and chapter 6.
10. The effect of this Western mood on the dialogue between Islamicists and Muslims is discussed by G. E. von Grunebaum, "Approaching Islam: a Digression," in *Middle Eastern Studies*, vi (1970), pp. 127–49.
11. On these controversies, see the excellent study by Gianni Sofri, *Il modo di produzione asiatico; storia di una controversia marxista* (Turin, 1969). For Turkish views, see Muzaffer Sencer, *Osmanli toplum yapısı* (Istanbul, n.d.) and Sencer Divitçioğlu, *Asya üretim tarzı ve Osmanlı toplumu* (Istanbul, 1967).
12. E. A. Belyaev, *Arabs, Islam and the Arab Caliphate in the Early Middle Ages* (tr. from the Russian by Adolphe Gourevitch; New York, London, Jerusalem, 1969).
13. Clifford Geertz, *Islam Observed: Religious Development in Morocco and Indonesia* (New Haven, 1968).

Chapter 2. Some English Travelers in the East

1. To cite a few examples: J. M. Carré, *Voyageurs et écrivains français en Égypte*, 2 vols. (Cairo, 1932); M. H. Braaksma, *Travel and Literature* (Groningen, 1938) (on English travel-books about Persia); N. Jorga, *Les Voyageurs français dans l'Orient européen* (Paris, 1928); W. Barthold, *Die geographische und historische Erforschung des Orients, mit besonderer Berücksichtigung der russischen Arbeiten* (Leipzig, 1913, translated from Russian; also available in French translation, Paris, 1947); M. Sommerfeld, "Die Reisebeschreibungen der deutschen Jerusalempilger," in *Deutsche Vierteljahrschrift für Literaturwissenschaft und Geistesgeschichte*, ii (1924), pp. 816–51; M. Leo, *La Bulgarie et son peuple sous la domination ottomane, tels que les ont vus les voyageurs Anglo-Saxons (1586–1878)* (Sofia, 1949); Mohammad Ali Hachicho, "English Travel Books about the Arab Near East in the 18th Century," in *Die Welt des Islams*, new series ix/1–4 (1964), pp. 1–206; M. Anis, "British Travellers' Impressions of Egypt in the late 18th Century," in *Bulletin of the Faculty of Arts, Cairo*, xiii/2 (1951), pp. 8–37; F. Dirimtekin, *Ecnebi seyyahlara nazaran xvi yüzyılda Istanbul* (Istanbul, 1964); M. Ish-Shalom, *Mas'ê Noṣerim be-Ereṣ Israel (Christian Travels in the Holy Land)* (Jerusalem, 1965). Besides the general bibliographical guide to travel by E. G. Cox (*A Reference Guide to the Literature of Travel . . .*, 2 vols., Seattle, 1935–38), there are invaluable specialized bibliographies by Shirley Howard Weber (*Voyages and Travels in the Near East Made During the XIX Century*, Princeton, 1952, and *Voyages and Travels in Greece, the Near East and adjacent*

regions made previous to the year 1801, Princeton, 1953); Berna Moran *(Türklerle ilgili Ingilizce yayınlar bibliografyası: xv yüzyıldan xviii yüzyıla kadar,* Istanbul, 1964); P. Thomsen, *Die Palästina-Literatur . . . ,* 6 vols. (Leipzig-Berlin 1911–56), article "Reisen."

2. "A Prefatory Discourse to an Essay on the History of the Turks," in *The Works of Sir William Jones,* ii (London, 1807), pp. 456–57.
3. Of these, it may be noted that Burkhardt, Lane, and Burton were Arabic scholars, and both Niebuhr and Doughty had some competence in the language.
4. Or rather pseudo-letters, copied by the authoress in two albums and possibly based on real letters sent to her friends. First published in 1763, without permission and from an imperfect manuscript, the Turkish letters were reprinted many times, the first critical edition appearing in 1861. These letters have now been published as part of a definitive scholarly edition, *The Complete Letters of Lady Mary Wortley Montagu, i, 1708–1720,* edited by Robert Halsband (Oxford, 1965).
5. *Letters,* pp. 315–16.
6. *Letters,* p. 368.
7. *Letters,* pp. 396–97.
8. *Letters,* p. 415.
9. Translated into Turkish by the well-known historian Ahmed Refik (Istanbul, 1933). Other travel books translated into Turkish include those of Chateaubriand, Moltke, Vambéry, and the *Letters from Turkey* of the eighteenth-century Hungarian author Kelemen Mikes. Translations into Arabic and Persian are also rare. Burckhardt was translated into both languages, Vambéry into Persian; Lawrence's *Seven Pillars* was published in Arabic in 1947.
10. *Records of Travels in Turkey, Greece, etc. and of a Cruize in the Black Sea with the Capitan Pasha, in the years 1829, 1830, and 1831,* 2 vols. (London, 1832), second edition 1854; *Turkey, Greece, and Malta,* 2 vols. (London, 1837).
11. *Turkey and the Crimean War* (London, 1867). The facts of Slade's career (he was born in 1804 and died in 1877) are briefly given in the *Dictionary of National Biography,* in O'Byrne's *Naval Biographical Dictionary,* and in an obituary notice in the *Times* of 15 November 1877.
12. Nassau W. Senior, *Journal Kept in Turkey and Greece in the Autumn of 1857 and the Beginning of 1858* (London, 1859), p. 36.
13. Slade, *Records,* i, p. 276; developed at some length in *Turkey, Greece. . . .* See further B. Lewis, *The Emergence of Modern Turkey* (revised edition, London, 1968), pp. 125, 144.
14. *Crimean War,* p. 20.
15. *Crimean War,* pp. 31–32.
16. *Records,* ii, p. 239.
17. *Records,* ii, p. 242.
18. *Crimean War,* pp. 30–31.

19. *Crimean War*, p. 25.
20. *Records*, i, p. 215.
21. *Records*, i, p. 216.
22. *Records*, i, p. 220.
23. *Records*, i, p. 214.
24. *Records*, i, pp. 214–15.
25. *Records*, i, p. 218.
26. *Records*, i, p. 230.
27. *Records*, i, p. 234.
28. *Records*, i, pp. 270–76.
29. Sir Charles Eliot, *Turkey in Europe* (London, 1965). A biographical memoir on Sir Charles Eliot, by Sir Harold Parlett, is prefixed to the posthumous edition of one of Eliot's major works of scholarship, his *Japanese Buddhism* (London, 1935).
30. *Turkey in Europe*, p. 56.
31. *Turkey in Europe*, p. 290.
32. *Turkey in Europe*, p. 90.
33. *Turkey in Europe*, p. 151.
34. *Turkey in Europe*, pp. 130–31.

Chapter 6. Slade on Turkey

1. A short biography of Slade will be found in the *Dictionary of National Biography*, s.v., where the date of his birth is incorrectly given as 1804. This account is based on O'Byrne's *Dictionary of Naval Biography*, p. 1077; the obituary notice in the (London) *Times*, of 16 November 1877, and on Slade's published books. See further chapter 2, above.
2. London, 1832; reprinted in one volume, 1854. Cited from the second edition, as *Records*.
3. London, 1837. Cited as *TG*.
4. London, 1840. Cited as *Germany*.
5. London, 1867. Cited as *Crimea*.
6. N. W. Senior, *Journal Kept in Turkey and Greece in the Autumn of 1857 and the Beginning of 1858* (London, 1859), p. 36.
7. *Türkiye ve Kırım Harbı* (Istanbul, 1943); *Sir Adolphus Slade'nin (Müşavir Paşa) Türkiye Seyahatnamesi ile yaptığı Karadeniz Seferi* (Istanbul, 1945). Both were translated by Ali Riza Seyfioğlu.
8. *Records*, p. 320.
9. The *harac*, the term commonly employed in Ottoman usage for the poll-tax, or *Jizya*, paid by non-Muslims.

10. *Records*, pp. 320–22.
11. *Records*, pp. 124ff; *TG*, i. pp. 208ff; *TG*, ii, pp. 92ff, pp. 476ff.
12. *TG*, i, p. 216.
13. *TG*, ii, pp. 92–94.
14. *Records*, p. 379.
15. *Records*, p. 379; *TG*, i, pp. 319, 425; *Germany*, pp. 172, 219–20; *Crimea*, p. 172.
16. *Ne var ne yok.*
17. *TG*, i, pp. 209–210.
18. *Records*, p. 124.
19. Slade's sensitivity about American slavery and British industrial exploitation is revealed in another striking passage: "Thus, the American citizen, while worshipping *his* liberty and denouncing monarchy in its mildest form as horrid, fosters and profits by slavery; the generous English emancipate their negroes and dogs, spread protection round their asses, yet toil hundreds of children in factories into disease and deformity. . . ." *Germany*, p. 107.
20. *TG*, ii, pp. 282–83.
21. *Records*, pp. 395.
22. *Records*, pp. 396–97.
23. *Crimea*, pp. 34–35.
24. Modern Turkish *vakıf*, from Arabic *waqf.*
25. *Salyane.*
26. *Harac.*
27. On the region assigned to the Kapudan Pasha, see M. Zeki Pakalın, *Osmanlı Tarih Deyimleri ve Terimliği Sözlüğü*, s.v. Kaptan Paşa eyaleti. See further *Encyclopaedia of Islam*, second edition, s.v. 'Kapudan Pasha' (by S. Özbaran).
28. *Crimea*, pp. 38–41.
29. *Crimea*, p. 41.
30. Mal-i miri denizdir, içmiyen domuzdur. Slade translates in a footnote: "The public treasury is a sea, who does not drink of it is a pig."
31. *Crimea*, pp. 30–32.
32. *Crimea*, pp. 114–15.
33. *Records*, p. 122.
34. *TG*, i, pp. 317–18.
35. *TG*, i, p. 318.
36. *Records*, pp. 137ff; *TG*, i, pp. 299ff; *Germany*, pp. 249ff; *Crimea*, pp. 17ff. Slade's description of the Janissaries as a kind of armed parliamentary body is paralleled in some Turkish writings of the period (*cf.* B. Lewis, *The Emergence of Modern Turkey*, 2nd edition, Oxford 1968, p. 144). Whether Slade's use of the term "Chamber of Deputies" is intended as a compliment to the Turks or a gibe at the French is not clear. He does not say "House of Commons."
37. *Crimea*, p. 43.

Chapter 7. Sources for the Economic History of the Middle East

1. For discussions of archival and documentary sources for Islamic history, see *Jean Sauvaget's Introduction to the History of the Muslim East: A Bibliographical Guide, based on the second edition as recast by Claude Cahen* (Berkeley and Los Angeles, 1965), pp. 16–21; C. Cahen, "L'histoire économique et sociale de l'Orient musulman," *Studia Islamica*, iii (1965), pp. 93–115, especially 98ff.; H. H. Roemer, "Über Urkunden zur Geschichte Ägyptens und Persiens in islamischer Zeit," *Zeitschrift der Deutschen Morgenländischen Gesellschaft*, cvii (1957), pp. 519–38; S. M. Stern, *Fāṭimid Decrees* (London, 1964), pp. 1ff.; H. Ernst, *Die mamlukischen Sultansurkunden des Sinai-klosters* (Wiesbaden, 1960, with detailed bibliography); Muḥammad Aḥmad Ḥusayn, *Al-Wathā'iq al-ta'rīkhiyya* (Cairo, 1954), pp. 58ff.; *Encyclopaedia of Islam*, 2nd edition, under "Diplomatic."
2. Brief accounts of the Ottoman archives, with bibliographical guidance, will be found in *Encyclopaedia of Islam*, 2nd edition, under "Başvekâlet Arşivi" (by B. Lewis) and "Daftar-i khāḳānī" (by Ö. L. Barkan); S. J. Shaw, "Archival Sources for Ottoman History: the Archives of Turkey," *Journal of the American Oriental Society*, lxxx (1960), pp. 1–12. Ottoman materials relating to Egypt and the Fertile Crescent are discussed in B. Lewis, "The Ottoman Archives as a Source for the History of the Arab Lands," *Journal of the Royal Asiatic Society*, 1951, pp. 139–55; S. J. Shaw, "Cairo's Archives and the History of Ottoman Egypt," *Report on Current Research, Spring 1956*, Middle East Institute (Washington, 1956), pp. 59–72; S. J. Shaw, "The Ottoman Archives as a Source for Egyptian History," *Journal of the American Oriental Society*, lxxxiii (1963), pp. 447–52.
3. B. Lewis, "Registers on Iran and Âdharbâyjân in the Ottoman *Defter-i Khâqânî*," in *Mélanges Henri Massé* (Tehran, 1963), pp. 259–63.
4. For a brief account in English see M. Yuldashev, "The State Archives of XIX Century Feudal Khiva," in *Papers Presented by the Soviet Delegation at the XXIII International Congress of Orientalists: Iranian, Armenian, and Central-Asian Studies* (Moscow, 1954), pp. 221–30, where other Russian publications are cited. See further H. H. Roemer, "Vorschläge für die Sammlung von Urkunden zur islamischen Geschichte Persiens," *Zeitschrift der Deutschen Morgenländischen Gesellschaft*, civ (1954), pp. 364ff. The archives of the Shaykhs of Jūybār, edited by P. P. Ivanov, *Iz arkhiva Šeykhov Džuybary* (Moscow-Leningrad, 1954), date from the sixteenth century.
5. The literature is reviewed by Roemer, "Über Urkunden . . . ," Stern, and Ernst. More recent publications include a group of articles, in Arabic, on documents in the St. Catherine's Monastery in the *Bulletin of the Faculty of Arts*, University of Alexandria, xviii (1964).
6. For an example, see Ḥasanayn Muḥammad Rabīʿ, "Ḥujjat tamlīk wa-waqf," in

Al-Majalla al-ta'rīkhiyya al-Miṣriyya, xii (1964–65), pp. 191–202. See further Muḥammad Aḥmad Ḥusayn, *Al-Wathā'iq,* pp. 97ff.

7. On the Arabic papyri, see A. Grohmann, *Einführung und Chrestomathie zur arabischen Papyruskunde,* i (Prague, 1954); A. Grohmann, *Arabische Chronologie, Arabische Papyruskunde* (Leiden-Cologne, 1966) [*cf.* the review by Claude Cahen in *Arabica,* xv (1968), pp. 104–6], and, more briefly, Cahen-Sauvaget, pp. 16–18.
8. Cahen-Sauvaget, p. 17.
9. On the *Geniza,* see S. D. Goitein, "Geniza," in *Encyclopaedia of Islam,* 2nd edition, where further references are given, and his *A Mediterranean Society: the Jewish Communities of the Arab World as Portrayed in the Documents of the Cairo Geniza,* i: *Economic Foundations* (Berkeley and Los Angeles, 1967). A bibliography has been published by S. Shaked, *A Tentative Bibliography of Geniza Documents* (Paris—The Hague, 1964).
10. At 'Awjā' al-Hafīr and in the neighborhood of Damascus and Sāmarrā. See Grohmann, *Einführung,* pp. 28–30.
11. See S. D. Goitein, *Studies in Islamic History and Institutions* (Leiden, 1966), Part 3.
12. Grohmann, *Einführung,* p. 56.
13. Janine Sourdel-Thomine and D. Sourdel, "Nouveaux documents sur l'histoire religieuse et sociale de Damas au Moyen Age," *Revue des Etudes Islamiques,* xxxii (1964), pp. 1–25; Janine Sourdel-Thomine and D. Sourdel, "Trois actes de vente damascains du début du IVe/Xe siècle," *Journal of Economic and Social History of the Orient,* viii (1965), pp. 164–85.
14. V. Minorsky, "Some Early Documents in Persian," *Journal of the Royal Asiatic Society,* 1942, pp. 181–94.
15. See *Encyclopaedia of Islam,* 2nd edition, "Diplomatic iii" (by H. Busse), and the two articles by H. H. Roemer, cited in notes 1 and 4 above.
16. For a brief account, see Cahen-Sauvaget, pp. 52–57, and, on recent work, G. C. Miles, "Islamic Numismatics: A Progress Report," in *Congresso Internazionale di Numismatica: Roma 1961, Relazioni,* i, pp. 181–92.
17. See for example T. Lewicki, "Il commercio arabo con la Russia e con i paesi slavi d'Occidente nei secoli ix–xi," *Annali, Instituto Universitario Orientale di Napoli,* new series, viii (1959), pp. 47–61, and J. Duplessy, "La circulation des monnaies arabes en Europe occidentale du VIIIe au XIIIe siècle," in *Revue Numismatique,* 5th series, xviii (1956), pp. 101–63.
18. Lewicki, p. 48.
19. Cited in Cahen-Sauvaget, p. 52.
20. For examples of both kinds see M. Sharon, "A Waqf Inscription from Ramlah," *Arabica,* xiii (1966), pp. 77–84; J. Sauvaget, "Décrets mamelouks de Syrie, 3," *Bulletin d'Etudes Orientales,* xii (1947–48), pp. 1–56.
21. See, for example, G. C. Miles, "Early Islamic Glass Weights and Measures in

Muntaza Palace, Alexandria," *Journal of the American Research Center in Egypt,* iii (1964), pp. 105–13; G. C. Miles, "Egyptian Glass Pharmaceutical Measures of the 8th Century A.D.," *Journal of the History of Medicine and Allied Sciences,* xv (1960), pp. 384–89; G. C. Miles, "Islamic Numismatics . . ." (cited in note 16 above), pp. 188–89.

22. Cahen-Sauvaget, p. 22.

23. Qur'ān, ii, 275ff. *Cf.* iii, 125; iv, 159.

24. Qur'ān, ii, 194, 276ff., 282ff.; iv, 33; vi, 153; lxii, 9–11.

25. Abū 'Amr Muḥammad al-Kashshī, *Ma'rifat akhbār al-rijāl,* Bombay A.H. 1317, p. 249. For other similar stories see Goitein, *Studies,* pp. 224–25; *cf.* Max Weber, *The Sociology of Religion,* trans. E. Fischoff (London, 1965), p. 263.

26. The original text is lost, but the work survives in an abridgment, with refutation, by the author's pupil Ibn Samā'a (d. 847), entitled *Al-Iktisāb fī'l-rizq al-mustaṭāb* (Cairo, 1938). It is examined in Goitein, *Studies,* pp. 220ff.

27. An incomplete and somewhat garbled edition in *Iḥdā 'asharata rasā'il* (Cairo, 1324/1906), pp. 155–61; partial translation of the edition in O. Rescher, *Excerpte und Übersetzungen aus den Schriften des . . . Ġaḥiẓ* (Stuttgart, 1931), pp. 186–88. *Cf.* C. Pellat in *Arabica,* iii (1956), p. 177.

28. On this literature, see W. Björkman, "Kapitalentstehung und -anlage im Islam," *Mitteilungen des Seminars für orientalische Sprachen,* xxxii (1929), pp. 81ff.; Sir T. W. Arnold, "Arab Travellers and Merchants," in A. P. Newton, *Travel and Travellers of the Middle Ages* (London, 1926), pp. 92ff.; "Tidjāra" in *Encyclopaedia of Islam,* 1st edition (by W. Heffening); Goitein, *Studies,* pp. 220ff.; Ann K. S. Lambton, "The Merchant in Medieval Islam," in *A Locust's Leg: Studies in Honour of S. H. Taqizadeh* (London, 1962), pp. 121–30.

29. *Rasā'il Ikhwān al-Ṣafā,* i (Cairo, 1928), pp. 210–26; *cf.* B. Lewis, "An Epistle on Manual Crafts," *Islamic Culture,* xvii (1943), pp. 142–51. For an earlier consideration of the crafts see Jāḥiẓ, *Rasā'il,* ed. Ḥasan al-Sandūbī (Cairo, 1352/1933), pp. 126–27.

30. On Ghazzālī, see Arnold, pp. 93–94: Ann K. S. Lambton, "The Merchant . . .," pp. 123ff.

31. On al-Dimashqī see H. Ritter, "Ein arabisches Handbuch der Handelswissenschaft," *Der Islam,* vii (1917), pp. 1–91; C. Cahen, "A propos et autour d'ein arabisches Handbuch der Handelswissenschaft," *Oriens,* xv (1962), pp. 160–71. The text was published in Cairo in A.H. 1318.

32. Jāḥiẓ (attrib.), "*Al-Tabaṣṣur bi'l-tijāra,*" ed. Ḥasan Ḥusnī 'Abd al-Wahhāb, *Revue de l'Académie Arabe de Damas,* xii (1932), reprinted Cairo 1354/1935; French translation by C. Pellat, "Ġāḥiẓiana, I: le *Kitāb al-Tabaṣṣur bi'l-tigāra* attribué à Ġāḥiẓ," *Arabica,* i (1954), pp. 153–65. The attribution to Jāḥiẓ is dubious.

33. Ibn Buṭlān, *Risāla fī shirā al-raqīq wa-taqlīb al-'abīd,* ed. 'Abd al-Salām Hārūn, in

Nawādir al-Makhṭūṭāt, iv, no. 15 (Cairo, 1373/1954), pp. 333–89. An English translation was prepared by the late Professor D. S. Rice but not published.

34. Al-Jawbarī, *Al-Mukhtār fī kashf al-asrār* (Cairo, A.H. 1353).
35. On this literature see "Filāḥa" in *Encyclopaedia of Islam,* 2nd edition (by various authors), where further references are given.
36. D. M. Dunlop, "Sources of Gold and Silver in Islam According to al-Hamdānī," *Studia Islamica,* viii (1957), pp. 29–49. See further the materials collected by Ḥamd al-Jāsir in the review *Al-'Arab* of Riyād, ii (1399/1968), pp. 798ff.
37. A. S. Ehrenkreutz, "Extracts from the Technical Manual on the Ayyubid Mint in Cairo," *Bulletin of the School of Oriental and African Studies,* xv (1953), pp. 423–47. The Arabic text of Ibn Ba'ra's manual was published in Cairo in 1966.
38. C. Cahen, "Le service de l'irrigation en Iraq au début du XIe siècle," *Bulletin d'Etudes Orientales,* xiii (1949–50), pp. 117–43; C. Cahen, "Documents relatifs à quelques techniques iraqiennes au début du onzième siècle," in *Ars Islamica,* xv–xvi (1951), pp. 23–28; C. Cahen, "Quelques problèmes économiques et fiscaux de l'Irâq Buyide d'après un traité de mathématiques," *Annales de l'Institut des Etudes Orientales,* x (1952), pp. 326–63.
39. A notable example is Professor Schacht's studies on the use of *Ḥiyal,* legal devices to extend the sanction and protection of the law to transactions, such as lending on interest, which are strictly speaking outside it. See J. Schacht, *Introduction to Islamic Law* (Oxford, 1964), especially pp. 76ff.; Schacht, "Ḥiyal" in *Encyclopaedia of Islam,* 2nd edition. On the special brand of legal writing concerned with the supervision of the markets, see "Ḥisba" in *Encyclopaedia of Islam,* 2nd edition.
40. For an introduction to Jewish Responsa, see S. B. Freehof, *The Responsa Literature* (Philadelphia, 1959); bibliography by Boaz Cohen, *Quntres ha-Teshuvot* (Budapest, 1930).
41. For an example, see C. Cahen, "Fiscalité, propriété, antagonismes sociaux en Haute-Mésopotamie au temps des premiers 'Abbasides, d'après Denys de Tell-Mahré", in *Arabica,* i (1954), pp. 136–52.
42. On the biographical literature, see Sir Hamilton Gibb, "Islamic Biographical Literature," and Ann K. S. Lambton, "Persian Biographical Literature," in B. Lewis and P. M. Holt, eds., *Historians of the Middle East* (London, 1962), pp. 54–58 and 141–51.
43. Al-Iṣfahānī, *Kitāb al-Aghānī,* Būlāq, xix, p. 18; third edition, iii, p. 45. *Cf.* Ibn 'Abd Rabbihi, *Al-'Iqd al-farīd* (Cairo, A.H. 1305); iii, p. 181 (Cairo, 1372/1953), vii, pp. 13–14; English translation in B. Lewis (ed. and trans.), *Islam from the Prophet Muhammad to the Capture of Constantinople* (New York, 1974), ii, *Religion and Society,* pp. 147–48.

Chapter 8. In Search of Islam's Past

1. Richard Knolles, *The General Historie of the Turkes . . . together with the Lives and Conquests of the Othoman Kings and Emperours* (London, 1603: later reprints and continuations).
2. Barthélemi d'Herbelot, *Bibliothèque Orientale, ou Dictionnaire Universel, contenant généralement tout ce qui regarde de la Connoissance des Peuples de l'Orient* (Paris, 1697).
3. J. Th. Zenker, *Bibliotheca Orientalis. Manuel de Bibliographie Orientale* (Leipzig, 1846). On traditional bibliographical writings see J. D. Pearson, "Bibliography," in the *Encyclopaedia of Islam* (Leiden, 1982), second edition, *sub voce.*
4. Giuseppe Gabrieli, *Manuale di Bibliografia Musulmana* (Rome, 1916).
5. Diana Grimwood-Jones, Derek Hopwood, and J. D. Pearson, eds., *Arabic-Islamic Bibliography* (Highlands, N.J., 1977).
6. *Handbuch der Islam-Literatur* (Berlin and Leipzig, 1923).
7. Ernst Bernheim, *Lehrbuch der historischen Methode und der Geschichts-philosophie* (Leipzig, 1889 and subsequent editions); Louis Halphen, *Initiation aux Etudes d'Histoire du Moyen Age* (Paris, 1946).
8. *Introduction à l'Histoire de l'Orient Musulman: Eléments de Bibliographie* (Paris, 1943).
9. *Jean Sauvaget's Introduction to the History of the Muslim East: A Bibliographical Guide* (Berkeley, 1965).
10. *Introduction à l'Histoire du Monde Musulman Médiéval, VIIe–XVe siècle: Méthodologie et Eléments de Bibliographie* (Paris, 1982).
11. For example, Bertold Spuler and Ludwig Forrer, *Der Vordere Orient in Islamischer Zeit* (Bern, 1954); Gustav Meiseles, *Reference Literature to Arabic Studies: A Bibliographical Guide* (Tel Aviv, 1978).
12. *The Mediaeval Islamic Underworld: The Banū Sāsān in Arabic Society and Literature,* two volumes (Leiden, 1976).
13. Joel L. Kraemer, *Humanism in the Renaissance of Islam: The Cultural Revival during the Buyid Age* and *Philosophy in the Renaissance of Islam: Abu Sulaymān al-Sijistānī and his Circle* (Leiden, 1986).
14. For example, L. I. Klimovich, "Suschchestvoval li Mokhammed? Kritika istochnikov," in *Voinstvuiushchii Ateism* (1931); N. A. Morozov, *Khristos* (Moscow, 1930), containing a chapter entitled, "Otkuda zhe Islam?"; S.P. Tolstov, "Ocherki pervonachal'nogo Islama" in *Sovietskaia Etnografiia 2* (1932). For a general review of these writings, see N. A. Smirnov, *Ocherki istorii izucheniia Islama v SSSR* (Moscow, 1954).

Chapter 9. The Use by Muslim Historians of Non-Muslim Sources

1. *"Accessit praeterea domini Almarici regis (cujus anima sancta requie perfruatur) illustris memoriae, et inclyptae in Domino recordationis jussio, non facile negligenda, et instantia multiplex, quae ad id ipsum nos maxime impulit, cujus etiam rogatu, ipso Arabica exemplaria ministrante, aliam Historiam a tempore seductoris Mahumeth, usque in hunc annum, qui est nobis ab Incarnatione Domini 1184, per annos quingentos septuaginta decurrentem conscripsimus: auctorem maxime secutivirum venerabilem Seith, filium Patricii, Alexandrinum patriarcham."* William of Tyre, Prologue.
2. *Cf.* A. Momigliano, "The Place of Herodotus in the History of Historiography," *History,* xliii (1958), pp. 1–13, for an illuminating discussion of these questions.
3. It is noteworthy that the first efforts to develop Sanskrit and Chinese studies in the Middle East were made in Ankara and Jerusalem.
4. "The Arabic Historiography of the Crusades," in B. Lewis and P. M. Holt, eds., *Historians of the Middle East* (London, 1962), pp. 98ff.
5. A possible exception is the account *(sīra)* "of the European Christians who in those years had come to the Muslim countries," mentioned by Ibn Muyassar (p. 70) and cited by F. Rosenthal, *A History of Muslim Historiography,* 2nd ed. (Leiden, 1968), p. 62. It is however symptomatic of the general lack of interest that this work has not survived even in quotation. See further above, pp. 92ff.
6. "The Influence of Biblical Tradition on Muslim Historiography," in Lewis and Holt, *Historians,* pp. 35–45.
7. The Persian sagas of the mythical emperors of ancient Iran and the Egyptian legends woven around the broken, massive remnants of the Pharaohs throw into relief the lack of real historical knowledge about the pre-Islamic past.
8. *Murūj,* iii, pp. 66–67, 69–72. *Cf.* the new French translation by C. Pellat, *Les Prairies d'or,* ii (Paris, 1965), pp. 344–45. See also B. Lewis, "Masʿūdī on the Kings of the 'Franks'," *Al-Masʿūdī Millenary Commemoration Volume* (Aligarh, 1960), pp. 7–10.
9. Ibn Khaldūn does indeed discuss the Mongols at some length, but this is preliminary to an account of their invasion of the lands of Islam. *Cf.* W. J. Fischel, "Ibn Khaldūn's Sources for the History of Jenghiz Khān and the Tatars," *Journal of the American Oriental Society,* lxxvi (1956), pp. 91–99.
10. *Cf.* G. Levi Della Vida, "La Traduzione araba delle storie di Orosio," *Al-Andalus,* xix (1954), pp. 257–93; W. J. Fischel, "Ibn Khaldūn and Josippon," *Homenaje a Millas-Vallicrosa,* i (Barcelona, 1954), pp. 587–98; W. J. Fischel, "Ibn Khaldūn: on the Bible, Judaism and the Jews," *Ignace Goldziher Memorial Volume II* (Jerusalem, 1956), pp. 147–71.

11. K. Jahn, "Les légendes de l'Occident chez Raşīd al-Din," *Mélanges Fuad Köprülü* (Istanbul, 1953), pp. 255–57; K. Jahn, *Histoire universelle de Raşid al-Din. . . .* I. *Histoire des Francs* (Leiden, 1951).
12. *Cf.* F. Babinger, *Geschichtsschreiber der Osmanen. . . .* (Leipzig, 1927), p. 107.
13. The *Tā'rīkh al-Hind al-Gharbī,* written *c.* 1580 for Murād III and printed at the Müteferrika press in 1142/1729. The same interest is reflected in other Turkish writings, notably in the geographical section of 'Ālī's *Künh al-akhbār.*
14. Babinger, p. 170.
15. *Encyclopaedia of Islam,* 1st edition, under "Ḥādjdjī Khalīfa," followed by Babinger, p. 200. There is some confusion here with a nother work by Ḥājjī Khalīfa—a history of Constantinople, based on the *Historia rerum in Oriente gestarum. . . .* (Frankfort, 1587), which included translations from Chalcocondyles and other Byzantine historians. See V. L. Ménage, "Kātib Čelebiana," *Bulletin of the School of Oriental and African Studies,* xxvi (1963), pp. 173–74.
16. Adnan Adıvar, *La Science chez les Turcs Ottomans* (Paris, 1939), p. 118, repeated with some modification in Adıvar, *Osmanlı Türklerinde ilim* (Istanbul, 1943), p. 129; Orhan Şaik Gökyay, in *Kâtib Çelebi, hayati ve eserleri hakkında incelemeler* (Ankara, 1957), pp. 54–56; V. L. Ménage, "Three Ottoman Treatises on Europe," in C. E. Bosworth, ed., *Iran and Islam, in memory of the late Vladimir Minorsky* (Edinburgh, 1971), p. 430, n. 13.
17. Ménage, pp. 421–23.
18. *Tārīkh-i Pechevī,* i, p. 106.
19. "Okuttuk ve ničesin türkīye terjüme ettik." The implication would seem to be that Pechevi had the chronicles read to him and then himself turned some of these into written Turkish prose—a procedure reminiscent of the Toledo school of translators. I owe this observation to Professor P. Wittek.
20. F. v. Kraelitz, "Der Osmanische Historiker Ibrâhîm Pečewi," *Der Islam,* viii (1918), pp. 252–60.
21. The MSS. are listed in Babinger, *Geschichtsschreiber,* pp. 229–30. I was able to consult one belonging to the Hunterian Museum in Glasgow (*cf. Journal of the Royal Asiatic Society,* 1906, pp. 602ff.). It was made at the French Embassy in Constantinople, according to the colophon by "Frānsīs al-Shahīr bi'l-Ṣalībī," presumably an Arabicized form of François Pétis de la Croix, the French dragoman to whom the manuscript originally belonged. On Hezārfen's dealings with Europeans, see Heidrun Wurm, *Der osmanische Historiker Ḥüseyn b. Ġa'fer, genannt Hezarfenn, und die Istanbuler Gesellschaft in der zweiten Hälfte der 17 Jahrhunderts* (Freiburg in Breisgau, 1971), especially pp. 122–49.

22. On Münejjimbashi see Babinger, pp. 234–35, Brockelmann, *Geschichte der arabischen Litteratur,* ii, p. 443, and Supplement ii, 637; A. Dietrich, "A propos d'un précis d'histoire gréco-romaine dans la chronique universelle arabe de Müneccimbaşī," in *Correspondance d'Orient,* xi, *Ve Congrès international d'arabisants et d'islamisants . . . Actes* (Brussels, 1971), pp. 172–88. The Turkish version, entitled *Ṣaḥā'if al-akhbār,* was published in 3 volumes, in Istanbul in 1285/1868–69. References are to the Turkish edition.
23. Faik Reşit Unat, "Ahmet III devrinde bir Islahat Takriri," *Tarih Vesikaları,* i (1941), p. 107.
24. Cited by Selim Nüzhet Gerçek, *Türk Matbaacılığı,* i (Istanbul, 1939), p. 44.
25. Ménage, "Three Ottoman Treatises . . . ," pp. 423–29.
26. For descriptions of these works see *Istanbul Kütüphaneleri tarih-coğrafya yazmaları katalogları.* 1. *Türkçe tarih yazmaları,* fascicule 1, *Umumi tarihler* (Istanbul, 1943), and fascicule 3, *Arab tarihi, Iran tarihi, Diğer milletler tarihleri* (Istanbul, 1945). On 'Os̱mān b. Aḥmed see R. F. Kreutel and Otto Spies, *Leben und Abenteuer des Dolmetschers Osman Aga* (Bonn, 1954) especially p. xxv. A topographic description of Istanbul, in Italian, by "Cosimo Comidas di Carbognano, Constantinopolitano," was published in Bassano, Italy, in 1794. My thanks are due to Professor Adnan Erzi for drawing my attention to this. Cosmo di Carbognano, who served as interpreter to the Spanish Embassy in Istanbul, was the grandson of a famous Armenian Catholic martyr; see A. Ubicini, *Lettres,* ii (Paris, 1854), p. 257.
27. On the productions of the Būlāq press see A. Perron, "Lettre à M. Mohl sur les écoles et l'imprimerie du pacha d'Egypte," *Journal Asiatique,* 4th series, ii (1843), pp. 5–23; J. H. Dunne, "Printing and Translation under Muḥammad 'Ali," *Journal of the Royal Asiatic Society* (1940), pp. 325–49. The most detailed study is that of the late Professor Jamāl al-Dīn al-Shayyāl, *Ta'rīkh al-tarjama wa'l-ḥaraka al-thaqāfiyya fī 'aṣr Muḥammad 'Alī* (Cairo, 1951), with full lists of publications.
28. E. Kuran, "Ottoman Historiography of the Tanzimat Period," in Lewis and Holt, *Historians,* pp. 422ff.

Chapter 10. The Cult of Spain and the Turkish Romantics

1. Henri Pérès, *L'Espagne vue par les voyageurs musulmans de 1610 à 1930* (Paris, 1937), pp. 52ff.
2. Pérès, pp. 55ff.
3. Pérès, p. 53.
4. On Munīf Pasha see Ahmet Hamdi Tanpınar, *XIX Asır Türk edebiyatı tarihi,*

2nd edition, i (Istanbul, 1956), pp. 150ff. For a contemporary impression [A. D. Mordtmann], *Stambul und das moderne Türkenthum,* i (Leipzig, 1877), pp. 173ff.

5. Osman Ergin, *Türkiye Maarif Tarihi,* iii (Istanbul, 1941), p. 802 (*cf.* p. 778). According to Ergin, despite his contributions to educational development he left a bad impression in Istanbul.
6. On Ziya Pasha see E. J. W. Gibb, *A History of Ottoman Poetry,* v (London, 1907), pp. 41–111; Tanpınar, *op. cit.*, pp. 279–321; Alessio Bombaci, *Storia della letteratura turca,* 2nd edition (Milan, 1969), pp. 420–23; B. Lewis, *The Emergence of Modern Turkey,* 2nd edition (London, 1968), pp. 138ff.
7. Gibb, p. 58.
8. *Encyclopaedia of Islam,* 2nd edition, under "ʿAbd al-Ḥaḳḳ Ḥāmid" (by A. Hamdi Tanpınar); Bombaci, pp. 430–36.
9. These derive in the main from the writings of the Young Ottomans.
10. For appreciations of *Ṭāriq* see Tanpınar, pp. 576–77; *cf. Islam Ansiklopedisi,* i, p. 70 (by Sabri Esat Siyavuşgil).
11. *Ibn-i Mūsā* was not published until 1917.
12. *Encyclopaedia of Islam,* 1st edition, article by Theodor Menzel.
13. Siyavuşgil, *loc. cit.*

Chapter 11. The Pro-Islamic Jews

1. T. P. O'Connor, *Lord Beaconsfield, A Biography* (1879), 8th ed. (London, 1905), pp. 607–10, 654.
2. E. A. Freeman, *Ottoman Power in Europe: Its Nature, Its Growth, and Its Decline* (London, 1877), pp. xviii–xx.
3. W. F. Monypenny and G. E. Buckle, *The Life of Benjamin Disraeli, Earl of Beaconsfield,* 1st ed. (London, 1910–1920), revised ed. (London, 1929), ii, p. 930.
4. Sir James Headlam-Morley, *Studies in Diplomatic History* (London, 1930), p. 206. *Cf.* R. W. Seton-Watson, *Disraeli, Gladstone and the Eastern Question* (London, 1935), p. 3; E. Kedourie, *England and the Middle East: The Destruction of the Ottoman Empire 1914–1921* (London, 1956), pp. 82–84; R. Blake, *Disraeli* (London, 1966), pp. 60, 204, 600ff. An amusing variant occurs in a letter written by Wilfrid Scawen Blunt to Wilfred Meynell in 1903: "His Semitic politics of course were genuine enough. For his fearlessness in avowing these I hold him in esteem—for a Jew ought to be a Jew—and I enjoy, as a tour de force, his smashing of those solemn rogues the Whigs, and his bamboozling of the Tories. Our dull English nation deserved what it got, and there is nothing funnier in history than the way in which he cajoled our square-toed aristocratic

Party to put off its respectable broad-cloth, and robe itself in his suit of Imperial spangles, and our fine ladies after his death to worship their old world-weary Hebrew beguiler under the innocent form of a primrose." W. S. Blunt, *My Diaries, Being a Personal Narrative of Events, 1888–1914*, ii, *1900–1914* (London, 1920), pp. 74–75.

5. Blake, *Disraeli,* p. 59.
6. *Tancred,* book iv, ch. vii; *cf.* ch. iii.
7. Monypenny and Buckle, ii, pp. 930–31.
8. *Contarini Fleming,* part iv, ch. xix; Monypenny and Buckle, i, pp. 170–71.
9. On the place of these scholars in the development of Arabic studies in Europe, see Johann Fück, *Die arabischen Studien in Europa bis den Anfang des 20. Jahrhunderts* (Leipzig, 1955), and, for Russia, Ignatii Yulyanovič Kračkovsky, *Izbranniye Sočineniya,* v (Moscow-Leningrad, 1958). On Gustav Weil, see Gustave Dugat, *Histoire des orientalistes de l'Europe du XIIe siècle au XIXe siècle,* i (Paris, 1868), pp. 42–48, and D. M. Dunlop, "Some Remarks on Weil's History of the Caliphs," in B. Lewis and P. M. Holt, eds., *Historians of the Middle East* (London, 1962), pp. 315–29. Biographies and appreciations of the work of individual scholars will be found in the obituary notices published in specialist journals. These are listed, together with articles on the history of Islamic studies, in J. D. Pearson, *Index Islamicus 1906–1955* (Cambridge, 1958), pp. 1ff., and supplements. Some are the subjects of articles in the *Jewish Encyclopaedia* and other works of reference. For critical assessments of the treatment of Islam by Western Orientalists, see Jean-Jacques Waardenburg, *L'Islam dans le miroir de l'occident* (Paris-The Hague, 1963), including a detailed consideration of Goldziher; Albert Hourani, "Islam and the Philosophers of History," in *Middle Eastern Studies,* iii (1967), pp. 206–67; Khurshid Ahmed, *Islam and the West* (Karachi, no date, ? 1958); A. L. Tibawi, "English-Speaking Orientalists," in *The Muslim World* (1963), pp. 185–204 and 298–313. For Western attitudes to Islam in general see Norman Daniel, *Islam, Europe and Empire* (Edinburgh, 1966).
10. On Davids see James Picciotto, *Sketches of Anglo-Jewish History* (London, 1875), pp. 316–18; Harold Bowen, *British Contributions to Turkish Studies* (London, 1945), pp. 43–44; A. Galante, *Recueil de nouveaux documents inédits concernant l'histoire des juifs de Turquie* (Istanbul, 1949), pp. 71–73; Şerif Mardin, *The Genesis of Young Ottoman Thought: A Study in the Modernization of Turkish Political Ideas* (Princeton, N.J., 1962), p. 250; and, in Turkish, Akçuraoğlu Yusuf, "Türkçülük," in *Türk Yılı,* i (1928), pp. 310–11, and Ahmet Hamdi Tanpınar, *XIX asir Türk edebiyatı tarihi* (Istanbul, 1949), revised ed. (Istanbul, 1956), pp. 220–22.
11. On Cahun see *Jewish Encyclopaedia,* article by Zadoc Kahn; Mardin, p. 61; Akçura, p. 359; C. W. Hostler, *Turkism and the Soviets* (London, 1957), p. 141.

12. The best sources of information on Vambéry are his own autobiographical writings: *Arminius Vambéry, His Life and Adventures Written by Himself* (London, 1884), and *The Story of My Struggles* (London, n.d.). There are short articles on him in the *Encyclopaedia of the Social Sciences* and in a number of general encyclopedias. For a Turkish appreciation, see Akçuraoğlu Yusuf, *loc. cit.*, pp. 313–15. On the influence of Davids, Cahun, and Vambéry on the growth of Turkish nationalism, see B. Lewis, "History-Writing and National Revival in Turkey," in *Middle Eastern Affairs*, iv (1953), pp. 221–22; Lewis, *The Emergence of Modern Turkey*, 2nd ed. (London, 1968), pp. 346–48; Niyazi Berkes, *The Development of Secularism in Turkey* (Montreal, 1964), pp. 314–15.
13. Arthur Lumley Davids, *Grammaire turke* (London, 1836), p. ix; L. Cahun, *Scènes de la vie juive en Alsace* (Paris, 1885).
14. For a rather interesting exception, see *The Memoirs of Ismail Kemal Bey*, edited by Sommerville Story (London, 1920), pp. 71–72. In general, however, even the contribution made by Jewish subjects of Muslim states attracted very little attention. Thus, the Jewish participation in the Young Turk movement, which aroused so much hostile comment in the West, is barely mentioned in Turkish sources. See Lewis, *Emergence*, pp. 212–13.
15. *Coningsby*, book iv, ch. x.
16. On the parallel cult of Spanish Islam among nineteenth-century Muslims see Aziz Ahmad, "Islam d'Espagne et Inde musulmane moderne," in *Etudes d'orientalisme dédiées à la mémoire de Lévi-Provençal*, i (Paris, 1962), ii, pp. 461–70, and chapter 10.
17. A. Vambéry, *The Story of My Struggles*, p. 395.
18. During the last half century a vast anti-Jewish—not merely anti-Zionist or anti-Israeli—literature has appeared in the Arab countries, in which racial, theological, and demonological themes, as well as political arguments, are used. It is significant that the ideas, the documentation, and often even the actual texts are overwhelmingly of Christian European origin. In the bookshops of the Arab Socialist states, Marx on the Jewish question is flanked by Hitler's *Mein Kampf*, the *Protocols of the Elders of Zion*, Henry Ford's *International Jew*, and a variety of local adaptations and imitations. Even the anti-Jewish cartoons that are common in the Arabic press reflect European anti-Semitic stereotypes, mostly German and Russian, and do not derive from any local tradition. See further B. Lewis, *Semites and Anti-Semites* (New York, 1986), pp. 164ff.
19. There are important direct Islamic influences on Jewish worship. See N. Wieder, "*Hashpa'ot Islamiyyot 'al ha-pulhan ha-yehudi*" (Hebrew), in *Melīla*, ii (1946), pp. 37–120. The self-conscious "Orientalism" of emancipated European Jews can also be seen in the pseudo-Moorish motifs that sometimes occur in modern synagogue architecture.
20. Cited by L. Massignon in B. Heller, *Bibliographie des oeuvres de Ignace Goldziher* (Paris, 1927), p. xvi, note i (*cf.* p. viii, note i).

Chapter 12. Palestine: On the History and Geography of a Name

1. The early Greek and Latin versions show interesting variations. The Vulgate has Philistiim, Philisthaea, and Palaesthinorum in the three passages respectively. The Septuagint has Phylistieim in the first, but in the second and third simply uses the word *allophylos*, "stranger" or "foreigner."
2. Palaistinê Syria, 1, 105, II, 106; Syria hê Palaistinê, III, 91, IV, 39; Syrioi en tê Palaistinê, II, 104, VII, 89.
3. Thus Aristotle, in a single reference (*Meteorologica*, II, iii), mentions the Dead Sea as lying in Palestine; Philo Judaeus equates Palestine with Canaan. On the other hand Pliny the Elder, who discusses Judaea at some length, speaks of Palestine as a former name for the borderland of Arabia (*Natural History*, v, xiii–xv).
4. Genesis 15: 18–21. *Cf.* the earlier definition of the land of Canaan in Abraham's time (Genesis 10:19).
5. Biblical definitions of both the promise and the conquest vary somewhat. The promise is in Exodus 13:31 and more fully in Numbers 34:2–12. See also Deuteronomy 1:7–8 and 11:24; Joshua 1:4, 12, and 13; I Kings 8:65. The country is often defined proverbially as "from Dan to Beersheba," for example in Judges 20:1 and frequently in the books of Samuel and Kings.
6. Nehemiah 11:27–30.
7. The text dealing with this matter has long been known in four variants, preserved in early rabbinical literature. A recently discovered inscription has added a fifth. See Y. Sussman, "The Boundaries of Eretz-Israel," *Tarbiz* (Jerusalem), XLV (1976), pp. ii–iii and 213–57 (Hebrew with English summary); S. Klein, "Das Tannaitische Grenzenverzeichnis Palästinas," *Hebrew Union College Annual*, v (1928), 197–259.
8. On the frontiers of Palestine in antiquity there are two useful articles by Michael Avi-Yonah: one in *Paulys Realencyclopädie der classischen Altertumswissenschaft*, new ed., Supplement vol. XIII (Munich 1973), s.v. "Palaestina," sections 1 and 2, "Namen" and "Grenzen," cols. 311–26; the other in the *Encyclopaedia Judaica*, s.v. "Israel, Land of: Geographical Survey; Boundaries," IX, cols. 112ff. See now also Louis H. Feldman, "Some Observations on the Name of Palestine," *Hebrew Union College Annual*, v (1990), 1–23.
9. On Arab Palestine see *Encyclopaedia of Islam*, 2d ed., s.v. "Filastīn" (by D. Sourdel), where further references are given.
10. The Biblical Hebrew Peleshet referred only to Philistia and became obsolete with the disappearance of the Philistines. The form Palestina occurs once or twice in the Talmud, to designate the Roman province of that name and was used by the British mandatary government in official Hebrew texts so as to avoid giving offense to the Arabs. It has never formed part of Hebrew usage.

11. Başvekalet Arşivi, Yıldız Katalogu, Kisim 39, no. 2131.
12. I owe my knowledge of this rare publication to Mr. Alan Makovsky, late of Princeton University. At my request, he has supplied the following note:

> In 1926 the Egyptian Foreign Ministry published the 1841 map—a copy of which Egypt had received from Turkey in 1925—in a pamphlet of documents related to the 1925 Italo-Egyptian agreement concerning Egypt's western border. A copy of this pamphlet (*La Frontière Occidentale de l'Egypte. Accord Italo-Eygptien du 6 Décembre 1925.* Documents Réservé, Royaume d'Egypte. Ministère des Affaires Etrangères, No. 1, 1926) is in the Map Room of the Royal Geographical Society in London.
>
> Although the 1841 map was included in the pamphlet in order to show the western limit of the area granted to Mehmet Ali in the 1841 firman of investiture, its eastern portion appears as well. The Sinai frontier there indicated is accurately described on page 12 of the pamphlet. "une ligne partant d'un point sur la Méditerranée situé au Nord d'El-Ariche et rejoignant le Golfe de Suez." According to the pamphlet, Egypt requested a copy of the map from the Turkish government on May 20, 1925, during the negotiations with Italy. Almost seven months later, on December 13, Turkey complied. Thus was retrieved a document which for decades had been thought lost.
>
> Doubt about the map's authenticity is largely alleviated by the fact that its western border lies several miles to the east of that claimed and won by Egypt in the 1925 negotiations. Consequently, the map could have served the Egyptians no useful purpose in advancing their claims, even had it arrived before the December 6 conclusion of the agreement, which—whether by design or circumstance—it did not.
>
> I was alerted to the existence of the pamphlet and the 1841 map enclosure (apparently unknown previously to historians of late Ottoman-Egyptian relations and the 1906 Aqaba crisis) by an undated note in the personal papers of W. E. Jennings-Bramley, also housed in the Royal Geographical Society.

13. There appear so far to be only two studies on the Aqaba crisis of 1906, one by an Israeli, the other by an Egyptian scholar. They are: Uriel Heyd, "Ha-mashber shel mifratz Elat bi-shenat 1906," in *Elath, the Eighteenth Archaeological Convention, October 1962* (Jerusalem 1963), pp. 194–206 (based in the main on published British and Turkish documents); Yūnān Labīb Rizq, "Azmat al-ʿAqaba al-maʿrūfa bi-ḥādithat Ṭāba 1906," *Al-Majalla al-Ta'rīkhiyya al-Miṣriyya Egyptian Historical Journal,* XIII, pp. 247–305 (based mainly on unpublished British documents). The delimiting of this and of the other frontiers was examined by H.F. Frischwasser-Ra'anan, *Frontiers of a Nation: A Survey of Diplomatic and Political History Relating to the Palestine Mandate* (London 1955). The Aqaba incident is also discussed in L.M. Bloomfield, *Egypt, Israel*

and the Gulf of Aqaba in International Law (Toronto 1957), pp. 108–43 (a legal examination, based entirely on British published documents).

Chapter 13. An Ode against the Jews

1. R. Dozy, *Recherches sur l'histoire et la littérature de l'Espagne pendant le moyen âge,* 3rd ed., i (Paris-Leiden, 1881), pp. 282–94 and lxi–lxviii; E. García Gómez, *Un alfaquí español: Abū Isḥāq de Elvira* (Madrid-Granada, 1944); García Gómez, "Abū Isḥāḳ al-Ilbīrī" in *Encyclopaedia of Islam,* 2nd ed.
2. Dozy, pp. 286 and lxii; García Gómez, xix, p. 125.
3. Dozy, *Recherches.* The French translation is reproduced in Dozy's *Histoire des musulmans d'Espagne,* revised ed., iii (Leiden, 1932), pp. 71–72.
4. *Geschichte der Juden,* vi, pp. 48–53. The poem and episode are discussed in S. W. Baron, *A Social and Religious History of the Jews,* iii, p. 158; v, p. 93; E. Ashtor, *Qōrōt ha-Yehūdīm bi-Sĕfarad ha-Moslemīt,* ii (Jerusalem, 1966), pp. 115–17, and also by H. Pérès, *La poésie andalouse en arabe classique au XIe siècle,* 2nd ed. (Paris, 1953), pp. 272–73.
5. Ed. E. Lévi-Provençal (Rabat, 1934), pp. 265–67.
6. García Gómez, *Un alfaquí español,* see note 1 above. The *qaṣīda* is no. xxv, pp. 149–53. The introduction is reproduced in E. García Gómez, *Cinco poetas musulmanes* (Madrid, 1944), pp. 95–138.
7. Nykl, *Selections from Hispano-Arabic Poetry* (Beirut, 1949), pp. 141–43; Nykl, *Hispano-Arabic Poetry* (Baltimore, 1946), pp. 197–200.
8. M. Perlmann, "Eleventh-century Andalusian Authors on the Jews of Granada," in *Proceedings of the American Academy for Jewish Research,* xviii (1949), pp. 284–90.
9. The poet is appealing to the Ṣanhāja, the dominant Berber tribe in the Zirid monarchy.
10. From Dozy's text; this line is missing in the *Dīwān.*
11. From Dozy's text. The *Dīwān* has a slightly different text for this line, meaning "And destruction approaches, and they do not know."
12. Thus *Dīwān:—fāḍil qānit.* Dozy reads *rāghib rāhib,* which might be translated: "[How many a Muslim] torn between fear and desire."
13. A standard insult. In the vocabulary of abuse, Jews are apes and Christians are pigs—though sometimes the latter term is also extended to Jews. The association with apes may be based on the Qur'ān (ii, 61; v, 65; vii, 166). See Pérès, *La poésie andalouse,* pp. 240–41; Perlmann, "Eleventh-century Andalusian Authors . . . ," pp. 287–88. The conventional association of certain animals with certain beliefs, in formalized abuse, still survives in part of Europe.
14. The poet may here be alluding to the ruler, Bādīs, or, more probably, to some

Muslim ally of the Jewish minister—possibly the colleague condemned in the poem cited above.

15. *Dīwān: akhrāj.* Perlmann translates "tatters"; Dozy reads *afwāj* and translates *"par troupes."*
16. *Mulawwana.* Perlmann suggests amending this to *mulawwatha,* filthy (p. 286, n. 52). This line is missing in both Dozy's text and the *A'māl.*
17. *Dīwān: wākabūhum,* in preference to Dozy's *rākabūhum,* "made them ride."
18. *Cf.* Qur'ān, v, 25–26, where the reference is specifically to Jews.
19. An allusion to an Arabic proverb which implies that one may begin by nibbling or gnawing with the front teeth, and end by crunching with the whole mouth. *Cf.* G. W. Freytag, *Arabum Proverbia,* ii (Bonn, 1839), pp. 245–46. The meaning seems to be approximately that of the English phrase "Give him an inch and he takes an ell."
20. Dozy reads *bi-asḥārikum* and explains *asḥār* as meaning *"les paroles que prononce le muézin au lever de l'aurore"*; *cf.* his *Supplément aux dictionnaires arabes,* i, pp. 635–36. It seems likely that Abū Isḥāq is alluding to the Hebrew word *Shaḥarīt,* the morning prayer; this would parallel the use of another Hebrew word in the next line. The *Dīwān* reads *bi-asmārikum*—presumably a copyist's attempt to cope with an unfamiliar term.
21. Thus Dozy; *Dīwān* reads *bi-aswāqihā.*
22. Not kosher—food which is ritually unclean for Jews. Dozy: *li-aṭrīfihim; Dīwān: li-aṭrāfihā.* In other words, the Muslims eat what the Jews reject.
23. A common Islamic formula. See for example Qur'ān, xxiii, 60.
24. Here the poet is addressing the king, with obvious intentions.
25. Thus *Dīwān: wa-kayfa takūnu lahum dhimma.* Dozy reads *lanā himma* and translates: *"Comment pourrions-nous aspirer à nous distinguer."*
26. Tha'lab, *Qawā'id al-shi'r,* ed. C. Schiaparelli, in *Actes du VIIIe Congrès international des orientalistes,* vol. ii, part 1 (Leiden, 1893), pp. 183–84; cited by G. E. von Grunebaum, *Medieval Islam: A Study in Cultural Orientation,* 2nd edition (Chicago, 1953), p. 262.
27. *Cf.* H. A. R. Gibb, *Modern Trends in Islam* (Chicago, 1947), p. 5; Jacques Berque, *Les arabes d'hier à demain* (Paris, 1960), pp. 173ff.; M. Berger, *The Arab World Today* (London, 1962), pp. 158–59; Hisham Sharabi, *Nationalism and Revolution in the Arab World* (Princeton, 1966), pp. 93–103.
28. See M. Canard, "L'Impérialisme des Fatimides et leur propagande," in *Annales de l'Institut des Études Orientales,* vi (1942–1947), pp. 156–93; E. García Gómez, "La poésie politique sous le califat de Cordoue," in *Revue des Études Islamiques,* 1949, pp. 5–11; S. D. Goitein, *Jews and Arabs: Their Contacts Through the Ages* (New York, 1955), pp. 161–63. On some economic uses of poetry, see above pp. 101–2. For examples of the poet as blackmailer, see *Encyclopaedia of Islam,* 2nd edition, articles "Al-Ḥakam b. 'Abdal," "Hidjā'," and "Hutay'a."

29. See for example F. Gabrieli, "La poesia hariǵita nel secolo degli Omayyadi," in *Rivista degli Studi Orientali,* xx (1943), pp. 331–72.
30. S. Moscati, "Le massacre des Umayyades dans l'histoire et dans les fragments poétiques," in *Archiv Orientální,* xviii (1951), pp. 88–115.
31. For a literary analysis of the poem see García Gómez, pp. 38–40; *cf.* Pérès, pp. 273–74.
32. Dozy, p. lxii (translation, p. 285).
33. Dozy, p. lxviii (translation, p. 289).
34. The sources differ on the number of Jews killed. For a brief discussion see Ashtor, *Qōrōt ha-Yehūdīm,* p. 363, n. 281.
35. Abraham ben David, *Sefer ha-Qabbālā,* in A. Neubauer, ed., *Mediaeval Jewish Chronicles* (Oxford, 1887), p. 73. Shĕlomo ibn Verga, *Sheveṭ Yĕhūdā,* ed. A. Shohat (Jerusalem, 5707), p. 22, with notes by I. Baer, p. 169; *Cf.* Samuel Usque, *Consolaçam ás tribulaçoens de Israel,* ed. Mendes dos Remedios (Coimbra, 1906), 3rd dialogue, ch. 24; English translation by Martin A. Cohen, *Consolation for the Tribulations of Israel* (Philadelphia, 1965), pp. 197–98 (*cf.* pp. 279ff.).
36. García Gómez, pp. 28–30; Perlmann, pp. 284–85; H. R. Idris, "Les Zīrīdes d'Espagne," in *Al-Andalus,* xxix (1964), pp. 74ff., pp. 88ff. The most important Arabic source, the memoirs of the Zirid ruler ʿAbdallāh, who reigned in Granada from 1077 to 1090, describes the crisis in Granada in detail, without saying a word about Abū Isḥāq or his poem. See E. Lévi-Provençal, "Les 'mémoires' de ʿAbd Allah, dernier roi Ziride de Grenade," in *Al-Andalus,* iii (1935), pp. 295ff.; ed. Cairo, *Kitāb al-Tibyān ʿan al-ḥāditha al-kā'ina bi-dawlat Banī Zīrī fī Gharnāṭa* (Cairo, 1955), pp. 55ff.
37. Dozy, *Recherches,* i, p. 293; García Gómez, pp. 50–51.
38. There is an extensive literature on the position of the non-Muslim in Muslim law and under Muslim rule. For a brief account, see the two articles "Dhimma" in the *Encyclopaedia of Islam,* 2nd edition, by Claude Cahen (history) and Chafik Chehata (law), where further references are given. On the Jews in particular see S. D. Goitein, *Jews and Arabs, passim,* especially pp. 62ff., and H. Z. (J. W.) Hirschberg, "The Oriental Jewish Communities," in A. J. Arberry, general editor, *Religion in the Middle East,* i (Cambridge, 1969), pp. 119–225 and B. Lewis, *The Jews of Islam* (Princeton, 1984).
39. On anti-*dhimmī* propaganda see M. Steinschneider, *Polemische und apologetische Literatur in arabischer Sprache* (Leipzig, 1877); R. Gottheil, "An Answer to the Dhimmis," in *Journal of the American Oriental Society,* xli (1921), pp. 383–457; M. Perlmann, "Notes on Anti-Christian Propaganda in the Mamluk Empire," in *Bulletin of the School of Oriental and African Studies,* x (1942), pp. 843–61; Perlmann, "Eleventh-century Andalusian Authors . . ."; S. W. Baron, *A Social and Religious History of the Jews,* v, pp. 95ff. Ibn Ḥazm's tract against Ibn Nagrella, cited by Perlmann, has since been published: *Al-Radd ʿalā Ibn al-Naghrīla al-Yahūdī wa-rasā'il ukhrā,* ed. Iḥsān ʿAbbās (Cairo, 1380/1960). For

other anti-Jewish poems, see W. J. Fischel, *Jews in the Economic and Political Life of Medieval Islam* (London, 1937), pp. 88–89 and 111; Pérès, pp. 268–73 (including some other contemporary attacks on Ibn Nagrella).

40. This theme, already discernible in the Qur'ān (ii, 61 and iii, 112), is common in later writings. *Cf.* the remarks of M. Perlmann, in his "Eleventh-century Andalusian Authors . . .," pp. 289–90.

Chapter 14. The Sultan, the King and the Jewish Doctor

1. See, for example, D. Yellin and I. Abrahams, *Maimonides* (London, 1903), pp. 113–14. "It may have been from el-Adil (the brother of Saladin and ruler of Egypt) that Richard heard of the fame of Maimonides as a medical practitioner. The 'King of the Franks in Ascalon' sought his services as his physician, but Maimonides declined the honour. He was well content with his position under the Vizir Alfadhel, and if he was acquainted with the events which had occurred at Richard's coronation, he must have felt safer in Cairo than in London."
2. Al-Qifṭī: *Ta'rīkh al-Ḥukamā'*, ed. Lippert (Leipzig, 1903).
3. *Bibliotheca Arabico-Hispana Escurialensis* . . . , i (Madrid, 1760), pp. 293–94.
4. Al-Qifṭī, p. 319. In Lippert's edition the word *Ghuzz*—a common term for the Turks—is misread as *Mu'izz,* thus adding to the confusion. Casiri gives the word correctly.
5. Casiri, *Bibliotheca Arabico-Hispana, loc. cit.*
6. H. Graetz, *Geschichte der Juden,* vi, p. 331.
7. M. Meyerhof, "L'Oeuvre médicale de Maimonide," *Archeion,* xi (1929), p. 138.
8. C. Cahen, "Indigènes et Croisés—un Médecin d'Amaury, *Syria* (1934), p. 353.
9. See the two important articles of Y. Prawer on Ascalon in the period of the Crusades: *Eretz Israel,* iv (1956), pp. 231–48, and v (1958), pp. 224–37; also, more briefly, *Encyclopaedia of Islam* (2nd ed.), "'Asḳalān."
10. Bahā' al-Dīn, *Sīrat Ṣalāḥ al-Dīn* (Cairo, 1903), p. 189; *cf.* Abū Shāma, *Al-Rawḍatayn,* ii (Cairo, 1872), p. 203; Ibn Wāṣil, *Mufarrij al-Kurūb,* ii (Cairo, 1957), p. 402; Richard of Devizes, *De Rebus gestis Ricardi Primi,* Rolls series (London, 1886), p. 445.
11. *Historia Rerum in Partibus Transmarinis Gestarum,* xx, ch. 31.
12. Ibn Abī Uṣaybi'a, *Ṭabaqāt al-Aṭibbā'* (ed. Müller), ii, pp. 121–23.
13. This often-cited letter has been printed a number of times. *Cf.* Yellin and Abrahams, *Maimonides,* p. 148.
14. Ibn Abī Uṣaybi'a, *op. cit.,* ii, p. 117.
15. *Relation de l'Egypte par Abd al-Latif* (Paris, 1810), p. 466.
16. *Geschichte der Arabischen Aerzte* (Göttingen, 1840), no. 198.
17. *Geschichte der Juden,* vi, p. 399.

18. S. Munk, "Notice sur Joseph ben-Jehouda," *Journal Asiatique* (1842), pp. 24, 29–30. *Cf.* B. Dünaburg, *Rambam* (Tel Aviv, 1935), pp. 13–14.
19. Munk, *Notice,* pp. 21–22. On this whole question see E. Ashtor-Strauss, "Saladin and the Jews," *Hebrew Union College Annual,* xxvii (1956), p. 312 and n. 25.

Chapter 15. The Mongols, the Turks and the Muslim Polity

1. Arnold Hottinger, "Patriotismus und Nationalismus bei den Arabern," *Neue Zürcher Zeitung,* 12 May 1957. On modern Muslim views of the Mongol invasions see further W. Cantwell Smith, *Islam in Modern History* (Princeton, N.J., 1957), pp. 32ff., 164ff.; G. E. von Grunebaum, *Modern Islam: the Search for Cultural Identity* (Berkeley and Los Angeles, 1962), pp. 44ff., 185, 213, 255–56.
2. E. G. Browne, *A Literary History of Persia from Firdawsi to Sa'di* (London, 1906), pp. 426–27; *cf.* Browne, *A History of Persian Literature under Tartar Domination* (Cambridge, 1920), pp. 14–15. Like most other Western writers, Browne bases his account of the Mongols largely on Baron C. d'Ohsson's *Histoire des Mongols,* 1st ed., 1824 (2nd considerably amplified ed., The Hague and Amsterdam, 1834–35).
3. V. V. Bartold, *Mussulman Culture,* translated from the Russian by Shahid Suhrawardy (Calcutta, 1934), pp. 110–12; *cf.* the very much better Turkish translation edited by M. Fuad Köprülü, *Islam medeniyeti tarihi,* 2nd ed. (Ankara, 1963), p. 62. The Russian original was reprinted in Bartold's collected works, *Sochineniya,* vi (Moscow, 1966). Bartold's views on the Mongol invasions and their effects are developed in many of his writings. In attempting a more positive assessment of the Mongols, he was to some extent anticipated by Sir Henry Howorth (*History of the Mongols,* London, 1876–88) and, still more, by Léon Cahun (*Introduction à l'histoire de l'Asie,* 1896). These works were, however, written without reference to oriental sources and are of no scholarly significance. Cahun's book, written with some skill and much enthusiasim, became a source of inspiration for Turkish and pan-Turkish nationalist theories.
4. I. P. Petrushevsky, *Zemledelie i agrarniye otnosheniya v Irane xiii-xiv vekov* (Moscow-Leningrad, 1960), p. 36; Persian translation by Karīm Kishāvarz, *Kishāvarzī va munāsabāt-i arẕī dar Irān 'ahd-i Moghūl,* i (Tehran, 1344 Persian solar era), p. 48. *Cf.* Professor Petrushevsky's introduction to the new edition of Bartold's collected works, *Sochineniya,* i (Moscow, 1963), especially pp. 32–33.
5. Ibn Wāṣil, *Mufarrij al-kurūb,* MS. Paris, Arabe 1703, folio 126 b, cited by D. Ayalon, "Studies on the Transfer of the 'Abbāsid Caliphate from Baghdād to Cairo," *Arabica,* vii (1960), p. 59.

6. Constantine K. Zurayk, *The Meaning of the Disaster,* trans. R. B. Winder (Beirut, 1956), p. 48; cited by G. E. von Grunebaum, *Modern Islam,* p. 255.
7. See Ann K. S. Lambton, *Landlord and Peasant in Persia* (London, 1953), pp. 77ff., Petrushevsky, *Zemledelie,* and, on the Mongol Empire in general, J. J. Saunders, "Le nomade comme bâtisseur d'empire: conquête arabe et conquête mongole," *Diogène,* no. 52 (1965), pp. 85–109, where other recent literature is cited.
8. Even in Iraq, however, the extent of the economic damage done by the Mongols has been exaggerated. See the important study by Dr. Jaʿfar H. Khesbak, "Aḥwāl al-ʿIrāq al-iqtiṣādiyya fī ʿahd al-Ilkhānīyīn al-Mughūl," *Majallat Kulliyyat al-Ādāb* (Baghdad, 1961), pp. 1–56.
9. Wladyslaw Kotwicz, "Les Mongols, promoteurs de l'idée de paix universelle au début du xiiie siècle," *Rocznik Orientalistyczny,* xvi (Cracow, 1950), p. 429.
10. Abu Shāma, *Tarājim rijāl al-qarnayn al-sādis wa'l-sābi',* ed. Muḥammad al-Kawtharī (Cairo, 1947), p. 208.
11. A. T. Hatto, "Ḥamāsa iv," in *Encyclopaedia of Islam,* 2nd ed., iii, p. 116. The whole problem of Turkish-Mongol relationships is discussed in an important article by Professor Ibrahim Kafesoğlu, "Türk tarihinde Moğollar ve Cengiz meselesi," *Tarih Dergisi,* v (1953), pp. 105–36.
12. W. Barthold, *Turkestan Down to the Mongol Invasion* (London, 1928), p. 305.
13. Ibn Khaldūn, *Kitāb al-'Ibar,* v (Cairo, 1867), p. 371. Professor Ayalon was the first to draw attention to this very important passage; "The Wafidiyya in the Mamluk Kingdom," *Islamic Culture* (1951), p. 90. English translation in B. Lewis (ed. and trans.), *Islam from the Prophet Muhammad to the Capture of Constantinople* (New York, 1974), i, *Politics and War,* pp. 97–99.
14. Osman Turan, "The Idea of World Domination among the Medieval Turks," *Studia Islamica,* iv (1955), pp. 80–81; Ann K. S. Lambton, "Quis Custodiet Custodes: Some Reflections on the Persian Theory of Government," *Studia Islamica,* vi (1956), p. 130. *Cf.* Fuad Köprülü, "Les institutions juridique turques au moyen-age," *Belleten,* ii, nos. 5–6 (1938), pp. 41–76; Köprülü, "Bizans müesseselerinin Osmanli müesseselerine te'siri hakkında bâzı mülâhazalar," in *Türk Hukuk ve Iktisat Tarihi Mecmuası,* i (1931), pp. 165–313; Italian translation, *Alcune osservazioni intorno all' influenza delle istituzioni bizantine sulle istituzioni ottomane* (Rome, 1953).

Chapter 16. Ottoman Observers of Ottoman Decline

1. The Turkish original was edited and published together with a German translation by Rudolf Tschudi, *Das Āṣafnâme des Lutfi Pacha* (Berlin, 1910). Another edition, giving a somewhat better text, was published by Shukrī in Istanbul, 1326. On Lûtfi Pasha see *Encyclopaedia of Islam,* article by Th. Menzel;

Islâm Ansiklopedisi, article by Tayyib Gökbilgin; and F. Babinger, *Die Geschichtsschreiber der Osmanen und ihre Werke* (Leipzig, 1927), pp. 80–81.

2. *Āṣafnāme,* p. 6; tr., p. 7.
3. *Āṣafnāme,* pp. 6–7; tr., p. 8.
4. *Āṣafnāme* pp. 10–11; tr., p. 11. Lûtfi Pasha was much concerned by the oppressive working of the courier system and discusses it at some length in his history *Ta'rīkh āl-i 'Os̱mān* (Istanbul, 1341), pp. 371ff. For a brief but very well documented account of the Ottoman courier system, see J. H. Mordtmann, in *Mitteilungen des Seminars für Orientalische Sprachen,* xxxii, section 2 (1929), pp. 23–25.
5. *Āṣafnāme,* p. 12; tr., p. 12.
6. *Āṣafnāme,* pp. 12–13; tr., p. 13.
7. *Ibid.*
8. *Āṣafnāme,* pp. 14–15; tr., p. 14. The asper was an Ottoman silver coin. On its value see below, note 19.
9. *Āṣafnāme,* p. 23; tr., p. 20. On the Ottoman system of price-control *(narh)* see R. Mantran, "Règlements fiscaux ottomans. La police des marchés de Stamboul au début du XVIe siècle," in *Cahiers de Tunisie,* no. 14 (1956), pp. 213–41; R. Mantran, "Un document sur *l'iḥtisāb* de Stamboul à la fin du XVIIe siècle," in *Mélanges Louis Massignon,* iii (Damascus, 1957), pp. 127–49; W. Hahn, *Die Verpflegung Konstantinopels durch staatliche Zwangswirtschaft* . . . (Stuttgart, 1926). Many documents from Turkish archives, relating to *narh* and *iḥtisāb,* were edited by Osman Nuri (in *Mejelle-i Umūr-i Belediye,* i, 1922), by Omer Lûtfi Barkan (in *Tarih Vesikaları,* ii, 1942), and by Ahmed Refik (in his four volumes of documents on life in Istanbul, *Istanbul ḥayatı,* Istanbul 1929–1935).
10. *Āṣafnāme,* p. 22; tr., pp. 19–20.
11. *Āṣafnāme,* pp. 32–33; tr., pp. 26–27. *Cf.* B. Lewis, *The Emergence of Modern Turkey,* 2nd edition (London, 1968), pp. 24ff.
12. *Āṣafnāme,* p. 35; tr., p. 29.
13. A well-known Turkish proverb. On Veysī, and the problems of his identity, see E. J. W. Gibb, *A History of Ottoman Poetry,* iii (London, 1904), pp. 208–18; Babinger, *Die Geschichtsschreiber,* pp. 152–54.
14. The first *risāle* of Kochu Bey was published in Istanbul in 1277; in London in 1862; in Istanbul again in 1303 and in a new edition, in the new Turkish script, by Ali Kemalî Aksüt (Istanbul, 1939), cited here. All these editions were preceded by the German translation of W. F. A. Behrnauer, "Kog'abey's Abhandlung über den Verfall des osmanischen Staatsgebäudes seit Sultan Suleiman des Grossen," *Zeitschrift der Deutschen Morgenländischen Gesellschaft,* xv (1861), pp. 272–332. A Russian translation, with an edition of the text, was published in St. Petersburg by V. D. Smirnov in 1873. Unpublished translations into French and Arabic exist in manuscript in Paris and Cairo. A second *risāle,*

presented to Sultan Ibrāhīm in 1640, was at first not recognized as the work of Kochu Bey. A German translation was published by Behrnauer in *Zeitschrift der Deutschen Morgenländischen Gesellschaft,* xviii (1864), pp. 699–740, but the text was not published until 1939, when it was included by Ali Kemalî Aksüt in his edition. It was translated into Russian by A. S. Tveritinova, in the Proceedings *(Zapiski)* of the Institute of Orientalism (Moscow-Leningrad, 1953), pp. 212–68. An important study on the memoranda of Kochu Bey was published by M. Çağatay Uluçay in *Zeki Velidi Togan'a Armağan* (Istanbul, 1955), pp. 177–99. See further the articles in *Encyclopaedia of Islam* and *Islam Ansiklopedisi,* and Babinger, *Die Geschichtsschreiber,* pp. 184–85.

15. *Risāle,* p. 18; tr. Behrnauer, p. 274.
16. *Risāle,* pp. 32 and 45; tr., pp. 288 and 301. The term "Turk" in these passages refers to the Anatolian Turkish peasants and Turcoman nomads, hitherto excluded from the imperial household and Janissary corps. A similar observation was made some decades earlier by the historian Selānikī Muṣṭafā, who says: "In the reign of the late Sultan Murād Khān [1574–95], a vile rabble of contemptible interlopers entered the respected household and, through bribery, the regiments of Janissaries, armorers and gunners were opened to peasants, to farmers who have abandoned their farms, to Tat, Chepni, Gypsies, Jews, Laz, Russians and townspeople. When these joined the ranks, tradition and respect disappeared entirely; the curtain of reverence of government was riven, and, in this way, men with neither aptitude nor experience of affairs came and sat in the seats of power . . ." (quoted from manuscript by I. H. Uzunçarşılı, *Osmanlı Devleti teşkilâtından Kapıkulu Ocakları,* ii [Ankara, 1944], p. 201).
17. In Turkish *bashmaklık* or *pashmaklık*—a term applied in Kochu Bey's time to appanages granted to certain ladies of the Imperial harem, for their personal needs in clothing, and so forth.
18. *Risāle,* p. 47; tr., p. 306.
19. The *jizye* was, in accordance with Islamic law, assessed in gold, though it could be paid in silver currency. The sharp rise in the rate of payment in silver aspers, mentioned by Kochu Bey, is attested by many documents of the period and was due to the devaluation of the Ottoman silver currency during the late sixteenth and early seventeenth centuries. Ottoman fiscal records of the early sixteenth century give the rate of the asper as 40 to the gold piece. By the time of Süleyman the Magnificent it had fallen to 60 and then 80 and under his successors dropped very steeply in value, at times to above 200. Kochu Bey, not unnaturally, fails to take account of these financial fluctuations. On Ottoman currency changes see J. von Hammer, *Histoire de l'Empire ottoman,* vii (Paris, 1837), pp. 410–25; I. S. Emmanuel, *Histoire des Israélites de Salonique,* i (Paris, 1936), pp. 233–34, 263 n. 51; R. Anhegger, *Beiträge zur Geschichte des Bergbaus im osmanischen Reich,* ii (Istanbul, 1944), pp. 432–33; Halil Inalcık, "Remarks on an essay on the economical [*sic*] situation of Turkey during the foundation

and rise of the Ottoman Empire" (in Turkish with English summary), in *Belleten*, xv (1951), pp. 629–90.

20. *Risāle*, p. 48; tr., p. 306. *Cf.* the remark of Lûtfi Pasha quoted above, n. 10. The sixteenth-century writer 'Ālī (on whom see the article in *Encyclopaedia of Islam*, 2nd edition) says: "The treasure of sovereigns is their subjects *(ra'iyyet);* the need of the subjects is for care *(ri'āyet)* and safeguarding from injustice," *Künh al-Akhbār*, v (Istanbul, 1285), p. 5. This phrase is repeated in a simpler and more direct form in the second *risāle* of Kochu Bey (ed. Aksüt, p. 105). The idea is already familiar to the ninth-century Arabic author Ibn Qutayba, who cites an unnamed Persian source: "The hearts of the subjects are the treasure-houses of their kings; what they deposit in them, they know is there." Ibn Qutayba, *'Uyūn al-Akhbār* (Cairo, n.d.), i, p. 10; *cf.* English version by J. Horovitz, in *Islamic Culture*, 1930, p. 194.
21. *Risāle*, p. 66; tr., p. 325.
22. The *Destūr al-'Amel li-Iṣlāḥ al-Khalel* was published in Istanbul in A.H. 1280 as an appendix to the *Qavānīn-i Āl-i'Os̱mān* of 'Ayn-i 'Alī. A German translation by Behrnauer had already appeared in *Zeitschrift der Deutschen Morgenländischen Gesellschaft*, xi (1857), pp. 110–32. Some account of the circumstances in which the memorandum was drafted is given by the Ottoman historian Na'īmā, under the events of the year A.H. 1063 (*Ta'rīkh*, 4th edition, v, pp. 281–83). On Kâtib Chelebi see *Encyclopaedia of Islam*, article on Ḥādjdjī Khalīfa; Babinger, pp. 195–203; and the collection of essays and studies published by the Turkish Historical Society, *Kâtip Çelebi, Hayatı ve Eserleri hakkında incelemeler* (Ankara, 1957). Another of his works, the *Mīzān al-ḥaḳḳ*, has appeared in English translation: Katib Chelebi, *The Balance of Truth*, trans. G. L. Lewis (London, 1957).
23. *Cf.* Ibn Khaldūn, *The Muqaddimah*, trans. F. Rosenthal (New York, 1958), i, pp. 339ff.; ii, pp. 117ff. On Ibn Khaldūn's influence in Turkey, see Fındıkoğlu Ziyaeddin Fahri, "Türkiyede Ibn Haldunizm," in *Fuad Köprülü Armağanı* (Istanbul, 1953), pp. 153–63, especially 156–57, and above, chapter 18. Already in antiquity, the Roman historian Florus divided the life of Rome into the four periods of infancy, youth, manhood, and old age. It may be noted that Florus's history was widely read in medieval Europe. For another version of the three phases, see Francis Bacon's *Advancement of Learning*, book II, x, p. 13.
24. *Destūr*, pp. 119–23; tr., pp. 115–91.
25. *Destūr*, pp. 124–29; tr., pp. 119–24.
26. *Destūr*, pp. 129–32; tr., pp. 124–26.
27. *Destūr*, pp. 132–35; tr., pp. 126–28.
28. *Destūr*, pp. 136–39; tr., pp. 129–32.
29. *Fezleke* (Istanbul, 1287), pp. 384–85; *cf.* Behrnauer, p. 115.
30. On Ḥüseyn Hezārfen see Babinger, pp. 228–31. The full Turkish text of his *Telkhīs al-Bayān fī ḳavānīn-i āl-i 'Os̱mān* has still not been edited, but some

extracts were published, together with a study, by R. Anhegger, "Hezarfen Hüseyin Efendi'nin Osmanlı devlet teşkilâtına dair mülâhazalar," *Türkiyat Mecmuası,* x (1951–53), pp. 365–98. A French translation, reputedly by Pétis de la Croix, was published in Paris in 1695.

31. The *Naṣā'iḥ al-Vüzerā va 'l-Umerā* of Sarı Meḥmed Pasha was edited with an English translation and notes by W. L. Wright (Princeton, 1935). *Cf. Sosyoloji Dergisi,* iii (Istanbul, 1946), pp. 141–45.
32. F. Babinger, "Die türkischen Quellen Dimitrie Kantemir's," in *Zeki Velidi Togan'a Armağan* (Istanbul, 1955), pp. 56ff.
33. Hezārfen, ed. Anhegger, p. 376; *cf.* Ibn Qutayba, *'Uyūn al-Akhbār,* i, pp. 8–9 (=Horovitz' version in *Islamic Culture* [1930], p. 192), and A. K. S. Lambton, "Quis custodiet custodes," *Studia Islamica,* v (1956), pp. 144, 147. In Ottoman usage the term *siyāset* frequently denotes capital or other bodily punishment inflicted under the discretionary authority of the ruler, as distinct from the penalties specified in the *Sharī'a.* On *siyāsa* in the sense of administrative, non-canonical justice, see the observations of al-Maqrīzī in *Khiṭaṭ,* ii, pp. 219–22. Al-Maqrīzī connects this meaning of *siyāsa* with the Mongol *yasa.*
34. For discussions of the larger historical problem, see B. Lewis, "Some Reflections on the Decline of the Ottoman Empire", *Studia Islamica,* ix (1957), pp. 111–27, reproduced with some modifications in his *The Emergence of Modern Turkey,* pp. 21–39; and H. A. R. Gibb and Harold Bowen, *Islamic Society and the West,* vol. i, part I, *Islamic Society in the Eighteenth Century* (London, 1950), pp. 173ff.
35. Some of these texts, with others, have been discussed, from different points of view, by Babinger, *Geschichtsschreiber,* p. 152, n. 1; I. H. Uzunçarşılı, *Osmanlı Tarihi,* iii, 2 (Ankara, 1954), pp. 501–502; Anhegger, pp. 365–69; E. I. J. Rosenthal, *Political Thought in Medieval Islam* (Cambridge, 1958), pp. 224–33 (from Behrnauer's translations only); A. S. Tveritinova, *Social Ideas in Turkish Didactic Politico-Economic Treatises of the XVI–XVII Centuries.* Papers presented by the USSR delegation to the XXV International Congress of Orientalists, Moscow 1960; and M. Tayyib Gökbilgin, "XVII. asırda, Osmanlı devletinde islahat ihtiyac ve temayülleri ve Kâtip Celebi," in *Kâtip Celebi . . .* (Ankara, 1957), pp. 197–218.
36. B. Lewis, *The Emergence of Modern Turkey,* pp. 56ff.

Chapter 17. The Ottoman Empire and Its Aftermath

1. Quoted in B. Lewis, *The Emergence of Modern Turkey,* 2nd edition (Oxford 1968), 352–53.
2. *Ibid.,* 466.
3. *Ibid.,* 325.
4. Falıh Rıfkı, *Taymis Kıyıları* (Istanbul, 1934), pp. 126–28.

Chapter 18. Ibn Khaldūn in Turkey

1. See the bibliographies by H. Pérès, "Bibliographie sur la vie et l'oeuvre d'Ibn Ḫaldūn," in *Studi Orientalistici in onore di Giorgio Levi Della Vida* (Rome, 1956), II, 308–29 and W. J. Fischel, "Selected Bibliography," appendix to Franz Rosenthal's translation of the *Muqaddima* (New York, 1958), III, 483–512.
2. Silvestre de Sacy, *Chresthomathie arabe* (1st ed. Paris, 1806), 2nd ed. (Paris, 1826–1827), I, 370–411; II, 168–169, 256–259, 279–336; III, 342–346.
3. J. von Hammer-Purgstall, *Geschichte des osmanischen Reiches* (Pest, 1827–1835), I, 301; III, 489; VIII, 253; *idem, Histoire de l'Empire Ottoman* (Paris, 1835), II, 71–72; XVI, 59.
4. For a pioneer survey of this topic, see Fındıkoğlu Z. Fahri, "Türkiyede Ibn Haldunizm," in *Fuad Köprülü Armağanı* (Istanbul, 1953), pp. 153–63.
5. *Keşf-el-Zunun*, eds. Şerefettin Yaltkaya and Kılıslı Rıfat Bilge (Ankara, 1941–1943), I, 278; II, 1124 and 1795.
6. *Destūr al-ʿamal fī iṣlāḥ al-Khalal*, printed in Istanbul in 1280/1863–1864, as an appendix to the *Ḳavānīn-i Āl-i Osmān* of ʿAyn-i ʿAlī. A German translation by Behrnauer had been published some time earlier, in the *Z.D.M.G.*, 11 (1857), 110–32. See above pp. 216–20.
7. Naʿīma, *Tārīkh* (Istanbul, 1281–1283/1864–1866), I, 5–6. For Naʿimā's own account, based on Ibn Khaldūn, on the stages of growth, stasis, and decline in the lives of states, *ibid.*, pp. 33–40. Naʿīmā also draws extensively on the *Destūr al-ʿamal* of Kâtib Chelebi.
8. *Ṣaḥā'if ül-Akhbār* (Istanbul, 1285/1868), pp. 32ff., pp. 282–83.
9. See F. Babinger, *Die Geschichtsschreiber der Osmanen und ihre Werke* (Leipzig, 1927), pp. 282–83.
10. Babinger, p. 379. The Turkish version of the *Muqaddima* was printed in Būlāq in 1274/1857–1858 and in Istanbul in 1275–1277/1858–1861.
11. Resmī, *Viyana Sefāretnāmesi* (Istanbul, 1304/1886–1887), p. 33.
12. ʿAẓmī, *Sefaretname 1205 Senesinde Prusya Kiralı Ikinci Fredrik Guillaum'ın nezdine memur olan Ahmed Azmi Efendinindir* (Istanbul, 1303/1885–1886), p. 52.
13. Silvestre de Sacy, *Chresthomathie arabe,* I, 309.

Chapter 19. Corsairs in Iceland

1. See Ch. A. Julien, *Histoire de l'Afrique du Nord.* 2nd edition, revised by Roger Le Tourneau, II (Paris, 1961), 274ff.; S. Lane-Poole, *The Barbary Corsairs* (London, 1890), 228ff.; Aziz Samih, *Şimali Afrikada Türkler* (Istanbul, 1937), I, 174; R. C. Anderson, *Naval wars in the Levant* (Princeton, 1952), 67ff.

2. Pierre Dan, *Histoire de Barbarie et de ses Corsaires* (Paris, 1637), Book III, 276. "En 1627 trois vaisseaux d'Alger, conduits par un Renegat Allemand, nommé Come Murat, furent si hardis que d'aller jusques'en Dannemarc, ou prenant terre en l'Isle d'Island, ils enlevèrent plusieurs mesnages escartes l'un de l'autre, & firent esclaves quatre cens personnes qu'ils emmenerent." In the Dutch translation of Dan's book (Amsterdam, 1684), the leader's name is given as Kure Murat.
3. Emanuel d'Aranda, *Relation de la Captivité,* 4th edition (Leiden, 1671), 368–72.
4. Oluf Eigilssen, *En Kort Beretning om de Tyrkiske Sørøveres onde Medfart og Omgang* . . . (Copenhagen, 1641).
5. Olafur Egilsson, *Lítil Saga um herhlaup Tyrkjans arid 1627* (Reykjavik, 1852). The difference between the Danish and Icelandic forms of the author's name will be noted.
6. Björn Jónsson, *Tyrkjaránssaga* (Reykjavík, 1866).
7. Sigfús Bløndal, "De Algierske Sørøveres Tog til Island aar 1627," *Nord og Syd* (Copenhagen, 1898–99), 193–208. This excellent article forms the main basis of the account given here.
8. Jón Thorkelsson, ed., *Tyrkjaránid á Íslandi 1627,* published by the Søgufjelag (Reykjavík, 1906–1909). A very brief account of the raid will be found in Knut Gjerset, *History of Iceland* (London, 1923), 319–20.
9. *En Kort Beretning,* 19–20.
10. Some of the other Icelandic sources severely criticize the negligence of the Danish governor Holger Rosenkrands on this occasion.
11. *The Life of the Icelander Jon Olafsson,* translated from the Icelandic edition of Dr. Sigfús Bløndal, by Dame Bertha Philpotts, ii (London, 1932), 258–59. To my knowledge this is the only one of the original sources available in translation.
12. *En Kort Beretning,* 22.
13. Bløndal, *loc. cit.,* 207–208.

Chapter 20. The Crows of the Arabs

1. ʿAbduh Badawī, *Al-Shuʿarāʾ al-Sūd wa-Khaṣāʾiṣuhum fi'l-Shiʿr al-ʿArabī* (Cairo, 1973), p. 21; my translation, as are all further translations in this essay. All further references to this work, abbreviated *S,* will be included in the text.

   In addition, the black Arabic poets have been examined in detail in several articles, notably by Muḥammad Bāqir ʿAlwān, "Aghribat al-ʿArab," *Al-Mawrid* 2, no. 1 (1973): 11–13, and ʿAwn al-Sharīf Qāsim, "Al-Sūdān fī ḥayāt al-ʿArab wa-adabihim," *Bulletin of Sudanese Studies* 1, no. 1 (1968): 76–92. Accounts (unfortunately very brief) of the group and of the individual poets may also be found in the standard histories of Arabic literature; see especially Régis Blachère, *Histoire de la littérature arabe des origines à la fin du quinzième siecle,* 2 vols. (Paris, 1952–66). On ʿAntara, see *Encyclopaedia of Islam,* 2d ed., s.v. "ʿAntara" (article by Blachère), where further references are given. Suḥaym's poems were collected and edited; see Suḥaym, *Dīwān,* ed. ʿAbd al-ʿAzīz al-Maymanī (Cairo, 1950); all further references to this work, abbreviated *D,* will be included in the text. See also the translation into German, *Beiträge zur arabischen Poësie,* trans. Oscar Rescher, 8 vols. (Istanbul, 1937–), 6, pt. 2:30–50. For the life and work of Nuṣayb, see Umberto Rizzitano, "Abū Miḥǵan Nuṣayb b. Rabāḥ," *Rivista degli studi orientali* 20 (1943): 421–71 and "Alcuni frammenti poetici di Abū Miḥǵan Nuṣayb b. Rabāḥ poeta ommiade del 1 secolo dell'egira," *Rivista degli studi orientali* 22 (1945): 23–35.

2. Abu'l-Faraj al-Isfāhānī, *Kitāb al-Aghānī,* 20 vols. (Būlāq, 1868–69), 7:149. See also R. A. Nicholson, *A Literary History of the Arabs* (Cambridge, 1941), p. 115.
3. Wilhelm Ahlwardt, ed., *The Divans of the Six Ancient Arabic Poets Ennābiga, ʿAntara, Tharafa, Zuhair, ʿAlqama, and Imruulqais* (London, 1870), p. 42. See *Encyclopaedia of Islam,* 2d ed., s.v. "ʿAntara."
4. ʿAntara, *Dīwān* (Cairo, 1911), p. 196.
5. *Ibid.*
6. Ibn Qutayba, *Kitāb al-Shiʿr wa'l-shuʿarā',* ed. M. J. de Goeje (Leiden, 1904), p. 196.
7. On Suḥaym, often named by Arab authors as "the slave of the Banū'l-Ḥasḥās," see al-Isfāhānī, *Kitāb al-Aghānī,* new ed. (Cairo, 1928–29), 20:2–9; Blachère, *Histoire de la littérature arabe* 1:318–19; and *Beiträge zur arabischen Poësie* 6, pt. 2:30–50.
8. Cf. Franz Rosenthal, *The Muslim Concept of Freedom* (Leiden, 1960), p. 91.
9. *Aghānī,* 1:140–41 (new ed. 1:352–54); and see Rizzitano, "Abū Miḥǵan Nuṣayb b. Rabāḥ," *Rivista* 20:453, 456 and "Alcuni frammenti," *Rivista* 22:24, 26.
10. *Aghānī,* 20:25; and see Badawī, *Al-Shuʿara',* p. 158.

Chapter 22. The Significance of Heresy in Islam

1. Cevdet (Jevdet), *Tarih,* 2nd edition, viii (Istanbul, A.H. 1309), pp. 147–48.
2. I. Goldziher, *Vorlesungen über den Islam,* 2nd ed. (Heidelberg, 1925), pp. 183–84. English translation by A. and R. Hamori, *Introduction to Islamic Theology and Law* (Princeton, N.J., 1981).
3. Al-Ghazālī, *Fayṣal al-tafriqa bayn al-Islam wa'l-zandaqa* (Cairo, 1901), pp. 10–18.
4. *Ibid,* pp. 18–19; *cf.* al-Ghazālī, *Al-Iqtiṣād fī'l-iʿtiqād* (Cairo, n.d.), p. 111ff.
5. *Ḥayawān,* 1st ed. (Cairo, 1325), I, p. 80: 2nd ed. (Cairo, 1938), I, p. 174; *cf.* Goldziher, *Vorlesungen,* p. 186.
6. *Fayṣal al-tafriqa,* p. 68.

7. Goldziher, *Vorlesungen*, pp. 185–86.
8. E. Strauss, "L'inquisition dans l'état mamlouk", in *Rivista degli Studi Orientali*, xxv (1950), pp. 11–26.

Chapter 23. The Revolutions in Early Islam

1. Al-Mas'ūdī, *Murūj al-dhahab*, ed. C. Barbier de Meynard and Pavet de Courteille, iv (Paris, 1861–77), pp. 253–55. New French translation by Charles Pellat (Paris, 1971), iii, pp. 616ff.
2. B. Lewis, "The Regnal Titles of the First Abbasid Caliphs," in *Dr. Zakir Husain Presentation Volume* (New Delhi, 1968), pp. 13–22.
3. Abu'l-'Aṭā' al-Sindī, cited in Abu'l-Faraj al-Iṣfahānī, *Kitāb al-Aghānī*, xvi (Būlāq, 1285), p. 84; *cf.* H. Lammens, *Études sur le règne du calife omeiyade Mo'âwiya Ie* (Beirut, 1906), p. 188.

Chapter 24. Islamic Concepts of Revolution

1. Attributed to Ibn al-Muqaffa', *Al-Adab al ṣaghīr*, in *Rasā'il al-bulaghā'*, ed. Muḥammad Kurd 'Alī, 4th ed. (Cairo, 1954), pp. 17, *cf.* p. 18.
2. *Al-Adab al-kabīr, ibid*, p. 50.
3. *Ibid*, p. 125; Ṭabarī, *Ta'rīkh*, ed. M. J. de Goeje and others, iii (Leiden, 1879–1901), p. 30.
4. Ṭabarī, p. 86.
5. O. Loth, "Al-Kindi als Astrolog," in *Morgenländische Forschungen, Festschrift . . . H. L. Fleischer* (Leipzig, 1875), pp. 263–309; *Rasā'il Ikhwān al-Ṣafā* (Cairo, 1928), i, pp. 106, 130–31; iii, p. 258; iv, pp. 234ff., 237; *cf.* A. L. Tibawi, "Ikhwān al-Ṣafā and their Rasā'il," in *Islamic Quarterly*, ii (1955), p. 37, n. 4. See further "Dawla" in *Encyclopaedia of Islam*, 2nd edition, by F. Rosenthal.
6. *Rasā'il al-Jāḥiẓ*, ed. Ḥasan al-Sandūbī (Cairo, 1933), pp. 295–96; French translation by Ch. Pellat, "La 'Nabita' de Djâhiz," in *Annales de l'Institut d'Etudes orientales*, x (Algiers, 1952), pp. 317–18.
7. Al-Muttaqī, *Kanz al-'ummāl*, iii (Hyderabad, 1312), pp. 201–203.
8. Al-Muttaqī, iii, pp. 197–98.
9. Al-Ījī, *Mawāqif*, viii (Cairo, 1907), p. 375; *cf.* p. 348ff.
10. *Risāla fi'l-Ṣaḥāba*, in *Rasā'il al-bulaghā'*, pp. 120–21. On the duty of disobedience see further H. Laoust, *Essai sur les doctrines sociales et politiques de . . . Ahmad b. Taimīya* (Cairo, 1939), pp. 310–25, and B. Lewis, *The Political Language of Islam* (Chicago, 1988), pp. 91ff.
11. 'Āṭif Efendi, "Memorandum of 1798," in Cevdet, *Tarih*, vi (Istanbul, A.H. 1309), p. 394; *Bonapart tarihi* (Turkish translation of Botta's *Storia d'Italia*) (Cairo, A.H. 1249); reprinted Istanbul, 1293, p. 8; *cf.* Shaykh Rifā'a Rāfi'

al-Ṭahṭāwī, *Talkhīs al-ibrīz* (Būlāq, 1834), new edition Cairo 1958, pp. 252, on the revolution of 1830, and 259, on 1789—*al-fitna al-ūlā li'l-ḥurriyya,* the first *fitna* for freedom. On classical usage, see "Fitna" in *Encyclopaedia of Islam,* 2nd edition, by L. Gardet, and E. L. Petersen, *'Alī and Mu'āwiya in Early Arabic Tradition* (Copenhagen, 1964), pp. 9ff. On *Bid 'a* see above, p. 226.

12. The name of the sect called the Khārijīs—those who go out—probably derives from an episode in their early history, the secret departure of the sectaries from Kufa, rather than from the general sense of seceders or rebels.
13. See "Ibn Faradj al-Djayyāni" in *Encyclopaedia of Islam,* 2nd edition, by H. Monés.
14. See for example M. Hamidullah, *Muslim Conduct of State,* revised edition (Lahore, 1945), pp. 168ff.
15. See for example 'Izzī, *Tarih* (Istanbul, A.H. 1199), pp. 128, 136, and *Tarih Vesikaları,* vol. ii, no. 7 (1942), pp. 65ff.
16. 'Āṭif, *ibid,* p. 395; Aḥmed Efendi, in *Tarih Vesikaları,* vol. iii, no. 15 (1949), p. 184; *cf. Bonapart tarihi,* pp. 8, 70.
17. Cevdet, ii (Istanbul, 1309), pp. 265ff.
18. Ṭabarī, iii, p. 30; G. C. Miles, "Al-Mahdi al-haqq, Amīr al-Mu'minīn" in *Revue Numismatique,* 6e série, vii (1965), p. 335; Abū Shāma, *Kitāb al-Rawḍatayn,* 2nd edition, ed. M. Ḥilmy M. Aḥmad, i/ii (Cairo, 1962), p. 563.
19. Examples in Ra'īf al-Khūrī, *Al-Fikr al-'Arabī al-ḥadīth* (Beirut, 1943), pp. 118f., 168, 220ff. English translation by Iḥsān 'Abbās, *Modern Arab Thought* (Princeton, 1983).
20. From the verb *raj'a,* "to return." The Arabic term *raj'ī* was probably inspired by the slightly earlier Ottoman Turkish neologisms *irtijā',* "reaction," and *mürteji',* "reactionary," both from the same root.
21. Loth, *loc. cit.,* p. 303; *cf.* pp. 274, 277.

Chapter 25. The Idea of Freedom in Modern Islamic Political Thought

1. See F. Rosenthal, *The Muslim Concept of Freedom* (Leiden, 1960).
2. Turkish text in Cevdet (Jevdet), *Tarih,* 2nd ed., i (Istanbul, A.H. 1309), pp. 358–59; *Mecmu'a-i mu'ahedat,* iii, p. 254; Italian text in G. F. de Martens, *Recueil des traités . . . ,* iv (Göttingen, 1795), pp. 610–12.
3. *E.g., Tarih-i Osmanī Encümeni mecmuası,* xxiii A.H. 1329, pp. 1458, 1460. On the display of the "symbols" of freedom by Frenchmen in Turkey, see Cevdet, *Tarih,* vi, pp. 182–83.
4. Cevdet, *Tarih,* vi, pp. 395, 400; *cf.* B. Lewis, "The Impact of the French Revolution on Turkey," in *Journal of World History,* i (1953), pp. 120ff. (revised version in G. S. Métraux and F. Croizet, eds., *The New Asia* [New York-

London, 1965], pp. 47ff., and *Slavonic Review,* xxxiv [1955], pp. 234–35). On the development of modern political thought in Turkey see Niyazi Berkes, *The Development of Secularism in Turkey* (Montreal, 1964), and B. Lewis, *The Emergence of Modern Turkey,* 2nd edition (London, 1968).

5. *ʿala asās al-ḥurriyya wa'l-taswiya;* versions in al-Jabartī, *Muẓhir al-taḳdīs* (Cairo, n.d.), i, p. 37; Niqūlā al-Turk, *Mudhakkirāt,* ed. G. Wiet (Cairo, 1950), p. 8; the text also appears in al-Jabartī, *ʿAjā'ib,* iii (Cairo, 1879), p. 4; Ḥaydar al-Shihābi's *Lubnān;* and elsewhere. The pioneer work on modern Arab political thought is the much-used and insufficiently acknowledged anthology of Ra'īf al-Khūrī, *Al-Fikr al-ʿArabī al-ḥadīth* (Beirut, 1943), a collection of excerpts, with an introduction, illustrating the influence on Arab thought of the French Revolution. This was followed by numerous other studies and books, the most notable of which is A. H. Hourani, *Arabic Thought in the Liberal Age 1798–1939* (London, 1962).
6. J. F. Ruphy, *Dictionnaire abrégé français-arabe* (Paris, An X [1802]), p. 120. As late as 1841 the Phanariot Handjeri renders *"liberté civile"* and *"liberté politique"* by *rukhṣat-i sherʿiye* and *rukhṣat-i mülkiye* respectively (*Dictionnaire français-arabe-persan et turc,* ii [Moscow, 1840–41], p. 397, with explanations and examples). The connotation of *rukhṣat* in Ottoman usage was permission, licence or, in the religious sense, dispensation.
7. Shanizade, *Tarih,* iv (Istanbul, 1291), pp. 2–3; *cf.* B. Lewis, *Emergence,* pp. 72–73.
8. Cairo, 1249/1834, reprinted Istanbul 1293/1876.
9. *Takhlīṣ al-ibrīz fī talkhīṣ Bāriz,* ed. Mahdī ʿAllām, Aḥmad Badawī, and Anwar Lūkā (Cairo, n.d. [1958?]).
10. Cairo, 1862, pp. 127ff. An unpublished Arabic translation of Machiavelli's *Prince,* prepared for Muḥammad ʿAlī Pasha c. 1825, renders the phrase in Chapter I "dominions . . . which have been free states" as *"amīriyyāt iʿtādat an takūn muḥarrara."*
11. See L. Zolondek, "Al-Ṭahṭāwī and Political Freedom," in *Muslim World,* liv (1964), pp. 90–97.
12. Text in Sadık Rıfat Pasha, *Müntehabat-i asar* (Istanbul), *Avrupanın ahvaline dair . . . risale,* p. 4; *cf. ibid, Idare-i hukumetin bazı kavaid-i esasiyesini mutazammin . . . risale, passim;* another version in Abdurrahman Şeref, *Tarih musahabeleri* (Istanbul, 1340), pp. 125f.
13. Text in *Düstūr,* first series, i, pp. 4–7; in modern script, in A. Şeref Gözübüyük and S. Kili, *Türk anayasa metinleri* (Ankara, 1957), pp. 3–5; English trans. in J. C. Hurewitz, *Diplomacy in the Near and Middle East,* i (Princeton, N.J., 1956), pp. 113–16.
14. Philippe and Farīd Khāzin, *Majmūʿat al-muḥarrarāt al-siyāsiyya wa'l-mufāwaḍāt al-duwaliyya ʿan Sūriyya wa-Lubnān,* i (Jūniya, 1910), pp. 1ff. *Cf.* Hourani, *Arabic Thought,* pp. 61–62.

15. Anṭūn al-ʿAqīqī, ed. Yūsuf Ibrāhīm Yazbak, *Thawra wa-fitna fī Lubnān* (Damascus, 1938), p. 87; English translation by M. H. Kerr, *Lebanon in the Last Years of Feudalism* . . . (Beirut, 1959), p. 53. See further P. K. Hitti, "The Impact of the West on Syria and Lebanon in the Nineteenth Century," in *Journal of World History,* ii (1955), pp. 629–30.
16. Ahmed Lûtfi, *Tarih,* iii (Istanbul, A.H. 1292), p. 100; *cf.* Ahmed Emin, *The Development of Modern Turkey Measured by Its Press* (New York, 1914), p. 28.
17. *Ghābat al-ḥaqq* (Beirut, 1866, reprinted Cairo 1298/1880–81).
18. *Aqwām al-masālik fī maʿrifat aḥwāl al-mamālik* (Tunis, 1284–85/1867–68); French trans. *Réformes nécessaires aux états musulmans* (Paris, 1868); Turkish version (Istanbul, 1296/1879); English translation by L. Carl Brown, *The Surest Path: the Political Treatise of a 19th Century Muslim Statesman* (Cambridge, Mass., 1969).
19. Cited in B. Lewis, *The Emergence of Modern Turkey,* p. 137.
20. See for example the article from *Hürriyyet* published by M. Colombe in French translation in *Orient,* xiii (1960), pp. 123–33. On the Young Ottomans see Şerif Mardin, *The Genesis of the Young Ottomans* (Princeton, N.J., 1962).
21. Namık Kemal, "Hukuk-i umumiye," in *Ibret,* no. 18 (1872); reprinted in Ebüzziya Tevfik, *Nümune-i edebiyat-i Osmaniye,* 3rd edition (Istanbul, 1306), pp. 357–58, and, in the new Turkish script, in Mustafa N. Özön, *Namık Kemal ve Ibret gazetesi* (Istanbul, 1939), pp. 96–97; English trans. in Lewis, *Emergence,* p. 140.
22. See *Encyclopaedia of Islam,* 2nd ed., under "Bayʿa."
23. Namık Kemal, *Hukuk-i umumiye, loc. cit.*
24. *Ibret,* no. 46 (1872), cited by Ihsan Sungu, *Tanzimat ve Yeni Osmanlılar,* in *Tanzimat,* i (Istanbul, 1940), p. 845; English translation in Lewis, *Emergence,* p. 167.
25. Sadullah Pasha, *1878 Paris Ekspozisyonu,* in Ebuzziya Tevfik, *Nümune* . . . , p. 288; English translation in B. Lewis, *The Middle East and the West* (London-Bloomington, 1964), p. 47.
26. Preface to *Shipsevdi* (Istanbul, 1912), English translation in Niyazi Berkes, *Secularism,* p. 292.
27. Cairo 1316/1898 and 1905; Turkish versions: Cairo 1326/1908, Istanbul 1329/1911, and, in Northern Turkish, Kazan 1909.
28. Reprinted in *Orient,* v (1958), pp. 29–38.
29. Cairo, n.d. See Sylvia G. Haim, "Alfieri and al-Kawākibi," in *Oriente Moderno,* xxxiv (1954), pp. 321–34; E. Rossi, "Una traduzione turca dell'opera 'Della Tirannide' di V. Alfieri," *ibid,* pp. 335–37.
30. *Risālat al-kalim al-thamān* (Cairo, 1298/1881).
31. *Risālat al-kalim al-thamān,* p. 2.
32. *Risālat al-kalim al-thamān,* pp. 36–37.

33. The writings and ideas of Luṭfī al-Sayyid have been examined by (among others) J. M. Ahmed, *The Intellectual Origins of Egyptian Nationalism* (London, 1960), and N. Safran, *Egypt in Search of Political Community* (Cambridge, Mass., 1961).
34. There is now an extensive if uneven literature devoted to the more recent ideological trends and expressions in Islamic lands. A useful selection of Arabic, Turkish, and Persian writings, in translation, will be found in Kemal H. Karpat (editor), *Political and Social Thought in the Contemporary Middle East* (New York, 1968). The authors cited are concerned mainly with nationalism, socialism, and various combinations of the two, and with few exceptions, mostly Turkish, show little interest in classical liberal values.

Chapter 26. On Modern Arabic Political Terms

1. On loan-words, see further Charles Issawi, "European Loan-Words in Contemporary Arabic Writing: A Case Study in Modernization," in *Middle Eastern Studies*, iii (1967), pp. 110–33.
2. See *Encyclopaedia of Islam*, 2nd edition, under "Djumhūriyya." The term *mashyakha* is still used for "republic" in an Arabic translation of Machiavelli's *Prince*, made for Muḥammad ʿAlī Pasha in about 1825. This text, a manuscript of which exists in the Egyptian National Library, is of considerable interest for the history of modern Arabic political terminology and deserves a critical edition.
3. Midhat Cemal Kuntay, *Sarıklı ihtilâlcı Ali Suavi* (Istanbul, 1946), pp. 58–59; Şerif Mardin, *The Genesis of Young Ottoman Thought* (Princeton, N.J., 1962), p. 372.
4. Mehmet Akif Ersoy, "Hakkın sesleri," in *Safahat*, 6th ed. (Istanbul, 1963), pp. 205–206; B. Lewis, *The Middle East and the West* (London and Bloomington, Ind., 1964), p. 89.
5. Ahmed Naim, *Islâmda dava-yi kavmiyet* (Istanbul, 1913), cited by Niyazi Berkes in *The Development of Secularism in Turkey* (Montreal, 1964), pp. 374–75.
6. U. Heyd, *Foundations of Turkish Nationalism* (London, 1950), p. 60; *cf.* Ziya Gökalp, *Turkish Nationalism and Western Civilization*, translated and edited by Niyazi Berkes (London, 1959), pp. 79ff., 97ff., 113ff., 126ff.
7. C. Ernest Dawn, "Ideological Influences in the Arab Revolt," in *The World of Islam: Studies in Honour of Philip K. Hitti*, ed. James Kritzeck and R. Bayly Winder (London, 1959), p. 240, citing *Revue du Monde musulman*, xlvii (1921), pp. 24–27 of Arabic text, 15–20 of translation.
8. See *Encyclopaedia of Islam*, 2nd edition.
9. See Ḥasan al-Bāshā. *Al-Alqāb al-Islāmiyya fi'l-ta'rīkh wa'l-wathā'iq wa'l-āthār* (Cairo, 1957), pp. 310–11; R. Dozy, *Supplément aux dictionnaires arabes*, 2nd

ed. (Leiden-Paris, 1927), i, p. 593; additional examples in Abū Shāma, *Tarājim rijāl al-qarnayn al-sādis wa'l-sābi'*, ed. Muḥ. Zāhid al-Kawtharī (Cairo, 1947), p. 81; Ibn al-Fuwaṭī, *Al-Ḥawādith al-jāmi'a*, ed. Muṣṭafā Jawād (Baghdad, A.H. 1351), p. 218; Ibn al-'Adīm, ed. B. Lewis, in *Arabica*, xiii (1966), p. 266.

10. See above, p. 320; also B. Lewis, *The Emergence of Modern Turkey*, 2nd edition (London, 1968), p. 156; Ş. Mardin, *The Genesis of Young Ottoman Thought*, pp. 23, 215.
11. In classical usage this was a legal, occasionally a social, but never a political term. On its modern development see above, chapter 25.

Chapter 27. Islam and Development: The Revaluation of Values

1. C. H. Becker, "Islam und Wirtschaft," in his *Islamstudien*, i (Leipzig, 1924) pp. 54–65.
2. See above, pp. 284f.
3. Mustafa Nihat Özön, *Namık Kemal ve Ibret Gazetesi* (Istanbul, 1938), pp. 42–43.
4. Abdülhak Adnan, *La Science chez les Turcs Ottomans* (Paris, 1939), p. 57.
5. See above, chapter 16.

Note on transcription

Arabic and Persian have been transcribed in accordance with a system of transcription commonly used by British and American orientalists. Turkish is written in some articles according to the same system, in others according to the official new Turkish orthography, with the following modifications (except in bibliographical references): for c - j, for ç - ch, for ş - sh

SOURCES

Note: All the contributions have to some extent been revised. Chapters 4, 25, 27, and 31 have been extensively rewritten.

I. The Western Approaches

1. The Study of Islam
Originally delivered as the third Marshall G. S. Hodgson Memorial Lecture at the University of Chicago. Published in *Encounter* 38, no. 1 (January, 1972) pp. 31–41.
2. Some English Travelers in the East
Middle Eastern Studies 4 (1968) pp. 296–315.
3. The Decolonization of History
Times Literary Supplement (London) 8 August 1968, pp. 853.
4. On Writing the Modern History of the Middle East
Middle East Forum (Beirut) June 1958, pp. 15–17, with some additional material from *Middle Eastern Studies* Vol. I, April 1965, pp. 283–295.
5. On Nationalism and Revolution
The Spectator (London) 26 June 1971.
6. Slade on Turkey
A paper presented to the First International Congress on the Social and Economic History of Turkey, held in Ankara, 11–13 July 1977. Published in *Turkiye'nin Sosyal ve Ekonomik Tarihi (1071–1920): Social and Economic History of Turkey (1071–1920),* edited by Osman Ikyar and Halil Inalcik, pp. 215–26. Ankara, 1980.

II. Muslim History and Historians

7. Sources for the Economic History of the Middle East
Studies in the Economic History of the Middle East from the Rise of Islam to the Present Day, edited by M. A. Cook, pp. 78–92. London and New York: Oxford, 1970.
8. In Search of Islam's Past
The New York Review of Books (5 December 1991), pp. 37–40

9. The Use by Muslim Historians of Non-Muslim Sources
Historians of the Middle East, edited by B. Lewis and P. M. Holt, pp. 180–90. London and New York: Oxford, 1962.
10. The Cult of Spain and the Turkish Romantics
Here published in English for the first time. Previously published in French as "Quelques Thèmes andalous de la littérature turque au xixe siècle." In *Études d'orientalisme dédiées à la mémoire de Lévi-Provençal*, pp. 185–90. Paris: Maisonneuve, 1962.

III. Muslims and Jews
11. The Pro-Islamic Jews
Judaism (New York) 17 (1968), pp. 391–404.
12. Palestine: On the History and Geography of a Name
International History Review 11 (January 1980), pp. 1–12.
13. An Ode against the Jews
Published as "An Anti-Jewish Ode: The *Qasida* of Abu Ishaq against Joseph Ibn Nagrella." In *Salo Wittmayer Baron Jubilee Volume*, pp. 657–68. Jerusalem: American Academy for Jewish Research, 1975.
14. The Sultan, the King, and the Jewish Doctor
Published as "Maimonides, Lionheart, and Saladin." *Eretz-Israel* (Jerusalem) 7 *(L.A. Meyer Memorial Volume)* (1963), pp. 70–75.

IV. Turks and Tatars
15. The Mongols, the Turks, and the Muslim Polity
Transactions of the Royal Historical Society 5th ser. 18 (1968), pp. 49–68.
16. Ottoman Observers of Ottoman Decline
Islamic Studies (Karachi) 1 (1962), pp. 71–87.
17. The Ottoman Empire and Its Aftermath
Journal of Contemporary History 15 (1980), pp. 27–36.
18. Ibn Khaldūn in Turkey
Published in *Studies in Islamic History and Civilization in Honour of Professor David Ayalon*, edited by M. Sharon, pp. 527–30. Jerusalem, Cana, and Leiden: Brill, 1986.

V. In Black and White

19. Corsairs in Iceland

Originally published in Turkish as "Izlanda'da Türkler" in *Türkiyat Mecmuası* 10 (1953), pp. 277–84. First published in English in *Revue de l'Occident musulman et de la Méditerranée (Mélanges Le Tourneau)* 15–16 (1973), pp. 139–144.

20. The Crows of the Arabs

Critical Inquiry 12 (Autumn 1985), pp. 88–97. Republished in *Race, Writing, and Difference,* edited by Henry Louis Gates Jr., pp. 107–116. Chicago: University of Chicago Press, 1986.

VI. History and Revolution

21. State and Society under Islam

The Wilson Quarterly (Autumn, 1989), pp. 39–51. Originally presented in August 1989, at a conference on "Europe and Civil Society," held at Castel Gandolfo (Italy) under the auspices of the Institut für die Wissenschaften vom Menschen (Vienna, Austria). The conference papers have been published in Polish and German.

22. The Significance of Heresy in Islam

Published as "Some Observations on the Significance of Heresy in the History of Islam." *Studia Islamica* 1 (1952), pp. 43–63.

23. The Revolutions in Early Islam

Published as "On the Revolutions in Early Islam." *Studia Islamica* 32 (1970), pp. 215–331.

24. Islamic Concepts of Revolution

Published in *Revolution in the Middle East,* edited by P. J. Vatikiotis, pp. 30–40. Totowa, N.J.: Rowman and Littlefield, 1972.

VII. New Ideas

25. The Idea of Freedom in Modern Islamic Political Thought

Encyclopedia of Islam, 2nd ed., s.v. "*Ḥurriyya.*"

26. On Modern Arabic Political Terms

Published as "On Some Modern Arabic Political Terms." In *Orientalia hispanica,* edited by J. M. Barral. Vol. 1: *Arabica-Islamica,* pp. 465–71. Leiden: Brill, 1974.

27. Islam and Development: The Revaluation of Values
    Published as "Problems as the Outcome of Changing Social Values in Developing Countries." In *Social Aspects of Economic Development,* pp. 109–24. Report of an international conference held at Istanbul, August 1963. Istanbul: Economic and Social Studies Conference Board, 1964.

VIII. New Events

28. Behind the Rushdie Affair
    The American Scholar 60 (1991), pp. 185–96.
29. The Egyptian Murder Case
    The New York Review of Books (31 May 1984), pp. 21–25.
30. How Khomeini Made It
    The New York Review of Books (17 January 1985), pp. 10–13.
31. The Revolt of Islam
    The New York Review of Books (30 June 1983), pp. 35–38.
32. The Middle East Crisis in Historical Perspective
    First delivered as the *Il Mulino* lecture in Bologna, September 1991. Published in Italian in *Il Mulino* (November 1991). The English text was first published in *The American Scholar* 61 (1992), pp. 33–46.

INDEX